MAX WEBER IN AMERICA

MAX WEBER IN AMERICA

Lawrence A. Scaff

PRINCETON UNIVERSITY PRESS

PRINCETON AND OXFORD

Library of Congress Cataloging-in-Publication Data

Scaff, Lawrence A.

Max Weber in America / Lawrence A. Scaff.

p. cm.

Includes bibliographical references and index.

ISBN 978-0-691-14779-6 (cloth : alk. paper)   1. Weber, Max, 1864–1920—Travel—United States.

2. Sociologists—Germany—Biography.   3. Sociology—United States—History.   I. Title.

HM479.W42S33 2011

301.092—dc22   [B]   2010037523

British Library Cataloging-in-Publication Data is available

This book has been composed in Goudy Old Style

Printed on acid-free paper. ∞

Printed in the United States of America

3 5 7 9 10 8 6 4 2

For my daughters
Janine and Rosalyn

CONTENTS

ILLUSTRATIONS

Figures

Tables

PREFACE

This is my second book about Max Weber, and until recent years I harbored doubts about writing it. Surely one contribution is enough in the vast sea of literature on Weber the man, thinker, scientist, and political intellectual. But the problems posed by Weber's life and work are a source of endless fascination. There are a number of reasons to be fascinated: the emotional range and psychological drama of the life; the breadth and depth of the work; the sense that our times share something important with his world; the apparent centrality of Weber's ideas to so many contemporary issues in science and politics; and, of course, the enduring questions about his most famous concepts, arguments, interpretations, and theses.

There are other reasons as well, however, for there is still a great deal we do not know about Weber and his life and writings and times. Despite the monumental efforts of the *Max Weber Gessamtausgabe* editors, we still do not have a complete published record of the correspondence and will not have that documentation for many years, if ever. Gaps persist in the critical edition of the published texts. Only in recent years, after nearly a century, have we recovered two texts Weber published in English translation in *The Encyclopedia Americana* in 1907–8. As for the historical period of Weber's life and work, we may well have a more comprehensive and nuanced understanding of the quattrocento in Italy or seventeenth-century New England than we do of the Wilhelmine Era in Germany, the Progressive Era in the United States, and the important transatlantic ties forged in the West before the disaster of the Great War—essential especially for social policy, the arts and sciences, and intellectual life generally. Above all, the crucial American connection to Weber and the story of his 1904 journey to the United States, despite repeated prior attempts, have never been fully documented and understood.

In this investigation I propose to take up these textual and historical challenges, though in an unusual way by focusing on the American dimension to Weber's work and experience. My first systematic treatment of Weber, *Fleeing the Iron Cage*, aimed for a comprehensive interpretation of his thought as a whole, juxtaposed to some of his most important contemporaries. This study is very different, for I use a particular focus in *Max Weber in America* to illuminate the thought, the life, and the historical era—especially in the United States, but with an eye on Germany and Europe. Readers will notice the two senses of Weber in America, the literal and the metaphorical: his 1904 travels with Marianne Weber in the United States in part 1, and the intellectual history of his work, texts and ideas in part 2. What unites these two inquiries is the biographical pursuit not of the man but of the work itself, for what we still need most of all is a biography of the work—or, if one prefers, a genealogy of the thinking that continues to challenge and provoke us.

My approach to the subject deserves an explanation. I have spent countless hours, days, and weeks in many archives in the United States and Germany, from the Knox County Public Library in Tennessee to the Prussian State Archives. It *is* a wonderful life, as Guy Oakes once said to me; if only the hours were better! For my interests (and considering the state of our knowledge) there is simply no substitute for reading the primary documentation—letters, reports, newspapers, records of all kinds, some neatly transcribed or printed, others hurriedly scribbled and barely decipherable. These materials were often frustrating, but always stimulating, raising questions I had not considered previously. I was impressed by the amount of documentation there is, particularly in American state and county historical societies' collections. Using such sources critically is essential, of course, and I hope that in doing so I have paid sufficient attention to the usual canons of scholarship and the interpretative literature, which for Weber alone would fill bookcases. I have dealt with the issue of sources and documentation by writing a readable narrative, uncluttered as much as possible by footnotes, endnotes, or other textual interruptions. Instead, I have included bibliographical essays for each chapter in which the relevant sources are identified.

There are conditions and contributions enabling this kind of work that I would like to acknowledge. It is a pleasure to express my appreciation to Guenther Roth, who has followed my work over the years, provided thoughtful comments and suggestions, defended the highest standards of scholarship, and supported this investigation with generous encouragement. He read the entire manuscript, assisting with a number of details. I also owe a special debt of gratitude to Wilhelm Hennis for his passionate engagement with Weber and his times. I benefited from conversations and correspondence with Edith Hanke and Keith Tribe, whose work assisted my own efforts. As general director of the *Max Weber Gesamtausgabe*, Edith Hanke assisted especially with the holdings of the Mohr-Siebeck Archive. I have enjoyed the counsel of numerous colleagues, among whom I would like to mention Kevin Anderson, Robert Antonio, Karl-Ludwig Ay, David Chalcraft, Uta Gerhardt, Peter Ghosh, David Kettler, Harold Orbach, Joachim Radkau, Alan Sica, Sandra van Burkleo, and Sam Whimster. Donald N. Levine arranged an affiliation at the University of Chicago that assisted my work in the Regenstein Library. Stephen Kalberg, Dirk Käsler, Laurence McFalls, Guy Oakes, and David Smith also expressed their interest in this project. Pat Riker and Marilee Scaff graciously donated their time as general readers of individual chapters. I am grateful to Pat Riker for her interest and support, and for the peaceful setting in Santa Monica, California, where much of the final text was written—shadowed, so to speak, by an earlier generation of European immigrants to American shores.

The study that I have written could not have been accomplished without the Webers' correspondence, both the nearly two hundred pages mailed home during the months in the United States, and the voluminous correspondence before and after the trip. The use of that handwritten correspondence is itself a challenge—Marianne's large, uniform, flowing, schooled, almost purely Sütterlin script, and by contrast Max's cramped, excitable, and highly individualized handwriting using a mixture of German and Roman scripts. If personality is revealed in the movements of the hand over the page, then here lies fertile ground for the analyst. As family members and other correspondents complained, reading Max Weber's letters was not a matter of reading but of deciphering. Thanks to early tutorials from Manfred Schön of the *Max Weber Gesamtausgabe* (MWG), the world's expert in such matters, my procedure has been to read the handwritten originals, compare my decoding with transcriptions or printed versions, as in Marianne Weber's *Max Weber: A Biography*, then return to the originals for a final comparison and correction. My translations are based on this final corrected version, and I have noted when printed versions are incomplete or incorrect, and when the originals are unclear or ambiguous. Much of this work would be unnecessary, of course, were these materials published through the careful editorial procedures of the MWG. However, no period presents more difficulties than the years from 1898 to 1906, and publication of letters from this period lies many years in the future. These difficulties will never entirely disappear, nevertheless, as the MWG publishes only Max Weber's complete letters, not those of other family members or the replies of his correspondents.

Working with primary sources can be an invitation to pay especially close attention to language, text, and context. And so it has been with my approach to Max Weber. In part 1, delineating the American journey of 1904 and its import, I have found it important to read what he actually wrote, to renew the engagement with his work by considering carefully *his* words, rather than following the projects proposed by subsequent commentators. Much of that commentary, as valuable as it may be in its own right, can still become a distraction. A great deal can be gained from learning to read Weber from the beginning, unencumbered by the various "creative misinterpretations" (in Guenther Roth's felicitous phase) that have been offered before. However, part 2 does indeed belong to those interpretations and misinterpretations, creative and otherwise. The chapters of part 2 explore the networks of scholars in America drawn to Weber and his work, to the politics and sociology of "reading" and translation, to the creation of the sacred Weberian texts—long after Weber the author could continue to explain and defend his own words. The intriguing question of how the two dimensions of such an inquiry might be

related—the historical-textual and the theoretical-interpretive, so to speak—
is one I have kept in mind throughout.

A few sections of this volume have been published previously. Parts of chapter
5, "Remnants of Romanticism," appeared in a modified form in the *Journal of
Classical Sociology* and *The Protestant Ethic Turns 100: Essays on the Centenary
of the Weber Thesis*. Some of the material in part 2, chapters 11 through 13,
appeared in *The European Journal of Political Theory*, *Max Weber Studies*, and
Das Faszinosum Max Weber: Die Geschichte seiner Geltung. I have completely
rewritten and revised these articles and chapters for the current study.

MAX WEBER IN AMERICA

INTRODUCTION

From the beginning, discussion of Max Weber's writings and ideas has been interwoven with a fascination for his life. Karl Jaspers established the point of view early in his retrospective appreciations: the work was seen to reflect the person, and the person the work. The fascination has never lost its attractions. This can seem surprising, for Weber's life was in some ways so unexceptional. What did he really *do*, after all? His meteoric rise in the university world was cut short by illness. He actually served on faculties only at the beginning and end of his career, and for barely six years. No school of thought bore his imprint, and his actual students were few in number. In public life his occasional efforts at a political career came to nothing. His interventions in political affairs and public debate left him an outsider in his own time. His efforts to establish new directions or new institutions in intellectual life similarly fell on deaf ears or, as with the Deutsche Gesellschaft für Soziologie, ended in misunderstandings and his sudden withdrawal. Even the great editorial project of his life, the encyclopedic *Grundriss der Sozialökonomik* (Basic Outline of Social Economics), became a casualty of World War I and remained a mere fragment when Weber died in 1920. Viewed as a whole, the life offers a sobering record of disappointment and failure.

And yet there was still the work, fragmentary as it may have been, covering the sweep of world history and culture, and raising the largest questions about the emergence of the modern world. Much of it remained unfinished or scattered throughout journals, handbooks, occasional publications, or newspapers. Weber's favorite medium was the extended essay, the handbook article, the encyclopedia entry, the exploratory investigation of indeterminate length—the kind of writing that would make an editor cringe today. With the exception of his dissertation and habilitation, he did not write a single book. Form seems to have counted for little; expressing the ideas in words on paper, often by dictation, was what mattered above all. Perhaps we should not be surprised, then, that much of this work was hidden or forgotten. It is astonishing, nevertheless, to note that two of his articles (on German agriculture, forestry, and industry) published in English translation in *The Encyclopedia Americana* in 1907–8 were unknown until this century, having escaped any of the previous bibliographical dragnets, starting with those cast in the 1920s by his wife and a few diligent Munich students.

Authors sometimes must await those who come afterward for their work to be brought together, read, interpreted, and remembered. Max Weber is an interesting and perhaps extreme instance of the phenomenon: dismissive of his own accomplishments, obscure in his own time, yet renowned and widely cited in ours, even in the popular media. How did this circumstance come about? What accounts for his present-day reputation? How did it become possible for us to speak of a "Weberian" perspective, approach, analysis, or theory?

Anyone who has read Weber's writings with care will be tempted to point to internal textual evidence for an answer, noting the compelling formulations and the subtexts of intense personal engagement, whether the subject is the Old Testament prophets, the ascetic practices of everyday life, the formation of Western music, or abstractions like patrimonial domination and charismatic authority. The effect of the cascade of sparkling ideas, the combination of factual detail and abstract generalization, the melding of the subjective and the objective, can be utterly breathtaking, as many readers have remarked. But such an answer comes too easily, for there is a far more complex and even more compelling narrative that needs to be set forth, one that requires close attention to the intellectual, historical, political, and social context of Weber's thinking. That narrative is the subject of this book. It requires bridging different fields of inquiry and writing a cultural and intellectual history, whose ultimate aim is to give an account of the intellectual biography not simply of the man but of the work itself.

The intellectual biography of the work and an adequate explanation of the Weber phenomenon is crucially dependent on understanding what happened to Max Weber and his work in America. Interestingly, the notion of a search for "Weber in America" can be pursued in two quite different but complementary ways, for Weber really *was* in the United States for nearly three months in 1904, traveling with his wife and occasionally others, an episode long familiar to readers of the biography written by his wife, Marianne Weber's *Max Weber: A Biography*, though a particularly important experience that has never been fully explored in all its dimensions and details. Indeed, the Webers' American journey in the age of Progressivism and the Theodore Roosevelt presidency is a worthy subject in its own right, reminiscent of Alexis de Tocqueville's and Gustave de Beaumont's earlier sojourn in Jacksonian America. My narrative of what the Webers did, who they met, and what they saw and thought opens onto an expansive cultural history of the United States, a recovery of our past at the very beginning of the "American Century." My discussion in part 1 gives the journey itself and the Webers' accompanying commentary a long-overdue comprehensive treatment. But what happened in 1904 was also a harbinger of what was to come following Max Weber's death in 1920—namely, the use, interpretation, and dissemination of his thought in the United States by American scholars, such as Frank Knight and Talcott Parsons, starting in the 1920s, and joined thereafter by German émigrés and others from the English-speaking world. The subsequent development of "Weberian" thought and perspectives in the human sciences is the subject of part 2.

With regard to Weber's months in the United States, nearly all of what we have known until now has come from Marianne Weber's account, published in 1926. The American journey played a pivotal role in the larger scheme of Weber's life and work, for it occurred just as he was beginning to emerge from the debilitating psychological collapse of 1898, a life-altering event brought on by a number of complex social and psychic factors, including overwork and exhaustion, severe unresolved conflicts within the family, and powerful libidinal tensions categorized under the heading "neurasthenia" in the diagnostics of the time. In writing her husband's biography, Marianne tended to stylize these months of emergence from illness, culminating in the 1904 journey, as the beginning of the "new phase," the critical turning point in Max's struggle to return to the world of thought, scholarship, and public activity. Rewriting Marianne's account recently, Joachim Radkau has placed the American journey on the path of escape from the furies of a vengeful nature and onward to personal "salvation and inspiration." Both have a valid point to make about the trajectory of Weber's experience. There is indeed a sense in which the American experience and its promise inspired Weber's imagination and enthusiasms, a passage in his life that Weber himself seems to have noticed in precisely such terms. Moreover, whatever explanation one chooses to give for the changed circumstances, it *is* noteworthy that the Weber whose work we have read, appropriated, criticized, modified, and incorporated into the discourse of modern social science and political life has been until recent years exclusively the Weber of the texts written in the last sixteen years of his life, starting in 1904, at age forty.

Now for all its heightened and sympathetic tone, Marianne Weber's narrative contains significant gaps, omissions, forgotten passages, and exaggerations from the standpoint both of Max's ideas and interests and of her own. It is thus essential to question her narrative edifice and begin anew, returning to the sources she used, such as the correspondence within the family or with colleagues, while also exploring new avenues of knowledge and interpretation; for the months in the United States we need to ask what Weber actually did, why he did it, whom he met and why, what he saw, and what significance this concentrated episode had for him and his work. And we need to ask the same questions of the earlier narrator, Marianne Weber herself, in order to construct a new foundation beneath her account. Such questions have biographical implications, of course, but they also contribute importantly to a biography of the texts Weber produced, and thus to a better understanding of the rationale underlying the appropriation of his work.

With an intellectual of Weber's stature, commonly considered a founder of sociology and the modern social sciences, we should be aware that a biography of the person and the work is also to some extent a biography of the sciences and the emergent scientific disciplines. For this reason my investigation does not end with Weber's experience and the 1904 journey but pursues in addition the question of the subsequent reception and deployment of his ideas. For peculiar historical and political reasons, the discussion of part 2 is to a large extent an American story, beginning in the 1920s with the codification and earliest translations of Weber's work, continuing in the 1930s and '40s with its pedagogical and professional deployment, and culminating after World War II with the reintroduction of that work into Europe. Retracing these steps might be viewed as a kind of "reception history" or *Rezeptionsgeschichte*. But it is much more than this, for it involves an investigation of the ambitious effort to define the subject matter of the new social science disciplines, to institutionalize a body of knowledge, and to create a particular kind of educational regime in the modern research university. Needless to say, forces far beyond the circumscribed horizon of those with access to Weber's writings were at work in these contexts. So to write about the construction and appropriation of Weber's thought is thus in unusual ways to plunge into the contentious debate over the modern university, educational policy, and the politics of the intellectuals, carried out in this instance initially in the United States beginning in the twenties, and then after 1945 extended elsewhere primarily in Europe, but then also in Asia. The result is a fascinating disciplinary, institutional, and intellectual history, a complex and shifting configuration of perspectives and commitments to a particular kind of inquiry that form one of the twentieth century's most important chapters in the politics and sociology of knowledge. Since Max Weber wrote comparatively about the world civilizations, capitalism, and the developmental tendencies of "rational" modes of social action and social and economic organization, the uses and extensions of his work beyond its circumscribed point of origin has been all the more remarkable and compelling.

I would like to add that writing about Weber and "America" today from this double perspective inevitably involves reflecting on the problem of the image or representation of America—the *Amerikabild*, to use the German expression—that is so unavoidable today, as it was throughout the twentieth century. To return through Weber to the age of his contemporaries, to prominent figures like Theodore Roosevelt and Woodrow Wilson, or the people he met, such as William James, Samuel Gompers, W.E.B. Du Bois, Florence Kelley, or Robert Latham Owen, offers not only an opportunity to view American society and intellectual life and the American polity as it was a century ago but also an opportunity to reflect on the passage of a century and its significance—its hopes and promise, disappointments and catastrophes. This is very much a book placed prior to the First World War at the beginning of the "American

Century." It is difficult to avoid the infectious optimism and potential of that moment, amplified by Weber's own exuberance in the United States and signaled by the dynamics of Teddy Roosevelt's fall presidential campaign that he witnessed. The picture of a Max Weber fleeing from the modern world, skeptical about "democracy" and issuing dark warnings about "the masses" is essentially a clever falsification, satisfying various unhistorical ideological needs of the intellectuals. The actual historical lessons of Weber's American journey are far simpler: History offers nations exceptional opportunities sometimes, and it offers little solace for those in need of definitive answers and unambiguous truths.

My approach to Weber in this study is, in a word, *historical*. Or using stronger language, one might call it radically "historicist" in the sense that I seek to improve our understanding of Weber's thought by investigating its genesis in the specific historical situation of his life and times, his social attachments and intellectual engagements. It has become popular to characterize such an approach as "genealogical." Whether or not the term might add a serviceable metaphor, it can only provide clarity if it means a tracing of the sources and development of ideas in language, social interactions, or experience. There are obviously approaches other than the historical to Weber or to any other major writer and thinker that are useful and important: systematic, analytic, comparative, topical, thematic, or problem-oriented. When skillfully deployed, each can contribute in significant ways to understanding ideas and advancing our thinking. Choosing one does not exclude the others. They also can be instructively combined, as I intend to demonstrate in some of the sections of this volume. Yet at this stage in the work on Weber, his generation, and the problems of the fin de siècle in both North America and Europe, there is a particularly compelling need to recover the contexts and relationships out of which emerged major bodies of work, as well as modern social theory, the contemporary social sciences and the institutions supporting them.

I must add a comment about the importance of the United States and "America" for Max Weber, a comment that also contains a word of caution. In Weber's mature work the United States returns again and again as a point of departure, a context for comparison, an illustration, an example, a source of observation and material for reflection. In this regard the only real competitor is Great Britain and England. By contrast, Weber says little about contemporary France or Italy. Thinking historically and comparatively, in the sweep of European civilization it was Rome that inspired his historical imagination, not the nation-states of the present. To the east his eyes were drawn to Russia, not out of intrinsic interest but for world historical reasons having to do with the revolutionary transformation of a traditional social and political order. The juxtaposition of America and Russia in his thought can appear as a reminder of Alexis de Tocqueville's similar ruminations on a Europe positioned between two great world powers. But unlike his French precursor, for Weber such a perspective was not a matter of seeing in America the face of the future, or of triangulating a European developmental path, though he sometimes expressed views about "convergence" between the Old and New Worlds. Instead, the American journey represented an opportunity for observation and illustration of a certain kind of moral and social order, and a cultural and political dynamic linked to capitalist development.

To make sense of this order and trace its dynamic has the effect, whether intentional or not, of moving the American presence toward the center of Weber's thinking about the modern world. But a word of caution is necessary, for it would be misleading to conclude that Weber's thought revolved around American themes or problems, or that the large innovative questions he posed, for example, about religious beliefs and economic activity could have been asked only as a result of the American experience. It is rather the case that Weber's *problematics* emerged from an immersion in social and cultural world history, the civilizations of the West and the East, and through engagement with complex debates in the sciences over the origins, nature and meaning for the contemporary world of "capitalism"—the "most fateful force in our modern life," as he called it.

"America" had a place in these discussions for well-known reasons, many of which Weber identified in his speech at St. Louis, Missouri: it was a new nation, possessing an immense territory, in the post–Civil War era without an old aristocracy, and in that respect unburdened by the power of tradition, but having both "democratic traditions handed down by Puritanism as an everlasting heirloom" as well as an economy exhibiting in unparalleled ways the "effects of the power of capitalism." Which of these contending forces would emerge victorious? How could their contrasting effects be reconciled? What would occur as the course of history caught up with the United States? Weber found a striking formulation for the historical context of such questions, noting, "It was perhaps never before in history made so easy for any nation to become a great civilized power as for the American people. Yet, according to human calculation, it is also the last time, as long as the history of mankind shall last, that such conditions for a free and great development will be given." What will then become of this most consequential of world historical experiments, and in the end what will be its enduring value?

This kind of questioning is the spirit in which Max Weber invoked America in his work—as actuality and symbol, as history and myth. The invocation involved a world historical perspective and assessment, like that voiced toward the end of his life in "Science as a Vocation," echoing Tocqueville: "Permit me to take you once more to America," Weber intoned, "because there one can often observe such matters in their most massive and original shape." Similarly, in the concluding paragraphs of The Protestant Ethic and the Spirit of Capitalism he referred to America exhibiting the capitalist spirit's "highest development" and "emancipation." Such statements appear to match the fin-de-siècle topos of America as a model for the most distinctive aspects of modernity. But they do more that this. They offer an opening appropriately onto the biography of the work, an invitation to join the quest. It is an invitation I have chosen to accept.

PART 1

THE AMERICAN JOURNEY

Wer den Dichter will verstehen
Muss ins Dichters Lande gehen.

*If it's the poet you want to understand,
Then you must go to the poet's land.*

—William James's Diary, January 5, 1905

ONE

THOUGHTS ABOUT AMERICA

Traveling to Progressive America

Max Weber was an indefatigable and enthusiastic traveler. In the two decades between his marriage to Marianne Schnitger in 1893 and the outbreak of World War I he journeyed to England, Scotland, Ireland, Wales, France, Spain, Switzerland, Corsica, Austria-Hungary, Holland, Belgium, the United States, and again and again to northern and southern Italy. These trips served different purposes: a honeymoon and tourism in the early travels with Marianne to the UK and France in 1893 and 1895; escape from the pressures of work and recovery from emotional turmoil in the many flights south into France and Italy after 1898; and now and then professional obligations, such as the lecture at the Congress of Arts and Science in St. Louis, Missouri, in 1904, or the meeting of the Verein für Sozialpolitik in Vienna in 1909. Whatever the purpose, these journeys helped renew his spirits and cultivate his historical imagination. Sometimes he seemed capable of his scholarly labors only with the prospect of these episodes of renewal beckoning like a muse on the horizon.

The associations among traveling, energizing the mind and the emotions, and acquiring knowledge based on observation of the new and unexpected is a well-known human experience. The ancient world captured these associations in the Greek verb *theorein*, a compound of *thea*, the view or look of something; *horan*, to see a thing attentively; and the noun *theoros*, the attentive observer or the emissary sent to observe foreign practices and to "theorize" about them—that is, to construct a rational explanation about the strange and unexpected. The discoveries of the great naturalists and ethnographers, figures like Alexander von Humboldt, Charles Darwin, or Bronislaw Malinowski would obviously have been inconceivable without experience in the field. But so too would have been the work of some of the keenest observers of political and social life, writers like Alexis de Tocqueville and James Bryce. Their classic commentaries of the nineteenth century on American politics and society, *Democracy in America* and *The American Commonwealth*, respectively, could only have been written with the benefit of observations made in the United States. What of Max Weber? As another astute observer of American life, Gunnar Myrdal, has once suggested, does he in this regard belong in the same company as Tocqueville, Bryce, and their counterparts in the sciences?

Of all of Weber's travels, the nearly three months in the United States in 1904 stands out in certain ways. It was a trip he had long anticipated, having canceled a plan in 1893 to visit the Chicago World's Fair with his friend Paul Göhre in favor of his secret engagement and subsequent marriage to Marianne Schnitger—replacing, it might be added, Göhre in her affections. His foreknowledge of American conditions had been cultivated for years by his father's 1883 Northern Pacific Railroad trip from Minneapolis–St. Paul to Portland, Oregon, and Seattle, orchestrated by the financier and family friend Henry Villard and accompanied by Carl Schurz, James Bryce, and Georg Siemens, among others. In discussing this episode Guenther Roth has quite rightly emphasized the interests of the "cosmopolitan bourgeoisie" in sizing up investment opportunities in the developing North American market, and residues of this interest may well have carried over to the son's probing of economic conditions two decades later. But Max Weber junior was also a self-conscious scholar, and his occasional statements about the 1904 journey show a desire to broaden his intellectual horizons and assess for himself what others had observed and written about American conditions, from Bryce's text (first published in 1888) that he read with care, to the commentaries and engaging enthusiasms of Friedrich Kapp; the important 1848 émigré, author, German American abolitionist politician and former associate of Karl Marx, Moses Hess; and other left Hegelians in the Rhineland. During Max's youth, Kapp, having returned to a unified Germany, frequented the Weber home in Charlottenburg and became a political ally of Max Weber Sr., both men holding liberal seats in the Reichstag. Within the family circle the American connection was formed not only through Villard and Kapp but also by the reports, exchanges, and disputes involving the descendants of Georg Friedrich Fallenstein, Max's maternal grandfather—some of whom had settled in the New World where the Webers were to visit them.

Weber's American interests were long-standing and well-established. It was Kapp, for example, who gave the eleven-year-old Max a copy of Benjamin Franklin's *Autobiography* in translation. Inscribed "to his dear young friend Max Weber," Kapp's own laudatory introduction included the unusual recommendation that German fathers teach their sons Franklin's practical maxims. Occasionally the engagements glimmer through in the collection of Weber's youthful correspondence, the *Jugendbriefe*, that his wife published posthumously, notwithstanding her tendency to suppress anything related to Max Weber Sr. and to omit or avoid documenting some family issues. Thus, at age fifteen the young Max recorded having "recently engaged a lot with the history of the United States of North America, which is very interesting to me" (October 11, 1879). Five years later he acknowledged the powerful effect of the frequent contact with Friedrich Kapp and the magic worked by his formidable memory, original judgments, and mastery of the "art of conversation" (November 8, 1884). And in two letters to his cousin, Emmy Baumgarten, he discussed the American misadventures and marriage of their half-cousin, Laura Fallenstein, whom he was to visit in Massachusetts (July 5, 1887; July 14, 1889). As Guenther Roth has shown, a thorough excavation of the family correspondence reveals the extent of the disputation over the American branch of the Fallenstein clan, a preoccupation thoroughly familiar to the young Max and later to Marianne.

The American journey was timely for another essential reason. It came just as Weber had turned his attention to the problems of his most famous work: the theme of the relationships among economic action, economic development, and the moral order of society, explored in the two-part essay he titled *The Protestant Ethic and the "Spirit" of Capitalism*. In view of this new project, whose publication and completion spanned the months in the United States, he was primed to search for those aspects of social life highlighted by his own thesis about the affinity between an ascetic religious ethos and economic activity. "My questioning," as he explained, "deals with the origins of the *ethical* 'style of life' that was spiritually 'adequate' for the economic stage of 'capitalism' and signified its victory in the human 'soul.'" It was a questioning that Weber carried with him during his travels. The possibility of connections among belief systems, with an emphasis placed on the voluntaristic Protestant sects and important features of social and economic activity—especially the aspect Weber called modern *vocational* culture—was never far from his thoughts.

In addition, it is important to emphasize that the months in America offered an opportunity to inquire more generally into economic and social conditions in the New World. As social historians have pointed out, the context of such an inquiry was shaped by two features of the fin-de-siècle intellectual world in North America; parts of the European continent, particularly Germany and Scandinavia; and Great Britain: the shared intellectual culture transmitted through the upper middle class or cosmopolitan bourgeoisie, promoted by educational exchange and the special attraction of studying at German universities; and the cosmopolitan "progressive" social and political outlook widely shared in professional circles, notwithstanding national differences and competition among the great powers. Both were important in Weber's travels.

In some ways the journey became a touchstone for a number of Weber's later reflections. The focus of his interests even reads like a list of leading issues on the agenda of American Progressivism: immigration and immigrant communities, class and status groups, race and ethnicity, gender and family life, education and the colleges, religion and the sects, democracy and electoral politics, political leadership versus administrative rule, the political economy of work and vocation, the politics of land tenure and rural life, the problems of the cities, the built environment, and the cultural problems of capitalism. The breadth of the subject matter gives credence to James Kloppenberg's view of Weber in the American context as "a progressive manqué" who differed from the other theorists of Progressivism primarily in mood while sharing "their philosophical perspective and their political ideals." Both Max and Marianne Weber devoted considerable effort to seeking out the areas of social policy and those social institutions that would speak to the need for reform. Max pursued his long-standing interests in social and economic organization, labor relations, agrarian society, religion, the social sciences, and university life. Among his professional contacts, nearly all had studied in Germany or had German connections. But he also met an astonishing array of people from different walks of life, so to speak—from land speculators in the Indian Territory to William James in Cambridge. He made a point of seeing different regions and a remarkably diverse cross-section of American society, from New England to the Deep South, from urban settlement houses to country life in rural Appalachia, from native and African American communities to German immigrant townships. At every opportunity he visited educational institutions, searched library holdings for material bearing on his work, and observed religious services—a long list of encounters that included Columbia University, Northwestern University, the new University of Chicago, the Tuskegee Institute, perhaps the University of Tennessee, Haverford College, the Johns Hopkins University, Harvard University, and Brown University (and for Marianne, Bryn Mawr and Wellesley Colleges). The services included numerous Protestant sects: principally Methodist, Baptist, African American Baptist, Quaker, Presbyterian, and Christian Scientist.

In national politics, the autumn of 1904 marked Theodore Roosevelt's presidential campaign, begun officially on September 12 with his appeal for "civic righteousness" and "national greatness." Roosevelt's open letter accepting the nomination for president and launching his campaign was printed in the *Chicago Daily Tribune* on that date when Weber was in Chicago. As a dedicated reader of newspapers, Weber would surely have read this text with its "pragmatic" characterization of Americans—"for fundamentally ours is a business people—manufacturers, merchants, farmers, wage workers, professional men, all alike"—and its call for a renewed national commitment to building civic "character." In style and substance the two months of campaigning became a landmark in the nationalization of the presidency and the creation of what Weber later called a truly "plebiscitary" executive office, underscored by the images of Teddy Roosevelt handshaking his way through the ethnic enclaves around Hull House. Social issues were everywhere: immigration, ethnicity, race, "the woman question," exploitation of labor, the plight of the cities, the crisis in education, trade policy, a growing gap between rich and poor. Questions persisted about what to do with a newly won overseas empire and the nation's new standing as a world power, celebrated as a theme at the St. Louis World's Fair in numerous ways, including most obviously a large Philippine exhibit. In addition, there were still questions to answer about the so-called "inland empire," the territories of the Southwest governed directly from

Washington, D.C., and given prominent public display in the Indian Building at the Exposition.

The invitation to travel to the United States was itself a stroke of good fortune. At the urging of Weber's Heidelberg colleague Georg Jellinek, in July 1903 Hugo Münsterberg extended an invitation to Weber to attend the St. Louis Congress of Arts and Science that was being planned in conjunction with the centennial celebration of the Louisiana Purchase. He was invited to present a paper in the economics section. Of course, Weber leaped at the opportunity, replying affirmatively within days. Münsterberg was then at Harvard University, enjoying an appointment in experimental psychology arranged by William James and serving as a point of contact among German and American scholars, politicians, and businessmen. Together with Albion Small, the University of Chicago sociologist, and Simon Newcomb, the well-known mathematician, Münsterberg had been appointed to the organizing committee responsible for recruiting Congress participants. Previously in the 1890s he had been associated with Weber and other junior faculty, such as Heinrich Rickert at the University of Freiburg. The earlier personal relationship was probably decisive for the invitation to St. Louis, for Weber was not well-known outside the circle of his German colleagues in economics, history, and law—unlike other invitees, such as the theologian Adolf von Harnack, the chemist Wilhelm Ostwald, or in the social sciences Georg Simmel, Ferdinand Tönnies, and Werner Sombart. From this group only Simmel, whose essays had already been translated by Albion Small and published in the *American Journal of Sociology*, declined to attend. For Weber, in any case, his reputation was based not on recent work, but on accomplishments in the meteoric early years of his career.

Planning for the Congress of Arts and Science turned out to be a contentious affair, a not uncommon occurrence with academic assemblies. In the verbal imbroglio leading up to it, Weber even considered avoiding the Congress altogether, while following through with his travel plans in order to exchange views with colleagues and see the American cities, as he wrote directly to Hugo Münsterberg on June 21 and July 17, 1904. But tempers subsided, the threat was unnecessary, and the conference turned out to be surprisingly beneficial. Once there, reporting from St. Louis to Jellinek, he then commented, "Many things here are *very* different than the travel writers, Münsterberg included, depict them" (September 24; BAK). The reference was to Münsterberg's sprawling two-volume treatise *The Americans* (1904), published in German early in the year and surely read by Weber. (An abbreviated American edition appeared shortly afterward.) Intended as a mediation between stereotypical American and German points of view, it was a work having few affinities with Weber's thought. Neither Münsterberg's mythic interpretation of America as the land of the "spirit," "desire," or the "instinct for self-direction," nor his uncritical patriotic view of Germany would have been congenial to Weber's outlook.

The comment to Jellinek poses important questions for our inquiry: if Münsterberg and other authors of the travel literature were mistaken, then why
and in what ways? What were the conditions that Weber thought he encountered? How and why did his perceptions differ from those of others? These
turn out to be complicated questions, and an answer must begin with Weber's
emergence after the turn of the century into a new period of intellectual engagement, which also involved a recovery and extension of some themes that
were close to his heart.

New Horizons of Thought

Max Weber returned home to Heidelberg on his birthday, April 21, 1902,
after an absence of nearly two years. He was thirty-eight. He would live only
another eighteen years, and not merely some but *all* of the work that would establish his reputation as one of the twentieth century's most important thinkers lay in front of him. The question of his life still had to be answered: Did the
return herald a rebirth of his capacities, or would he fade into oblivion?

The America journey falls at the beginning of these years of intensive mental labor and extraordinary accomplishment. The four years leading up to it
might be described as the most crucial in Weber's life, for it was during these
years that he found the resources, essentially on his own, to answer the question. Yet this period is veiled in silence. Very little is known about what Weber
did, read, or thought, and most of what we know is transmitted through his
wife Marianne, on whom for lengthy periods he was thoroughly dependent as
his "only connection to the world," as he once acknowledged.

By 1903 Weber had taken the very first painful steps back to intellectual
engagement, interspersed with travel, as always, and with publication of the
labored first section of his critical essay on the historical economics of Wilhelm Roscher and Karl Knies, his own Heidelberg economics professor. Marianne reported to Max's mother Helene Weber that the first installment was
mailed to Gustav Schmoller for his journal on February 20. The essay was not
an auspicious beginning, with the critical commentary on the logical problems
of historical method (and specifically Roscher's naive pre-Hegelian "emana-
tionism") buried in forty pages of dense prose. The year's trips recapitulated
the normal routine: following the struggles with Roscher and methodology,
an escape to Italy in early spring, Holland in the summer, then Hamburg for
a meeting of the Verein für Sozialpolitik, on to Helgoland for another meeting, finally a return to Holland in October. It was on the Hamburg-Helgoland
excursion with Edgar Jaffé, Werner Sombart, and Alfred Weber, Max's brother
who had been featured recently in the pages of the *Frankfurter Zeitung*, that
the final details had been worked out covering the important editorial assignments for the *Archiv für Sozialwissenschaft und Sozialpolitik*. That coeditorship

(with Sombart and Edgar Jaffé, the journal's owner) was to occupy Weber's energies for the rest of his life and contribute to some of his most important publications.

The likelihood of an American trip was first mentioned by Marianne Weber in a letter to Max's mother, Helene, on August 28. Having remained in Heidelberg while Max discussed plans for the *Archiv* in Helgoland, she followed the news three weeks later with expressions of delight that Max was "for the first time in five years" together with colleagues, "though probably without taking part in the discussion," she surmised. However, Max's absence and the anguish and disappointments of the preceding years also combined to provoke Marianne's revealing confession to her mother-in-law:

> But I long so that *my* star, my celebrated Max, might shine once again, to our delight and the notice of others! Oh my god, how difficult it is to cast about in the harbour of resignation and to see others forge ahead while he is shut down. Does he feel it the same way? I don't know, but I would like to believe that the summons right now from the old circle of colleagues has made it obvious. But he is so different from most of the others—perhaps it is still the illness, the need for self-protection that shields him from the kinds of thoughts that often rage through me. The day after tomorrow is our 10th anniversary. Ten years full of love and living together and growing closer together, and of those 6 full of a hard and troubled fate! And my greatest wish to grow together *fully* with *him* in love and understanding, that is now fulfilled through this fate. But at *this price?!* No, that wasn't necessary and can't be rationally explained, though I want to embrace it with thanks as the greatest gift of this year—this consciousness of growing together with him, as only a few married couples can experience. And now we will continue to bear our fate well, even if the burning desire for his creative power *consumes* me and can't be stamped out or overcome. But enough of this. When I'm alone everything comes over me in a stronger and more elemental form than when he is here and the claims of the happier present silence and numb all the old wishes and sorrows. (September 18, 1903; DWS)

The lure of the happier affirmative present and hopes for the future was one of the most striking features of the couple's joint planning for the voyage to the New World that took place the following year.

What occurred in these months leading up to the departure for the United States from Bremen on August 20, 1904? Marianne naturally immediately turned her attention to Max's well-being—reporting, for example, that his health and mood was "up and down," and that "after bad nights he's very gloomy, and then occupying himself with Baedeker on America helps" (October 30). Karl Baedeker had published his first North American handbook in time for the Chicago World's Fair of 1893, with a second revised English edition appearing in 1899. The second expanded German edition was on the way for the St. Louis attendees. Weber presumably began reading the first with its topical introductory chapters, including James Bryce writing on American government and politics. At nearly five hundred pages the Baedeker would have kept him occupied.

Returning home from Helgoland, Max Weber had, to be sure, brought an important writing assignment with him: the editors' introduction to the new *Archiv für Sozialwissenschaft und Sozialpolitik* and the position paper that became the well-known essay, "The 'Objectivity' of Knowledge in Social Science and Social Policy," published before departure for the United States in 1904. The usual struggles ensued: "Max is now completely 'finished,'" wrote Marianne on February 15, 1904, as the project neared completion, for, as she noted, he

> sleeps poorly, has increased sexual irritations, and cannot work. In short, we will surely send him traveling, for until the America trip he'll never last here without a break. He really needs to recuperate now, for the inability to work makes him much more inconsolable and irritable than before, and that's entirely natural in view of the increased demands on us. His travel plans aren't clear yet, but probably he'll take a trip from Genoa to Amsterdam, though there isn't much one can do with nature, as it's still too early in the Romagna. He is waiting for the manuscript corrections, and I think he will probably depart at the end of the week. (DWS)

Joachim Radkau has explored the psychological dimensions of such clinical assessments in some detail—in particular the ambivalent meanings attached to "nature." Suffice it to say that Marianne's worries were overstated: Max never left for a vacation or another location in the months leading up to the America trip, instead immersing himself in his work and the preparations for transatlantic travel. The work included two more occasional writings completed in the spring and summer, one on the problem of entailed estates in Prussia and the other on the controversy in agrarian history and economics over ancient Germanic social structure. Weber noted that the latter was begun as a contribution for his lecture in St. Louis, but then turned into an independent article. The thematic connection among these writings, including what came to be the presentation in St. Louis, was formed in his mind by their concerns from different points of view with the problem of capital accumulation and the conditions for *modern* capitalist development.

In addition to these assignments, partly occasioned by his new editorial responsibilities, Weber also found time to engage in a spirited defence of parliamentary institutions in the pages of the *Frankfurter Zeitung*, his first political polemics since 1898. And, drawn back to science, he began participating in one important Heidelberg discussion group, the Eranos Circle, a select number drawn from the university professoriat at the initiative of the New Testament theologian Adolf Deissmann and the classical philologist Albrecht Dieterich. Weber attended a meeting on February 28, 1904, and probably another on July 3, when his colleague Georg Jellinek spoke on the "religious and

metaphysical foundations of liberalism," a topic stemming from his discussion
of the relationship between religious belief and political-constitutional forms
in *Die Erklärung der Menschen- und Bürgerrechte* (translated as *The Declaration
of the Rights of Man and of Citizens: A Contribution to Modern Constitutional
History.*) Jellinek's study had just appeared in its second edition, and it was
filled with numerous American examples from state constitutional practices.
The author argued that the defense of human rights emerged historically from
the struggles over religious freedom, and that the American states' bills of
rights provided the model for the better-known *French Declaration of the Rights
of Man and the Citizen.* Jellinek's was a work of fundamental importance for
Weber, a key for understanding the American contribution to the modern
language of rights, toleration, and the rule of law. Like Jellinek and Weber,
the other Eranos participants—among them theologian Ernst Troeltsch, philosopher Wilhelm Windelband, and historian Erich Marcks—were concerned
with the deeper significance of religion for human communities considered
historically, cross-culturally, and in relation to the many aspects of modern
life. It was the perfect setting for Weber to work out his ideas and express them
to a well-informed, critical, but sympathetic audience.

Completing the work schedule, then, was the lecture for St. Louis and the
new text that had increasingly consumed Weber's attention: *The Protestant
Ethic and the"Spirit" of Capitalism.* Using the available correspondence, Hartmut Lehmann has pointed out that to some extent the new direction was
entangled in Weber's effort to persuade Lujo Brentano, his Munich economics colleague (and the man he was to replace at the University of Munich in
1919), to write a review of Sombart's *Modern Capitalism* (1902) and divide
up the "colossal literature" on Puritanism. But the effort failed, leaving the
field to Weber and his other colleague and Eranos Circle participant Ernst
Troeltsch.

In October 1904 Weber was already immersed in reading the Puritan sources.
It is intriguing to note that he mentioned in a letter to Brentano, whom he had
just seen in Hamburg, the possibility that his presentation in St. Louis would
deal with some of the literature of the Reformation: "I think with pleasure on
the recent get-together, even if it was brief, and hope to be able eventually to
be useful to you in some way, in case you engage more closely with the question of Calvinism. During the winter I'll be working through the sources for
my St. Louis lecture and an essay for the Archiv" (October 10, 1903; BAK).
The result of this work over the months that followed was actually two separate manuscripts: the lecture on agrarian economics and sociology that drew
upon his earlier writings in the 1890s, and part 1 of *The Protestant Ethic and the
"Spirit" of Capitalism,* published as the first three of what were eventually five
chapters under the succinct and ambivalent heading "The Problem."

Weber began writing this three-chapter essay of fifty-four pages in April
1904, finishing it in July. By the end of that month Marianne was writing to

Helene Weber, "Our thoughts are indeed directed largely toward America" (July 22; DWS). With departure less than a month away, Marianne was immersed "with pleasure," she said, in Hugo Münsterberg's new two-volume book on America and the Americans. At the same time Max was reading the proofs of part 1 of his own *Protestant Ethic*, returning them to his publisher, Paul Siebeck, before leaving Heidelberg. He concluded the manuscript with a discussion of Luther's conception of the calling, and in the final paragraph appended an all-too-often ignored warning that read

> we have no intention of defending any such foolishly doctrinaire thesis as that the "capitalist spirit" . . . let alone capitalism itself, *could only* arise as a result of certain influences of the Reformation. . . . We intend, rather, to establish whether and to what extent religious influences *have in fact* been *partially* responsible for the qualitative shaping and the quantitative expansion of that "spirit" across the world, and what concrete aspects of capitalist culture originate from them. In view of the tremendous confusion of reciprocal influences emanating from the material base, the social and political forms of organization, and the spiritual content of the cultural epochs of the Reformation, the only possible way to proceed is first to investigate whether and in what points particular *elective affinities* between *certain* forms of religious belief and the ethic of the calling can be identified. At the same time, the manner and general *direction* in which, as a result of such elective affinities, the religious movement influenced the development of material culture will be clarified as far as possible. Only *then* can the attempt be made to estimate the degree to which the historical origins of elements of modern culture should be attributed to those religious motives and to what extent to others.

These words of caution and qualification were in fact published in the *Archiv für Sozialwissenschaft und Sozialpolitik* only as Weber's American journey was coming to a close. While in the United States, then, Weber was not known at all for the "thesis" announced in the text that surely became his most daring and controversial essay.

The most challenging issue at this juncture, however, is not so much the reading and interpretation of the work but its genesis. What went into the preparation, the "prehistory" of the famous *Protestant Ethic* thesis? What clues can we assemble for understanding the origins and direction of Max Weber's thinking as he set his sights on America?

A "Spiritualistic" Construction of the Modern Economy?

Weber never really completed his study of the "Protestant Ethic and the Capitalist Spirit," the working title he first used. After visiting the United States he mentioned wanting to return to work through sources he had uncovered in the sectarian libraries of Protestant denominations and colleges, a project never accomplished. He elaborated the work in the heated and lengthy exchanges with Karl Fischer and Felix Rachfahl between 1907 and 1910, refining his argument as he wrote. As part of the multivolume essays in the sociology of religion he planned a comparative study of Christianity in its many facets, a work barely begun. In revising the text of *The Protestant Ethic and the Spirit of Capitalism* in 1919, he added some new passages and expanded the footnotes by one-third, particularly the critique distancing his views from those of others, such as Brentano and Sombart. Weber said a great deal about the original text by way of explanation and elaboration in these writings and in occasional comments. Among these commentaries, two remarks stand out in bold relief: his notation in the first reply to Rachfahl in 1910 that he had lectured on the same topic "in part as much as 12 years ago"—that is, in 1897–98; and the provocative announcement about part 2 in a letter to Heinrich Rickert: "In June/July [1905] you will receive a cultural historical essay that may interest you (asceticism of Protestantism as the foundation of modern *vocational* culture), a sort of 'spiritualistic' construction of the modern economy" (April 2, 1905; MWP).

Questions about the genesis, sources, descent, or "origins" of Weber's ideas about the "Protestant ethic" and the "spirit," the *Geist* of capitalism (invariably in distancing inverted commas) have persisted over decades. Guenther Roth has investigated at length the ways in which Weber's life circumstances and family background in the "cosmopolitan bourgeoisie" of Europe, the German men of affairs on his father's side of the family and the French Huguenot connections on his mother's side, prepared him to take a larger view of the relationship between economic action and religious ethics. Similarly, Hartmut Lehmann has urged that we view Weber's text as a kind of testimony about himself, and by extension the family circle and personae he knew and observed at close range. In addition, there is substantial commentary on Weber's immersion in the theological and popular literature related to the subject, from the writings of English reformers like Richard Baxter and John Bunyan to the work of scholars like Albrecht Ritschl on pietism or his colleague Otto Pfleiderer on the philosophy of religion. There is also speculation about the period of gestation in the hidden years before 1904: his observations in the Netherlands, or his long sojourn in Italy and contacts in Rome's German Historical Institute with the Counter-Reformation scholars Johannes Haller and Karl Schellhass, the latter a friend from Weber's youth. In sum, *The Protestant Ethic and the Spirit of Capitalism* has become, in Wilhelm Hennis's accurate phrase, an "overdetermined" text.

Nevertheless, a few signposts are worth mentioning. We should remember that the problem of establishing the relationship between aspects of culture and the economic system—especially capitalism—had already been formulated in general terms by the Historical School of economics. One striking piece of evidence comes from the lectures of Karl Knies, the professor and former teacher Weber was to replace at the University of Heidelberg in 1897. Three semesters before he enrolled in Knies's class on applied economics at Heidelberg, his American colleague and acquaintance Edwin R. A. Seligman took the same course. Seligman's extensive handwritten notes (in German) have survived, and in one section dated October 25, 1880, under the heading "praktische Nationalökonomie und Volkswirtschaftpolitik" (meaning, roughly, "applied political economy and national economic policy") he cataloged Knies's discussion of different "intellectual influences" on the economy, especially in relation to "religion and confession." Knies discussed in sequence the Indian Brahmans, the ancient Greeks, the Jews, Christianity, and Islam. Within Christianity, a "universal religion," Knies distinguished Catholicism from Protestantism. The latter was characterized by "the principle of individualism. Here the individual is responsible for his belief," Seligman wrote, adding the fragments, "Also the rational principle. Progress revealed in the texts. Profound contradictions." Seligman also recorded the contrast with Islam, according to Knies: "Belief in unconditional fatalism, leading to a certain apathy. Lack of development," he summarized.

When Weber enrolled in Knies's courses in 1882 he would surely have heard the same framing of the problem: How did different religious belief systems affect the formation and development of economic activity and the economic system? There were, of course, manifold causes accounting for economic action, including financial interests and various other "material" factors. In his later work Weber extensively discussed the material factors on the "other side of the causal chain," so to speak, as in his last course of University of Munich lectures collected under the heading *General Economic History*. But it was the contents of the human mind and the nature of conviction and confessional belief that inspired his youthful imagination. We should thus expect that when he replaced Knies fifteen years later and began lecturing on the same subject Weber would return to this very question. It was a question about the conditions for the emergence of the modern economy, in part framed comparatively in relation to the world religions, a question that stayed with him the rest of his life.

The complex biography of the "Protestant Ethic" thesis can be pursued further in Weber's habit of observing religious services and practices. It was a habit begun early in life and continued in the United States. One truly exceptional instance of the practice appears in a long letter Weber wrote to his mother at age twenty-two. He was on military duty in the reserves at Strasbourg between semesters, spending time intermittently at the home of his mother's sister, Ida Baumgarten, her husband Hermann, the well-known historian, and their children and friends, including on one occasion Karl Schellhass. On the Sunday celebrating Saint Simeon's Feast Day (February 3), Weber was given responsibility for representing the officer corps at a Catholic service in the Église Saint-Étienne:

On Sunday two weeks ago I heard a very interesting sermon and church service here in the Stephans[kapelle of Saint-Étienne]. The service began with a short musical introduction and a verse sung by the church choir, then a sermon on the well-known parable of the workers in the vineyard [Matthew 20: 1–16]. The sermon was delivered with a common touch and easily understandable, without any echo of pious platitudes, but really practical and in its dialectic carefully thought out, so that it was a pleasure to be able to recognize the intellectual work put into it. Logically considered, much of it was surprising, especially for someone who is used to Protestant deductions and modes of reasoning [Gedankenzusammenhänge]. The train of thought was the following, for example: The worker who has done the least receives as much pay as those who have done the most. Therefore, it is not a matter of *what* one does, as the contrast between the sacrifice of Cain and Abel also shows—but a matter of the sense or meaning with which ones does it [mit welchem Sinn man es tut], as a Protestant preacher would continue saying—however, instead came: but a matter of one possessing divine grace or mercy [himmlische Gnade] and being accepted as a righteous person in the eyes of the Lord, as was not the case with Cain. But this divine grace must be *earned* [erworben], and for that purpose only love helps; "'if only I had belief that I could put to good use," etc., from which follows that belief alone is not sufficient. That was then discussed using very practical examples, on the one hand at the level of the unproductiveness of dead belief, and on the other the misfortune of those who not withstanding concentrated activity [angestrengte Tätigkeit] have not earned divine grace. The entire sermon, skillfully and powerfully delivered, lasted about 20 minutes, including the reading of the text (appearing to be a translation of the Bible that at first I thought was from the Latin, as it sounded in speech pattern like the latter.) Then followed more than half an hour of liturgy accompanied by songs. The entire event interested me a lot and in general spoke to me, especially the way in which the sermon addressed the relationships of the individual and the skill shown in adapting and adjusting to the situation and outlook of the soldiers. At any event [it was] a striking difference from the Protestant chaplain here, who spoke about the scene in the temple [Luke 2: 25–35] and thus presented the old Simeon in two parts, namely: (1) the child in his arms, (2) the hope in his heart, followed by the usual sentiments. (February 19, 1887; DWS)

For inexplicable reasons, in her collection of Max's youthful correspondence Marianne Weber missed this lengthy epistle Max wrote to his mother Helene. It has never been cited before, for it lies buried within Marianne's massive archive. But the omission is singular: in the spiritually charged environment of his aunt's home, the setting for Weber's early conversations about William Ellery Channing, Theodore Parker, and the American Unitarians, he begins to reflect on the distinctions in practical religious ethics that would guide the argument of *The Protestant Ethic and the Spirit of Capitalism*.

The issue in these comments involves the familiar distinction between faith and "works." Lutheran theology advanced the notion of justification by faith alone, or in the words of Luther's own sermon on the meaning of Simeon's affirmation of salvation through faith in Luke 2, "You will perceive therefore how the whole of scriptures speak only of faith, and reject works as useless, nay, as standing in the way of justification and preventing us from rising." Weber takes up Luther's line of reasoning, noting that in explicating the parable of the vineyard and the paradox that "the last will be first, and the first will be last," the Protestant pastor would have emphasized the quality of a person's inner faith, exemplified by Simeon, whereas the Catholic priest emphasized earning divine grace through demonstrated good works. The performance of one's duty in one's calling or vocation as a condition for salvation, an idea in Luther's discourse "That Soldiers, Too, Can Be Saved" and other texts, is of course developed at length later by Weber. But in the church in recently annexed Alsace there was some consolation to soldiers facing danger, whatever their religious affiliation, to hear that having either achieved faith or earned grace, they were able to "depart in peace."

In this youthful letter it is not only Weber's familiarity with the biblical texts that strikes our attention but above all his perception about a theological difference, a difference in interpretation and emphasis, and the implications of that difference for practical ethics and action in the world. In his observations the *Protestant Ethic* thesis starts to emerge as a kind of intuition that will provoke further reflection, a search for historical evidence, and an effort to sort through and make logical sense of the "profound contradictions" mentioned by Knies. It is a search that would continue in the churches and sects of the United States.

TWO

THE LAND OF IMMIGRANTS

Arriving in New York

Max and Marianne Weber left Heidelberg on August 17, 1904, and they returned home by train through Paris after docking at Cherbourg, France, on November 27—a journey of over three months. The Atlantic passage to the United States was aboard the *Bremen* of North German Lloyd, a 10.5-thousand-ton vessel built in Gdansk (Danzig) that departed from Bremerhaven, Germany, on Saturday, August 20, and proceeded to Southampton, England, for additional passengers. The ship was sighted south of Fire Island as it approached New York's Ellis Island the evening of August 29, according to the *New York Times*. Passengers disembarked the following day. The Atlantic voyage took a normal 8 days, but it was well short of the record of exactly 5 days, 11 hours, and 54 minutes held by the luxury liner *Deutschland*. The *Bremen* continued its Germany–to–New York service until the outbreak of war in 1914, and after the war flew the British flag as reparations under the terms of the Treaty of Versailles.

Thanks to the diligence of archivists for the Ellis Island Foundation, the ship's manifest for the Webers' 1904 passage is available on the Internet. The manifest lists 1,679 passengers, nearly 60 percent of them immigrants from Russia and the Hapsburg lands of central and eastern Europe, including the provinces that now comprise Poland. A majority of the men and women were under twenty-five, and many were Jewish ("Hebrew" in the code of the immigration statutes), crowded into third-class steerage and the lower decks. In her letters home Marianne accurately reported five hundred Jewish immigrants. Of the other passengers, numerous German and other European travelers were headed to the International Exposition in St. Louis, Missouri. Among them were the impressionist painter Max Schlichting, who exhibited an oil painting, *Strandvergnügen* (Pleasures of the Beach), at St. Louis; and Professor Guido Biagi, the royal librarian in Florence, who spoke at the Congress of Arts and Science on the library as an institution of learning. Marianne noted that Schlichting, an influential member of the *Kunstgenossenschaft* (art association) who had affiliated earlier with the Berlin Secession, had been sent to the exposition by the German government to observe and serve as an art jurist, an important political appointment. On the first day at sea he introduced himself to Max Weber. Having just published a tract on art and the state, *Staat und Kunst*, that attacked his former associates in the secession and defended the official call for a "unified" presentation of German art, Schlichting's apologetics apparently allowed him to slip through the screen of court-sanctioned disapproval of modern styles in painting. To my knowledge he was the only (former) secessionist to present his work in St. Louis. One can only wonder how his ambivalent double role would have appeared to Weber, who became increasingly critical of the strident and crude antimodern cultural policies and pronouncements of Kaiser Wilhelm II.

The names of Schlichting and Max and Marianne Weber and their traveling companion Ernst Troeltsch appear late in the complete manifest for the *Bremen* as passengers 1638 and 1647 to 1649, respectively. Max is amusingly misidentified as a clergyman, a title probably intended for Troeltsch. Perhaps he looked the part. Their Atlantic passage had gone well, without seasickness, Max eating his way through the lavish menu, to Marianne's distress. She noted they were seated at dinner with two American women schoolteachers, one of whom was probably a Chicagoan named Ida Pahlman, who were glad to assist with their English. But Marianne saved her longest substantive comment for one of the enduring social policy issues that would weave in and out of their travels: immigration. It was an obvious concern, considering the circumstances on board. Having observed the cramped quarters of the eastern European immigrants, pressed together "like sheep on the heath," she noted that the relative cost of the Atlantic crossing meant the privileged few actually lived at the expense of others—"really dreadful," she complained, and "it should be given public attention" (August 24; MWP). The struggles of immigrants and the substandard living conditions in immigrant communities was receiving attention in some quarters in the United States, as she would soon discover.

The pattern of post–Civil War immigration should be well known, especially for New York, as it was the major port of entry and destination for many immigrant groups. By 1904 legal immigration into the United States exceeded 800 thousand people annually, topping a million for the first time the following year. The large numbers recorded in the decade before 1914 would not be seen again until the end of the twentieth century. For the five boroughs of New York City itself, approaching four million in 1904, the foreign-born percentage of the population was headed to an estimated high of 40 percent by 1910. (In recent decades the metropolitan area has once again approached such percentages.) By 1900 the surge in German and Irish immigrants had begun to subside, to be replaced by the wave of new immigrants from central, eastern, and southern Europe—Hapsburg territory, the Russian Empire, and Italy. Of the 8.2 million immigrants entering in the first decade of the twentieth century, two-thirds came from these locations in Europe. Among them were Jewish immigrants, estimated at about 950 thousand over the decade in one official report from the 1910 census. Many settled on Manhattan's Lower East Side, served there by settlement houses and social workers the Webers would visit in November 1904.

The Webers stayed in New York City twice: upon arrival for about five days with Ernst Troeltsch at the Astor House on Broadway, then for a more intensive and consequential two weeks at the end of their travels. The weeks in November were reserved for some serious work, observations of numerous urban institutions, and a fast-paced social schedule. By contrast, the days on arrival offered little more than a whirlwind of first impressions: the ethnic and economic contrasts of the city, the crush of different nationalities, the mansions of the wealthy along Fifth Avenue, the noise and poor condition of city streets (confirming the warning in the Baedeker guide), the oasis of calm in Frederick Law Olmsted's Central Park (duly noted by the Webers as a reminder of Berlin's Tiergarten), the celebrated Green-Wood Cemetery in Brooklyn, and the Wall Street stock exchange. This last location was considered a tourist destination at the time, though it would have attracted Weber's professional interest in any case, since he had published a few hundred pages explaining to a skeptical German public the rationale and inner workings of stock and commodities exchanges, including the futures market. He also had served in 1896 as an academic expert on the German Ministry of the Interior's thirty-member Committee on the Stock Exchange. The transcript of the committee's sessions shows his acute awareness of the operation of other exchanges in Europe and North America,— particularly the emerging futures market. The stop on Wall Street was an imperative: it gave him a firsthand look at one of the famous institutions of modern market capitalism.

If the popular imagination of the time represented America in visible monuments, then it surely found them in the Brooklyn Bridge and the steel-frame urban skyscrapers, a distinctive new American architectural innovation and style of building. Crossing the East River, the Webers commented on the "painterly" vistas, with Max juxtaposing the impressions left by the bridge and its masses of humanity in motion with the views from a distance of the "fortresses of capital" on lower Manhattan, reminiscent of the towers of the *grandi* in the medieval Italian cities. Directly across from their hotel stood the St. Paul Building and the thirty-story Park Row Building, the latter recognized by Baedeker and praised by *King's Views of New York City* as "the tallest structure of its kind in the world." "Ground rent drives buildings into the heights" was Max's dictum. Marianne captured the mood, writing, "Two of the powerful 'beasts,' 30-story 'skyscrapers,' arise directly across from us. One must see them to believe they are real. I still ask myself whether they are simply dreadful, grotesque and showy, or whether they display their own beauty and dignity. In any case, like the tower of Babel, they nullify everything else in the vicinity, such as the little church [St. Paul's Chapel] with its gothic tower that tries to assert itself like an island of peace amid the untamed din of the streets" (September 2; MWP). Today the curious traveler can still judge for herself the outcome of this face-off between spiritual "culture" and materialistic "capitalism." Taking sides in the debate, for his part Max announced that the new imposing

Figure 1. A postcard of New York City from the era shows the view across Broadway of the Park Row and St. Paul skyscrapers that provoked Marianne Weber's ambivalent comments about the "powerful beasts directly across from us" and Max Weber's quip about the "fortresses of capitalism." Courtesy Archive of American Architecture.

structures stood beyond the usual categories of aesthetic judgment. They were symbols of a new kind of American sublime.

The main encounters with American university and college life were to come later in the trip, though they began right away in September in conversations with Professor and Mrs. William Hervey. A Columbia University Germanist educated in Leipzig, Hervey with his wife provided a brief introduction to the political economy of academic life in the metropolis: small apartments, cramped offices, high rents, time-consuming commutes, expensive shopping, difficulty finding satisfactory domestic help, general constraints on "individualism" in everyday life. Little has changed in a century.

As for the traveling companions, in these first few days Weber established a reputation for being one step ahead of everyone, "until now better than *ever* since his illness" Marianne observed, an enthusiast in pursuit of the new, distinctive, and unusual. His complaints were reserved for those, like Troeltsch, who instead of engaging with the new experience quickly found "the outward symbols of the American spirit antipathetic and repulsive" in the words of Marianne's reporting. The spirit of adventure set Weber apart from Troeltsch and other colleagues, such as Werner Sombart, and contributed importantly to the range of his personal contacts, the depth of his inquiries into the details of American life, and the sheer variety in his itinerary.

Following the first days in Manhattan, the threesome boarded a Pullman car for the trip up the Hudson Valley to Albany and on to Buffalo. Alert to the abrupt change of environment, Marianne commented that the natural spectacle "awakened completely new feelings about the new world," as if revealing the unspoiled edenic landscape celebrated by the nineteenth-century Hudson River painters. The immediate goal for seeing the power of nature, of course, was Niagara Falls, almost an obligatory pilgrimage for the European traveler. Alexis de Tocqueville and Gustave de Beaumont had stopped there in August 1831, donning rain gear for a dangerous exploration behind the falls. But there was another, more important destination: the German immigrant community in North Tonawanda at the terminus of the Erie Canal.

Church and Sect, Status and Class

The Webers' correspondence from North Tonawanda and Niagara Falls, where they stayed in Andreas Kaltenbach's hotel, contains a surprising amount of detail. In her account Marianne chose to include only a few sentences from Max's commentary, emphasizing the stark contrast between the urban metropolis they had just left behind and the modest wood-frame single-family homes of the immigrant community of about ten thousand they visited in North Tonawanda. But more was at stake than the obvious differences between the cosmopolitan metropolis and smalltown America.

First of all, the traveling party expanded to include three more university colleagues. At Niagara Falls they were joined by the Erlangen philosopher Paul Hensel, who had arrived in New York two weeks earlier, also bound for St. Louis, where he would deliver a lecture titled "Problems of Ethics." Johannes E. Conrad, a professor of economics and then rector at the University of Halle, was also in town visiting his daughter and son-in-law, Margarethe and Hans

Haupt, before continuing to St. Louis. As a prominent representative of the Historical School of economics, Conrad presented a paper at the Congress of Arts and Science titled "Economic History in Relation to Kindred Sciences." Weber knew both scholars; indeed, some of his important early contributions to political economy, including handbook articles about the stock exchange, had been published by Conrad as editor of the *Jahrbücher für Nationalökonomie und Statistik* and the *Handwörterbuch der Staatswissenschaften*.

In his later reconstruction of this particular episode, Hans Rollmann has mentioned these professional connections, deftly using the alternative perspective provided by Ernst Troeltsch's travel letters to his wife Marta. However, the circle needs to be completed, for it also included the American economist and educator, Edmund J. James, and his German-born wife and two university-age sons, both fluent in German. The James and Haupt families had known each other for years, starting in Germany. Graduating from Harvard University, James had gone on to study in Berlin and Halle, completing his doctorate under Conrad in 1877. In Halle he also had met and married Anna Lange, the daughter of a Lutheran pastor. Having taught already at the Wharton School at the University of Pennsylvania and at the University of Chicago, James had advanced quickly through the academic ranks, founding the American Academy of Political and Social Science and editing its *Annals*, among many other accomplishments, and then advancing to the presidency of Northwestern University. In these days in upstate New York he was in the process of accepting an offer to become president of the University of Illinois (at a salary of $8000.) James was a well-known figure in the founding generation of American economists—many of them, such as Richard Ely and Edwin R. A. Seligman, educated like James in Germany. Weber thus found himself not only in a German immigrant community with colleagues from home but also in the company of an influential educator, political economist, university president, and one of the founders of the American Economic Association.

In North Tonawanda, Hans Haupt was pastor for the German Evangelical and Reformed Church, located centrally in a working-class neighborhood at 174 Shenck Street. Partially supported by the Johannesstift in Berlin, and called the Deutsche Vereinigte Evangelische Friedens Gemeinde at its founding in 1889, like many such congregations it was eventually absorbed into the United Church of Christ in the 1950s. Services in this Protestant congregation were conducted in German well into the twentieth century. Haupt had grown up in Halle, the son of the theologian Erich Haupt, a well-known New Testament scholar at the Martin Luther University who became caught up in some of the historicist controversies of the time over the life and teachings of the historical Jesus of Nazareth. After leaving home, Hans Haupt moved away from his pietistic background and into liberal Protestant circles that would have included people Weber knew, such as Friedrich Naumann, Paul Göhre,

Figure 2. The German Reform "Friedens Gemeinde" Church in North Tonawanda,
New York, as seen today, a site in 1904 for considering the importance of the
Protestant sects in North America. Author's photograph.

or Martin Rade, editor of the *Christliche Welt*—or later on, the American Walter Rauschenbusch, whom Haupt met during a trip to Germany. Haupt wrote
for Rade's journal, and he was primarily interested in practical ethics and the
human meaning of the scriptures rather that their dogmatic or literal content.
His writings on religion in America, published in German, are concerned with
the relation between church and state and the nature of preaching. They reveal above all an intellect attuned to the political and social context of religious life in the United States. The practice of using Bible study to promote
"character building" was one among many examples he explored.

Weber's central interest in North Tonawanda had to do with the general
relationships across the religious community, an individual's religious or spiritual beliefs, and economic activity. This interest was expressed in a number of
comments that served as the starting point for two sets of ideas: first, the formulation of an essential distinction between the religious community as either an
institutionalized "church" or a voluntary "sect"; and second, a similarly crucial

distinction between considerations of social "status" or socioeconomic "class" and their interplay in nascent immigrant communities that found themselves embedded within a preexisting "democratic" social order.

His informal commentary documented the political and domestic economy of North Tonawanda, starting with the made-to-order wood-frame houses, priced from $1000 to $3000, one of which was the Haupts' parsonage that the travelers visited next to the Friedens Church. Weber's comments also included a brief sketch of the Church's economic and moral foundations:

> The congregation consists of 125 families, and church attendance appears excellent, especially with the men. Of course the congregation itself—*almost all unskilled* workers in the lumber mills and on the docks—supports the church and the minister. The individual worker's share *costs* him about $20–30 (80–120 Marks) annually, along with the offerings. The ministerial teaching is a quite *undogmatic* Christian message, freely interpreted. The congregation pays attention to the minister's personality and talent as a preacher, and according to Haupt, if the general synod caused problems, the congregation would simply leave. The minister can be terminated with 3 months' notice (like nearly everyone), though apparently this happens rarely. When he was on the prairie [earlier in his career in Iowa], for a salary Haupt, who reminds one of [Martin] Rade in appearance and speech, received $250 (1050 Marks) *a year*. The farmers would invite him for dinner on Sunday and would send him ham, etc., while the women donated rabbit pelts. According to Haupt, in [North] Tonawanda his income now is about $1000 (4200 Marks). A mason in New York earns 1½–2 times as much, and a worker in Tonawanda just as much. The *15-year-old* maid (a girl from the congregation) earns $104 (422 Marks) a year. . . . a minister's salary appears often to vary between $600 and $1000, except for the "stars" in the metropolis. What a contrast with the income of the president of the steel trust [a reference to J. P. Morgan] of $1 million or 4.2 million Marks! (September 8; MWP)

The Haupts' domestic economy, supporting four children, was similarly constrained and labor intensive, resting on a kind of division of labor reminiscent of the *autarkeia* (self-sufficiency) of the ancient *oikos*, or household. Weber had difficulty understanding how they could make ends meet.

According to Rollmann and to Wilhelm Pauck, who asked Haupt about the scholars' visit many years later, Weber and Troeltsch had requested beforehand that he gather as much information as possible on the moral teachings of the Protestant denominations, particularly as they bore on economic activity. Haupt reported being unimpressed by their scientific curiosity, perceiving Weber and Troeltsch to be suffering from a professorial conviction that they already had all the answers they needed. Nevertheless, in 1906 when Weber came to write his sequel to *The Protestant Ethic and the Spirit of Capitalism*, the essay on the Protestant sects and the spirit of capitalism, first for the *Frankfurter Zeitung* under the title "Churches and

Sects," then revised for Rade's *Christliche Welt*, he alluded in the introductory paragraphs to Haupt's figures, though without identifying their source. It was the combination of *voluntary* support for a largely independent and self-governing congregation, substantial tithing of family income, and high rates of Church attendance that attracted Weber's attention. The comparison with Europe became explicit in his last 1920 revision of these reflections: "Everyone knows that even a small fraction of this financial burden in Germany would lead to a mass exodus from the church. But quite apart from that, nobody who visited the United States fifteen or twenty years ago, that is, before the recent Europeanization of the country began, could overlook the very intense church-mindedness which then prevailed in all regions not yet flooded by European immigrants. Every old travel book reveals that, formerly, church-mindedness in America went unquestioned, as compared with recent decades, and was even far stronger."

Weber may have overestimated the long-term trend toward *secularization*, depending on what one means by the term, and his claim about "Europeanization" raises interesting questions about "American exceptionalism" that need to be explored. But at the time his question was, How can the difference between America and Europe be explained?

The answer for Weber, supported by the conversations with Haupt and observations of his congregation, could be found in the form and quality of the personal legitimation offered by membership in the religious community. Such legitimation depended on a certain kind of social and moral dynamic made possible only in the voluntary community of believers, the "sect" form of organization, typical of reform Protestantism. The "personal" character of the attachment was evident not only in the "testing" of individual members but also, as Weber emphasized, in the attention given to the minister's personal qualities. The ministerial position was not an "office" backed by ecclesiastical structures of authority but an appointment or "election" subject to the popular will of the membership. Thus, in Weber's classic and widely cited formulation, so essential to the sociological understanding of religious life, the church was "a compulsory association for the administration of grace," whereas the sect was "a voluntary association of religiously qualified persons." In Protestantism, as Weber noted, the conflict between these two opposed organizational forms played itself out again and again over the centuries. Nowhere was this truer than in America, which for Weber was the preeminent land of sects and sectlike associations, whose strength was reinforced politically by the formal constitutional separation of the church from the state, and culturally by egalitarian or antiauthoritarian norms.

A source of continual puzzlement and misunderstanding, the generalized religiosity or "church-mindedness" found in the United States was grounded in the voluntaristic quality of the sect form of association and its social functions. In new immigrant communities, however, the exclusive nature of the religious sect could have paradoxical consequences, as Weber noted in his comments about the Haupt family:

> They are limited in their efforts to get ahead by their German *"accent,"* which almost eliminates any opportunity for advancement by a minister. Haupt is thus already anglicized in appearance and intonation. He still preaches most of the time in German, but now and then in English. The *high schools* (advanced public schools or roughly the third through sixth year of a Gymnasium) are, of course, entirely in English. He must urge his children and his congregation to learn English if they don't want to remain *second rate* forever. Enjoying "good company" is rendered difficult by the distances, but also by the residential situation. It is customary for people living on the same street to socialize together, but Haupt lives amid his workers. The doctor and the pharmacist two streets over don't visit him, nor do the *"first rate"* families from other parts of town. For having a home in a street regarded as belonging to the *"first set"* is an indication of being a *"gentleman"* and leads to acceptance in *"society,"* even for the most well-to-do. This is a remarkable result of the purely mechanical characteristics according to which democratic society is ordered here. We have great respect for the Haupts (and their children), as they are faced with such conditions, and for the fact that they have stayed and become what they are. (September 8; MWP; emphasis added.)

Though he was writing in German, as if to illustrate the point about the significance of language, in this commentary Weber even used the English terms I have italicized.

Spoken native language as a badge of cultural identity is an issue familiar to immigrant communities, sometimes dividing the generations. In North Tonawanda, public opinion generally supported having German used in the schools, according to Haupt, but a New York State law required that English be used for at least half the instruction. The larger issue was not simply language, however, but the nature of the criteria according to which social status, social distinctions, exclusivity, and inequalities would be practiced in an allegedly "democratic" social and political order—and how and by whom those criteria would be recognized. Class position determined economically or by "wealth" was one obvious answer, a way of defining the structure of opportunity and privilege—that is, "life chances" in Weber's vocabulary. But in the absence of wealth or inherited status, what else could be used to express the "passion for distinction," as our second president, John Adams, called this human propensity? The answer implicit in Weber's commentary is "education."

Education and the problems of the modern university formed one of the great themes of Weber's lifework, culminating in the well-known lecture in the last years of his life on the pursuit of science as a vocation or calling. In the figure of Edmund James he encountered a model educator enthusiastic about German scholarship and self-consciously committed to adapting German practices to American requirements. James's Midwestern Methodist and

Huguenot origins may help account for his passionate interest in educational improvements at all levels for men and women, including advocacy for the kindergarten, for coeducation, and for the free public high school, all post–Civil War innovations in American life. Weber was clearly impressed with James and the *grandezza* of his presence, noting that his position as an American university president represented a synthesis of the political skills of a German minister of culture, the financial acumen of a corporate trustee, and the administrative and ceremonial presence of a German university rector—an astute sizing up of this unique institution.

As an educator, James's views were an instructive combination of what Weber later referred to as the "dual tendency" in American higher education: encouraging specialized professional training for teachers and businessmen, successfully implemented by James at the Wharton School as a case in point, while also advocating broad preparation for undergraduates across a variety of scientific and humanistic subjects. Weber surely would have had James in mind when he reflected on these issues. Writing for the Berlin press in 1911, for example, he noted that in contrast to the tendency toward specialization, which seemed "European,"

> There is another quite opposite tendency found in American business circles—so I was repeatedly told, to my surprise—although I could not assess how widespread this tendency is or how enduring it will be. According to this view, the college, with its particular impact on the character—in the sense of the Anglo-Saxon ideal of the "gentleman"—and the particular type of general education which it offers, seems, according to the experience in these circles, a setting especially adapted for education towards independence—and, it should be added, for the healthy civil self-respect of the embryonic businessman, both as a human being and in his job; as such it is better than a specialized course of study.

It hardly needs to be said that the discussion of "general education," a subject of intense scrutiny at the time by James and other educators, such as presidents Charles Eliot of Harvard University and Martha Carey Thomas of Bryn Mawr College, and typical still today of American but not European universities, has indeed endured and never abated; it has only waxed and waned in the face of competing claims on the curriculum, conflicting ideals for the educated man and woman, and uncertainties about the requirements for informed citizenship.

What about the object of these discussions, the university students themselves? Weber met many of them, starting at Niagara Falls and North Tonawanda with Anthony and Hermann, the two sons of Edmund and Anna James who were graduates of Chicago's South Side Academy. Anthony, the older of the two, was a cadet at the Annapolis Naval Academy. The episode returned to Weber's thoughts during World War I, in the context of a series of speculative comments about the fate of democracy in America in an age

when, as he put it, "everywhere in the large states modern democracy is becoming bureaucratized democracy." The hypothesis, in brief, was that in the
large modern democratic polity, educationally certified expertise and organized
bureaucracy would challenge the egalitarian status conventions embedded in
the self-governing sects:

> As a consequence of this war America will emerge as a state with a large army,
> an officer corps, and a bureaucracy. When I was there previously, I spoke with
> American officers who were not entirely sympathetic with the demands placed on
> them by the American democracy. For example, once I was with the family of the
> daughter of a colleague [Margarethe Conrad Haupt], and the maid was off work.
> (House maids could take a two-hour break.) The two sons arrived, both navy ca-
> dets, and their mother said: "You must go out and shovel the snow, otherwise I'll
> be fined 100 dollars." The sons, who had just been visiting with German navy of-
> ficers, replied that wasn't appropriate for them, provoking the mother's response:
> "If you don't do it, then I'll have to myself."

This story drawn from everyday life in the James family is an apocryphal but
harmless falsification of the actual circumstances described in the Webers'
correspondence. But it served its purpose, not simply as a comment about
the status conventions promoted by specialized training or service in the
officer corps but also about the role of women in a culture promoting "democratic" norms.

Appearing early in Weber's 1918 speech in Vienna to Austrian officers, the
comment is set up provocatively by a reference to Thorstein Veblen's sardonic
critique of "predatory national policy" as a "sound business proposition" in
the last pages of *The Theory of Business Enterprise*, a text Weber knew well.
It would go too far to suggest that Weber shared all of Veblen's iconoclastic
views. But on these matters they did agree on the sources of unresolved conflict in American public life: the radical self-sufficiency and independent spirit
promoted "from below" by the self-governing sects, and the status conventions
and dependencies promoted "from above" by the administrative state and its
orders and agencies. The modern university is caught in this vice, acknowledging the demands of collegiality on the one hand, but bound to the standards
of administrative rule on the other. The microcosm of North Tonawanda provided a beginning hint of these competing possibilities.

Settlements and Urban Space

The dual challenge of the "social question" and the "woman question," posed
often in stark ways by immigration and the conditions of working-class families, elicited other responses in North America and Europe, many of which
the Webers were to observe. Marianne had a particularly strong interest in

the settlement movement that had sprung up in the late nineteenth century, following the lead of Toynbee Hall in London. On her last full day with the Haupts she chose to explore the situation in Buffalo, leaving Max writing letters, and Troeltsch exploring Goat's Island with Hensel.

With a population of nearly 400,000 in 1904, Buffalo ranked eighth among American cities, and as a major urban center it had a sizable immigrant population. A large majority of the foreign-born were German. It was the site of the Pan-American Exposition in 1901, the national sequel to the Chicago's World's Fair, and memories at the time linked the exposition with President William McKinley's assassination on its grounds three years previously. The Haupts had actually been present at the fair the day the shooting occurred.

Marianne was accompanied by Grete Haupt and her father, Johannes Conrad. Of the six settlements serving Buffalo's immigrant communities, they toured only two, probably the Neighborhood House and the Westminster House, the latter close to the German Lutheran Seminary that was surrounded by homes built by German carpenters for their own families. Both of these settlements served ethnic German neighborhoods, and she found them similar to the practice in Germany of establishing "homes" for employees, offering a full range of manual training, especially for young women and men, along with entertainment, theater, and sports. Marianne's brief observations marked the beginning of her effort to make sense of American social policy and the circumstances of women, an interest that extended well beyond the trip itself. They were supplemented by her extensive conversations with Grete Haupt, a rich source of insight into the position of women in American life that informed her feminist views and the sympathetic perspective on American women that she would articulate upon her return to Germany.

As for the city itself, Marianne was especially taken with the contrast between the downtown streetscapes, the ethnic neighborhoods, and the system of parkways and residential streets designed more than two decades earlier by Frederick Law Olmsted and Calvert Vaux, in 1904 at the height of their magnificence:

> My trip to Buffalo yesterday was very pleasant, even though all the walking around along lengthy streets was fairly strenuous. Despite the magnificent buildings, the shopping streets as a whole look no more inviting than those in New York: Everything is obscured with a black sooty haze, windows are sometimes dirty—in short, new and yet already falling into disrepair, somewhat like our own suburbs. By contrast, the residential district in the world of elegance is attractive, nothing but tree-lined green streets with charming wood-frame houses that look as if someone had just taken them out of the toy box and placed them on the velvety green lawn. They are the only completely new and original architecture that I've seen here so far, and aesthetically far more satisfying than the imposing stone palaces in New York. (September 9; MWP)

The reference was to two contributions from Chicago's architectural inno-
vators: the Prudential (Guaranty) Building designed by Dankmar Adler and
Louis Sullivan, and the Ellicott Square Building of D. H. Burnham, a fitting
prelude to the modern cityscape of Chicago that the Webers were about to
experience.

In later decades "progress" had its costs. Unfortunately for the city that Olmsted called America's best planned urban space, in the 1960s his system of connected parkways and residential streets was decimated by the construction of
expressways from the suburbs bulldozed through established urban parks and
neighborhoods. Only recently have efforts to restore at least some parts of the
original design achieved limited success.

Hans Haupt took up pastoral duties in a different German Reform church in
Cincinnati in 1910, thriving in an environment with an educated congregation more congenial to him, Grete, and their children. The couple remained
there the rest of their lives. When in old age Grete lay dying from cancer,
Hans read to her between three and five in the afternoon from Marianne
Weber's recently released biography of her husband, "a few pages to her every
day." What would they have thought had they been able to savor all the comments from a few days in 1904 about their lives of service to the immigrant
community? The community they left behind succumbed slowly to the blight
left by deindustrialization and globalization. At the beginning of the twenty-
first century the once-vibrant Friedens-Gemeinde Church has been converted
to the Ghostlight Theater, an irony that should not be lost on those who now
attend its shows and perform on its stage.

THREE

CAPITALISM

On September 9, 1904, Max and Marianne Weber left Niagara Falls by train for Chicago, where they remained for eight days, with Ernst Troeltsch and Paul Hensel following a day later. They had accommodations in the new Auditorium Building on Michigan Avenue, the early contribution to a modern American style of building by the German-born Dankmar Adler and his partner, Louis Sullivan, completed in 1889 and today the home of Roosevelt University. The stop at the German immigrant community in North Tonawanda, New York, had been the first objective prior to arriving in St. Louis, Missouri, for the Congress of Arts and Science. The second and very different major objective in keeping with Max Weber's fascination with urban life was the week in Chicago, an opportunity for him to satisfy his curiosity about the American cities. He was not disappointed by the city James Bryce characterized as "perhaps the most typically American place in America" and Carl Sandburg in his well-known tribute "Chicago":

> Hog Butcher for the World,
> Tool Maker, Stacker of Wheat,
> Player with Railroads and the Nation's Freight Handler;
> Stormy, husky, brawling,
> City of the Big Shoulders.

Weber had said he wanted to travel to America to see its cities, and he saw nearly all the major urban centers east of the Mississippi River. But Chicago would have had a special appeal. His father had stopped there in 1883 with Bryce, Carl Schurz, and Henry Villard, staying in the Palmer House. He had set aside his own plans for visiting the city's Columbian Exposition a decade later. By 1904 Chicago had grown to become the world's fifth largest urban center (behind London, New York, Paris, and Berlin), with a metropolitan area twice the size of the city of London, as he noted. Like Berlin, it was a new industrial and commercial magnet and transportation hub, with a rapidly increasing working class and staggering labor, public health, and social issues. Nowhere else could one experience so immediately the raw, untamed energy of the New World, as well as the kind of dynamic pace and assault on the senses that Weber's colleague, Georg Simmel, had described in his remarkable essay of 1903 on the modern metropolis. The language Weber himself was to use on a later occasion would have suited Chicago well: "The modern metropolis with its streetcars, subways, electric lights, show windows, concert halls, restaurants, cafés, smokestacks, massive buildings, and the wild dance of impressions of sound and color that play on the sexual fantasy, affect the constitution of the soul, and encourage us to brood about all of the apparently inexhaustible possibilities for the conduct of our lives [*Lebensführung*] and happiness."

When the Webers arrived in Chicago, the twentieth century's first major strike by butchers, packinghouse workers, teamsters, and affiliated trades in the stockyards had just ended in defeat for the Amalgamated Meat Cutters and Butcher Workmen's Union. The AMCBW, an affiliate of the American Federation of Labor and chartered by Samuel Gompers as recently as 1897, had been engaged over the previous four years in organizing the packing industry. As AFL president, Gompers (whom Weber was to meet a month later in Washington, D.C.) had urged caution and argued unsuccessfully against a strike, concerned about lack of discipline in the union, a surplus of unskilled workers in the labor market, and the organizational strength of the "Big Five" packing companies—Armour, Swift, Morris, Wilson, and Cudahy. When contracts expired in May the union membership became impatient, especially in the skilled crafts, and the strike began in July and was settled temporarily by arbitration, but then resumed and continued for another six weeks. Despite the union membership's apparent support for continuing the strike, the executive leadership, led by Michael Donnelly, declared the struggle at an end on September 8. Union leaders issued positive pronouncements for the press, but the outcome was in fact disastrous. Unionization of the stockyards failed completely. Some workers and leaders were blacklisted—Donnelly included—and nothing was achieved related to the main demands: a ten-hour working day, a minimum wage of 18.5 cents an hour for unskilled workers, and a preference for hiring men rather than women in the slaughterhouses. The outcome provoked Finley Peter Dunne's (Mr. Dooley's) ironic reprise in the *Chicago Daily News*, "If I was a wurrukin' man I'd sigh f'r th' good ol' days whin Labor an' Capital was friends. Those who lived through thim did." At the very least the strike and its aftermath added to the passions and drama of the Webers' week.

The City as Phantasmagoria

Max Weber's descriptions of Chicago are unparalleled in their vivid metaphors and memorable imagery. He wrote two letters about the city, and Marianne wrote one, covering about one-tenth of their entire American correspondence. In *Max Weber: A Biography* Marianne selected parts of the most colorful passages, but she also missed a lot: their comments about Hull House, Jane Addams and her circle; Max's asides about churches and religion; and the day spent in Evanston at Northwestern University (confused by later editors with the University of Chicago). Max's topic was the anatomy of the city; for good reason Marianne cited his first lengthy reflections, written with a clinical eye and apt comparisons upon their arrival in St. Louis:

Chicago is one of the most unbelievable cities. By the lake there are a few comfortable and beautiful residential districts, mostly with stone houses of a very heavy and cumbersome style, and right behind them there are little old wooden houses such as one finds in Helgoland. Then come the tenements of the workers and absurdly dirty streets that are unpaved, or there is miserable macadamization outside the better residential district. In the city among the skyscrapers the condition of the streets is utterly hair-raising. Soft coal is burned there. When the hot dry wind off the wastelands to the southwest blows through the streets, and especially when the dark yellow sun sets, the city looks fantastic. In broad daylight one can see only three blocks ahead, even from the observation towers. Everything is mist and thick haze, the whole lake is covered by a purple pall of smoke from which the little steamers suddenly emerge and in which the sails of the departing ships quickly disappear. It is an endless human desert. From the city one travels on Halsted Street—which, I believe, is 20 English miles long—into the endless distance, past blocks with Greek inscriptions, Xenodochien [Hotel], etc., and then past others with Chinese taverns, Polish advertisements, German beer halls, until one reaches the stockyards. For as far as one can see from the Armour firm's clock tower there is nothing but herds of cattle, lowing, bleating, endless filth. But on the horizon all around—for the city continues for miles and miles until it melts into the multitude of suburbs—there are churches and chapels, grain elevators, smoking chimneys (every big hotel here has its own steaming elevator, etc.), and houses of every size. The houses are usually small, for at most two families each (hence the enormous dimensions of the city), and they are graded in cleanliness according to nationality. All hell had broken loose in the stockyards: an unsuccessful strike, masses of Italians and Negroes as strikebreakers; daily shootings with dozens of dead on both sides; a streetcar was overturned and a dozen women were squashed because a nonunion man had sat in it; dynamite threats against the Elevated Railway, and one of its cars was actually derailed and plunged into the river. Right near our hotel a cigar dealer was murdered in broad daylight; a few streets away three Negroes attacked and robbed a streetcar at dusk, etc., etc.—all in all, a strange flowering of culture. There is a mad pell-mell of nationalities: up and down the streets the *Greeks* shine the Yankees shoes for 5 cents. The Germans are their waiters, the Irish take care of their politics, and the Italians of the dirtiest ditch digging. A very instructive illustration in Hull House (which Marianne probably wrote about) showed how this residential mixing together of nationality groupings actually worked. The table of wages next to it showed (to my surprise) that the *Italians* have the lowest wages, lower than the *Russians*. With the exception of the better residential districts, the whole tremendous city—more extensive than London!—is like a human being with its skin peeled off and whose intestines are seen at work. For one sees everything—in the evening, for example, on a side street in the city the prostitutes are placed in a show window with electric light and prices on display! Characteristic here as in New York is the maintenance of a specifically Jewish-German culture. Theaters perform in Yiddish [Judendeutsch] "the Merchant of Venice" (with Shylock prevailing, however) and stage their own Jewish plays that we want to see in New York. The role of the Germans in Chicago is not very significant, despite their large number. They have even sold their "Schiller" theater because of dissension. By contrast St. Louis has a large number of highly regarded German families (with Americanized children, of course) and German wealth is equal to [that of] the Anglo-American. Carl Schurz lived here [in St. Louis] earlier, and he still owns 2/3rd interest in the Mississippi newspaper, which manages the novel task of publishing a strictly *Republican morning* edition, and with other editors, an equally partisan *Democratic evening* edition. That speaks volumes about the party system here and its particular orientation only to office-holding, or even more so its unprincipled character. (September 19; MWP)

The city as a human body with its skin peeled off and inner workings made visible: for urban sociology, a midwestern Chicago invention, there is surely no better fantastical vision of the organic, fully transparent life of the metropolis.

The Webers marveled at the extreme contrasts: wealth and comfort alongside poverty and squalor, civility together with criminality, decency with vice (in the words of the *Chicago Daily News*)—as well as the mapping of social structure and ethnic demographics onto the urban grid and the built environment. The steel-frame skyscrapers first seen in Manhattan were a Chicago invention, and Marianne now noted the "several magnificent and aesthetically satisfying structures," while Max called them "an expression of economic strength" evoking the capitalist spirit—allusions to the new architecture of Dankmar Adler and Louis Sullivan, D. H. Burnham and John W. Root, Charles Atwood, and William LeBaron Jenney.

Max Weber's description of sex, violence, and crime were perhaps somewhat overdrawn, depending on one's perception and expectations in the confused aftermath of the failed strike. The *Chicago Daily Tribune* editorialized that although "there was some violence during the strike . . . the accounts of it have been greatly exaggerated." But the *Tribune* and the *Daily News* continued to report attacks in the stockyard district as the strikebreakers departed. The violence reflected not only labor and economic issues, but also ethnic and racial tensions. The AMCBW was dominated by Irish and German workers, especially higher-status butchers, though with a new influx of Polish, Lithuanian, and other eastern European nationalities. The ethnic mix was accurately depicted in Upton Sinclair's best-seller of the period, *The Jungle* (1906), based on firsthand observations in the stockyards in 1904. The packing companies hired large numbers of African Americans and probably some Italians and Greeks as strikebreakers, and much of the mob violence was directed toward them, adding to ethnic and racial conflict that existed already *within* the union itself. The union's inability to maintain working-class solidarity by mediating internal ethnic conflict was often given as one of the main reasons for the strike's failure. The *Tribune* did on September 13, 1904, report the mob assault on streetcars loaded with men, women, children, and two alleged (black) strikebreakers, listing the injured by name. The press also reported the cigar store holdup and murders on West Lake Street, as well as the activity at Hotel Casino with its "nocturnal debauches" on Madison Street.

Americans found their own depiction of the city in muckraking journalism, the term drawn by Theodore Roosevelt from an impeccable moral source and one of Weber's favorites: the man with the muckrake in John Bunyan's *Pilgrim's Progress*. In addition to Sinclair's novel, the most famous tract of the times was Lincoln Steffens, *The Shame of the Cities* (1904), serialized in *McClure's* magazine, where he was managing editor. Steffens published a lengthy chapter on Chicago, matching Weber's metaphor with one of his own: "First in violence, deepest in dirt; loud, lawless, unlovely, ill-smelling, irreverent, new; an overgrown gawk of a village, the 'tough' among cities, a spectacle for the nations." But he also credited Chicago with the spirit of adventure, a love of audacity and the "sporting spirit," a city that had not just talked reform but actually done something about it. "Chicago should be celebrated among American cities for reform," he wrote; "real reform, not moral fits and political uprisings."

The prospect for political reform and the consequences of it in the face of corruption, rule by bosses, and the big city political machines was of course the larger problem for Weber and the American Progressives. Chicago offered the perfect setting for addressing the issue: Jane Addams's Hull House.

Hull House, the Stockyards, and the Working Class

The Webers visited Hull House on their first weekend in the city, and Marianne returned for a Sunday evening meeting of the Women's Trade Union League (WTUL), a chapter of the association founded by Jane Addams earlier in the year. They toured the facility and examined the social surveys. Having already seen the Buffalo settlements, Marianne reported,

> The most interesting thing I've seen here is a large settlement that has been built at considerable expense in a workers' district by a quite extraordinary and engaging woman. It includes a day nursery, accommodations for 30 women workers, a sports facility for young people, a large concert hall with a stage, an instructional kitchen, a kindergarten, rooms for all kinds of instruction in needlework and manual tasks, etc. During the winter 15,000 people of both sexes come here and

receive instruction, inspiration, counsel, and enjoy themselves. It is truly remarkable and requires not only superior organizational skill but also a sense of design
and good taste. Miss Addams, the founder and leader, always with a lot of men
and women volunteers at her side, is an engaging, gentle, distinguished person.
One believes immediately that she has earned the appellation "angel" Joanna.
Her ability to persuade the wealthy to provide support and to recruit working
assistants is to me no less impressive than her ability to attract the poor and the
workers and gain their trust. (Undated, probably September 13; MWP)

Marianne was particularly interested in the question of women's employment,
access to occupations, working conditions and wages, and participation in
trade union organizations. These topics had already begun to occupy her as an
activist and essayist in Germany, centered at the time in her leadership of the
association known as the Verein Frauenbildung-Frauenstudium:

> Miss Addams and her circle promote the working women's organizations as much
> as possible and in that respect work hand in hand with the male trade union lead-
> ers. Clearly here they already have had greater success than we've had with the
> women's organizations. They have succeeded even in organizing the women home
> service and outworkers—that is, making them trade union members and forcing
> employers to hire only such "labeled" women (i.e., members of the unions).
>
> In the meeting [of the WTUL] only the failure of the great stockyard strike
> was discussed, the strike of the men and women butchers (20–30,000) that still
> agitates all of Chicago and keeps it partly in the grip of a rebellion. The train of
> thought and viewpoints about the event expressed completely those of my circles.
> Thus I felt surrounded immediately by the atmosphere of home and the tasks I
> know so well, but had to be impressed once again by the charming eloquence of
> American women. Like American men, they have a delightful way of expressing
> their views vividly and with warmth and humor.

This evening ended with Jane Addams insisting that Marianne make a statement, which she reluctantly agreed to do, singing a "hymn of praise" for her
hostess, as she put it, much to Addams's chagrin. Parenthetically, in the weeks
of the strike's collapse, Addams did mediate between the union and management, Michael Donnelly and J. Ogden Armour, using her prestige and powers
of persuasion to wring a desultory agreement from the packers' firms and thus
save the union for battle another day, which came again well into the twentieth century.

It was only years later in 1930 in the pages of the *Frankfurter Zeitung* that
Marianne Weber gave a full account of Hull House and the "angel of Chicago." The occasion was Addams's seventieth birthday. Both a biographical
remembrance and an homage to women's culture, Marianne's essay went
about tracing the contours of moral resistance to the penetrating realities of
what she called the monstrous, demonic modern city. After nearly three de-

cades Chicago had become a more "harmonious" place, she thought. Through its evolution Addams had remained the city's best guide and exemplar, and Hull House the realization, in Marianne's words, of the "democratization of the spirit," the possibility of all "to lift themselves up" that she had found most admirable and enduring in the American experience.

While Marianne's interests focused on Hull House and the WTUL, Max's turned to the stockyards themselves. Even Karl Baedeker's pages extolled the drama and spectacle: "The processes of killing the cattle and hogs are extremely ingenious and expeditious, and will interest those whose nerves are strong enough to contemplate with equanimity wholesale slaughter and oceans of blood." Weber could not resist the opportunity for direct observation: "Everywhere one is struck by the tremendous intensity of work," he wrote,

> most of all in the stockyards with their "ocean of blood," where several thousand cattle and pigs are slaughtered every day. From the moment when the unsuspecting bovine enters the slaughtering area, is hit by a hammer and collapses, whereupon it is immediately gripped by an iron clamp, is hoisted up, and starts on its journey, it is in constant motion—past ever-new workers who eviscerate and skin it, etc., but are always (in the rhythm of work) tied to the machine that pulls the animal past them. One sees an absolutely incredible output in this atmosphere of steam, muck, blood, and hides in which I teetered about together with a boy who was giving me alone a guided tour for fifty cents, trying to keep from being buried in the filth. There one can follow a pig from the sty to the sausage and the can. (September 20; MWP)

Assembly-line mechanization was already well advanced in the packing plants, with line-speed efficiency and calculations of profitability driving the processes of production, and specialization of tasks allowing management to replace skilled craft workers with unskilled labor. The plants served as a perfect illustration of Fordism in practice well before Henry Ford's first automotive assembly line in 1913, though one should note that the change at Ford was accompanied by an extraordinary increase in wages to $5.00 a day.

For the working class, dehumanizing rationalization of the working and living environment was not limited to the stockyard plants. As Weber noted,

> When they finish work at 5 o'clock, people often must travel for hours to get home. The streetcar company is bankrupt; as usual it has been administered by a "receiver" for years, and he is not interested in expediting the liquidation and hence does not purchase any new cars. The old ones break down all the time. Around 400 people are killed or crippled in accidents every year. According to law, each death costs the company $5000 (to the widow or the heirs), an injury costs it $10,000 (to the injured party), if the company does not take certain precautionary measures. The company has now calculated that those 400 indemnities cost it less than the required precautions, so it does not bother to introduce them.

The irrationality of "rational" calculation extended to public health and safety issues as well:

> The city of Chicago uses the water of Lake Michigan unfiltered, and until a short time ago the filth of the city flowed into the water supply; some still does. An Austrian colleague came down with a gastric infection, and typhus is a daily occurrence. Recently they blocked the Chicago River and used the watershed to divert it to the Mississippi and let the city's filth descend on St. Louis. The tunnel of the subway under the river is threatening to cave in, as the ships with a deeper draught almost always scrape against it. No one considers doing anything about it *before* it caves in, etc., etc., ad infinitum. It is a wild life notwithstanding the refined layer of culture that overlies everything.

Cases of typhoid in St. Louis did number in the hundreds annually, but scientific evidence of Chicago's complicity in water pollution was not conclusive. In one of the early decisions of environmental law, *Missouri v. Illinois and the Sanitary District of Chicago*, decided in 1906, Justice Oliver Wendell Holmes expressed the U.S. Supreme Court's view that the cause of water pollution had not been proven and dismissed the suit, but "without prejudice."

Closed finally in 1971, at the turn of the century the packing plants, animal pens, packaging and shipping facilities bounded by Halsted and Ashland, Thirty-ninth and Forty-seventh streets in south Chicago, were a microcosm of the struggle between capital and labor. The statistics of the time are breathtaking, reaching into the millions of head of cattle, hogs, sheep, and horses, but the most impressive figure was a simple one: when Weber visited the yards, over 80 percent of all the meat consumed in the United States came from this single location, and it was an era without uniform public health standards, regulation, or oversight. Hastened in part by Sinclair's writings on conditions in the stockyards, however, the U.S. Food and Drug Administration legislation was signed by President Roosevelt two years later. That was one valuable result of the bright spotlight cast by the strike, though hardly the radical solution that Sinclair as a socialist had intended.

The assembly line mechanization and rhythms of labor that Weber saw were a capital intensive production process. But it still required a significant labor force, numbering about 25,000. The AMCBW began as a craft union, with its members considering themselves skilled workers. However, rationalization of the enterprise had the effect of deskilling the labor force, replacing skilled with unskilled workers, and driving down wages. Skilled workers tended to be men from the older immigrant population, while unskilled workers tended to be newer immigrants, women, or African Americans. There were exceptions, of course: the union had about five hundred black members, for example, and women tended to dominate the packaging operations. But the economic trend was unmistakable in 1904: skilled workers and their craft orientation were under siege. For the skilled workers the loss of jobs, status, wages, and vocation had become more than a mere threat.

Max Weber devoted a massive amount of attention to capitalism and labor relations from the beginning of his career—capitalism as a system of production, the institutions of market finance and the market economy, and the historical development of capitalist economic systems. His reputation at the time rested largely on his work on agrarian labor. But in 1908 he did take up questions of industrial labor, completing the Verein für Sozialpolitik's study of work and vocation in heavy industry, *Zur Psychophysik der industriellen Arbeit.* The text remains untranslated and is rarely cited today. It is scarcely known even to specialists. But in it Weber explicitly addresses the problem of mechanization and its consequences, the effects (quoting his words) "on the personal qualities, vocational fate and extravocational 'style of life' of workers," as well as the "ethnic, social, and cultural" factors affecting the entire conduct or way of leading one's life, the *"Lebensführung,"* of the workforce. Such questioning would only have been reinforced by the observations in Chicago.

Weber was alert to the totality of working-class life in the cities, both in Germany and in the United States. His frank exchanges about social democracy with Robert Michels always vigorously underscored the sociocultural dimensions of labor relations and labor organization, a point of view apparent in his assessment of the "moral order" seen in Chicago. Commenting on the working-class districts, for instance, he noted an apparent contrast with New York related to ethnicity and religious institutions, and then elaborated on the theme of secularization:

Because of its ethnic mix Chicago is less religious [*kirchlich*] than New York. Nevertheless, precisely in the workers' districts the number of churches supported by the workers themselves is quite large. Here lie the most characteristic features of American life, as well as the most fateful factors for a deep inner transformation. Up to now it was the orthodox sects here that gave to all of life its special character. All sociability, all social cohesion, all agitation in favor of philanthropic and ethical and even political concerns (such as the campaign against corruption) are held in their grasp. Now along with the Catholics (who maintain or even increase their number because of immigration) only the large Lutheran Missouri Synod is a rock of orthodoxy. Everything is now in flux. The Presbyterians have abandoned the theory of predestination and belief in the damnation of the unbaptized. The large sects are adopting "pulpit change"—that is, their ministers often exchange preaching in each others' churches—and the workers are not interested in hearing about dogmatism. The "Ethical Culture" has a temple with preaching on Sundays in New York. Temples of Christian Science are present everywhere, often enormous in size, and the states have to enact laws to deal with the immorality of refusing to acknowledge illness and seek medical attention for patients. The old harsh strain of Methodism is likewise fading away. It's difficult to say how these matters will develop further. (September 20; MWP)

If the trend toward secularization was interpreted as a shift away from ortho-dox theology in the mainline denominations, then the trend did not neces-sarily also indicate a decline in religiosity or the public and social importance of the religious sects. Weber thought this was a distinctive American pattern, replicated even in newer immigrant enclaves: matter-of-fact skepticism about dogma, combined with a sectlike form of social organization, still permeating working-class public life.

Character as Social Capital

The week in Chicago was also an occasion for events leading up to the Con-gress of Arts and Science, some hosted by Albion Small and William R. Harper, president of the University of Chicago. Because a large number of Congress delegates were in the city, there was a reception scheduled for the University of Chicago campus at the Reynolds Club, a banquet at the Webers' hotel, and tours of the city and the museums. Weber most likely met Small during the week, an inconsequential encounter, and his attendance at these events is uncertain. One excursion that left a deep impression, however, was a Wednesday (September 14) spent with Marianne and Ernst Troeltsch in Evanston at Northwestern University, the first of a growing list of stops at educational institutions and inquiries into American educational practices.

Weber would have heard already about Northwestern through Edmund James. With James having just resigned as president, the campus tour was con-ducted by James Taft Hatfield, a professor of German literature and language, son of a Methodist minister who in Hatfield's words "represented the authen-tic Puritan-Methodist tradition of the eighteenth-century." Hatfield was en-dowed with "a high and noisy tenor" voice and was attracted to the *Volkslied* tradition and the use of music to express spiritual longings and religious devo-tion—quite the opposite of the Calvinist sentiments of the primitive Baptists and the Quakers. Active in the Methodist Church and as a faculty advisor to the Beta Theta Pi fraternity, he also led the nondenominational Friday student chapel service. He was one of seven Northwestern faculty members participating in the Congress of Arts and Science, presenting a paper titled "Germanic Literature." Much later in his career he presided over the Modern Language Association, delivering as his presidential address a rousing defense of "standards" in academia.

During the day Hatfield recruited an unsuspecting freshman and together with him treated his guests to a rendition of the Beta Theta Pi melody, sung to the tune of "O Tannenbaum." Weber acknowledged being moved by this sort of entirely local patriotism, and puzzled over its other characteristics: "something childlike, a strange mixture of robust human understanding, enthusiasm and naïveté." Weber described his visit thus:

> The visit to Northwestern University in the suburb of Evanston was very pleasant, in the beautiful countryside along the lake with large playing fields and attractive wood-frame and masonry homes of the faculty. Once again the small and often tiny rooms of the professors' houses—a puff on my pipe would permanently darken the study—and a very pretty house of a student fraternity ("Greek letter society") that (except for dueling and drinking bouts) does everything we do. Also nice albums of a similar *women's* sorority with amusing illustrations of the way the "old gentlemen," or rather "old ladies" of the sorority show up at the beginning of the semester to help "recruit" the first-year students ("freshmen"), etc., etc.—in short, a lot of nice insights into the American student life that is *just as* full of hard work as of poetry. (September 20; MWP)

Weber acquired a surprisingly detailed knowledge of the American school system, the colleges and universities, the students' way of life, college degree requirements, faculty appointments and workloads, teaching methods, student costs and fees, and faculty and administrative salaries. But the point of his curiosity was singular: it had to do with the ethos of education—the cultivation of habits, the formation of mind and character, and the attitude toward life related to work and accomplishment:

> While the American youth has to work little and slowly in primary school, grammar school and high school, at about 17–18 (before he's as far along as a 6th year Gymnasium student) he enjoys the greatest amount of freedom (thus for our taste [in Germany] difficult to accept), but nevertheless has become vigorous and independent. The college student (17/18 to 21/22 years old) normally enters a dormitory, has to submit to the rules, is controlled if not formally then in practice with respect to drinking, etc. His course of study is prescribed with the exception of certain electives, failure to attend classes is impossible, there is weekly chapel, and exams occur every quarter. Despite all this the magical memories of youth are focused on this period of life. Sports on a massive scale, attractive forms of sociability, endless intellectual stimulation, countless lasting friendships are the results, and above all, far more than with our students, learning the habit of work. The son-in-law of our host [in St. Louis] confirmed that a college-bred man would learn the business in half a year, others in 2–3 years.

The specific reference (as we shall see in the next chapter) is to the very successful iron and steel manufacturing magnate Frank Mesker, whose views seem entirely representative. But the more general reference is, in a word, to *asceticism*. The question is, what are the sources and the institutional reinforcements for the formation of the type of person who is committed to action in the world?

In pursuit of an answer to this question, among the "habits" that most startled Weber none was more impressive than the requirement of chapel attendance:

> It seems incredible when one reads in the *statutes* of Northwestern University in Chicago (originally Methodist, the large University [of Chicago] founded by Rockefeller is Baptist, and both compete in *the same* city!) that a student must attend either 3/5 of the daily services or one additional hour of lectures *instead* of 3 hours of services. If he has a bigger "*chapel record*" (!!) than required, he is *given credit for the next academic year*, and then he needs that much less attendance. If the "chapel record" is inadequate for two years, the student is expelled. Yet the "religious service" is peculiar: sometimes it is replaced by lectures, for instance on [Adolf von] Harnack's *History of Dogma*. At the conclusion the dates of the next football, baseball, cricket match, etc., are announced, as the harvesting used to be announced in German villages. The whole thing is utterly confusing. It is hard to say how great the *indifference* is at this time; that it has increased, particularly because of the Germans, is fairly certain. But the power of the church communities is still enormous in comparison with our Protestantism.

Weber's memory was essentially correct. The *Northwestern University Bulletin* cataloged the pertinent rules:

> The charter of the University provides that "no particular religious faith shall be required of those who become students of this institution." The University was not established with the view of forcing on the attention of students the creed of any particular church, but for the promotion of learning under influences conducive to the formation of a manly Christian character. This continues to be its aim and purpose.
>
> Students in the College of Liberal Arts are expected to attend public worship on Sunday in the church of their choice.
>
> Chapel service is held at noon on each week day except Saturday, throughout the college year. Attendance upon at least three-fifths of these services is required under the following regulations:
>
> 1. When a student's record of chapel credits is deficient as many credits as he is expected to secure in one-half of a semester, his registration in all studies is cancelled, and it may be restored only on the recommendation of the faculty committee on chapel attendance.
>
> 2. Surplus chapel credits in excess of the three-fifths required in any semester are carried forward to the chapel record of the following semester.

Northwestern University was not exceptional. Similar requirements existed at the University of Chicago and the University of Tennessee, for example. But the "utter confusion" Weber registered was surely his own. Having lived through a similar modified "weekly chapel" regimen at the coeducational college I attended, I have no doubt that the students found the requirement completely understandable and rationally manageable. Needless to say, the culture of the "college" has changed; the practice by now has gone the way of in loco parentis and other survivals from an earlier era.

In 1904, however, the invocation of "character" was an expression of the times, essentially a topos linked by Americans to the educational regime of the college as an institution and a formative life experience. The idea appeared everywhere: in the pages of the *Chicago Daily Tribune*, where the vice president of the First National Bank announced to an audience that "character is real capital"; or during President Theodore Roosevelt's visit to Northwestern, accompanied by Edmund James, when his message to students was, "Now it is a great thing to have a safe and strong body. It is a better thing to have a sage, a strong and a vigorous mind. But best of all is to have what is partly made up of both, partly made up of something higher and better—Character." On such matters Roosevelt was often a bellwether: "character" signified not merely personality or learning but an existential quality, a synthesis of mental and physical agility, an inner spiritual strength and independence of judgment. To appeal to "character" and its qualities—honesty, modesty, frugality, hard work—was to restate Benjamin Franklin's homilies in more modern terms. The college was supposed to embody the ideal.

For Max Weber the observations at Northwestern were repeated elsewhere over the next two months: at the Tuskegee Institute, the Johns Hopkins University, Haverford College, and Harvard and Columbia Universities. They were generalized into a full-scale argument that appears in different locations: the controversy over Friedrich Althoff's policies as the Prussian minister of education; wartime texts, such as the speech "Socialism" in Vienna; and in their best-known form, "Science as a Vocation," where the entire problematic is introduced through a comparison of American and German university life. The Althoff debate is perhaps the most intriguing of these discussions, as the retrospective and prospective orientation of Weber's thinking is unmistakable. His position in these heated exchanges, dependent on American points of reference, was rarely understood.

Consider the striking language Weber used in a passage from his address to the professoriat at the *Deutsche Hochschullehrertag* in Dresden in October 1911:

The classic older type of American university grew out of the college. Colleges were located not in large cities but wherever possible in the countryside, in any case in small towns. Furthermore, the older colleges were predominantly established by religious sects. Traces of this can be seen everywhere. Nowadays, however, American universities are becoming to a certain extent metropolitan and, furthermore, there is no doubt that at least in some of them the old collegiate system, with required residence in college and strict control over the mode of life of the students, is partly in process of being discarded and partly has already been discarded. At the same time, I have been assured in American business circles that these latter conditions were responsible for maintaining the college and the particular kind of college education, which does not aim primarily at training for science and scholarship, but rather at the formation of character through the experience of holding one's own in the society of similarly situated students, at the formation of adult citizens, and at the development of an outlook which serves as the foundation of the American governmental and social systems.

The "business circles" would have included the college-educated Frank Mesker. Of course, Northwestern fit the classic model, and though the University of Chicago was by contrast decidedly newer, more urban, and more oriented toward specialized scientific graduate training, it too had remained strongly committed to the residential undergraduate "college" with its healthy respect for education instead of training. The University of Chicago has stubbornly persisted to do so to this day, although with occasional bouts of self-doubt and struggles over "general" education and curricular reform. The modern debates over so-called general education, so often misunderstood and characteristic *only* of American universities, are important precisely because they touch on the ideal of the college and informed citizenship.

The alternatives to this original American model were the source of provocation in Weber's critique of German conditions:

> All the while we find that schools of economics are being founded in Germany. To express ourselves in vivid form we may say that a driving force propelling these schools of economics is the commercial employee's wish to attain the status in which he may accept a challenge to a duel and thereby be made capable of becoming a reserve officer: a pair of sabre scars on his face, a bit of student life, a short rest from the habit of work—all things about which I ask myself: will we be able to compete with the great productive powers of the world, particularly the Americans, if the new generation of our business class is educated into such an ethos?

Substitute another nationality—citizens of China, India, or Brazil, for example—and today the question has remained the same. The problem of the relationship between education in the sense Weber discovered in the American college and the challenges of global competition has perhaps never been more visible to the public. Scarcely a week passes without another editorial, speech, report, tract, or anecdote bemoaning the erosion of the educational and civic ideals and social capital that were attached originally to the idea of the college.

However, the problem is hardly ever grasped in the way that Weber, educators like James, Harper, or Hatfield, or even politicians like Roosevelt understood it, for what they saw in the college was the beneficial effects of quite specific institutionalized forms of association and sociability for the disciplining and testing of the self and the construction of the social order. These forms embodied a pragmatic logic, of course. Max Weber was less interested in their narrowly construed utility, however, than in their implications for the totality of practical ethics and a distinctive way of life within the confines of capitalist culture. How could the ethos represented by the college be reconciled with the capitalist rationalization of the material world? The question had now been formulated. Weber was still searching for a compelling answer.

FOUR

SCIENCE AND WORLD CULTURE

The St. Louis Congress: Unity of the Sciences?

The Congress of Arts and Science was scheduled for the week of September 19, 1904, in St. Louis, Missouri; it was a massive affair of 128 sections assessing the state of knowledge in the human, biological, and physical sciences; medicine; law; the humanities; religion; and education. Some three hundred papers were presented, not including the short papers and commentaries. Weber spoke in a social science panel concerned with rural communities on the afternoon of September 21. At the same time Ernst Troeltsch delivered his paper discussing William James's *The Varieties of Religious Experience*, a "masterpiece" of "remarkable richness" as he called James's lectures, in a session on the philosophy of religion. That morning their colleague Ferdinand Tönnies had shared the stage with Lester F. Ward on a sociology panel dealing with social structure, commenting on the development of modern social forms and his theory of community and society, or in his terminology, *Gemeinschaft* and *Gesellschaft*. The following day Werner Sombart discussed socialism, the urban proletariat, and industrial society on a panel with Richard Ely. Johannes Conrad and Paul Hensel gave their presentations the next day. Other sessions featured an impressive cast of participants: among those whose reputations have lasted were Woodrow Wilson, James Bryce, Jane Addams, and Martha Carey Thomas; the German and French scientists Wilhelm Ostwald and Henri Poincaré; and the American social scientists and reformers Frederick Jackson Turner, Franz Boas, W. I. Thomas, Edward A. Ross, Charles Merriam, and Felix Adler.

The evenings were reserved for the obligatory array of oversized receptions and dinners, most of which the Webers appear to have attended, Max complaining all the while. But the daytime sessions proved beneficial, much to Weber's surprise, considering his initial skepticism about the Congress. Among the benefits were contacts with American colleagues. He appears to have attended the other sessions in economics, thus giving him an opportunity to hear and meet, among others, Edwin R. A. Seligman of Columbia University, and Jacob H. Hollander from the Johns Hopkins University, both of whom he was to visit again in the last month of his stay.

That the Congress came about at all must be credited to a small group of persistent academics. Planning for it was a remarkably contentious affair. The discussions started in 1901, and involved essentially a select group of five men: William R. Harper, president of the University of Chicago, the earliest to support the idea; Nicholas Murray Butler, president of Columbia University; Simon Newcomb, the mathematician and astronomer who served as the Congress's president; and his two vice presidents, Albion Small, the chair of the University of Chicago sociology department, and Hugo Münsterberg, the Harvard University psychologist and Weber's former colleague in Freiburg. Although the extensive correspondence among these educators produced more heat than light, it manages in retrospect to yield a glimmer of insight into the state of the sciences at the beginning of the twentieth century.

For the historian of science the important intellectual issues that emerged during the discussions about the Congress had to do with a sharp disagreement about a claim for what today would be referred to as the methodological unity of the sciences. Following the terminology the late Richard Rorty popularized, it would be accurate to say that it set a foundationalist conception of the logical structure of knowledge against a pragmatic conception of scientific interests and activity. Münsterberg, advocating a unified system of scientific knowledge, stood on one side of this issue; Small, defending the diversity of science and its methods as actually practiced, represented the other. In the public arena the dispute was joined in an interesting way by John Dewey, who formulated a pragmatic version of science in opposition to Münsterberg's neo-Kantian metaphysics that found expression in Dewey's later works, such as *Democracy and Education* and *The Quest for Certainty*.

Münsterberg and Small submitted competing plans for the Congress. Writing in the *Atlantic Monthly*, Münsterberg declared that his proposal had "the definite purpose of working toward the unity of human knowledge" and giving the meetings "the mission, in this time of scattered specialized work, of bringing to the consciousness of the world the too much neglected idea of the unity of truth"—fighting words for a pragmatist. Münsterberg believed the time had arrived to overcome the legacy of the nineteenth century's materialism, of Auguste Comte's positivism and Herbert Spencer's social Darwinism, by working out a new foundation for knowledge. "Our time longs for a new interpretation of reality," he wrote, and that interpretation was to be found in postulating the interrelations of all knowledge and the "fundamental principles" or "philosophical foundation" that bind the sciences together. These principles were articulated essentially in the construction of a system of knowledge, reminiscent incongruously of Comte and Spencer. But now it was a system built around a distinction between the "objectifying" sciences dealing with "phenomena" and the "subjectifying" sciences concerned with "purposes." This terminology reflected an earlier neo-Kantian distinction between the "nomothetic" natural sciences oriented toward specifying invariant universal "laws" and the "idiographic" Geisteswissenschaften that aimed for culturally or psychologically informed "understanding." For the Congress, however, it was not so much clarification of the distinction or classification that interested Münsterberg, already set forth in his main treatise, *Die Grundzüge der Psychologie* (1900), but rather the desirable totality, the interconnections, and the shared underlying commitment to the ideal of the "unity of knowledge."

On the other hand, in his submission Small started from the radically different premise, typical for a Progressive sociologist schooled in pragmatist modes of thought, that the Congress should make an effort to assess the achievements and "progress" of the previous century, with science or knowledge only one sphere of activity among others, such as health, economic well-being, social justice, aesthetics, and religion. Even in the sciences themselves, Small argued, "methodological progress is a very small subsidiary fraction of scientific progress as a whole, while the more important development of science consist[s] in the solution of real problems and in the proposal of new problems on the present frontiers of our knowledge"—a statement closely parallel to Weber's reservations about the "methodological pestilence" invading the sciences. From this point of view the project of establishing the logical interrelationships of the sciences as the Congress's highest purpose was either willful scholasticism or a misunderstanding of the way the sciences and the growth of knowledge actually worked. Rigidly applied, Small cautioned in a letter to Harper, Münsterberg's scheme would put on display not the unity of science but the disunity of scientists.

As if to demonstrate Small's warning, others who joined the fray invariably objected to the scholastic narrowness of Münsterberg's vision of science. In his response, for instance, Dewey quite correctly complained that the proposed scheme offered "a particular methodology emanating from a particular school of metaphysics" and amounted to a "sectarian intellectual idea." To assert the integration a priori of the different kinds of science and the theoretical and practical levels of science into a system within which each had its proper place would have been to place regressive restrictions on scientific practice. Corresponding later with Münsterberg, James similarly castigated the "resolute *will to have a system* of absolute principles and 'categories.'" For James the difference between his viewpoint and Münsterberg's was fundamental: "But were it not for my fixed belief," James wrote to his colleague,

> that the world is wide enough to sustain and nourish without harm many different types of thinking, I believe that the wide difference between your whole *Drang* in philosophizing and mine would give me a despairing feeling. I am satisfied with a free wild Nature; you seem to me to cherish and pursue an Italian Garden, where all things are kept in separate compartments, and one must follow straight-ruled walks. (June 28, 1906)

Dewey gave James's untamed nature an apt political characterization, insisting, "The essential trait of the scientific life of to-day is its democracy, its give-and-take, its live-and-let-live character."

Reading these arguments today, in the extended aftermath of Thomas Kuhn's work in the philosophy and history of science, we might assume the

It is unclear whether Weber intended to write "chair*man*" or "chair*men*" of the Indian Commission, and if in the latter case he also would have met Thomas B. Needles and Clifton R. Breckenridge, the other two commissioners in this powerful triumvirate. He concluded by noting the informality of these office conversations: "All officials have received me in their shirt sleeves, of course, and together we put our legs on the windowsill. The 'lawyers' etc. struck me as somewhat audacious, but there is a marvelously free-and-easy atmosphere, and yet mutual respect is never lost sight of."

Weber accurately expressed the official efforts to eliminate land speculation or at least curtail its abuses through legal and administrative means, a truly Herculean undertaking. He also acknowledged that "there is a colossal 'boom' and land speculation flourishes despite all the laws; no wonder, because here land costs $10 and in Oklahoma the price already stands at $75," prices per acre that are probably accurate, with the proviso that land values varied considerably depending on quality and location. Twenty years earlier Max Sering had found farmland values in the plains ranging from $5 to $50 per acre, in the Midwest from $40 to $200, and in California from $60 in the Central Valley to a high of $250 in the Santa Clara Valley (popularly known today as Silicon Valley). Weber's optimistic assessment of land allotment reflected the hopes of Bixby and the commission. But in reality the tasks of establishing accurate citizenship rolls (officially closed on March 4, 1907) and allocating land continued for several years, with the commission itself persisting as a legal body for another decade.

In describing federal agency activity Weber actually conflated two different events, both of which he attended: The land auction itself in the Indian Agent's Office, widely announced in the press for the regular weekly time on Friday, September 30; and the following day the distribution of a legal payment to members of the Creek tribe. Shoenfelt was personally responsible for these transactions, which received generous press coverage. The *Muskogee Daily Phoenix* on October 1 reported that of twenty-three tracts offered, four sold for a total of $6,871, while the others either received no bids or received bids that were rejected because they were below the minimum assessed value. It also reported the beginning of the Creek payment, lasting a week and distributed by the Indian agent to qualifying individuals in the amount of $12,500, adding that the total claim of $1 million dated from the 1830s and was based on losses incurred by the Creeks in the forced resettlement from Alabama to Indian Territory.

The Creek payment afforded an unusual opportunity for ethnographic observation: "Today I watched whole troops of Indians arrive to get their money; the full-bloods have peculiar tired facial features and are surely doomed to decline, but among the others one sees intelligent faces. Their clothes are almost invariably European," Weber reported on October 1 (MWP). For Indian agent Shoenfelt these would have been routine business transactions, but for Max Weber they seemed to take on the representational quality of the fate of a people and the unfolding of historical destinies.

Nature, Traditionalism, and the New World

As an outsider, Weber obviously did not become an advocate in the debate he encountered between those favoring protection of Native American culture and those favoring economic, political, and social development, stating the rival positions in somewhat simplified terms. But his views about "development" generally, as expressed already in the debates over industrialization and economic policy during the 1890s in Germany, were congruent with the positions articulated by Robert Owen. Weber was alert to the causes, significance, and consequences of the forces driving the debate in the Indian Territory, and he was fascinated by the transformation occurring there from traditional society and attitudes to modern "capitalist" economic conditions and modern social and political relationships. He observed the shifting coalitions of homesteaders, railroad interests, land speculators, developers, financial interests, different tribal groups and interests, and federal agents that produced the transition from the old Indian Territory to the new state of Oklahoma. Among the most basic causes, his record of conversations and observations can be read to support the view that the destruction of the Five Civilized Tribes was in large part brought about, paradoxically, by the federal government itself and its local representatives acting for political reasons, not from commercial motives, and accomplishing this unintended result through the use of the law, the courts, and legal authority. Owen and tribal members like him surely took part in writing this last chapter of the old Indian Territory, but the main authors were in the federal administration itself.

Weber also had no doubt that the coming of modern industrial civilization meant the rapid disappearance of the romanticized past. "The virgin forest's hour has struck even here," as he put it, and the "Leatherstocking romanticism" of native life and the frontier was coming to an end. After touring Muskogee he pronounced it "a marvelously attractive [fabelhaft reizvoll]—that is, not aesthetically attractive—picture of growth that next year will already have assumed the character of Oklahoma City etc., that is, that of any other Western city" (September 28; MWP). The following day the same thought crowded into another passage: "Too bad; in a year this place will look like Oklahoma, that is, like any other American city. With almost lightening speed everything that stands in the way of capitalistic culture is being crushed" (September 29; MWP). His very last lines about the territory repeated the sentiment: "But enough of this trip to the 'old romantic land.' The next time I come here, the last remnant of 'romanticism' will be gone" (October 1; MWP).

It is precisely these passages that Marianne Weber chose to excerpt in her account. Emphasizing them can leave open the impression of Max's frontier excursion as a sentimental journey into a more authentic past and an opportunity to express thinly veiled antimodern or anticapitalist sentiments. But to reach such a conclusion would be a serious error. In Weber's commentaries something far more subtle and interesting is at stake than casting a vote for indigenous culture and against industrial civilization.

In no other place in his entire correspondence does Weber have as much to say about the construction of "nature" than in his descriptions from Indian Territory. He announces the theme in the first letter: nature in its "original" or "primary" form *as we represent it to ourselves*, and then the blending and mixing of the fictional "romance" or "poetry" of nature as experienced on the frontier together with the most modern aspects of a capitalist civilization that is coming into being:

> Nowhere else does the old Indian romanticism [*Indianerpoesie*] blend with the most modern capitalistic culture as much as it does here right now. The newly built railroad from Tulsa to McAlester first runs along the Canadian River for an hour through veritable virgin forest [*Urwald*], although one must not imagine it [*sich vorstellen*] as the "Silence in the Forest" with huge tree trunks. Impenetrable thicket—so dense that except for a few vistas one doesn't even notice that one is only a few meters from the Canadian River; dark trees—for the climate is already southerly, rarely with snow—overgrown with climbing plants right up to the top; in between yellow, quiet forest brooks and little rivers completely covered with greenery. The large rivers, like the Canadian River, have the most Leatherstocking romanticism [*Poesie*]. They are in an utterly wild state, with enormous sandbanks and thick dark greenery on their banks, their waters rolling along in bends and branches, leaving a peculiar impression of something mysterious. One doesn't know where they're coming from and where they're going. They were empty, with the exception of a single Indian fishing boat that I saw.

This passage, written at the end of his first day in Muskogee (and confusing the Canadian and Arkansas Rivers), continues with a step-by-step entry into modern civilization:

> But the virgin forest's hour has struck even here. In the forest one does occasionally see groups of genuine old log cabins—those of the Indians recognizable by the colorful shawls and laundry hung out to dry—but also next to them quite modern wood-frame houses and cottages from the factory on stone foundations, from $500 and up, and next to them a large clearing planted with corn and cotton. The bases of the trees had been smeared with tar and ignited. They are dying off, stretching their pale smoky fingers into the air in a confused tangle, which together with the fresh crops among them creates a peculiar [*wunderlich*] but in no way comforting

impression. Then there are large stretches of prairie, partly grazing land, partly again fields of cotton and corn. And suddenly it begins to smell like petroleum: one sees the tall Eiffel Tower–like structure of the drilling holes, right in the middle of the forest, and comes to a "town." This kind of place is really an incredible thing [*tolles Ding*]: tent camps of the workers, especially section hands for the numerous railroads under construction; "streets" in a natural state, usually doused with petroleum twice each summer to prevent dust, and smelling accordingly; wooden churches of at least 4–5 denominations (Muskogee had 4,000 inhabitants four years ago and now has 12,000, most of whom are Methodists). As an obstacle to traffic on these "streets" wood-frame houses are placed on rollers and thus moved along. The owner became rich, sold the house, built a new one, and the old house is moved to a site where a newcomer who purchased it moves in. Add to this the usual tangle of telegraph and telephone wires, and electric train lines under construction, for the "town" extends into the unbounded distance. For this reason we drove around in a small carriage pulled by a huge horse, saw four schools of the different sects, also public schools (gratis)—compulsory attendance is in sight—a hotel with modest rooms (September 28; MWP).

The narrative obviously combines observations on the train trip from Guthrie to Muskogee and the subsequent tour of Muskogee and vicinity, where the first oil wells appeared in 1903. Weber's statistics, probably learned from Douglas and Owen, appear correct: in the 1900 census Muskogee had a population of 4,254: McAlester and South McAlester, 4,125; and Fort Gibson, 606.

In these few sentences Weber records the passage from primeval nature, the *Urwald* of the American wilderness that so impressed Tocqueville as well, to the amazing phantasmagoria of emergent civilization, with various transitional stages in between where the intermingling of "natural" and "created" forms is immediately perceptible. This is not Jean Hector St. John de Crèvecoeur's well-known depiction of a condition in which "everything is modern, peaceful, and benign" and "Nature opens her broad lap to receive the perpetual accession of newcomers." In the New World, Crèvecoeur continued, "everything would inspire the reflecting traveller with the most philanthropic ideas; his imagination, instead of submitting to the painful and useless retrospect of revolutions, desolations, and plagues, would, on the contrary, wisely spring forward to the anticipated fields of future cultivation and improvement, to the future extent of those generations which are to replenish and embellish this boundless continent." What inspires Weber's reflective imagination, however, is the experience of dynamism, transformation, and the excitement of the new, but also displacement, conflict, and the prospect of encountering limits in the future. He never cites Crèvecoeur, but he does employ instructive substitutes to provide weight and measure for the "poetry" of the imagined natural order: from German literature, Ludwig Ganghofer's *Das Schweigen im Walde* (The Silence in the Forest), "the quintessence of German sylvan sentimentality," as Harry Zohn has noted; and from American literature the popular adventures of Natty Bumppo in James Fenimore Cooper's five Leatherstocking novels, where the founding mythology is created of an "American Odyssey" with the *Deerslayer* as Odysseus, quoting D. H. Lawrence, and the themes are struggle, strife, inner loneliness, and mastery of self and world. "And when *this* man breaks from his static isolation," Lawrence concludes, "and makes a new move, then look out, something will be happening."

If Weber sides with anyone, it is with Lawrence. To be sure, to "see" nature is a matter of representation, of *Vorstellung*, for which fiction may or may not be an adequate guide. But benign, sylvan, and sentimental are not the terms of Weber's discourse. For him the "natural" must be represented as untamed, inexplicable, sublime, and therefore mysterious. And it is under assault, for the engineering of invasive "civilization" can be conveniently depicted through a reminder of the quintessential symbol of the fabulous modern sublime—the Eiffel Tower—which is visibly present, dotting the landscape. It is a symbol of dynamism and development but also of mechanization, expropriation, and domination.

Precisely the same mental constructions and emotional tone frame the other episode on the Indian frontier where nature and civilization are juxtaposed: Weber's unusual excursion to Fort Gibson. Marianne Weber failed to include the lead-in recorded in her husband's letters, "Today or tomorrow evening I'll take a 'trip' to Fort Gibson and the Canadian River with several local lawyers I've got to know, and thus enjoy some primeval romanticism [*Urwald-Poesie*], for the Clubhouse in which we are supposed to have supper lies in a place known because of Longfellow and others—even the Hiawatha legend can be attributed to it" (September 29; MWP). The short trip occurred the following day, and Marianne then excerpted the colorful passages describing the clubhouse set above the Arkansas River, the American form of *Gemütlichkeit* hosted by an "Aunt Bessie and 'Uncle Tom,'" the exclusiveness and culture of the club itself—equivalent to the symposium of classical antiquity translated into the American vernacular—and the experience of getting lost in the wilderness or "wildness" (*Wildheit* is Weber's word), while traveling some twenty miles back across the Arkansas River to Muskogee.

Hiawatha, *Uncle Tom's Cabin*, and memories of Plato's *Symposium* are added to Cooper's and Ganghofer's tales. Weber was quite wrong about Fort Gibson as the setting for *Hiawatha*, however, as Henry Wadsworth Longfellow placed this most American of sagas in Lake Superior and the Great Lakes Basin. But the mistake is itself revealing and understandable, for he had only picked up this bit of mythology from his American hosts. It had become part of the local folkways to imagine that Hiawatha must have had a connection to the Indian Territory. The fiction was convenient, furthermore, for it fused together two of the founders of American letters: Longfellow and the most important of the "others," Washington Irving. Irving had in fact passed up an opportunity to

Figure 7. The clubhouse at Fort Gibson, perched on a bluff above the Arkansas River, is no longer in use as a restaurant or tavern. In 1904 it served as an imagined American symposium and destination for Max Weber's adventure into the poetic *Urwald*. Author's photograph.

create a suitable literary form for the Hiawatha legend and left it for Longfellow. But it was actually Irving, not Longfellow, who had first given Fort Gibson and Native American life on the frontier a place in the American imagination, publishing *A Tour on the Prairies*, his "brilliantly drawn pictures of frontier life" that recorded a month of travels on horseback in 1832 in the Indian lands from Fort Gibson to a location near Guthrie and back—essentially the same territory Weber had traversed.

Weber never cited this work by Irving, though he may have known about it, as the German translations were widely reprinted and read. But toward the end of *The Protestant Ethic and the Spirit of Capitalism* he did refer to Irving's earlier writing that established his reputation, and in particular the notion of ascetic Puritanism and the calculating spirit of capitalism "breaking down the spontaneity of the *status naturalis*" and evincing "less play of the *fancy*, but more power of *imagination*." In this respect Irving can be said to deliver the Weberian theme: inner-worldly asceticism's mastery of nature and the "natural" condition with a loss of romance and *Poesie*, but with a gain in the power of the kind of imagination that can master the self and the world. Personal and political "freedom" and "sense of responsibility" become the leitmotifs of the new age. This would be one way—albeit unusual—to describe the historical destiny of those individuals, like Robert Owen, a devout Presbyterian, and those social groups, such as the Methodist newcomers, whom Weber encountered in Muskogee. They *were* the social agents, using Weber's own words, for that "*ethical* 'style of life' that was spiritually 'adequate' for the economic stage of 'capitalism' and signified its victory in the human 'soul.'"

The Significance of the Frontier

Weber spent barely a week in the Oklahoma and Indian Territories, and yet there are echoes of the conditions he encountered there scattered through his work. Some are general and have to do with the conceptualization of analytic categories as social constructions, such as "race" and "ethnicity," both in impromptu discussions, like those in the Deutsche Gesellschaft für Soziologie, and in the systematic presentation in *Economy and Society*. But some are much more specific: In the final version of the *Agrarian Sociology of Ancient Civilizations*, for example, he followed Sering's brief allusion in noting a similarity between Roman and North American colonization and settlement: the *ager occupatorius* in Rome involved a rationalization of measurement and "a regulated form of land development," as in the work of the Dawes-Bixby Commission in Indian Territory. This helped account for the comprehensive, relatively rapid, and "individualistic" pattern of settlement of vast territories in both cases, far more fast-paced in America than even Thomas Jefferson had forecast when he purchased the Louisiana Territory and with the stroke of a pen doubled the size of the country.

Most significantly for the understanding of American democracy, in the different texts of his essay on "The Protestant Sects and the Spirit of Capitalism" Weber used a conversation in Indian Territory to illustrate one of his major themes: the significance for personal legitimation, the social standing of the individual, and the formation of civil society of one's membership in a religious sect or voluntary association in which sociation is conditioned by moral testing. Consider the 1906 version of this encounter:

> Membership of a church community "of good repute" (according to American criteria) guarantees the good standing of the individual, not only socially, but also, and especially, in terms of business. "Sir," said an older gentleman who was a commercial traveler for Undertakers' Hardware (iron tombstone lettering), with whom I spent some time in Oklahoma, "as far as I am concerned, everyone can believe what he likes, but if I discover that a client doesn't go to church, then I wouldn't trust him to pay me fifty cents: Why pay me, if he doesn't believe in anything? This is an immensely vast and sparsely settled land, where people are often on the move, where there is an excessively formal Anglo-Norman legal system, where the law of seizure and impounding is lax and, indeed, has practically ceased to exist, thanks to homestead privileges granted to the mass of farmers in

the West. In such a land, it was inevitable that *personal credit* would have to be supported on the crutches of a church guarantee of creditworthiness like this.

Not only personal legitimation was at stake either, for it was especially these processes of sociation that counteracted the corrosive and invasive effects of capitalist culture so evident on the frontier, giving American democratic life its distinctive character. American civil society was never a "sand pile" or a "mass fragmented into atoms," Weber pointed out several times, but a highly varied and differentiated social order permeated with processes of sociation—group affiliations, voluntaristic attachments, and "'exclusivities' of every kind."

More generally, the combination of moral-religious, social, and economic considerations was never far from Weber's thoughts. His evocative comment about land speculators, homesteading, and community development seems to come straight from the tour of Muskogee:

> Even today it is perfectly normal for a land speculator, wishing to see his sites occupied, to build a "church," that is, a wooden shed with a tower, looking for all the world like something out of a box of toys, and to employ a young graduate just out of a seminary run by some denomination or other for five hundred dollars as its pastor. He will come to an agreement, spoken or unspoken, that this position will be a life-long post provided only that he can soon succeed in "preaching the building sites full." And usually he does succeed.

Such a convergence of spiritual, social, and economic interests offered another way to get at the processes of association that Weber thought were the key to making sense of this new order of civilization.

Similarly, Weber made use of these materials in his important discussions in *Economy and Society* and elsewhere of status, class, bureaucracy, domination, and the "civic culture" of democracy: the notion of equality of status as a "gentleman;" the sacrifice of social honor by the "big speculator" to gain the naked power of money; the relatively low standing of officials in newly settled areas where entrepreneurial initiative is valued and the constraining conventions of a traditional order are weak; the opposition between bureaucratic rule and political democracy, particularly in the governance of townships; and the antiauthoritarian civic norms and willingness to question authority that can be "so irritating or so refreshing." Already in the Indian Territory Weber had observed the conflicts among a professional bureaucracy, political leadership, and advocates of democratic accountability. He had witnessed the clashes among traditional tribal authority, the rationalizing forces of modern law and administration, and the independent stance of a charismatic figure like Robert Owen. It is thus not surprising to find such notions making their appearance in his mature political sociology.

Among the people he met, one interesting subsequent development was Robert L. Owen's stewardship of the Federal Reserve Act in the U.S. Congress. As the chairman of the U.S. Senate Committee on Banking and Currency, Owen coauthored the Owen-Glass Bill that established the current Federal Reserve System and governing board in the United States, his most impressive and lasting legislative accomplishment. Weber was aware of this Wilsonian reform of the banking system "discussed over a *long* period of time," as he wrote to Edgar Jaffé in response to the banking crisis of 1907, which he had also followed. After considering taking on the subject himself, Weber commissioned Jaffé to write the article on banking and finance for the *Grundriss der Sozialökonomik* in which the reform was discussed. Though Owen is not mentioned by name in the correspondence with Jaffé, it is difficult to imagine Weber failing to connect this legislative triumph with Owen's criticisms of federal policy that he had heard nearly a decade earlier.

Yet in the last analysis the journey to the Oklahoma and Indian Territories is about the emergence of a new world and a unique occasion to view it: "the last time," in Weber's phrasing at St. Louis, "as long as the history of mankind shall last, that such conditions for a free and great development will be given." The world it has given us is the one Weber himself described at the end of *The Protestant Ethic and the Spirit of Capitalism*, written after his return home: "that powerful cosmos of the modern economic order, bound to the technical and economic presuppositions of mechanical and machine production that today determine with overpowering force the style of life of all individuals who are born into this mechanism, *not* only those directly engaged in the economy—and perhaps will so determine them until the last amount of fossilized fuel is burned up." The sentence actually comes from the paragraph that finishes in a rhetorical flourish with Weber's most celebrated and contested image: the "iron cage" of John Bunyan's *Pilgrim's Progress* becoming our own modern fate. But ending it as I have, invoking the images and aromas of the oil fields, and the transformed lives of the natives, settlers, administrators, politicians, professionals, entrepreneurs, and dispossessed alike in the Oklahoma and Indian Territories, is an equally compelling way to capture the questioning of what remains from this journey into the American frontier.

SIX

THE COLOR LINE

Max Weber's resolve to travel through the American South probably was a matter of long standing, connected to the fate of his relatives, the descendants of Georg Friedrich Fallenstein, and encouraged by the commentaries of Friedrich Kapp. However, the reasons for choosing the lengthy trek from St. Louis, Missouri, through Memphis, Tennessee, to New Orleans, then north through Tuskegee, Alabama, to Atlanta and beyond are not entirely clear. Like Alexis de Tocqueville and Gustave de Beaumont, he was interested in questions about race and the consequences of slavery, and he might well have been curious about the survival of French influences in the southernmost reaches of the Louisiana Purchase. His interest in agrarian economies also would have attracted him to the post–Civil War South. The idea for the itinerary could have been planted in conversations during his earlier visit to Jane Addams's Hull House in Chicago, where connections had formed with the Tuskegee Institute and the work of Booker T. Washington. During Max and Marianne's stay in St. Louis, August and Willamina Gehner probably offered advice about the train route headed south. The stop at Tuskegee was obviously planned, perhaps at the suggestion of W. E. B. Du Bois, Jacob H. Hollander, Edwin R. A. Seligman, or others at the St. Louis exposition, such as William I. Thomas or Edward A. Ross. On September 25, 1904, Weber first mentioned the intention to visit Tuskegee, just four days after his St. Louis speech, in a letter to Booker T. Washington, also noting that he had spoken with Du Bois. Among those who might have attended the speech, aside from Du Bois, Seligman had firm ties to Tuskegee, and from the Midwestern reform circles in 1904 Ross even moved to Tuskegee to become Washington's personal assistant, a position first offered to Du Bois, who had turned it down.

Whatever the origins of the idea, Weber clearly saw this part of the trip as an opportunity to observe firsthand the problems of race and race relations in the former Confederacy, only forty years after the end of the Civil War. Unlike other St. Louis attendees and colleagues, such as Karl Lamprecht or Werner Sombart, Weber deliberately sought out leaders of the African American community and paid special attention to their educational institutions, expressions of culture, and political aims. Class relationships, status conventions, ethnicity, labor relations, the transition to a capitalist economy, the flight to the cities—those were the topics and categories Weber carried with him from his previous work. There were others, too, related to culture, religion, education and the "spirit" of this region characterized historically by slave labor plantation economies. As an agrarian economist, Weber had published studies on the *latifundia* of Roman antiquity and the large grain-producing estates of eastern Germany. He had observed the break up of the "second serf-dom" in the German east—as Friedrich Engels had called the socioeconomic system—and the transformation of the region under the pressures of global market competition, the introduction of capitalist modes of production, technological innovation, and immigration. He had commented sympathetically on the role played by the irreversible "desire for freedom" at the expense of the traditional security provided by patrimonial rule. By comparison, what would he find in the American South?

Preparation in the literature of the day was meager, which partly explains Weber's enthusiasm for Du Bois's published work, and especially *The Souls of Black Folk*. Friedrich Kapp's competent pre–Civil War history of slavery, dedicated to his abolitionist compatriot, Frederick Law Olmsted, was very dated by 1904. Karl Bücher, Weber's economics colleague in Leipzig, had just published engaging material on African American folk songs—the "soul of American music" in Du Bois's words—in his book on work and rhythmics. His investigation had been aided by the efforts of University of Chicago professor Charles Henderson and his students in collecting fieldwork songs. Weber knew Bücher's study, but its perspective on race and the postbellum South was obviously limited. In volume 2 of *The American Commonwealth*, James Bryce had followed his discussion of immigration with chapters on Reconstruction and its aftermath in the South and the problematic political and social situation of African Americans in both the South and the North. The discussion was a mere sketch, however, and in any case race and ethnicity were not central to Bryce's account of American life. Hugo Münsterberg made a more extended effort to address the problem of what he called the "social exclusion" of blacks in American society, noting that any kind of social equality was at best a very distant prospect, not only in the former Confederacy but also in the North, where discrimination was sometimes harsher than in the South. He also devoted some pages to the two tendencies within the black community, setting Washington's program for gradualist reform from below against Du Bois's appeal for a special mission and the development of exemplary black leadership. Münsterberg's was at least a balanced and sympathetic account. Considering his familiarity with this literature, Weber was thus aware of the general contours of the issues, including the division of opinion among the leading black spokesmen and intellectuals. But he lacked any analysis approaching a sociology or politics of race and ethnicity, with the exception of the work that Du Bois had begun to publish, including *The Philadelphia Negro* in 1899, and the continuing series of investigations reported in the Atlanta University Publications and the Occasional Papers of the American Negro Academy.

Du Bois and the Study of Race

The immediate political and intellectual context for Weber's contact with Du Bois in St. Louis, the correspondence with both Du Bois and Washington, and Weber's subsequent stop at Tuskegee was established by the events of the preceding years. He had indeed arrived at a propitious moment, for over the previous decade tensions had been building in the African American community and among proponents of racial equality and advocates for civil rights, starting with Washington's accommodationist "Atlanta compromise" address of 1895 and continuing with the 1900 Pan-African Congress in London. The former is still remembered for Washington's slogan of economic self-help, "Cast down your bucket where you are," while the latter served as a forum for Du Bois's most famous political counterpoint, which is worth quoting in full: "The problem of the twentieth century is the problem of the color line,—the relation of the darker to the lighter races of men in Asia and Africa, in America and the islands of the sea." This observation, with its global reach and inviting varied interpretations, became the opening sentence of chapter 2 in *The Souls of Black Folk*. It also found a remarkable echo in one of Weber's last letters from New York, addressed to Du Bois: "I am quite sure to come back to your country as soon as possible and especially to the South, because I am absolutely convinced that the 'colour-line' problem will be the paramount problem of the time to come, here and everywhere in the world" (November 17). Though Weber never succeeded in returning, he did manage to follow up with a line of inquiry leading into his own work.

In the struggle over equality and civil rights in the United States, divergent positions began to surface as the older leadership and the younger generation of educated African Americans wrestled with urgent questions of organization, objectives, political strategy, and social policy. Behind these strains lay even more fundamental questions about the identity, control, and definition of the struggle, increasingly oriented around what Du Bois referred to as the "Tuskegee Machine." Though not contradictory in principle, the political, educational, and commercial interests as expressed by different groups started to clash with each other. The potential for conflict became apparent in the violent confrontation in July 1903 between supporters and opponents of Washington when he spoke to the Boston chapter of the National Negro Business League, and then again the following January with the public presentations and standoff between Washington and Du Bois at a small gathering of civic leaders, including Andrew Carnegie, in Carnegie Hall. The division of opinion and lack of progress on civil rights encouraged Du Bois to take the lead in establishing the Niagara Movement the following year, and several years later the National Association for the Advancement of Colored People.

Figure 8. W.E.B. Du Bois was the only person to follow through on Max Weber's invitation to write an article for the *Archiv für Sozialwissenschaft und Sozialpolitik*. Having met Du Bois in St. Louis, Weber later praised him as "the most important sociological scholar anywhere in the Southern States in America." Harvard University Archives, call # HUP Du Bois, W.E.B. (1). Reproduced by permission.

The potential dimensions and significance of the struggle had been announced already by Du Bois in his chapter "Of Mr. Booker T. Washington and Others" in *The Souls of Black Folk*, published a year before the Webers' arrival. A revision of an earlier article, Du Bois's critique praised Washington's doctrine of "Thrift, Patience, and Industrial Training for the masses" but excoriated the renunciation of political power, the struggle for civil rights, support for higher education, and the commitment to black self-assertion that in Du Bois's view had to be presupposed as conditions for the success of Washington's doctrine and program. Weber read Du Bois's book, that "splendid work" as he later called it, probably during the American journey. The fact that he mentions to Washington "having read your works" (presumably at least *Up from Slavery* and *Character Building*) in one of his letters from New York suggests that Weber, an omnivorous reader, was collecting and devouring these materials as he traveled. With regard to *The Souls of Black Folk*, he was captivated by the style and the vocabulary, as he noted, and so impressed that after returning to Germany he suggested to Du Bois his former doctoral student, Else Jaffé, as a translator for the book, with Weber himself contributing an introduction. Unfortunately the project foundered on Jaffé's maternal responsibilities, the turmoil in her life, and her doubts about doing justice to the power and elegance of Du Bois's prose. It took another century, to the year, for a complete German translation of Du Bois's masterpiece to finally appear.

It is important to emphasize that Weber and Du Bois had crossed paths in the early 1890s, when Du Bois was studying at the Humboldt University of Berlin. Du Bois later recalled having heard Weber lecture, probably when he served as a substitute instructor in commercial and Roman law for his ailing doctoral dissertation director, Levin Goldschmidt, under whom he had written *The History of Commercial Partnerships in the Middle Ages* (1889). It is also possible, as Nahum Chandler has suggested, that Du Bois heard Weber address the influential Verein für Sozialpolitik (Association for Social Policy) on the East Elbian question. In any case, Du Bois, along with Seligman, would have been among the few American scholars to know Weber's early work and reputation. It was only in St. Louis, however, that they met as colleagues for the first time, most likely over breakfast (according to Weber's memory) and perhaps at the time of Weber's speech as well. What they discussed is a matter of conjecture, though it surely would have included the question of race and African American labor in the post–Civil War South. Writing from New York in November, Weber then invited Du Bois to contribute an article to the *Archiv für Sozialwissenschaft und Sozialpolitik* on the problem of race and race relations in the United States. Du Bois wrote the article several months later, the only person to follow through on Weber's numerous editorial initiatives during his travels, publishing in translation "The Negro Question in the United States" in 1906, with a brief editorial note appended by Weber. Du Bois must also have invited Weber to stop at Atlanta University, as Weber seems to have had the visit in mind; but the plan misfired for a number of reasons, among them Du Bois's absence when he passed through the city on October 8.

The relationship between Weber and Du Bois is thus strikingly unique, as it involved not only the questions of the day about race relations, social equality, and social policy but also a common core of intellectual assumptions about the investigation of social and economic life. The latter should not be surprising, however, as it was a product in part of educational exchange between Germany and the United States prior to 1914, of which Du Bois's experience was entirely representative. There are thus two sides to the relationship, one made visible through Du Bois's education at the University of Berlin from 1892 to 1894, where he was attached to Gustav von Schmoller's well-known political economy seminar and absorbed the best scholarship that German social science had to offer, and the other becoming evident a decade later in the course of Weber's travels and their aftermath in his commentaries and writings.

In his biography of Du Bois, David Levering Lewis has emphasized the importance of the German Historical School of political economy for Du Bois's intellectual development. It is noteworthy that his university program of studies closely paralleled Weber's: Du Bois studied primarily with the political economists Schmoller and Adolf Wagner while attending lectures by the two historians Heinrich von Treitschke and Max Lenz. His instructor in statistics was August Meitzen, the man under whom Weber had written his habilitation on Roman agrarian and legal history, *Die römische Agrargeschichte* (1891). The significance of Schmoller's political economy seminar, where Du Bois read parts of his planned doctoral thesis in December 1893, "Die landwirtschaftliche Entwicklung in den Südstaaten der Vereinigten Staaten" (The Development of the Agrarian Economy in the Southern States of the United States), cannot be overestimated for both German and American scholarship in the social sciences. The Berlin seminar provided the setting for numerous apprentice scholars—among them Richard Ely and Albion Small from the United States, and Georg Simmel and Werner Sombart from the German ranks— to sharpen their conceptual and empirical skills, as becomes so evident for Du Bois in texts like *The Philadelphia Negro*, the turn-of-the-century Atlanta University Publications, his work on the 1900 census, or his own contribution to the *Archiv*, the leading social science journal in Germany.

Like Weber's 1890s studies of the agrarian economy, agricultural workers, and immigrant labor in the German East, Du Bois's early works demonstrate a command of survey methods and statistical generalization, combined with a skillful interpretation of status groups, class and caste, socioeconomic structure, developmental relationships, and the role played by race or ethnicity. In a sense it was not only race and ethnicity but also the connected interests in comparative agrarian economies, the dynamics of industrialization and urbanization, exacting methods of social research, and the prospects for structural reform that led Weber to Du Bois's writings in the first place—interests in fact advanced in the more institutional and sociological version of political economy favored in Berlin, and then represented in American universities by Ely, Small, Seligman, Hollander, William Z. Ripley, Robert Park, and even Thorstein Veblen. The larger point deserving emphasis for the history of the social sciences is that "a native tradition of inquiry," as Dorothy Ross has called it, which was "allied to communal and Progressive reform" and backed by the authority of German social science, contributed to the institutionalization of sociology in the black colleges and Small's own University of Chicago, which itself became a center, as it remains today, for educating African American social scientists. These developments were consistent, of course, with Du Bois's early educational program as it took shape at Atlanta and in his disputations with Washington.

An important clue to Weber's general perspective was present already in his St. Louis speech on the problem of rural society in which, as we have seen, he held that in the old plantation economy of the South, the presence of both unfree slave labor and capitalist production for a market led to insupportable contradictions and fueled a bitter civil war. In the postbellum present, however, the most urgent social problems of the South were "even in the rural districts, essentially ethnic and not economical," he asserted. His journey through the South; his visit to Tuskegee; his conversations with Southern whites and then subsequently with Northern reformers like Edwin R. A. and Caroline Beer Seligman and Helen Francis and Julia Sandford Villard in New York in November 1904; and his reading of Washington, Du Bois, and the literature stemming from Du Bois's Atlanta University efforts and the work of the American Negro Academy seemed to confirm this conclusion.

Du Bois's *Archiv* contribution was a response in part to Weber's observations about the relationship between race and class, which were penned in Weber's characteristic English longhand (with occasional Latinized spellings) in his very first letter to Du Bois from New York:

> Until now, I failed in finding in the American (and, of course, in any other) litterature [sic] an investigation about the relations between the (so-called) "race-problem" and the (so-called) "class-problem" in your country, although it is impossible to have any conversation with white people of the South without feeling the connection. We have to meet to-day in Germany not only the dilettantic litterature [sic] à la H[ouston] St[ewart] Chamberlain & Com., but a "scientific" race-theory, built up on purely anthropological fundaments, too,—and so we have to accentuate especially those connections and the influence of social-economic conditions upon the relations of races to each-other. I saw that you spoke, some weeks ago, about this very question, and I should be very glad, if you would find yourself in a position to give us, for our periodical, an essay about that object. (November 8)

Weber's comments open an important window onto his critical thinking about race, well before his sharp attack on Alfred Ploetz, a proponent of allegedly "scientific" theories of race, at the Deutsche Gesellschaft für Soziologie in 1910. His intellectual position regarding the social construction of race is already clear, and his complaint about the absence of a serious discussion of class and race is accurate, with the exception of a few of Du Bois's essays. Contemporary writing that Weber consulted, such as Thomas Page's *The Negro: The Southerner's Problem* (1904), serialized in *McClure's* magazine, were indeed "superficial," as he commented later to Du Bois.

The exchanges with Du Bois thus illuminate Weber's focused interest in the problem of race in America. He must have read a press account of Du Bois's speech, a copy of which has survived in the Du Bois papers (with his own handwritten corrections). Du Bois delivered the address, "Caste in America," to the Twentieth Century Club in New York, and he repeated it in other forums as well; a version titled "Caste: That Is the Root of the Trouble" was printed in the Des Moines, Iowa, *Register Leader* on October 19, 1904. His argument at the time was important for emphasizing that the "race problem" was embedded in a contradiction between the Jeffersonian promise of equality and the reality of discrimination and servitude or "bondage," a problem thus connected to "the spirit of caste that is arising in a land which was founded on the bed-rock of eternal opposition to class privilege." Recognizing the inevitability of the rise of socioeconomic distinctions based on differences in individual ability and accomplishment, Du Bois pointed out that social stratification and a structure of opportunity based on achievement and economic success was entirely different in its social consequences from an iron "system of class privilege and unchanging caste gradations" based on race. The attempt, as he saw it, "to establish a new slavery by using the economic power of race prejudice to erect barriers of color caste" was fueled by economic interests and racial fears. Public resistance to this kind of repression was muted since victims of the new slavery were "largely black people," the ranks of the poor and powerless. Warning that such trends had "buried civilizations," Du Bois called in these passages for a new moral order of truth-telling and policies aligned with what later in American public life came to be called "equal opportunity."

Essentially the same line of reasoning found its way into the framing of Du Bois's *Archiv* contribution, particularly the last section concerned with the "new caste mentality." The manuscript was accompanied upon its submission in English by a list of recent literature on "the Negro problem" or "the question of questions," in his words, and a modest disclaimer that the essay "is a rather hurried piece of work & if it is not just what you want do not hesitate to cut it down or reject it." Weber did reduce its length slightly, appending an editorial comment that Du Bois and others had looked closely at the issues under discussion in the Atlanta University Publications, numbers 1–9, reporting on research discussed at conferences from 1896 to 1904, as well as *The Philadelphia Negro* and *The Souls of Black Folk*, and the eleven Occasional Papers published to date by the American Negro Academy—all literature that Weber wanted to have reviewed for the *Archiv*, a project that remained uncompleted in the face of his own immediate, intensive, and unexpected engagement with the Russian Revolution of 1905—an event that perhaps more than any other ushered in the twentieth century as the century of revolution, war, and unprecedented mass violence, obscuring for a time Du Bois's prescient forecast about the "color line."

When Du Bois's essay is read today, his modesty about the contribution to Weber's journal seems misplaced, for in its first two sections he sets forth a comprehensive political sociology of postbellum class relations in the South and their convergence with race, drawing on parts of his previously published work on the Freedmen's Bureau, the Negro farmer, and agrarian labor. He shows that the system that evolved in the "black belt" amounted to the continuation of slavery by other means as a combination of peonage or bondage and the exploitation of convict labor. The division of agrarian labor into four socioeconomic strata—renters of land at the top, followed by sharecroppers and then croppers (those entirely without capital), and wage laborers at the lowest level—was supplemented by formal legal and informal social and political constraints designed to hinder African Americans' mobility and stifle their initiative. Class structure overlapped with race; the vast majority of black Americans were confined to a marginal existence as sharecroppers, with little chance of escaping their plight. Du Bois called it a system of villeinage or "patronage domination," fitting the characteristics that appeared as a particular variant of traditionalism in Weber's early writings on agrarian labor and his later sociology of domination in *Economy and Society*: patriarchal *Herrschaft*, or domination. Their well-known contemporary, Carl Schurz, writing in *McClure's* magazine in January 1904, simply called these labor relations "serfdom": There will be a movement either in the direction of reducing negroes to a permanent condition of serfdom—the condition of the mere plantation hand, 'alongside the mule,' practically without any rights of citizenship—or a movement in the direction of recognizing him as a citizen in the true sense of the term. One or the other will prevail." Based on his firsthand knowledge of the conditions, Schurz's blunt assessment and political framing of the choices converged with Du Bois's investigations and Weber's observations.

There are some striking parallels between Du Bois's analysis and Weber's discussion of agrarian relations in eastern Germany in the 1890s. The two accounts breathe the same air of historical economics. Both dissected the problem of labor dependency, a "second serfdom," within systems distorted by an unsustainable contradiction between a fractured traditional order and capitalist productive modes. The relationship between class and the problem of "race" stood out in the one account, and that between class and the problem of migrant ethnic labor in the other. Both authors recognized that the two most common paths of escape from servitude were ownership of land outright or flight into the cities. Needless to say, they were also aware of the dynamics of associative life as a protective barrier against a hostile surrounding world, exemplified most vividly by the African American church. There was also the less traveled alternative path of education and entry into the professions and the bourgeois world of business enterprise. But, of course, in its developmental dynamics the South was not East Elbia. It was the "anomalous" South and the differences separating it from the old societies of Europe, the emphatic playing out of the struggle between class and race in America, the dangers of the color line becoming a determinant for caste that challenged Weber's and Du Bois's understanding.

They were not alone. Another outside observer, Gunnar Myrdal, was also aware of the legacy. In *An American Dilemma* he explicitly extended one of Weber's generalizations about associational life to the black community, an application Weber would have welcomed, noting, "Max Weber has sought to explain the numerous social clubs in America as a means of helping people to business, political and social success. This is only partly true for American Negroes. . . . [who] are active in associations because they are not allowed to be active in much of the other organized life of American society. . . . the tremendous amount of club activity among Negroes is, in one sense, a poor substitute for the political activity they would like to participate in but cannot because of caste." While "caste" may have disappeared from popular discourse, it should be said that a century after the exchanges between Du Bois and Weber the tense struggle over inequality is still with us—that is, socioeconomic inequalities defined by "race" versus inequalities defined by "class" or socioeconomic "status," to use the often preferred term. Notwithstanding our apparent reluctance to discuss class and race, much less caste, the veil of forgetting is still pierced occasionally by episodes that engage the public's consciousness. For his part, Du Bois never forgot the class problem; it figured centrally in his later migration to radical political positions.

One last point about Weber's enthusiasm for Du Bois's work, particularly the *Souls of Black Folk*, has to do with the way that work transcended the more prosaic categories of social science and probed areas of experience a narrowly construed science might overlook. Du Bois was also, we should not forget, a protégé of William James, judged by some to be James's most famous student. The reflective and lyrical quality of his writing appears even in the *Archiv* essay when Du Bois turns to what he sees as the most essential problem, the "intellectual" and "spiritual struggle," and imagines how the "occasional visitor to the South" might in a moment of estrangement and sudden awakening peer into "the shadows of the color line," imagery he borrowed from an earlier essay, "The Relation of the Negroes to the Whites in the South." It is a telling insight into the psychology of the traveler from afar, the shock of recognition, and the effect on the outside observer of the social conditions of the South.

Weber had prepared for the experience and was drawn into it with an uncommon intensity. In reading *The Souls of Black Folk* he would have been struck already by Du Bois's use of the "sorrow songs," his invocation of an emotional life and affirmation of an expressive musical culture reminiscent of the German romanticism that Weber knew so well. He noted that in this respect African American life and institutions did not share the austere aesthetics found in some of the Protestant sects. Having made an effort to hear the singing in the tobacco fields of the South, he expressed regrets later to Karl Bücher for having failed to do so during his travels. But two weeks after leaving Tuskegee he did succeed in hearing the musical performances at the large African American Baptist church on Nineteenth Street in Washington, D.C. Weber had a finely tuned ear for such cultural expressions and the connections across work, music, poetry, and spirituality. He was, after all, before Theodor Adorno the only major social theorist to write importantly about music in its worldwide cultural context. He would have inevitably felt drawn, we might suppose, to the emotional alternatives expressed in this different and yet very familiar spiritual realm that Du Bois perceived as "unvoiced longing toward a truer world, of misty wanderings and hidden ways."

At the end of their correspondence Weber expressed the hope that Du Bois would spend a sabbatical in Germany, then repeated his hope that "I shall come to the United States, I think, 1907 or 8" (May 1, 1905). Du Bois had a lifelong interest in German intellectual and cultural life and did visit again, but not until 1926, well after Weber's death.

The Lessons of Tuskegee

In her account of the American journey Marianne Weber missed an opportunity by not mentioning Du Bois or the emerging political debate in African American and reform circles, and she failed to include Weber's comments about Du Bois in her 1924 edition of Weber's collected essays on sociology and social policy, the *Gesammelte Aufsätze zur Soziologie und Sozialpolitik*. Of the journey through the South by train from Memphis through New Orleans, to Tuskegee, to Knoxville, Tennessee, and into North Carolina only a phrase appears, along with two pages devoted to Tuskegee, quoting one of her husband's letters at length, though ignoring explicit comments of her own. The reason for this emphasis seems clear enough: on the positive side the strong impression left on her by Margaret Washington and her circle at Tuskegee, an impression in line with her feminist interests and one that she interpreted in a characteristic and revealing way. But she also suffered from the hot and humid weather and then developed a migraine that lasted for days. The two weeks after St. Louis could not have been pleasant and must have tested her endurance.

New Orleans was a disappointment: a suffocating heat wave, sleepless nights, swarms of mosquitoes in the parks, the old French Quarter "Americanized" and in decline. Fleeing the city with relief, the Webers traveled by train to Mobile, Alabama, and along the Alabama River through Montgomery to

Tuskegee. Along the way Weber observed the "traces of the dreadful over-exploitation of the old cotton plantations," the "wretched Negro huts," and the return of the region to pine forests and an economy of wood exports.

Tuskegee, by contrast, offered an inspiring and welcome prospect that left (in Marianne's words) a "very moving impression." As she wrote with even greater emphasis in the biography, "What they found probably moved them more than anything else on their trip." This compelling emotional response was her own. Tuskegee appeared an oasis of reformist zeal, committed social action, and a well-defined educational program. Writing from New York, Max summed up his impression in a letter to Booker T. Washington: "It was—I am sorry to say that—*only* at Tuskegee I found *enthusiasm* in the South at all" (November 6). The choice of the word revealed an important idea, for *enthusiasm*, the quality of spiritual or "divine inspiration" borrowed by ascetic morality from the ancient Greek ἐνθουσιασμός, had since Plato always held a special attraction for the creators and protectors of cultural values, historic figures like Washington and Du Bois.

Washington himself was absent when the Webers arrived, having departed for one of many fund-raising trips in the North, so they were graciously hosted by his wife and the staff. They had lunch with Margaret Washington, observed the Tuskegee Institute's operation, and met the teaching and administrative personnel. Weber mentions especially Jane E. Clark, the dean of women, the person who accompanied the Washingtons' oldest daughter, Portia, to Berlin the following year for two years of music study with Professor Martin Krause; Warren Logan, the treasurer and second in command; Robert R. Taylor, the MIT-educated architect and superintendent of buildings and grounds; and the "Professor of Agriculture," who could have been either George Washington Carver or George R. Bridgeforth. During the brief stay Max browsed Washington's writings and perhaps consulted the library, as he did on other campuses, while Marianne attended an evening meeting of the Tuskegee Woman's Club, organized and chaired by Margaret Washington. Max noted the unusual combination of a "socially and intellectually free atmosphere," practical vocational training, and nondenominational Bible study with the "conquest of the soil" ideal. Marianne found herself once again in her element, as at the meetings in Hull House, and was impressed by the "idealism and striving" of the educated women she met. In Chicago her observations had centered on women and labor, but in the Alabama setting they shifted to women and race.

Both the Webers noted the differentiation and social stratification within the black population, Marianne commenting that some of the teachers were "nearly as white as I am," and both wrote about racism and its effects. In Max's words, among whites,

Everyone has a different opinion of Booker Washington and his work, from deepest revulsion at any education of Negroes which deprives planters of "hands," to the opinion, not rare among southern whites, that he is the greatest American of all time except for Washington and Jefferson. But without exception they share the view that "social equality" and "social intercourse" are *forever* impossible, also or even more *especially* with the educated and often nine-tenths white Negro upper stratum. Yet the whites are bleeding to death because of this separation intended as "racial protection," and the only enthusiasm in the south is found among this Negro upper class. Among the whites there is only aimlessness and impotent hatred of the Yankees. I have spoken with probably a hundred white southerners of all parties and social classes, and based on these conversations the problem of what should become of these people seems absolutely hopeless. (October 12; MWP)

The "people" Weber referred to were not the educated African Americans, but the segment of the white population, like his uncle Fritz, who belonged, using his words, to the "brave, proud but confused people who are lost in today's struggle for existence." Weber placed some of his other relatives in the same category, a judgment Marianne suppressed in her account.

Marianne's reflections took on a highly personal tone that questioned the definition and social construction of race itself. Recording her favorable impression of the college-educated Jane Clark, she pointed out that in her basic feelings, personal needs and outlook on life Clark was closer to educated white women than to poor rural blacks:

> But a social community will never come about between her and the whites. *She will* be counted among the most despised race; she may never hope to have her education and sensibility recognized as equally valuable as theirs. A drop of Negro blood in her veins excludes her forever from any legitimate living in common with a white man. In fact, any white person who was unprejudiced enough to interact socially with these people would be boycotted by his own race. And one calls that Christianity and recognition of "human rights"! I find the entire relations of the whites in the South to these highly educated people of mixed race simply outrageous. (October 12; MWP)

In the final analysis, she added, there was an economic motive: racial hatred and division served the purpose of protecting the supply of black "hands" with limited education who would perform the least attractive kinds of manual labor. This challenging conversation about race continued with the relatives— Max Weber's half cousin William ("Bill") Miller in particular—a few days later in Knoxville. "We spoke with Bill about the problem of race," she wrote, "and he is much too good-hearted not to admit that the relations of the whites to the higher stratum of Negroes is an injustice, but still shrugs his shoulders about it."

There was a possible way to break the stranglehold of caste, however, expressed for Marianne on the one hand through the German word *Bildung*—

that is, education and cultivation of the personality—and on the other through the practice of social action and social solidarity. The Woman Club's slogan of "lifting as we climb" conveyed the didactic moral, social, and educational message, the "Tuskegee spirit," as expressed by both Margaret and Booker T. Washington. In Marianne's view Tuskegee's educational regime for women, led by participants like Clark and the Quaker-educated Washington, thus bore essentially the same features of personal cultivation and education of the free personality embedded in a web of supportive social relations as she was to observe at northern women's colleges like Bryn Mawr and Wellesley, and Max at Northwestern University, Haverford College, Harvard University, and elsewhere. In this view the contemporary model for Tuskegee's moral regime was the "college," and deep beneath it in the American past the urtext of the voluntary sect. But Tuskegee also represented more than that: in the heart of the South it was an oasis in which the social forces of class and caste were held at bay.

One of the principal expressions of moralizing didacticism to emerge at Tuskegee was appropriately Booker T. Washington's Sunday evening addresses, thirty-seven of them collected in *Character Building*. By today's standards Washington's message of moral rectitude, individual responsibility, and hopeful optimism can seem both quaintly archaic and subversively modern. "Character is a power," he reminds his audience. "If you want to be powerful in the world, if you want to be strong, influential and useful, you can be so in no better way than by having strong character." The Franklinesque tone is unmistakable, complete with a disquisition in one talk on the "penny saved is a penny earned" homilies that Weber appropriated from Benjamin Franklin for his characterization of the "spirit of capitalism." But the classic voice of race-blind moral equality is present too in Washington's teachings: "In the sight of God there is no colour line," he intoned, "and we want to cultivate a spirit that will make us forget that there is such a line anywhere. We want to be larger and broader than the people who would oppress us on account of our colour." Such phrases offered a kind of moralist's reply to Du Bois.

Weber would have mediated the differences between Washington and Du Bois in an interesting way, seeing at Tuskegee evidence for the power of an ethos emphasizing the dignity of labor and the disciplining of the self in service to a secular ideal. In *The Protestant Ethic and the Spirit of Capitalism* the virtues of this kind of essentially ascetic attitude were traced to notions of vocation and calling, which then reemerged in the vastly different setting of Franklin's rules for living a purposeful and productive life, aiming at "moral perfection," and getting ahead in the world. So Weber would have read *Character Building* and *Up from Slavery* in the "spirit" of Franklin's *Advice to a Young Tradesman* and *Autobiography*, just as he interpreted the Washingtons' educational project at Tuskegee in terms not simply of practical vocational training but as an effort aiming at the reconstitution of the moral order and the human personality.

The shaping of character would surely have been in his mind when, at the end of the subsequent debate over the *Protestant Ethic*, Weber referred to Washington's comments in the fifth chapter of *Up from Slavery* emphasizing the crucial distinction between the claim to have received a "divine call" as an expedient way of avoiding personal responsibility, deceiving others, and gaining worldly benefits, and the genuine "calling" as an expression of absolute devotion to a vocation and its ascetic demands. The former was merely self-deception, a "parasitic mission." But the latter could be said to inspire a revolution from within, a program for authenticity brought about through disciplining and transforming the individual person. That was in the best sense the true meaning of Tuskegee.

Washington's was a moral message, nevertheless, and that was its strength and inspiration. The difficulty is that it tended to look away from deeply entrenched historical and social realities, the challenging threat of caste, and it could be at best only indirectly political. It could not dislodge or compensate for the sociology of race that Du Bois wanted to establish, nor could it adequately address the problem of social equality and civil rights that Du Bois identified in his *Archiv* article with his question of questions: "Can the white and black race live together in America in freedom and equality? What does 'living together' mean in a free, modern state?" It could not mean accepting the injustice of social caste. If living together meant living separately, even in moral rectitude, then the Jeffersonian promise of the American experiment would have been irretrievably compromised and lost.

Race and Ethnicity, Class and Caste

Weber's contact with Du Bois, travel through the South, his brief stay at Tuskegee, and the numerous conversations along the way all contributed to an enlarged horizon for his intellectual interests. Reflecting on the major categories of the experience, he found ways of abstracting them from the American context and reworking the ideas in parts of his well-known discussions of race, ethnicity, and nationality; class, status, and caste; domination and authority; and the sociology of religion. The conceptual apparatuses of these discussions, subsequently canonized in American scholarship, certainly owe some of their richness to this formative episode.

One immediate consequence of this aspect of the American travels, noted previously by American sociologists and an émigré scholar, was the debate in 1910 at the inaugural meeting of the Deutsche Gesellschaft für Soziologie. In one of the sessions on "the concepts of race and society" the issue of racial inequality surfaced as Max Weber tangled in heated exchanges with Alfred Ploetz, the proponent of what purported to be a "scientific theory" of race supported by notions of biological determinism. Weber had already mentioned

Ploetz in his letters to Du Bois, and he used this opportunity to pay homage to Du Bois and his work. He repudiated Ploetz's arguments by once again accentuating the socioeconomic determinants of race relations while reminding his audience that "race" is a category of culture and that prejudice is (in his words) "a product not of facts and empirical experience, but of mass beliefs." To Ploetz's claim that "inferiority" could be demonstrated using the methods of empirical science, he gave the trenchant reply, "Nothing of the kind is proven. I wish to state that the most important sociological scholar anywhere in the Southern States in America, with whom no white scholar can compare is a Negro Burckhardt [sic] Du Bois. At the Congress of scholars in St. Louis we were permitted to have breakfast with him. If a gentleman from the Southern States had been there it would have been a scandal. The Southerner would naturally have found him to be intellectually and morally inferior. We found that the Southerner like other gentlemen would have deceived themselves." And on the general question of group characteristics or personal qualities attributable to race, Weber's retort was unequivocal: "But does there exist even today a single fact that would be relevant for sociology—a single concrete fact which in a truly illuminating, valid, exact and incontestable way traces a definite type of sociological circumstance back to inborn and hereditary qualities which are possessed by one race or another? The answer is definitively—note well—definitively no!" The commonplace folklore of alleged racial differences conceived in terms of such varied characteristics as attitudes toward work or bodily odor were social 'inventions' or instances of a sociology of the natural senses of the kind Weber's colleague, Georg Simmel, had begun to investigate. There was no factual, natural, or "anthropological" basis for such claims. Contempt for manual labor, for example, could be treated hypothetically as part of the "feudalizing" tendency identified by American economists or, in Weber's words, "simply as a Europeanizing process which accidentally matures in America with a secondary effect."

The same topic returned two years later at the second meeting of the Deutsche Gesellschaft für Soziologie, with Weber once again intervening to warn that "with race theories you can prove and disprove anything you want." It was a "scientific crime," he added, to attempt to circumvent the difficult sociological analysis of a problem by using uncritical and confused racial concepts and hypotheses.

Two scholars widely separated in time and milieu have attended to the issues raised by Weber's discussion and uses of the American materials. The German Jewish refugee and Plato scholar Ernst Manasse, who after fleeing Nazi Germany spent his career teaching at North Carolina Central University in Durham, a traditionally black college, noted, "The direct observation of racial conflicts in the United States, more than any other experience, seems to have convinced Weber of the necessity to analyze the social implications of race." Manasse's is an insightful comment, conditioned no doubt by his own experiences in the South. In Manasse's view Weber's analysis of the social implications of race became manifest primarily in the sociology of religion and the discussion of caste, class, status, and ethnicity in India, China, and ancient Judaism. Such categories are undoubtedly important in these studies—especially the discussion of caste and caste taboos in Hinduism. More recently Karl-Ludwig Ay has sharpened the focus by emphasizing Weber's critical assessment of the conceptual, logical, and methodological issues plaguing "race" and its use as an explanatory category, as well as the setting for the scientific issues in the discipline of political economy. He has also pointed out that Weber tended to use North American examples in developing his systematic critique of the concept of race, though he could have chosen the problem closer to home—namely, anti-Semitism.

How did Weber propose to clarify the problems of race and class? Political economy had already framed the discussion, for in his Heidelberg political economy lectures of 1898 Weber had systematized the contemporary literature on race and ethnicity under the heading "The Biological and Anthropological Foundations of Society," a listing of thirty sources from Ludwig Gumplowicz to Adolphe Quetelet. This early bibliographic exercise served as the starting point for his political economy lectures, and then the mature formulations in his unfinished master treatise *Economy and Society*, with its canonical treatment of the central concepts of race, ethnicity, nationality, class, status, and caste.

If anything stands out in the carefully worded pages of *Economy and Society*, it is Weber's extreme skepticism about the use of *race* or *ethnicity* without explanation as serviceable terms. In his last word on the subject in the revised section on basic sociological terms, for example, he asserted that "the possession of a common biological inheritance by virtue of which persons are classified as belonging to the same 'race' naturally implies no sort of communal social relationship [*Vergemeinschaftung*] between them." Other factors, such as shared language, history, tradition, religious beliefs, or feelings of belonging together that lead to a common action orientation are decisive for the formation of a social community. Or in the section on ethnicity, the source of ethnic consciousness is treated as highly ambiguous, derived more often from "common political experiences" than "common descent." The formal definition makes the social or "artificial" quality of ethnicity clear:

> The belief in group affinity, regardless of whether it has any objective foundation, can have important consequences especially for the formation of a political community. We shall call "ethnic groups" those human groups that entertain a subjective belief in their common descent because of similarities of physical type or of customs or both, or because of memories of colonization and migration; this belief must be important for the propagation of group formation; conversely, it does not matter whether or not an objective blood relationship exists. . . . In our sense,

ethnic membership does not constitute a group; it only facilitates group formation of any kind, particularly in the political sphere. On the other hand, it is primarily the political community, no matter how artificially organized, that inspires the belief in common ethnicity.

Simply stated, far from being a category given in "nature," ethnic and racial identities were socially and historically constructed and politically conditioned. The definition is followed by a coup de grace:

> The notion of "ethnically" determined social action subsumes phenomena that a rigorous sociological analysis . . . would have to distinguish carefully: the actual subjective effect of those customs conditioned by heredity and those determined by tradition; the differential impact of the varying content of custom; the influence of common language, religion and political action, past and present, upon the formation of customs; the extent to which such factors create attraction and repulsion, and especially the belief in affinity or disaffinity of blood; the consequences of this belief for social action in general, and specifically for action on the basis of shared custom or blood relationship, for diverse sexual relations, etc.—all of this would have to be studied in detail. It is certain that in this process the collective term "ethnic" would be abandoned, for it is unsuitable for a really rigorous analysis.

The same cautionary warning applied to the concept of "race."

The questioning of collective concepts and the need to disaggregate their constituent meanings and references carried over to "class" as well, set forth in a section of Weber's master treatise widely known by the title given to it by Hans Gerth and C. Wright Mills, "Class, Status and Party." The text is really about the distribution of power within the political community, considering the effects of economic power (class), social honor or prestige (status), and organized parties. Weber tended to illustrate status conventions with American examples—the equality among "gentlemen," the social mingling of bosses and clerks in public settings, the usurpation of social distinction based upon a claim of ancestry and pedigree (e.g., descendents of the first families of Virginia or the Pilgrim forebears). Status segregation in its most extreme and thoroughgoing form became a closed "caste," a condition that Weber found most likely "where there are underlying differences which are held to be 'ethnic'"—an apt comment on what he saw in the United States.

Weber started to rewrite the discussion of social class in *Economy and Society*, but the revision remained a mere fragment, like Karl Marx's in the third and last volume of his *Capital*. On this crucial topic both theorists procrastinated until it was too late. But in these last passages Weber did return to the American South to illustrate the *absence* for "cultural" or other reasons of class conflict and action based on economically determined class interest, precisely where one might have expected to find such conflict, writing, "A classic example of the lack of class conflict was the relationship of the 'poor white trash' (non-slave owning whites) to the plantation owners in the Southern States. The poor white trash were *far* more anti-Negro than the plantation owners, who were often imbued with patriarchal sentiments." The displacement and trumping of economic class with caste, social status group, or cultural conundrums is an old American story, with suitable modern analogues. Though unaware of Weber's work or exchanges with Du Bois, John Dollard's and Hortense Powdermaker's classic landmark studies of Indianola, Mississippi, *Caste and Class in a Southern Town* (1937) and *After Freedom: A Cultural Study in the Deep South* (1939), addressed precisely that issue—the persistence of the cross-cutting dynamics of race, class, and caste.

The journey to the United States had begun aboard the *Bremen* with ethnic immigrants from central and eastern Europe, and it would end amid the settlement houses and Jewish immigrant neighborhoods of Manhattan's Lower East Side. The exact midpoint was the encounter with the "color line" at the Tuskegee Institute. What Weber discovered there and in the South was the interplay of class and caste, and the differentiation among socioeconomic classes *within* the caste orders, both white and black. To visualize the "color line" and its social effects was to recognize the problem of caste tugging at the fibers of the democratic social ideal. It was also to recognize the high degree of differentiation and stratification within *both* the black and white communities. Weber had not anticipated this observation. Conditions far harsher and more complex than Münsterberg's reference to "social exclusion" were at issue. Indeed, the accounts of American democracy written by Münsterberg, Bryce, and Tocqueville would have provided no guidance whatever in this respect. Weber had traveled this road on his own.

In the last analysis Max Weber thought any social group, "society," or "social system" would structure the life opportunities or life chances of its members, from "open" to "closed" relationships, from "positively" to "negatively" privileged conduct, actions, occupations, or ways of life. How would it do so, and using what criteria? The society's answer to that question was the crucial test of its merit and standing in the world. Weber had now edged closer, if not to a definitive answer to this question, then at least to a much more complex understanding of how his question was to be addressed in America.

SEVEN

DIFFERENT WAYS OF LIFE

Colonial Children

After leaving the Tuskegee Institute the Webers' route through the South to Washington, D.C., followed the railroad lines through Atlanta; Chattanooga and Knoxville, Tennessee; Asheville and Greensboro, North Carolina; and Richmond, Virginia—five states and over a thousand miles in ten days—arriving in Washington on the evening of October 18, 1904. These ten days were especially fast-paced, as they included the visits with the American relatives, descendents of Georg Friedrich Fallenstein and his first wife, Elisabeth Benecke, an aspect of the journey under discussion with Max's mother, Helene Weber, before leaving Germany. She was concerned about the circumstances of the American relatives and awaited a firsthand report. The condition of the "colonial children" (as the family referred to them) and their prospects in the New World had been under discussion in the family for years, creating a certain amount of strife and ill will, as Guenther Roth has pointed out in his finely crafted family history. As late as August 12, Helene wanted to make sure Max and Marianne had the addresses for Bill Miller and James Miller, and as a reminder promised to send them once again after they arrived in the United States. Like the Indian Territory adventure and the stop in Tuskegee, this part of the itinerary was arranged only after Max and Marianne were in St. Louis. But unlike Max's exploration of the southwestern frontier, it requires little explanation: seeing the relatives was a matter of keeping up with the family, reporting on their circumstances, and satisfying Helene Weber's expectations.

Our knowledge of what occurred during this part of the trip depends almost entirely on Max's and Marianne's letters. There is an unusual gap in the correspondence, however, from October 1–2 at the stopover in Memphis to October 12–14 in Asheville and Greensboro. When letter-writing resumed in the relaxed and temperate mountain air of The Manor at Albemarle Park, Asheville, there was even confusion about the date and day of the week. In addition, the conclusion to Max's letter from Asheville is missing, as Marianne indicated in her later notation. These gaps contribute to the challenge of reconstructing the record of travel and the significance of their stay with the relatives.

In *Max Weber: A Biography* Marianne handled the episodes with the relatives by devoting three and one-half pages to the brief stay at Mt. Airy, North Carolina, using Max's letter and a few lines of her own written in Washington,

D.C. The Sunday, October 16, events at Mt. Airy are well-known for the colorful account of the afternoon baptism. Max described it himself (in somewhat more elaborate form than his letter) in his 1906 article "Churches and Sects in North America," using the scene as illustrative material for the significance of religious affiliation and, as during the Webers' visit to North Tonawanda, New York, his central distinction between an institutionalized church and a voluntarist religious sect.

The opinions expressed in the accompanying text of the biography, however, are more characteristically Marianne's than Max's. At the very least they reflect her poor health (a cold and an asthma attack) and, more significantly, her feminist point of view, whose intensity she tends to soften and blur when writing in the 1920s. Consider the more complete 1904 version of her complaint about the social scene at Mt. Airy:

> For these people the driving force of the inner life and all activity is above all the feeling for the family, the love and care for their children and all the family concerns. Otherwise not much stirs the hearts and minds of the women, and why should it? Their school education is at best elementary—attendance is not required—and the so-called free school is in session for only four months. One notices it, too. The intellectual engagement of the women is much more limited than that of the men, and thus it is difficult to get anywhere with them. The men experience and learn about the operation of the world through their business relations, and despite reading newspapers irregularly, were well-informed about what's going on. For the most part I was left with the women, of course, while Max walked around outside with the men and captivated them with his delightful stories. One simply assumed that I would be best off with companions of my own sex. But *how* I longed to be with the men!! How I pricked up my ears to try to snatch bits of their conversation, and how much I once again pitied the lot of my sex, whose field of vision and range of interests remain as limited as its sphere of activity! In a word, the women were very pleasant and nice, but boring; in contrast something was always going on with the men. (October 21; MWP)

It is not difficult to sympathize with Marianne's plight, or to understand her decision to suppress these ungracious but honest passages. Her observations about schooling were correct: public school attendance was optional, and the school year averaged barely twenty weeks. Unlike Hull House and the Jane Addams circle in Chicago where she had been in her element, with the relatives in Appalachia she felt completely out of place. "As long as we were there I really felt rather uncomfortable," was her summary of the two full days at Mr. Airy. There is indirect evidence from the oral histories of surviving family members in North Carolina that the feeling was reciprocated by the relatives, who found Max a "mighty jolly fellow" but did not know what to make of the woman they called "Mary."

For Marianne the trip had reached its nadir. Max's continued high spirits and the male camaraderie would understandably have been a source of envy and annoyance. Indeed, for Marianne the entire visit with relatives might have been captured in a paragraph or two, had it not been for the happenstance of being in Mt. Airy on a Sunday and attending both a Methodist and a Baptist service, two of the sects in which Max was most interested, and the subject of sections he was to write for the second part of *The Protestant Ethic and the Spirit of Capitalism.*

What has not been understood previously, however, is that Marianne omitted not only a full account of her own reactions but also an accurate description of the journey itself, for there were in fact two visits with relatives in the South: the first with William (Bill) Miller and his family in Knoxville, Tennessee; the second with the other members of the Miller (Fallenstein) clan across the mountains in North Carolina. Marianne conflates the two, writing a single sentence about the former: "One of them [Bill Miller] had been at first a miner and then an elementary school teacher and was now owner of a law office and associated with a smart Irishman for whom he did the work; he, at any rate, was on his way toward becoming a notable." Nothing more is said about the three days in Knoxville. However, like the Mt. Airy church services involving the rest of the Miller clan, the days there offered some unexpected insights.

Nothing Remains except Eternal Change

When the Webers arrived in Knoxville, probably on October 9, they were returning a visit of Bill Miller's to Freiburg in 1895, accompanied then by his father, Friedrich (Fritz) Fallenstein, also known as Francis Miller, Helene Weber's half brother. As Guenther Roth has shown, the Millers' visit to Freiburg gave Helene, also at the time a visitor at her son's home in the Schillerstrasse, a welcome lift in the months following the death of her sister. In Freiburg Uncle Fritz and Bill seem to have hit it off with Max as well, notwithstanding his foul mood brought on by overwork, family tensions, and preparation for a trip to England.

Bill's father, the "Old Captain" as he was called locally in North Carolina, had lived an adventurous early life, escaping from the ship that brought him to the New World, fighting in the Jacksonian-era Seminole Wars in Florida and Georgia, heading north for New York to make his fortune, making his living from cabinetmaking and then getting diverted by Moravians into the Virginia mountains, where he married and remained as a farmer—"to his misfortune," as Max wrote. Max must have heard the saga from his cousins and perhaps the uncle's banker, whom they met by chance on the train through the Blue

Ridge Mountains. He recorded the details in one of the letters home, adding in a revealing reference that his uncle's life reminded him of Gottfried Keller's imaginative tale of ill-fated but self-inflicted decline and failure among Swiss mountain farmers, *A Village Romeo and Juliet*. When Max reached for a literary point of reference it was always a tip-off of the images forming in his mind: in this case not the romantic tragedy of Keller's adaptation of William Shakespeare but the rustic conditions, peculiar habits, and hardscrabble existence of rural folk seemingly trapped by fate.

In the Civil War, Uncle Fritz chose to serve in the Confederate Army, attaining the rank of captain, and apparently he was held as a prisoner of war. One of his sons, Jefferson Miller, described to Max the terrible conditions of imprisonment in what he called this "foolish war." After his release Fritz returned to the family in the mountains of North Carolina, scraped by as a farmer, and at one point was elected a county commissioner. Max referred to his uncle's loyalty to Virginia and his belief in its right to secede overriding his strong abolitionist views, following John C. Calhoun's interpretation of the U.S. Constitution in his *Disquisition on Government*, though the evidence about Fritz's actual political convictions seems ambiguous.

The entire family story line did not follow Gottfried Keller's, however. Bill Miller must have absorbed some of his father's early ambition, as he was the only one of Uncle Fritz's surviving six children, unlike those in the next generation, to break away from the confines of rural Appalachia to pursue a professional career. Upon his return to the United States from the trip to Germany, he decided at age twenty-nine to enroll at the University of Tennessee in Knoxville, a new state land-grant university created in 1879 that had been founded with the merger of Blount College (established in 1794) and East Tennessee University. The university showed its progressive side by admitting women in 1893; it remained true to the practices characteristic of its founding, and like the Chicago universities in 1904 still required chapel attendance for students. The university's register listed Bill Miller as a student in the two-year law program from 1895 to 1897, noting that his bachelor of law (LLB) was one of ten bachelor's degrees awarded in 1897. He also continued with graduate studies the next year, though there is no record of further degrees. Perhaps anticipating completion of his degree and a career in law, he married Magnolia ("Nola") Brittian on December 23, 1896, and they settled permanently in Knoxville.

Bill began practicing law upon graduation, and then in 1898 entered into a partnership that lasted twenty years with a man named John P. Murphy, the first-generation "smart Irishman" referenced by Marianne. The firm of W. F. Miller and J. P. Murphy occupied space in the Miller Building in downtown Knoxville. Listed in all the city directories of the period, it appears to have been a well-connected and successful partnership, though in the early years Bill certainly brought in additional income through employment as an elementary school teacher, a miner, and a speculator in land. He must have been well regarded, as he was also called upon to substitute for his professors at the university. The family relied on his legal expertise as well, as Max noted that he managed the financial affairs both for his brother, Hugh, who suffered from epilepsy, and his sister, Elisabeth, who was married to a man named Robert Rawley whom the family considered a "gambler."

In the correspondence addressed to Helene Weber in Berlin and the aunts in Oerlinghausen, both Max and Marianne wrote about the Knoxville experience, especially in the lengthy letter from Asheville. Having just come from Tuskegee, some of their attention was focused on race relations. This was one setting in which the Webers could explore racial attitudes with white Southerners in a relatively unconstrained way. Moreover, Knoxville itself was a city where the travelers experienced at close range the effects of post-Reconstruction segregation and discrimination against blacks: separate public facilities, transportation, parks, neighborhoods, churches, and schools. The mechanisms of disenfranchisement were also firmly in place: restrictive voter registration requirements, the poll tax, the secret ballot, vote tallies ratified by partisan election commissions, and manipulation in apportioning electoral districts.

To be sure, Knox County and eastern Tennessee participated in the wave of progressive reform after 1900. But as historians have shown, Progressivism as a political doctrine or outlook was a complicated and multifaceted movement with significant variations by region and social circumstance, marked only by a general core of shared views about industrialization, government, and the uses of "science" in public policy. In East Tennessee the "ethos of reform" encompassed several generalities: improving public education and health, supporting the rights of labor, building new roads, expanding public services, and regulating corporate interests and public utilities. It could also include support for woman suffrage, though not other forms of gender equality. As was true elsewhere, the progressive creed did not extend to racial justice; it was "for whites only," as C. Vann Woodward pointed out in his classic history of the New South; it did not affect the lingering effect of "caste" relationships.

Progressivism in this regional variant also left the "separate spheres" for men and women untouched, a point Marianne underscored in her continuing complaint about the political economy of the household. As would occur a few days later at Mt. Airy, in Knoxville she was shunted off to the domestic sphere with the women and children: Nola, Bill's wife, whom she found "kind-hearted and nice, but passive and phlegmatic"; her engaging and helpful mother; a visiting cousin; and two energetic children—six year-old Fritz and four year-old Ida, Bill's adored "blue-eyed lily." Meanwhile, Max was free to engage in important and lively discussions with Bill and the men. In the household division of labor, the educational regime for children was left to the adult women, Marianne noted, and she seemed to appreciate their approach—"simple" and "democratic" in her words—while expressing the standard cultural worries about overindulgence and lack of obedience. "Democratic" in the domestic context stood for a kind of personal ethos (with obvious political correlates): independence, self-reliance, unpretentiousness, questioning of authority. But in this Knoxville household it did not include social equality: Nola refused to allow son and daughter to play with workers' children in the neighborhood, Marianne reported: "Status-consciousness shoots up from the ground like a mushroom."

With Helene Weber's concerns about the relatives in mind, Marianne also observed that compared to nine years previously, as head of a family Bill's maturity stood out and he appeared more like one of the "notables." But contrary to her suggestion in the biography there is little evidence that he had the desire or the means to become a member of the influential local elite, notwithstanding his professional success and public engagements. Always alert to the material foundations of life, Max noted that Bill's annual income was

> about $1000 (4200 M), and from that he saves something and must deduct debts for setting up his office. He speculates some in real estate; he bought his small house and lot for $900, half the actual value. Nola's monthly household budget comes to $20–25 (80–100 M), as she grows sweet potatoes and the like. Such numbers are possible only in the southern states, where land in Tennessee, for example, is worth about half, or in Alabama a tenth to a fifth the value of the land in the former Indian regions settled already for a number of years by the Yankees in Oklahoma." (October 12–13; MWP)

Indeed, Knox County records show that Bill was involved in at least ten land transactions by 1903, including the purchase of two adjacent lots on Cornelia Street in what was then a northern suburb on which the home was built. The family income may seem close to the poverty line, but Morgan Kousser has shown that for the Southern states it would have ranked easily in the upper quartile. (In 1900 the lowest 76 percent of the population averaged a mere $64 per capita annually!) "Bill always commented to me that he will probably never be a 'rich man,' but he is a 'very happy man,'" Max noted, continuing,

> And in fact that's the case, as Marianne will probably write: this mixture of democratic instincts and Jeffersonian ideas, combined with that Fallenstein inability to bring things to a conclusion, as found in most of Uncle Fritz's children, make it difficult to get ahead. The combination of this mixture of ideas with the aristocratic instincts of the old miner, white Southerner and upwardly mobile notable is really quite peculiar, and it reveals questionable educational principles that make it difficult for the children to accomplish much. Bill works with an Irishman—that is, *Bill* does the work, while the Irishman is a deputy in the state assembly, a politician and jovial backslapping type, the kind of person who often has a political career here. He was very friendly toward me, quick-witted and mischievous, thought that I was like a man from Tennessee, or indeed from Kentucky,

etc. Nevertheless the connection is advantageous for Bill, as I realized after his explanation of the relationship. The Irishman doesn't do anything, to be sure, but pays one-third of the office expense and his portion of the profit is very small. The old fellow [he was forty-seven!], who showered me with some very valuable books, saw Bill on the street one day after his two-year "university course," called him into his office, immediately proposed the partnership and thus "made" him. Everything is really an amazing game of chance in these half-finished relationships. Until now I didn't know that Bill was a miner for seven months, primary school teacher for five, and his brother a miner who was let loose on the public as a physician. Not too long ago Bill (whose knowledge of jurisprudence is akin to administrative training in Germany) assumed the "professorship" in common law for two weeks, that is, he drilled the students on the basis of textbook reading, etc. etc.—a remarkable confusion in which nothing remains except the eternal change of everything, above all "vocation." (October 12–13; MWP)

Max seems to have hit it off with Bill and his law partner, enjoying the give-and-take of these relationships. The evidence is circumstantial, but suggestive: he spent at least one and perhaps two nights in town with the men, undoubtedly engaging in discussions of public topics and perhaps attending a political meeting related to the election campaign. In the correspondence he continued to quote Bill's opinion on social issues. And at least one of Murphy's gifts, Arthur S. Colyar's two-volume *Life and Times of Andrew Jackson* (1904), returned with Weber to Heidelberg. We might anticipate this kind of engagement anyway, as Weber had landed in one of his most familiar and favorite settings: local electoral politics.

Weber especially enjoyed the life story of his cousin's Irish partner. Like Weber's father, John P. Murphy had become a vocational politician, living *for* as well as *off* politics. At the end of his life he was described by the *Knoxville Sentinel* as a "well known citizen and active in city, state and national politics for more than 40 years." He was the son of Irish immigrants, a Democrat and a Catholic, first employed at age eleven as a printer for the *Knoxville Journal*. Essentially self-educated, later in life he had studied law before setting up the partnership with Bill Miller. His political career seems to have received a helpful push during one of Grover Cleveland's presidential terms, presumably the first from 1885–89, when he served in the U.S. Postal Service, no doubt a patronage appointment of the kind that Weber attributed to the "spoils system." He was then twice elected to the lower house of the Tennessee Assembly (1893–95 and 1901–3) representing Knox County, and in October 1904 he was campaigning for the assembly again (and was not, as Weber suggests, an incumbent representative). But he did hold office as one of eleven aldermen on the Knoxville City Council, a salaried position, where he served continuously from 1891 to 1912, when a five-member commission replaced the elected council in the wave of progressive reform sweeping the country.

The fall election campaign found Murphy at the center of a raucous intra-and interparty electoral battle in Knox County that pitted the Democratic Party machine (to which he belonged), then in control in the city and county, against another party faction as well as against the Republican nominees. Murphy's wing of the party was dubbed variously the "organized Democracy," the "Tyson Regulars" after one of its leaders, Colonel L. D. Tyson, or simply "the Ring" by the Republican *Journal and Tribune*, which enjoyed comparing it to New York's Tammany Hall; the opposing faction became the "reformers" or "Bate democracy" for Senator William B. Bate, one of its leading "Bourbon" members, or more colorfully in the Democratic *Knoxville Sentinel* the "natural mugwumps" or "goo-goos." As William R. Majors has noted, such electoral contests in Tennessee were certain to be "bitter and confusing." The campaign revolved around the usual blend of personal ambition and charges of corruption, election fraud, patronage appointments of the unqualified, and complaints about "unprincipled" politicians in "the Ring" and hypocrisy and disloyalty among the "mugwumps." (One can imagine this setting as the source of the American political lexicon's wry definition of a mugwump as a fence-sitter with his "mug" on one side and "wump" on the other.) But to this mixture must be added the baffling complexity of post-Reconstruction politics in Tennessee before Prohibition. It was a border state but also a Southern state, and one composed of three distinct historical and geographical sections; Knox County, in eastern Tennessee where a quarter of the population resided, was the center of a Republican electoral majority in a state otherwise solidly Democratic.

In his pathbreaking study *Southern Politics in State and Nation*, V. O. Key has noted that through this period Tennessee effectively had two one-party systems: Democrats ruled in the west and central regions, distinguished by the legacy of a plantation economy, slaveholding, and support for the Confederacy; whereas Republicans controlled the east, characterized instead by small farms, a relative absence of slavery, and abolitionist and unionist sentiment. In view of these realities it is not surprising that during Reconstruction, Tennessee was the first secessionist state to have democratic rule restored. The state's partisan alignment—forged during the Civil War and its aftermath—showed remarkable durability, persisting in voting patterns into the current century. It also made the state as a whole a relatively competitive electoral environment when compared with other Southern states, and the competition encouraged vote trading, unusual alliances, and urban party machines.

In this political context a member of a local Democratic minority but a statewide Democratic majority, Murphy aligned himself with the reform-oriented and more progressive "New South" wing of the party, as distinct from the state's dominant "Bourbon" faction. These shifting labels must be used cautiously, but in general they referred to the main division between those committed to a vision of "progress" in education and the economy (that is, support for industrial development, railroads, transportation, urbanization) versus those who kept the "Lost Cause" alive; emphasized states' rights, laissez-faire, and white supremacy; and traced their roots to the old planter aristocracy. The "New South" orientation was evident in organizations like the Southern Good Roads Association, formed in 1901, or the East Tennessee Education Association of 1903. One of its leading proponents was Arthur S. Colyar, who had a reputation among contemporaries as a brilliant captain of industry. He was also an important power broker who ran unsuccessfully for governor three times, in addition to being the author of the study of Tennessee's most famous politician that Murphy had recently purchased before bestowing it upon Weber. Murphy would surely have known Colyar personally from their years of political activity in more progressive Democratic circles.

Like many parts of the country at the turn of the century, Tennessee was increasingly faced with the regional challenges of economic development, the growth of corporate power, and the need for educational reform—in short, the kinds of problems characteristic of the emerging modern American state. Murphy selected one of these issues—education—as the key to addressing all the others. He outlined his campaign position at an electoral rally on October 8, 1904, the day before Max Weber arrived; as the local press reported,

> Mr. Murphy said that he had not yet been attacked by the enemy and that he would not discuss them as the hour was growing late, but that he favored an appropriation of $50,000 for the University of Tennessee. That he wanted to see 1000 free scholarships instead of 275; furthermore he was for better schools in the country districts and such should be the case. He favored a bill making the school books free and also the compulsory educational law. We should do all in our power to place the education of the children as cheap as possible. He was for good roads and longer terms of the schools in the country districts.

Over the next month Murphy elaborated this message of educational reform and a larger University of Tennessee appropriation, emphasizing the importance of educational opportunity and stressing that he wanted "to make education as close to the poor man as it could be." Among his legislative accomplishments, he expressed pride in securing the position of factory inspector in his previous service in the assembly, an issue with which Weber would have identified.

The press reported numerous local election-related gatherings, and if not in attendance at one of these Weber would surely at the very least have heard the debates of this overheated electoral season—grist for the mill on the theme of the political party as a "machine," or the fifteen pages in "Politics as a Vocation" in which Weber compared party organization and structure in England, the United States, and Germany. "The creation of such machines signifies the advent of *plebiscitarian* democracy," Weber wrote. In America the "plebiscitarian" principle stood out in bold relief. In Weber's interpretation it was set in motion at the national level by Andrew Jackson, an antitraditional-ist politician from a new "western" state, and in 1904 reinforced by Theodore Roosevelt's campaign and his conception of presidential leadership.

Politics is a local affair, however, and so the machine must have local roots. Americans of the time agreed. According to the editor of the *Knoxville Sentinel*, summing up the fall campaign,

> Every political party must have organization. So in Knox county the active ma-chine for doing the party work has been an executive committee of about 600 members. The chairman was given power to add to or take from this committee at his pleasure. It is the largest, most democratic committee in the state. Of course a smaller number of influential men consulted together and had great influence. Thus the cry of "ring" arose, but there was no more ground for such cry than has always been the case. . . . No more than now in the ranks of the bolters them-selves. We do not claim this organization has been free from error, but we do claim it has been less open to criticism than is usually the case in a large county like this. There is another class of people who oppose all political methods and these furnished recruits to the disgruntled. These were the natural mugwumps. . . . They are good men, many of them, and are sincere. [But] they are of the class which is never satisfied and always in the opposition. (November 5, 1904)

The sense of politics and political method in this statement, and the moraliz-ing oppositions and alternatives—all entirely representative of the rough-and-tumble of local American politics—bear an uncanny resemblance to Weber's point of view. If Louis Hartz is correct about a "natural Lockeanism" in Amer-ica, then one is tempted to call such statements evidence of a kind of "natural Weberianism." The outlook about the necessity of organization is homegrown and unpolished, a kind of political vernacular that took shape with the emer-gence of the modern American state. Cataloged in the pages of James Bryce's *American Commonwealth*, it is a way of conceiving politics that is consistent with the premises and categories of "Politics as a Vocation."

What of the outcome? Faced with divided support from the local press, "the Ring" (and Murphy) lost this battle, electing only one of six candidates for state office, and returning the Knox County Democratic Party to its divided condition of the 1890s. The "natural mugwumps" were evidently better orga-nized than the "organized democracy." But Murphy continued to serve on the Knoxville City Council for another eight years, earning $100 annually while continuing the partnership with Bill Miller.

Max and Marianne would never see Bill Miller again. He outlived his cousin Max by more than two decades, passing away quietly and suddenly at age seventy-four on May 17, 1941, at his home in Knoxville, remembered as a graduate of the University of Tennessee College of Law and a member of the

Washington Pike Methodist Church and the Bright Hope Lodge of the Masons; he was survived by his wife, Nola, and his daughter Ida Miller Harbison, his "blue-eyed lily."

Ecological Interlude

The Webers left Knoxville midweek. Had they stayed the evening of October 12, Max could have heard one of Murphy's many election speeches. Instead he and Marianne treated themselves, perhaps with Bill's knowledgeable advice, to the pleasures of an off-season vacation retreat in Asheville, North Carolina—"one of the most beautiful places we saw," Max wrote, "surrounded by blue forested mountains and the forest at the height of its fall colors." It was not only fall scenery and posh accommodations that awaited them. Nearby was also the attraction of the new Biltmore estate, which they toured on October 13.

Following the Civil War, Asheville had benefited from an infusion of Northern investment, including the Vanderbilt's capital. Cornelius Vanderbilt had launched the family's philanthropic endeavors with a $1 million endowment establishing a university in 1879 about three hundred miles away in Nashville. One of his grandsons and heirs, George Washington Vanderbilt II, then turned his attention to a quite different public works project: the Biltmore estate. Hiring Richard Morris Hunt, the architect of choice for the social stratum that Thorstein Veblen called the "leisure class," George teamed up with him to tour France's Loire Valley chateaux and returned with their design: a French Renaissance palace reminiscent of Blois and Chenonceaux with a banquet hall, winter garden, indoor swimming pool, and 250 rooms—all at a cost of $4 million. The Baedeker guidebook called it "probably the finest private residence in America," eclipsing Thomas Jefferson's Monticello, which had become only "an interesting example of the architecture of the period" (missed by the Webers), not to mention George Washington's Mount Vernon, merely "an old-fashioned wooden mansion" (which the Webers did see). Jefferson, who thought he was establishing a distinctive architectural idiom for the American home, would have been scandalized. Weber seems to have been fascinated. "The famous Vanderbilt 'estate,'" he wrote, was

> as large as the principality of Lippe, with 71 miles of avenues, as far as from Heidelberg to Strasbourg; black pigs, washed daily and massaged with oil, like Odysseus; cows of every imaginable kind, each in its own stylish cottage. The little houses for pigs, built in a Swiss style, have dimensions greater than Bill's house. Wonderful fresh ice-cream, that is, *here* it's actually frozen cream; magnificent chickens, etc. etc. Hunting grounds that encompass numerous hills and many square miles

of dense forest. He [George Vanderbilt] bought out the farmers, à la "Jakob der
Letzte," built a magnificent castle on a hill (unfortunately visible to us only from
the rear, since he was in residence), then a very "stylish" village with a church,
rented partly to the 500 personnel and foresters and others, and partly to guests—
an incredible impression of possessions and squandering of labor, land, and people.
But it is certainly marvelous anyway. (October 14; MWP)

The European and literary references were piled on top of each other in an
effort to make sense of this new efflorescence of the moneyed leisure class.
Veblen, one of Weber's favorite American social critics, would have adroitly
summed it all up under the heading "conspicuous consumption."

For Biltmore, however, Veblen's tagline was not quite accurate. From the
beginning Vanderbilt and Hunt had worked closely with Frederick Law Olmsted, Friedrich Kapp's old associate, to plan a self-sustaining community. The
Webers had already encountered and commented favorably on Olmsted's
landscapes in New York City's Central Park; Brooklyn's Prospect Park; the
parkways in Buffalo and Niagara Falls, New York; and Chicago's 1893 World's
Fair site at Jackson Park and the Hyde Park midway. Olmsted not only designed the Biltmore grounds but managed the feat of blending Renaissance
classicism with the primeval forested expanses of the New World. This success
required a massive reforestation project covering more than 100,000 acres of
degraded hardwood forest, the introduction of ecological practices developed
in Europe, and the employment for the first time in the United States of a
scientifically trained forester, the progressive conservationist Gifford Pinchot,
who during Theodore Roosevelt's presidency became the first head of the U.S.
Forestry Service. The project served multiple human and commercial purposes, including local economic development and a sustainable forestry and
woodworking business. It was an experiment in responsible social ecology, an
effort to re-create the institutions of the working village.

Weber's startling allusion to Peter Rosegger's *Jakob, der Letzte. Eine Waldbauerngeschichte aus unseren Tagen*, published in 1888, refers to be sure to the
Steiermark novelist's favorite themes: the expropriation of farmers, the exploitation of nature, the management of wildlife for personal sport—in short,
the victory of urban capital over rural tradition. The age's defender of Edenic
nature and pastoral life, of sacred *Heimat*, or the idea of home bound to the
soil, Rosegger told a story about the last Jacob, whose ladder is broken and
covenant violated. (The biblical reference is to Genesis 28:12–17.) As in
Keller's tale of Romeo and Juliet, the novel ends in tragedy and a form of life
vanishes—although, not quite, for young Jacob the son has run away to sea,
like young Fritz Fallenstein, finally coming to rest (like Fritz) in America. But
instead of a misfortune, such as in Ferdinand Kürnberger's odd potboiler *Der
Amerika-Müde* (The America-Weary), which Weber cites in *The Protestant
Ethic and the Spirit of Capitalism*, the event opens the path to self-discovery.

So the tale is also about America, the ethic of conservation, and the project of what today would be called sustainable ecology. In Rosegger's fiction, after making and losing a fortune in California's goldfields, young Jacob returns to his true self through a pilgrimage of testing and retrieval of Homeric proportions. Finally, from the fertile and unspoiled reaches of a Sierra Valley (located by the author carelessly in Oregon), he writes to his doomed father that his new multiethnic community of German, French, English and Native American settlers has reestablished the old harmony of life in nature, "like the first humans after the earth's creation." Rosegger's vision is thus a mythic narrative of escape, tribulation, recovery, healing, and salvation. The oldest myth of America has triumphed: Europe succumbs to the ravages of industrialization, while the New World glories in humanity's redemption and rebirth. The story becomes an allegory for the vision of Biltmore's creators, Vanderbilt and Olmsted.

Familiar with Keller's work, Weber would also have known Rosegger's popular novellas. Invoking the "last Jacob" as he gazed at Olmsted's creation, he might have had any number of images in mind: the irresistible Jeffersonian myth of American *societas*, the daring hubris of an effort to remake the world, the reconciliation of classical European culture with the natural order of America, or the healing power of human artistry and ingenuity even in the face of the rapacious exploitation and depletion of resources that he saw in the Indian Territory. The ambiguities in Rosegger's tale and the solitude of the mountain retreat invite conjecture. Could Weber also at some level have had in mind the meaning of his own American odyssey?

Inner Life and Public World

From Asheville to Mt. Airy was a journey from quiet repose and a glimpse of the "rich and famous" to something very, very different. Travel was circuitous and strenuous, boarding the train at 5:00 a.m. and arriving by horse-drawn buggy well after dark. The journey from Ashville onward was a change from the expected, a ride in a local train packed with passengers and not the comfortable Pullman cars the Webers were used to, with their impeccable service, lounge chairs, dining car meals, libraries, and writing and smoking rooms. Max was wearing his standout travel attire of knickers and high socks, misidentified by traveling companions as the German "national costume," a source of mirth for all. He assumed cultural parochialism: no one had seen a German before. After a scenic ride through the Blue Ridge Mountains, reminiscent of the Black Forest vistas of southwest Germany, there was a brief stop in Greensboro, North Carolina, at the Hotel Huffine. Lunch consisted of three kinds of meat, a fish steak, beans, green corn, noodles, turnips, cabbage, fresh wheat bread, butter, pie, and coffee, at a cost of fifty cents per person; only in the South, he noted, cheaper than Germany, and yet another opportunity to sample everything on the table. As Marianne slept, still in recovery mode, Max penned his curiosity about what they would find at Mt. Airy: no longer the petit bourgeoisie, but perhaps authentic farmers.

If Marianne Weber was frank about her response to the relatives, Max was no less forthcoming about the results of the Mt. Airy adventure. The brief stay there turned out unexpectedly to be an opportunity to observe religion in action. His observations about religion in America had started immediately at the beginning of their U.S. visit in North Tonawanda and continued in Chicago and beyond. Over the next month they were to take a slightly different turn: attendance at religious services, seven in all, beginning at Mt. Airy on October 16 and concluding with a service of the Ethical Culture Society in New York City on November 13.

There are four versions of the Mt. Airy events, one of which Max Weber published for an informed general readership in the *Frankfurter Zeitung* after returning home, then amended slightly for Martin Rade's journal *Die Christliche Welt*. It was his first effort to clarify the distinction between a religious sect and an institutionalized church that had crept into his consciousness already in North Tonawanda, a distinction that he thought was particularly pronounced in American practices. The Sunday at Mt. Airy must have been especially memorable, as the morning was spent in a Methodist service, the afternoon at an outdoor Baptist service that included a mass baptism, and between them a family dinner with the circuit-riding Methodist preacher as guest.

James ("Jim") Miller, Bill Miller's younger brother, was a devout Methodist. He was also the most successful member of the local clan—"'busy' like a Yankee," Weber quoted the relatives saying, a characterization that conveyed a mixture of admiration, envy, and disapproval. With an annual income of $1,000 from farming, Jim also ran a business on the side in horses and buggies. He took the Webers and some other family members to the service at the Zion Methodist Church, a simple, austere barnlike structure in a rural location. Weber noticed the sharp contrast between the plain solemnity of the interior and the brilliant autumn colors of the surrounding landscape. The sermon was "purely practical," and yet it had an "emotional" quality and revealed the preacher's strong inner convictions. Congregants who felt "awakened" by the experience came forward, kneeling and praying aloud at the altar. The minister, who served eight churches in the circuit, preached "entirely like a political speaker," Weber remarked, still fresh from the campaign in Knoxville. The only jarring element was the music, the "unspeakably dreadful singing of the shrill voices," a source of continuing comment: "In America," he wrote a few months later in *The Protestant Ethic and the Spirit of Capitalism*, one "hears as community singing in general only a noise which is intolerable to German ears."

Weber showed some awareness of the purpose of this musical aesthetic, both in the New World and in European centers of the reformed church such as the Netherlands; it brought the listener back to the "sobriety" of the setting and the occasion, as he said of the Mt. Airy service. Given additional time, he might have probed more deeply into this dimension of the musical culture of Appalachia. As anthropologists and musicologists have subsequently pointed out, the strict Calvinism of the primitive Baptist influence in Appalachia favored elimination of plain chant, bel canto, or the use of vibrato of any kind, and instead favored slow, stately, dissonant, and unaccompanied singing, without the organ or any other instrumental accompaniment. Austerity of expression was supposed to hew as closely as possible to the mode of religiosity in the original Puritans, an aural witness to the inner-worldly asceticism of the congregation.

Over dinner at Jim Miller's after the service Weber conversed with the young Methodist preacher about religious trends, and the minister agreed that the older practices of periodic "revivals" and weekly confessional "class meetings" of individual members among like-minded neighbors were going out of style. This view confirmed Weber in his belief, as he put it, that "an enormous number of 'orders' and clubs of all kinds have begun partly to take on the functions of the religious community," a development that he elaborated in the Frankfurt newspaper report:

Almost every small businessman who wants to make something of himself wears some kind of badge in his lapel. But the Ur-form of this practice that serves to guarantee *every* kind of "honor" for the individual is surely the religious community. This function is most fully developed . . . in those communities that are "*sects*" in the specific sense of the word to be discussed here. This was made especially clear to be personally when I attended a Baptist baptism on a cold Sunday in October in the foothills of the Blue Ridge Mountains in North Carolina. About ten people of both sexes in "*full dress*" stepped one after another into the ice-cold water of the mountain stream, in which the minister dressed in black stood waist-deep through the entire procedure. After the usual professions of conviction, they placed themselves in his arms, bent their knees, leaned back until the face disappeared under water, climbed out puffing and shaking, and were "*congratulated*" by the farmers who had come by horse and wagon in large numbers, and quickly driven home, sometimes hours away. ("*Faith*" protects them from catching a cold, it's said.) One of my cousins, who had accompanied me from his farm and showed his disdain for the event by disrespectful spitting (he maintains his *lack* of church affiliation as a sign of his German heritage!), showed a certain interest when an intelligent looking young man undertook the procedure: "*Oh see: Mr. X! I told you so!*" Asked for an explanation, he only replied that Mr. X intended to open a bank in Mr. Airy and needed considerable credit. Further discussion revealed that for this purpose acceptance into the Baptist congregation had to have a decisive value not primarily on account of the Baptist customers, but rather much more for the customers who were *not* Baptists. This was because the detailed investigation into moral and business conduct of one's life [*Lebensführung*] that the congregation conducts is considered by far the strictest and most reliable.

The cousin to whom Weber referred was one of James and Bill Miller's older brothers, Jefferson ("Jeff") Miller, a man in his late fifties who had managed only to scrape by as a farmer, an occupation and a life he detested. The generational gap and the tension over "success" within the family were readily apparent: twenty years separated these brothers, Jeff brandishing his native cynicism and hostility to the sects, while both Jim and Bill were firmly embedded in the social fabric of Methodism. Weber referred to Jim belonging to other unnamed "orders," and Bill was also a Freemason. Differences in the forms of sociability could not be missed: at Jeff's house religious or spiritual expression was avoided, whereas at Jim's a prayer preceded dinner and the form of address was "brother" (or "sister") so-and-so. ("Faith protects them from catching a cold" was actually Jim's pronouncement.) It hardly needs to be said that cousin Max would have noticed that it was not Jeff but Jim and Bill who had made their way successfully in the world. (Parenthetically, in defense of Jeff's manners, I should point out that the habit of chewing tobacco was widespread, even among the women relatives—to Marianne's consternation. Fortunately today the appropriate cultural substitute has become chewing gum, with the exception, apparently, of the baseball dugout.)

The outdoor baptism was most likely sponsored by the Mt. Carmel Baptist Church. Notwithstanding uncertainty about the actual participants, the event in itself for Weber captured an important social relationship across religious affiliation, moral approbation, and economic action. One aspect of the connection was symbolic, such as wearing a badge or a lapel pin as an outward symbol of authentication and conviction. The practice was not exclusively American, though in Weber's view in the United States its use reflected a sacred religious origin and point of reference. When displayed for secular political purposes (the ubiquity of the American flag and the flag lapel pin is the obvious example, inserted even into presidential campaigns today), the symbolic bona fides could thus be witness to a strong emotional appeal.

More was at stake than the manipulation of symbols, however, for the relationships across sect membership, morality, and economic action that Weber perceived had a direct bearing on the totality of a way of life or life conduct. Among the relatives in America the relationships were revealed in an especially unforgettable way. It was the authentication of the individual's moral standing through social action and group membership that attracted Weber's attention, as it had in the quite different settings of Northwestern University, the Tuskegee Institute, or the Indian Territory. At Mt. Airy, however, the example was not just the "Mr. X" or "Bem" of the baptism, but the different ways of life of the cousins as well. The language Weber chose to describe the process—moral examination, ethical probation, moral testing, methodical way of life, proving oneself through sober diligence in one's calling—emphasized the institutionalization of access to group membership, of course. Yet it also captured the frictions and tensions of the family history set out vividly before him.

As for the sects, the crucial claim still had to be substantiated. Though the process of joining was voluntary, it was also competitive and demanded success of the applicant: the successful challenge of holding one's own in a circle of social equals provided a test of personal legitimation. In its social consequences, sect membership thus extended to the individual "a certificate of moral qualification and especially business morals," as Weber expressed the idea. It provided proof of one's reputation, honesty, trustworthiness—hence, proof of one's credit worthiness and access to credit. It was then a short step logically to understanding the sect, and *all* sectlike associations, as social carriers of the orientation that Weber called matter-of-factly "the bourgeois capitalist business ethos among the broad strata of the middle classes (the farmers included)."

In sum, in America the sects were the original model. All other processes of sociation and forms of group life followed their lead. Today we would say they were the guarantors of "middle-class values," of a wealth of social trust and social capital.

The Cool Objectivity of Sociation

In Chicago's stockyards and again in the oil fields of Muskogee in the Indian Territory, Max Weber explored the dynamics of American society as an expression of modern industrial capitalism—one dominant way of thinking about the United States as the most advanced example of the world to come, prefigured already in Alexis de Tocqueville's sense in the Jacksonian age of seeing the European future in the American present. In Knoxville and Mt. Airy, however, a quite different picture began to emerge: not economic rationality and its problematic and alienated effects, but an image of the processes and patterns of associational life characteristic of the American democratic social and political order. Weber's reading of this order was "progressive" in an interesting way, calling attention to the power of associational life, the sects and orders and parties, and to the formation of the self, the certification of the individual, and the creation of citizens through the dynamic of what he called the "cool objectivity of sociation." The phrase poses an enigma: what exactly did Weber have in mind?

At the conclusion of the *Frankfurter Zeitung* article Weber arrived at a formulation of the issue, giving it a polemical edge by setting up a double opposition: democratization properly understood (using the American example) versus the bureaucratization of German life that he abhorred; and more surprising, the processes of forming *social* groups versus the romantic nostalgia for "community":

> Whoever represents "democracy" as a mass fragmented into atoms, as our Romantics prefer to do, is fundamentally mistaken so far as the American democracy is concerned. "Atomization" is usually a consequence not of democracy but of bureaucratic rationalism, and, therefore, it cannot be eliminated through the favored imposition of an "organizational structure" from above. The genuine American society—and here we include especially the "middle" and "lower" strata of the population—was never such a sand pile. Nor was it a building where everyone who entered without exception found open doors. It was and is permeated with "exclusivities" of every kind. Where the old relationships still exist, the individual does not have firm footing, either at the university or in business life, when he has been unable to be selected into or to *hold his own* in a *social organization* (earlier almost always religious, today of one kind or another). And the old "sect spirit" holds sway with relentless effect in the intrinsic nature of the associations. The latter are always "artifacts" or "societies" [Gesellschaften] and not "communities" [Gemeinschaften], to use the terminology of Ferdinand Tönnies. In other words, they neither rest on "emotional needs" nor aspire toward "emotional values." The individual seeks to claim *his own* position by becoming a member of the social group. That undifferentiated peasant-like, vegetative "comfortableness" [Gemütlichkeit] is missing, without which a German is unable to cultivate a sense of community. The cool *objectivity* of sociation [*die kühle Sachlichkeit der Vergesellschaftung*] promotes the precise placement of the individual in the purposive activity of the group, be it a football team or a political party. But this objectivity never means a diminution of the necessity for the individual to care constantly for his self-assertion. On the contrary, precisely *within* the group, in the circle of acquaintances the task *of "proving" oneself* really makes itself felt for the first time. For that reason the social group that one belongs to is never something "organic," a mystical unified essence hovering above a person and enveloping him, *but* much more a quite conscious mechanism for one's own material or ideal *purposes*. . . . the connection of the inner isolation of the individual, which signifies a maximum development of his powers of action, with his capacity for forming social groups having the strongest coherence and the greatest impact, has emerged with its highest potential on the foundation of the *sects* and their formation.

Weber might have written "material or ideal *interests*," as he did in a later text. But the point would have been the same: both material "goods" and ideal "values" were promoted by social action within a group.

At first glance, it appears that Weber has discovered an important source, perhaps *the* essential historical source of social capital in America. But the passage is more extraordinary than such a conclusion might suggest, for in the hills of Appalachia amid relatives he had stumbled across evidence for an idea that had been maturing through the preceding weeks, a provisional answer to the question posed in Chicago by the tension between economic rationalization and an ethos of asceticism. Could it be that the capitalist rationalization of social and economic life might be countered by a distinctive process of sociation and a conscious promotion of associational life?

The idea required rethinking the nature of *social* action, or the process of forming social relationships, the verbal noun *Vergesellschaftung* rendered imprecisely in English as "sociation" or "association." Consider that the radical critique of capitalism in Europe, from the young Karl Marx to Pyotr Alekseyevich Kropotkin and Leo Tolstoy, had always set fragmentation against wholeness, atomization against authenticity, mechanization against organic connection, the alienating forces of civil society against the healing powers of community. The "other" of alienating capitalism was its overcoming in the species life of classless community, a conceptual placeholder borrowed from romanticism. But Weber has suggested that such mutually exclusive, reified categories are entirely misleading. The reason they mislead is that they miss the modern alternative—namely, the kind of *purposive process* of forming social relationships that attaches individuals both to the local and particular, and to the universal and general. The process both unifies and differentiates, and it does so on the basis of *social* rather than communal norms, relying on the "cool" rationality of matter-of-factness, of *Sachlichkeit*, instead of the warm congeniality of *Gemütlichkeit*, that untranslatable noun of comfort and contentment. The social norms are "objective" because they are external to the individual and have a pragmatic logic; they describe a *practice*. The norms are not inscribed in the "inner self" or dependent on subjective inwardness.

Stated more abstractly, this kind of sociation or process of forming social relationships combines purposive action oriented toward rational ends with the rational value orientation of egalitarian participation in group life. In that sense it is democratic; it is also thoroughly *modern*. The ends of coming together in a social relationship are radically different across social groups, from an election committee to a Bible study group or an athletic team, but the means of forming the social relationship are the same, replicating in the modern social setting the "sect spirit" with its matter-of-fact public, participatory, and collegial norms. The untraditional, public, impersonal, voluntary, and purposively rational solution to the problem of individual action within group constraints was what made for such an unusually potent and original variation of previous social forms—a solution romanticism and neoromantics of all stripes have consistently misjudged.

Weber's insight follows the thread woven through the experience of the American journey to this point, discovering the basic model for social differentiation and democratization in the antiauthoritarian and nontraditional sects. The advantage of the insight is its comprehensive character, for it sets in motion the basic dynamic of American social life: on the one hand the drive toward exclusivity, toward purposive goals and distinctive individual achievements; and on the other hand the commitment to inclusiveness, to social democratization and a common, shared fate. Paradoxically, voluntaristic sociation promoted both.

How and why these two sets of contending forces are constrained, combined, split apart, and recombined is the next problem Weber would have to engage. Whether his generalizations from a century ago still hold is, of course, another matter, widely discussed and much disputed. It is an issue that we will have to judge for ourselves.

EIGHT

THE PROTESTANT ETHIC

After saying farewell to the North Carolina relatives, the Webers set their sights on continuing by train to the two Civil War capitols—Richmond, Virginia, and Washington, D.C.—followed by a return to the East Coast. Marianne had conquered her migraine but still suffered from asthma and a cold, recovering at last only in Philadelphia. Max commented that they might have stayed longer at Mt. Airy had it not been for her poor health, and he gave a similar reason for not returning to Atlanta after October 20 to visit W.E.B. Du Bois.

The stop in Richmond offered nothing more than a brief glimpse of the city, but the short week in the District of Columbia provided for the first time a much more leisurely pace—some days of recovery for Marianne, an opportunity to be ordinary tourists, and two instructive appointments for Max. Staying in the fashionable new Raleigh Hotel on Pennsylvania Avenue four blocks from the White House, the Webers followed the usual Baedeker itinerary: a trip down the Potomac River, and visits to George Washington's Mount Vernon, Arlington Cemetery, the home of Robert E. Lee (Fritz Fallenstein's commander, Weber noted), the Washington Monument, Olmsted's newly landscaped Capitol, and the redesigned Mall as approved by the McMillan Commission. It was a fall tour mixing natural beauty with colonial America, memories of the Civil War, and neoclassical republican grandeur: commanding vistas, plantation culture, broad urban avenues, stately architecture, the poignancy of sixteen thousand gravestones stretching row upon row into the distance.

Max Weber broke away from this program of sightseeing for two engagements, both connected to interests explored previously. One was a meeting with the well-known president of the American Federation of Labor (AFL), Samuel Gompers. An immigrant himself, though opposed to unrestricted immigration, the London-born Gompers had played a restraining role in Chicago's stockyard strike. We can only speculate about why the meeting was arranged and what was discussed, as Weber's description was terse: Gompers was "hyperdiplomatic and always felt he was being interviewed, so always swallowed the second half of a sentence that contained something interesting. Thus instead of learning about his thoughts, I had to guess at them" (November 2; MWP). The idea for a meeting probably originated either in Chicago, where the strike was the issue of the day, or in St. Louis at the suggestion of Jacob Hollander. The session could well have had the feel of an interview, as

Weber had a long-standing interest in labor relations and labor organization, and as an editor of the *Archiv für Sozialwissenschaft und Sozialpolitik* he was always in search of information, statistics, reports, contributions—and, from the previous month, an explanation of the failure of a major strike. That failure and AFL policy concerning unskilled and immigrant labor surely would have been on his mind.

A few months later the task of reviewing the American labor literature fell to Weber's coeditor, Werner Sombart, a review preparatory to his writing *Why Is There No Socialism in the United States?* However, Weber also took up labor issues in comments at the Verein für Sozialpolitik in 1905 and thereafter, as well as in the monograph *Zur Psychophysik der industriellen Arbeit.* In these statements and writings it was invariably the "matter-of-fact men" of labor leadership in the United States that most impressed him, a reasonable characterization of Gompers, in contrast to the ideological disputes and tendentiousness found in the German socialist and labor movements. But Weber also recognized that in the American setting, too, the protest against the embourgeoisement of the labor movement was contributing to an upsurge of a more radical politics, both in a domestic Socialist Party and by 1905 the formation of the Industrial Workers of the World as an alternative to Gompers's moderate craft unionism.

The second engagement was a continuation of the practice begun during the visit with relatives in Mt. Airy, North Carolina: an opportunity the very next Sunday to observe an entirely different kind of religious service, that of the the Nineteenth Street Baptist Church, a large urban and middle-class black Baptist congregation established in 1839. Cited in Du Bois's Atlanta University study *The Negro Church*, the church was served by the legendary preacher and former slave Walter H. Brooks, a tireless campaigner for temperance and respectability, opposed even to dancing. Nineteenth Street Baptist played a prominent role among regional African American churches. Unfortunately Brooks was away at the time, but the service did not disappoint Weber for its emotional expressiveness, the style of preaching, the interactions within the congregation, and the engaging response of the listeners that built from low rumblings and whispers to a rousing crescendo: "the last words of each sentence [of the sermon] first repeated softly, then in a shrill voice, with 'Yes, Yeas!' or 'No, No!' in response to the apostrophizing of the preacher, who was no more impassioned than the young Methodist minister in Mount Airy, and not even close to [Adolf] Stöcker" (November 2; MWP). The Webers sat in the back pews, feeling out of place, and noticing once again the remarkable contrasts and differentiation *within* the African American community. The service seemed to come from another world, mysterious and beyond the expected—"uncanny" (*unheimlich*) was the word that kept coming to Weber's mind.

The emotion was to be felt again soon, but in a radically different, austere setting, one of silently awaiting the movement of the spirit. Though the Webers could not have known, the Nineteenth Street Baptist service was a kind of watershed, pointing the way for the final four weeks of their American tour. The physical and mental pace of the journey was about to quicken, then remain at a high pitch until the very end. In *Max Weber: A Biography* Marianne captured a few of its engaging moments, but she also overlooked much of what was most important in the encounters with colleagues, friends, institutions, the social world, the everyday, and the moral and spiritual life.

Spirit and World

Arriving in Philadelphia on a Monday, the Webers settled for a few days into the Aldine Hotel on Chestnut Street between Nineteenth and Twentieth Streets. In America's third largest city the familiar skyscrapers had returned, similar to those of New York and Chicago. D. H. Burnham's Land Title Building was just down the street, a reminder of his Fisher and Reliance edifices in Chicago. But there was an important difference in Philadelphia, duly noted by Marianne: numerous buildings in the federal style; the blocks of uniform red brick row houses set up "like one egg after another"; and the contrast among the rectilinear cityscape, the "painterly" vistas of the colleges on the city's outskirts, and the spare, unadorned, "sober" style of vernacular building that seemed to express the "Quaker spirit."

As Marianne finished recovering from the visit to Mt. Airy, Max took the following day to travel by train to Baltimore with an invitation from Jacob Hollander to visit the Johns Hopkins University and its economics department, or seminary, as it was then called. In American higher education Johns Hopkins was well known for having introduced the German seminar method of instruction, perfected at the University of Berlin by the historian Leopold von Ranke. Arriving in the morning, Weber certainly attended one and perhaps two undergraduate classes: Hollander's seminar "Economic Theories since Adam Smith" with seventeen students, and the general "Economic Seminary" Hollander taught jointly with his colleague, associate professor George E. Barnett, attended by thirteen students.

Hollander and Barnett were an interesting pair with quite different backgrounds: Hollander was active in Jewish circles, his father a recent Bavarian immigrant; Barnett came from an established Methodist family, and his father was an ordained minister. Their political views differed, as Hollander served Republican presidents while Barnett became a "New Freedom" Democrat. Nevertheless, they became close personal friends and remained intellectual partners for decades. Weber was intrigued by their methods of instruction, noting that "the student studies about 30–40 pages of a political economy text at home (Hobson's *Evolution of Capitalism*) and then will be *questioned*. Here it was quite adroitly combined with a kind of lecture. Then came a seminar: a *good* seminar paper was (very severely) criticized" (November 2; MWP). It was one occasion where Weber could not resist intervening, perhaps motivated by John A. Hobson's book on the subject of capitalism and its "evolution" through machine production. Hobson's thesis relied on work on the cotton industry by Weber's colleague, Gerhart von Schulze-Gaevernitz, that demonstrated a correlation between higher wages, shorter working hours, improved rates of production, and lower prices of products. (Only in the revised second edition of 1906 did Hobson introduce a chapter on the origins of modern capitalism and the "capitalist spirit," using Sombart's *Der moderne Kapitalismus* and his concept of "economic rationalism," but not Weber's more directly relevant work.) Weber admitted that in the seminar he had the "audacity to monopolize the discussion with the students." Thanking Hollander afterward, he promised to improve his English for a return engagement. He also praised the "intensity of the work" and the "high standards of scientific investigation" that he found, contrasting them favorably with the financial pressures in German universities to attract large numbers of students (undated letter, probably November 2).

Weber and Hollander shared a concern for the problems of the Indian Territory, a topic they discussed with the advantage of Weber's firsthand knowledge of Muskogee and the Dawes-Bixby Commission. More generally, however, they shared an interest in the field of labor economics and in the critical evaluation of historical economics. Hollander and Barnett were well known among economists for focusing their instructional program and field research on labor relations and trade unionism in the United States, though Hollander was also at home in economic theory, economic history, public finance, and international economics. Weber would have been attracted to his view that the small-bore empiricism and historicism of Gustav von Schmoller and the German Historical School had run its course and now needed to be supplemented by "a new body of economic theory," as Hollander argued. He also would have appreciated Hollander's sense that the United States presented unparalleled opportunities for scientific inquiry—"perhaps the most efficient substitute for a great economic laboratory that the world has ever known," a formulation close to a few of Sombart's comments. It is difficult to imagine that the day would have passed without a discussion of labor relations, the AFL, Weber's meeting with Gompers, and the effort to organize the stockyards.

Weber (and Sombart) as coeditors wanted to enlist Hollander to write for the *Archiv für Sozialwissenschaft und Sozialpolitik*, either on the problems of the Indian Territory—especially finance and taxation—or on the history of American economics and economic theory. Hollander knew Sombart and corresponded with him about these matters as well. He seemed inclined to contribute, but like most of Weber's entreaties, this one also succumbed to the pressure of work and other competing demands on Hollander's energies.

Returning to Philadelphia, Weber encountered another kind of worldly student culture: the high-spirited evening send-off at the Broad Street Station, featuring a student snake dance, of the University of Pennsylvania football team for the off-campus training camp preparatory to the annual Harvard University game, to be played in Cambridge. It was a glimpse of events to come. But first there were other educational matters to consider. Weber had written to the president of Haverford College, Isaac Sharpless, asking about a visit to the campus, and he had received a friendly and positive reply. The Bryn Mawr College president, Martha Carey Thomas, could well have been the source of the idea, as at the Congress of Arts and Science in St. Louis, Missouri, or earlier in Berlin she must have invited Marianne to spend a day at her women's campus. So the morning following Max's invigorating conversations with colleagues and students at Johns Hopkins, the couple took the Pennsylvania Main Line to Haverford Station, and toured two more colleges founded by Quakers; while Marianne visited Bryn Mawr and lunched with Martha Carey Thomas, Max spent the day at Haverford and dined with its dean, the economist Don Carlos Barrett.

As at Northwestern University, Marianne continued to be impressed with the culture of the college. Her hostess, Martha Carey Thomas, had delivered the speech on "the college" at the Congress of Arts and Science, a speech Marianne may well have heard. An outspoken participant in the debate over liberal education, Thomas had defended the ideal of the residential four-year undergraduate college as a special location for liberal learning and intellectual awakening, offering students in her words a "wider vision, broader intellectual sympathies, deeper personal happiness . . . [and] all the intangible and ineffable things of the spirit." In this address her real target was twofold: educators, such as president Charles Eliot of Harvard, who advanced arguments for educating men and women differently, based on alleged differences in their "natures." Lecturing at Bryn Mawr, Hugo Münsterberg had also toyed with such ideas from the perspective of psychology, though with greater circumspection. The other target was those (Eliot again was an example) who were urging a course of studies with more elective subjects and a curriculum more attuned to the demands of the professional graduate schools introduced at newer campuses like Johns Hopkins and the University of Chicago.

The latter discussion of curricular requirements was the first round of a debate on American college and university campuses that has never ended and probably never will, as the hidden text touches upon the historical rationale for college education in the first place: the intellectual and emotional struggle not merely over the formation of "character," but over the human soul and spirit. Thomas was central to the early debate, for she embodied perfectly the effort to develop institutions with the aim of shaping and reforming the person, the "inner self."

Marianne Weber met Thomas for the first time at the International Women's Congress in Berlin, where they shared the platform for a panel on the "university studies of women." The personal battles they had waged and their feminist interests in women's education and occupations brought them together. Marianne Weber was one of the first women accepted for university matriculation in Germany at the University of Freiburg, and Thomas had graduated in 1882 with a doctorate (summa cum laude in English literature) from the University of Zürich, having been turned down at home by Cornell University and Johns Hopkins and in Germany by the Universities of Leipzig and Göttingen. She was also the first woman president of a major college. By 1904 Thomas had become the leading spokesperson on education for women, enjoying celebrity status in part because of her ability to take on established authorities, all male, and to press the case for equal education for women and for coeducation—the latter notwithstanding her commitments to Bryn Mawr as a women's institution.

In St. Louis Marianne had seen coeducation in practice at the high school level, and if she had still harbored any doubts they had quickly disappeared. At Bryn Mawr and the following week at Wellesley College she could take the full measure of the advantages of the college for women, attending lectures in philosophy and political economy and observing residential life. She was once again in her element. Most impressive to her were the institutionalization of arrangements promoting independence, self-government, rigorous work habits, and what she called the "perfection of the personality"—in her view a remarkable balance between personal freedom and social control. This "sanctuary of idealism" was marred, however, by the racial prejudice that emerged once again in a luncheon conversation with Thomas about the "Negro question"—that is, the paired issues of social equality for African Americans, and class and status distinctions within the black community—negating in Marianne's phrasing the "Christian and democratic ideals" that the college sought to instill. The episode was a stark reminder of the "color line" in the North. For Marianne the contradiction and the lesson were obvious: in the oasis of liberal learning, especially, racial (and religious) prejudice had no place and no defense.

Haverford College's president Sharpless was away from campus, and thus it was Max Weber's good fortune to spend much of the day with economics colleague Don Carlos Barrett, recently appointed dean of the college. Barrett had just returned from a sabbatical in Germany, where in Berlin he had heard a lecture by Alfred Weber, Max's younger brother. A specialist in public finance, Barrett also distinguished himself (according to a student publication) as left guard on the faculty football team that defeated Swarthmore College in the annual Thanksgiving game. Haverford offered confirming evidence of the college environment and student life: residential living, small classes (the student-to-faculty ratio was seven to one, virtually identical to today's figure), the resortlike setting, the signs of wealth, and a nearly Platonic combination of intellectual and athletic prowess. Weber heard about the cricket team, reportedly the best in the country; it had just toured England, playing fifteen games (fine wins, two losses, eight draws). Maintaining that tradition, Haverford today boasts the *only* varsity cricket team in America.

Weber used the occasion to consult the Haverford Library (holdings of 45,452 volumes in 1904) for his work on the Quakers, a topic for the soon-to-be-written fourth chapter of *The Protestant Ethic and the "Spirit" of Capitalism.* He did not mention meeting Rufus M. Jones, the eminent Quaker scholar and professor of philosophy, though a conversation is possible. Jones became important for his effort to recover an active, affirmative, and worldly mysticism found in early Quakerism, requiring involvement in the world rather than quietism and withdrawal. "This-worldly" mysticism, or mysticism oriented toward action in the existing world, was one of the most intriguing orientations for Weber. Jones did appear later in Weber's revised text as the editor of the *American Friend,* and along with John W. Rowntree, the driving force behind the definitive seven-volume history of the Society of Friends. Whether or not Weber met Jones, he certainly did encounter the university librarian and professor of history Allen Clapp Thomas, and either through him or Barrett was invited to attend the Haverford Friends Meeting. Weber leaped at the invitation; he had read George Fox and Robert Barclay, but this opportunity offered something utterly new and unique.

The Fifth Day Service the following morning was held weekly at the Quaker meeting hall next to campus on Buck Lane. The college required student attendance at the meeting until 1965. Still an active meeting house, the site has hardly changed over the last century, the dark wood paneling of the hall's interior inviting quiet repose, contemplation, and mindfulness. Sitting on the hard oak bench in the dimly lit room, the visitor has little difficulty imagining the dramatic impression the service would have made on an outsider from the land of Martin Luther.

Both Max and Marianne described the "service"—a misleading term, they recognized, as there was no organ, altar, choir, singing, Bible reading, or pastor but instead a coming together that began in deep silence and remained that way until the spirit moved members of the congregation, men or women alike, to speak, to convey a religious experience, to utter a prayer, to comment on a Biblical passage. Marianne thought it to be "like the most ancient Christian congregations, as simple and unadorned as one can imagine, as anti-Catholic as possible, excluding any manner of sensual or aesthetic influence, and thus enormously impressive, particularly the silence and the collective anticipation about what the holy spirit will announce through the mouth of one of the members of the congregation" (October 27; MWP).

Figure 9. The Haverford Friends Meeting House, unchanged since 1904, except for a new coat of paint and the banner reading "There is no Way to Peace. Peace is the Way." The Webers attended a Fifth Day Quaker service, an experience that left a strong impression and found its way into Max's written work. Author's photograph.

The event seemed like an annunciation. Only the fireplace crackling and a few coughs revealed something about the time and place. Of the six women and three men seated most prominently in front, Marianne and Max hoped an elderly woman, praised for her "charisma" and reputed to be the best speaker, would rise to the occasion. Instead, the voice they heard was that of Allen Clapp Thomas, a church elder, and Martha Carey Thomas's older uncle.

Raised a devout Quaker, Martha Carey Thomas had gradually moved away from the requirements of orthodoxy, inspired partly by her neoromantic aesthetic sensibilities and her love of Algernon Charles Swinburne's poetry and Richard Wagner's music. Her life was given over entirely to the college and women's education. But Allen Clapp Thomas was one family member who had remained true to the Quaker teachings, attending the local meeting and participating in church governance.

As a historian with a philological bent, Allen Thomas had prepared a rather formal discourse on the saints, perhaps aware that with visitors expected, spontaneity might have its limits. Weber found the talk's early going tedious, but then warmed to Thomas's carefully prepared, learned, and "practically oriented interpretation of the different designations the New Testament gives the Christians." The text of Thomas's presentation has not survived, but something of its contents can be inferred from Max Weber's notation a few months later: "I myself have listened to a Quaker sermon which laid the entire emphasis on the interpretation of 'saints' = *sancti* = *separate*." Weber does not identify the speaker, but the "Quaker sermon" was Thomas's talk at the Haverford Friends Meeting.

The experience of the Fifth Day Meeting stayed in Weber's mind because it went to the heart of his own thesis about the Protestant ethic. The reference came in the two concluding paragraphs of the long fourth chapter of *The Protestant Ethic and the "Spirit" of Capitalism*, where the only footnote is to Thomas's "sermon." Weber is summing up his investigation and outlining the task of the final chapter—namely, to consider the effect of the idea of the calling on business life and economic activity. So far, he notes, he has only outlined the religious foundation for the calling:

> To recapitulate, what has been crucial for our consideration was always the view (which occurs in all denominations) of the religious "state of grace" as a status that separates man from the depravity of the creaturely and from the "world." Possession of this status, however . . . could only be guaranteed by *proving oneself* in a specific form of conduct unambiguously distinct from the style of life of the "natural" man. The consequence for the individual was the drive to *keep a methodical check* on his state of grace as shown in how he conducted his life and thus to ensure that his life was imbued with *asceticism*.

In his lecture on the "saints" Thomas had apparently emphasized precisely the radical separation between the believer and the world, the opposition between the asceticism of the saints and the unredeemed "natural" cycle of life. This separation or opposition was a precondition for "the *rationalization* of the conduct of life in the world," as Weber phrased the idea. But the question was, could asceticism lead not to a renunciation of the world, but to an effort to *master* the world? Weber thought it could:

> Christian asceticism, which was originally a flight from the world into solitude, had already once dominated the world on behalf of the Church from the monastery, by renouncing the world. In doing this, however, it had, on the whole, left the natural, spontaneous character of secular everyday life unaffected. Now it would enter the market place of life, slamming the doors of the monastery behind it, and set about permeating precisely this secular everyday life with its methodical approach, turning it toward a rational life *in* the world, but neither *of* this world nor *for* it.

Weber had thus found a way provisionally to formulate the paradox of the "saints." It was a language for describing a transformation of the world brought about by ascetic practices: a type of action that aimed to master the world of human affairs, though paradoxically it had not emerged from this world nor was it bound to the present world or justified by it.

The Quaker meeting was not in any sense monastic, though because of its remove from the everyday present it could have seemed that way to an outsider. The austere setting, silent waiting, and collective anticipation were psychologically important as a preparation for the descent of the spirit or, in Weber's phrasing, "the overcoming of the instinctive and irrational, the passions and subjectivity of the 'natural' man." Only in such a state could God speak and could actions be considered by searching one's conscience. Not quiescence or contemplative withdrawal, but an active and questioning *conscientiousness* in one's worldly calling was the outcome of the silent waiting for the spirit to do its work.

It has become a commonplace to define the Protestant ethic as the "work ethic"—that is, as a moral injunction to work hard, which in popularized versions conveys a sense of humorless resolve, long hours, and little time for amusement, play, leisure, or inspiration. But this notion is at best a poor caricature of the ethos Weber was attempting to describe, an ethos characterized by constant, methodical, ascetic mastery of the self and the world as an end in itself that required no independent justification. This kind of asceticism was transformative in its unintended consequences; it sought to discipline the natural self and change the everyday world by bringing both self and world under "rational"—that is to say, "conscientious" and "mindful"—control. The ethic was thoroughgoing and continuous, not episodic; it defined a totality, a specific kind of life conduct, a complete way of life. The ethic had a sociological basis: the Protestant sects were its social agents and carriers. But it also had a mental dimension, a psychological premium placed on worldly action. And as Weber already knew, no one had explored the psychology of religious experience and belief, and their consequences for human action, more exhaustively than William James.

William James and His Circle

The Webers' send-off for Boston and their introduction to Cambridge, Massachusetts, must have left a strong impression. They encountered the throng departing for the Penn-Harvard game and accompanied them on the ten-hour train trip through New York. The following day, after checking into Young's Hotel on Court Street in downtown Boston, they saw the contest at the new coliseumlike Harvard Stadium, completed the previous year as the world's first reinforced concrete structure. Seating 22,000 when it opened, the stadium was filled with boisterous fans and "thunderous chanting." Penn ended Harvard's undefeated season and six consecutive victories over its Ivy League rival with an 11–0 victory, sending Cambridge into a "deep depression" (Weber's words) and igniting celebrations in Philadelphia. Explaining the unexpected victory, the *Philadelphia Inquirer* found a justification in the team's "zeal" and "spirit." "The great characteristic of the Pennsylvania team was their businesslike earnestness," one observer intoned; or in the modest appraisal by the Penn coach, victory was achieved because "We did not make any rash claims" but proceeded "with complete reliance upon our methods and with a determination to play conscientiously." At Monday Chapel the university's dean sanctified the outcome as "a vindication of Penn spirit and determination."

The interpretation of athletic competition as a test of character and proof of moral worth is a cultural commonplace, of course, and not only in America. But something else was at stake in these remarks from a century ago: the need to demonstrate that a physical activity that might be considered self-indulgent, instinctively pleasurable, merely entertaining, or an expression of unbridled personal ambition was on the contrary a "rational" expression of the methodical zeal of a worldly asceticism. Sports *had* to be justified in terms associated with the Protestant ethic—a modest, disciplined, earnest, methodical, zealous, conscientious activity, thus within the bounds of reason and a socially acceptable way of striving for accomplishment in the world. Weber was struck by the newspaper coverage: many more pages on the game and its aftermath than on the presidential campaign or the Russo-Japanese War in Asia. It was an important lesson not so much about the civic culture but about the sociology of sports that Weber explored soon afterward in the pages of *The Protestant Ethic and the "Spirit" of Capitalism.*

Years later Robert Merton would launch his career by writing an impressive monograph on the origins of modern science, starting from one line in Weber's treatise about the relationship between ascetic salvation religion and modern science. Inspired by similar comments about asceticism's cultural effects, the same kind of investigation could have been initiated with respect to the deeper sources of the modern mania for sports.

The atmosphere of the annual Harvard-Penn football game was an improbable, though suitable, preparation for that Sunday's events. Max Weber almost surely met William James at an afternoon gathering that day at the home of Hugo and Selma Münsterberg in Cambridge. Twice the Webers visited the home, two blocks west of the new Emerson Hall where the questioning inscription read, "What is man that thou art mindful of him?" (Psalms 8:4). At the University of Freiburg the equivalent verse had been a more direct imperative, nearly Kantian in spirit: "You shall know the truth, and the truth shall make you free" (John 8:32). Located at 7 Ware Street, the Münsterbergs' spacious residence was ideal for entertaining friends, students, colleagues, scholars, and foreign dignitaries. At this location the couple managed a salon for nearly two decades, creating a center of social and intellectual exchange, especially between America and Germany. Their efforts collapsed in the bitterness and misunderstandings of World War I. In recent years the university has preserved the home as an office for development and alumni fund-raising, an appropriately ironic counterpoint to its distinguished and long-forgotten past.

In early October the prearranged tour for Congress of Arts and Science participants, fifty strong, had already descended on the Harvard campus, feted and dined by its president, Charles Eliot. Weber had missed these events, un-doubtedly to his great relief, because of his decision to head off alone into the Oklahoma and Indian Territories. Before leaving Philadelphia he had written to Münsterberg to say that while in Cambridge he would enjoy seeing one of the Congress attendees, the Harvard political economist and transporta-tion expert William Z. Ripley, who was teaching economics and statistics for the fall semester. Weber had probably heard him speak in St. Louis on the panel with his Vienna colleague, Eugen von Philippovich. He also expressed an interest in meeting with the progressive reformer and consumer advocate John G. Brooks, who had studied in Germany and probably had met Weber previously. The semester having begun, Weber said he wanted to avoid impos-ing on his Harvard host, though he also expressed an interest in meeting any-one else Münsterberg might recommend. Münsterberg's fall assignments were demanding: in addition to directing the laboratory and teaching a psychology seminar, he had teamed with Josiah Royce to offer the introduction to philos-ophy to 215 students, a setting in which his theatrical gravitas had earned the undergraduate witticism, best vocalized in a Lutheran key, "Ein Münster-Berg ist unser Gott." At the same time Royce and James had taken on metaphysics with 21 undergraduate and 14 graduate students. Notwithstanding his work-load, Münsterberg seized the opportunity to make sure that James and Weber met. Aside from his contact with Du Bois, this conversation was surely Max Weber's most consequential encounter during the American journey.

The Webers were already somewhat familiar with the circle around William James from the years at the University of Freiburg, where Weber and Mün-sterberg were colleagues. Interested in giving up the psychological laboratory at Harvard to devote more time to philosophy, in 1892 James had recruited Münsterberg as his replacement. A student of Wilhelm Wundt and the famous applied psychology laboratory at the University of Leipzig, Münsterberg was reluctant to cut his ties to Germany. But after a three-year trial period at Har-vard, and a return to Freiburg for two years, he yielded to James's and Eliot's entreaties; about the time Max Weber moved from Freiburg to the University of Heidelberg in 1897, Hugo Münsterberg moved to Cambridge. For Münster-berg the change proved salutary: already in the following year he was elected president of the fledgling American Psychological Association.

One of Münsterberg's Freiburg students was Ethel D. Puffer, a talented and vivacious Smith College graduate who became a mainstay in the group of young scholars and wives centered on the Münsterbergs, the Webers, Schulze-Gaevernitz, and Heinrich and Sophie Rickert. In addition to her work with Münsterberg, she studied ethics and aesthetics with Heinrich Rickert, meeting Marianne Weber in the process, followed the artistic work of Selma Münster-berg and Sophie Rickert, and traveled to Italy for some weeks of aesthetic edu-cation one summer with Selma. Sophie painted Ethel's portrait and sculpted a bust of her that in 1904 resided in Marianne's study, next to her desk. Returning home, Ethel Puffer became a regular participant in the circle around James, Münsterberg, Royce, and George Santayana, moving back and forth between psychology and philosophy, and completing her Radcliffe College doctorate in 1902, the second awarded to a woman. She accepted a faculty appointment at Wellesley College, first in philosophy and then in psychology, remaining on the faculty until her marriage in 1908. Together with Charlotte Perkins Gilman, she was the founder of a way of thinking that became known as "material feminism," a set of progressive ideas and practices concerned with radically transforming the conditions of women's labor, production, and consumption, especially in the home. The issues would have captivated Marianne, as in her essays she worked through many of the same problems regarding women's work, domestic roles, and professional employment. Later in the 1920s Ethel Puffer Howes became director of the Institute for the Coordination of Women's Interests at Smith College while also teaching sociology there. The Smith venture was the earliest effort to institutionalize women's studies, and in the words of the *Christian Science Monitor*, "one of the most novel and far-reaching experiments ever before tried in women's education." The institute failed after six years, sacrificed to entrenched local interests.

The gathering on Sunday, October 30, would certainly have included Ethel Puffer, and perhaps Ripley, Brooks, and Royce as well. It gave Marianne and Ethel an opportunity to renew their friendship, and the two women arranged to visit Wellesley twice, inviting a comparison with Bryn Mawr. Marianne attended one of Ethel Puffer's lectures on aesthetics, the subject of the major study Puffer was about to complete, *The Psychology of Beauty*; the book presented a wide-ranging investigation of "the means by which the end of Beauty is attained" in the different spheres of culture. The two women also stopped at recently opened Simmons College, where Marianne picked up useful tips about a low-fat diet, a reminder that the "life reform" movement was already underway in the United States and Germany.

Before arriving in Cambridge Weber had surely thought about and discussed some of James's work, if not because of Münsterberg then through his colleague and traveling companion Ernst Troeltsch. At the Congress in St. Louis Troeltsch had presented a paper with the forbidding title, "Main Problems of the Philosophy of Religion: Psychology and Theory of Knowledge in the Science of Religion." But the real subject of the text was William James's thought and the challenge of *The Varieties of Religious Experience* to Kantian rationalism. Crediting James with having written a "masterpiece" characterized by "freshness and impartiality," "remarkable richness," originality and a complete command of the subject, Troeltsch tried to rescue something of Immanuel Kant's claims about the rational substance, validity or truth of religious belief. The admirable effort proceeded to revise what Troeltsch saw as Kant's no longer tenable position. It offered a series of concessions of Kant's "over-rigorous" rationalism to James's empiricism and profound insight into the religious state as "the sense

Figure 10. William James, the "outstanding scholar" whose *Varieties of Religious Experience* captured Max Weber's attention. The two men met on an autumn afternoon in Cambridge, Massachusetts. Harvard University Archives, call # HUP James, William (5). Reproduced by permission.

of presence of the divine." By the end of the discussion Troeltsch had reduced Kant's "religious apriori" to a quaint formalism, and the best he could do by way of revision was worry about the path to a vague, otherworldly mysticism lurking in the actualization of religious experience in James's work. He concluded with an appeal for a synthesis of "the empirical and psychological with the critical and normative"—that is, of James with Kant! Troeltsch brought the paper with him aboard the *Bremen*. Considering Weber's own intellectual preoccupations, it strains credulity to suppose that he and Troeltsch never discussed the subject and James's impressive contribution while in transit, or in the months before when they were active in the Eranos Circle. Weber read Paul Hensel's paper for the St. Louis Congress, "Problems of Ethics," probably while traveling; and if Hensel's short essay then surely also Troeltsch's.

The subject of Weber's conversation with James is a matter of conjecture. It could have touched upon any number of shared interests, including the topic of a special lecture James was to give that week in October, "The Vocation of the Scholar," a theme more commonly associated with Weber's ideas than with James's thought. There is no evidence Weber heard this talk, but there is a clue to their conversation provided by Weber in his very last reference to James, which he inserted into the revised text of "Churches and Sects in North America." After reviewing the phenomena of religiosity that he had observed in America, from North Tonawanda, New York, through Philadelphia, Weber offered, "Some cultured Americans often dismissed these facts briefly and with a certain angry disdain as 'humbug' or backwardness, or they even denied them; many of them actually did not know anything about them, as was affirmed to me by William James. Yet these survivals were still alive in many different fields, and sometimes in forms which appeared to be grotesque." It was a point that both scholars had made in their writings. Traces of the religious and sacred past were often overlooked in the modern and more secular present, especially by the literati or intellectuals. Weber even underscored the idea in the very last paragraph of *The Protestant Ethic*, reminding the reader that "modern man is in general, even with the best will, unable to give religious ideas a significance for the conduct of life [*Lebensführung*], the culture, and the character of a people which they deserve." The remark recalls his earlier conversation with James, which must have dwelled in some measure on questions about religious experience and its cultural significance.

In Weber's work this is only one of any number of allusions to James, many of them concealed, as Wilhelm Hennis has pointed out. The extent of the intellectual relationship is indeed much larger and more intriguing than the few remarks about the traces and survivals of the religious life in American society.

Ideas and Experience

"The Religious Foundations of Inner-worldly Asceticism" is the title Weber gave to the fourth chapter of *The Protestant Ethic and the Spirit of Capitalism*. It is by far the longest of the five chapters, covering nearly half the original text, and dealing with the four main branches of ascetic Protestantism: the Calvinists, the Pietists, the Methodists, and the Baptists. Few contemporaries are cited in the notes, which bristle with historical figures like John Calvin, John Milton, Richard Baxter, and John Bunyan. But there is one important exception: William James, the "outstanding scholar" and his monumental work *The Varieties of Religious Experience*.

Weber's text is not usually read alongside James's discussion , but the parallels, overlaps, and points of contact and compatibility between the two scholars is unmistakable: a similar formulation of the categories of asceticism and mysticism, an unwavering focus on practical conduct and the pragmatic effects of religious beliefs, and insightful portrayals of the types of spiritual life or "personality" formed by religious experience. Even their methods invite comparison: James introduced his lectures by insisting on two "orders of inquiry" governed by the logical distinction between existential judgments and value judgments (or because of the subject at hand, "spiritual" judgments), a position usually associated with Weber's thought. Propositions about value, meaning, and "truth," James warned, cannot be deduced from propositions about the nature, constitution, or history of a phenomenon. The approach of his inquiry, he cautioned, called for considering religious phenomena from a "purely existential point of view." Then when questioned by Charles Eliot about accepting the veracity of a person's account of religious conversion, James noted that the narrator "aims at reproducing an ideal type which he thinks most significant and edifying" and not a description that is "literally true," which is indeed an impossibility. "I think my account has been fairly objective," James replied to Eliot, "for persons of all sorts of dispositions towards religion seem to find material for corroboration of the prepossessions they may start with." James's methodological defense of his scientific investigation is one that Weber could have provided himself.

Considering the content of the empirical analysis, Weber would have had no difficulty making sense of James's central contrast among spiritual types—the tender- or tranquil-minded versus the tough-minded—or his fundamental distinction between the religion of optimistic "healthy-mindedness" and the disenchanted and melancholy search for salvation of the "sick soul," the religion of "morbid-mindedness." The Ethical Culture movement and Christian Science counted among the former, the two scholars agreed, while John Bunyan and Leo Tolstoy exemplified the latter. Weber's interest in such movements and exemplary spirits is well documented, from his observations of the penitents at Lourdes on a trip to France in 1897 to his later unfinished study of Tolstoy. Closer to home, he had ample evidence for these types and orientations among his own relatives. The Baumgarten household in Strasbourg that young Max knew so well served especially as a case study of the struggle between "mind cure," as James called the movement of therapeutic optimism, encouraged by the sermons of Theodore Parker and William Ellery Channing, and in James's terms the "double-storied mystery" of unhappy souls. James presented the struggle as two opposed ways of looking at life residing within the "divided self." It is no wonder that Eduard Baumgarten, a survivor of this emotional incubator, was struck by the extensive marginalia that he found later in Weber's personal edition of *Varieties* (in German translation), a book that unfortunately has so far eluded recovery by the archivists.

James and Weber knew full well where they belonged as "cleric-academic-scientific" types, and why:

> Unsuspecting from the bottom of every fountain of pleasure, as the old poet said, something bitter rises up: a touch of nausea, a falling dead of the delight, a whiff of melancholy, things that sound a knell, for fugitive as they may be, they bring a feeling of coming from a deeper region and often have an appalling convincingness. The buzz of life ceases at their touch as a piano-string stops sounding when the damper falls upon it.
>
> Of course the music can commence again;—and again and again,—at intervals. But with this the healthy-minded consciousness is left with an irremediable sense of precariousness. It is a bell with a crack; it draws its breath on sufferance and by an accident.

The words are William James's. They can be read as autobiographical, but they can also be understood as an insight attuned to the ambivalence of the "religiously unmusical" intellectual, as Weber once described himself, who in a fateful turn has become a passionate observer of the inner recesses of the spirit, and who knows what it means for life's music to stop and to recommence, "again and again." For Weber's work, James's lines offer another metaphor for illuminating some of the most distinctive passages of *The Protestant Ethic*, namely the pathos of the "feeling of unprecedented inner *loneliness of the single individual*" and the "restless and systematic struggle with life" characteristic of the state of consciousness that Weber referred to as "that *disillusioned* and *pessimistically* tinted *individualism*" found among peoples with a Puritan past—William James among them. Weber sometimes sought the same temperament of ascetic mastery within himself, and complained bitterly if it eluded his grasp. When scholars like Hartmut Lehmann speak of Weber's text as a kind of projection, a testament about himself, it is such passages that they have in mind.

The dialogue that Weber conducted at a distance with James is framed by a problematic that Weber continuously reworks. In *The Protestant Ethic* that problematic only begins to emerge in chapter 4, when Weber suddenly announces that he is not primarily interested in theological doctrine, church dogma, sermonizing or moral teachings; instead, he claims, "the main thing is to discover the psychological *drives* which led people to behave in a certain way [*die Ermittelung der psychologischen Antriebe, welche der Lebensführung die Richtung wiesen*] and held them firmly in this path. These drives usually originated from purely religious ideas." The phrasing in German is important. Talcott Parsons translated this key passage rather differently as, "We are interested rather in something entirely different: the influence of those psychological sanctions which, originating in religious belief and the practice of religion, gave a direction to practical conduct and held the individual to it. Now these sanctions were to a large extent derived from the peculiarities of the religious ideas behind them."

While a psychological "drive" may imply a "sanction," it is not a sanction in itself. In the first three chapters of *The Protestant Ethic* Weber had uttered not a word about such "drives" or "sanctions," or issues of a psychological order. But with James's work hovering in the background, notwithstanding some rhetorical hedging, Weber was now compelled in chapter 4 to turn his attention to the psychology of belief. Acknowledging that religious ideas had to be presented in "their most logically consistent form"—that is, as an ideal type—the inquiry now took this direction for a specific reason: it turns out that the notion of personal testing and "proof" of spiritual convictions had become, according to Weber's interpretation, "the psychological starting point for methodical morality." In other words, one could not fully understand practical conduct only by thinking about the effects of social organization, economic, and political interests, or moral and religious doctrine; psychological forces had to be considered as well.

The concept of a "drive" embedded in the psyche is hardly self-evident. Weber seemed to have in mind not a physiological or natural endowment but a predisposition of mind conditioned by cultural and religious factors. This view emerged most strongly in his critique of Lutheranism, which in his words "as a result of its doctrine of grace, simply failed to provide the psychological drive to be systematic in the conduct of life, and thus to enforce the methodical rationalization of life." In this critical view, by contrast with Lutheranism, Calvinism and the other Protestant sects *did* unleash such forces and thus achieved a practical effect on human conduct that Weber called "psychologically efficacious." Stated somewhat differently, in the particular circumstance of the ascetic sects whose practices are oriented toward transforming the world, the sociology of religion is compelled to take a pragmatic or "behavioral" psychological argument into account.

Such different outcomes had a historicopolitical corollary as well, which Weber often underscored. Thanking Adolf von Harnack for reading the first part of *The Protestant Ethic*, for instance, he observed that in opposition to his senior colleague, theologian, and church historian, his views about the asceticism of the sects oriented toward worldly activity borrowed a page from Georg Jellinek's thesis about the historical origins of modern liberty and rights. "I have a *very* different opinion about American freedom," he wrote. "In my work Luther *necessarily* appears too briefly, for it cannot be denied that from *this* point of view, which is *peripheral* when considered *religiously*, his great accomplishment is essentially *negative*. We really should not forget that we have the sects to thank for things that *none* of us could give up in the present day: freedom of conscience and the most elementary 'human rights,' all of which are self-evident possessions for us today. That could *only* be created by *radical* idealism." By "idealism" Weber meant properties of the mind conditioned psychologically by a practical solution to the problem of salvation: Who had achieved salvation, and how? Along what path, and with what amount of sacrifice? With which accomplishments? With what type of worldly recognition? With what kind of relationship to God, to fellow humans, and to the spiritual life? Theology could answer such questions, and did so in impressive detail. But Weber was interested, as was James, in the existentially compelling answers that men and women invented and lived through daily in their moral choices and practical decisions.

Thus, for Weber and James there are two fundamental issues—issues large enough to have bedeviled Western philosophy from the beginning: the problem of the relationship between ideas and action, and the question of the "rationality" of experience. In Weber's work the former takes a particular form: the tension between the *logical* and the *psychological* consequences of religious ideas for practical conduct. The problem arises in this way because of the strict Calvinist theory of predestination, according to which certain knowledge of salvation is concealed from the faithful. Because of such absolute uncertainty, the logical result could be fatalism. But Weber insisted that because of the additional requirement of "testing" and "proving" oneself in a calling, the doctrine's psychological effect was instead to promote a committed and worldly activism. Logic seemed to suggest one course of action, while psychology dictated an opposite outcome. This is one important observation about the problematic relationship between abstract dogma and concrete action, one could say, that James had repeatedly demonstrated in his lectures.

Not satisfied with this conclusion, however, Weber wanted to continue and refine the dialogue with James. Having ceded some ground to psychological determinants of practical action, "On the other hand," he wrote,

> religious *ideas* [*der* Gedankengehalt *einer Religion*]—as Calvinism demonstrates particularly well—are of *far* greater significance than someone like William *James* (*The Varieties of Religious Experience*, 1902, pp. 444f.) is inclined to admit. The significance of rationality in religious metaphysics is classically shown in the far-reaching effects which the *idea* [gedankliche *Struktur*] of the reformed concept of God has exercised on life. If the God of the Puritans has had an effect in history like no other before or after him, this is thanks to the attributes with which the power of the *idea* [*die Macht des* Gedankens] has equipped him. James's "pragmatic" evaluation of the significance of religious ideas according to the degree to which they have been "proved" in life, is, by the way, itself a true child of that Puritan set of ideas [*Gedankenwelt*] in which this outstanding scholar is at home.

Weber's precise language is critical once again: this is a commentary not on the philosophical "idea," whether Kantian or Hegelian, but on the process of *thought* or the quality of reasoning a pragmatist could have called *thought in action*. The specific reference, remarkably, is to the passages at the conclusion of James's eighteenth lecture in *Varieties*, in which he challenges the claims of "transcendentalist idealism" to have established the impartial, universal, and rational grounds of religious belief. The long shadow of the old Kant is still casting its spell. Of course, James sides with the facts of experience against transcendental reason. But this is not to deny the *historical* and *practical* effect (or "rationality") of a particular conception of divine will. Practical rationality is not identical with metaphysical reason. The final aside gives away Weber's intention. Who had insisted on the importance of the *practical* testing and proof of ideas, if not Weber himself?

In seeming to correct James's line of thought, Weber mainly succeeds in showing that he shares the same premises: validity according to abstract reason is not the issue; rather, it is significance in relation to culture. "Proof" of the idea in action should be the measure of its significance. Weber writes as much in the next paragraph, though with the obverse problem in mind—the rationality not of thought in action but of "experience":

> Religious experience [*Erlebnis*] as such is, of course, irrational, like *every* experience. In its highest, mystical, form it is indeed *the* experience κατ ἐξοχήν and—in James's fine description—is distinguished by its absolute incommunicability. It has a *specific* character and appears as *knowledge* [*Erkenntnis*] but cannot be adequately reproduced by means of our linguistic and conceptual apparatus. It is also true to say the *every* religious experience loses substance as soon as an attempt to formulate it *rationally* is made, the more so, the further the process of conceptual formulation has advanced. Herein lies the basis of the tragic conflicts of all rational theology, as the Baptist sects knew as early as the seventeenth century.

James's lectures were awash with examples of efforts by his subjects, especially the saints and spiritual virtuosi, to convey in ordinary language the rational core of their extraordinary experience. On the problem of the rational meaning of experience Weber wanted to have the last word, writing, "The irrationality, however—which, by the way, is *by no means exclusive* to *religious* experience, but is common to *every* kind, although in different sense and degree—does not alter the fact that the *nature* of the system of *ideas* that, so to speak, seizes and directs the immediate religious 'experience' in its own paths, is of the greatest practical significance. It is *this* that determines the majority of those important practical ethical differences in the various world religions." These notations offer a sensible observation about pure experience in any aspect of life: it is only comprehensible and communicable when provided with a framework of interpretation, and for the spiritual life that framework is often (though not always) found in a preexisting system of ideas. The last sentence reveals Weber's reason for insisting on this point: his fascination with explaining the different practical ethical outcomes in the major religions of the world, especially the differences in their *economic* ethics.

Weber's final actual reference to James is in an obscure place in his writings, a book review from 1909 in which the subject is the problem of "truth" in the contemporary philosophy of science. The passage has not been translated or even discussed previously, and yet it reveals a great deal about Weber's position in relation to James. The book under review, a defense of political economy as a science by Adolf Weber (no relation to Max), included a brief critique of James's pragmatic conception of truth in the lectures on *Pragmatism* (1907), which Max Weber probably also read. Alluding to the notion of "cash value" in lecture 2, the author asserted, "Truth remains for us [in German thought] something independent and absolute." Max Weber could not resist a rejoinder to this embrace of high-minded Kantianism, remarking that for James the concept of "cash value" as a measure of truth content had both a "practical utilitarian" meaning and a meaning attached to its "value for the simplest description of empirical facts, whose knowledge contents validate our scientific interest." It is not a coincidence, he added, that the pragmatist conception of truth arose in the United States and England:

> From the time of nominalism and [Francis] Bacon the theory of the multiplicity of truth had one of its main headquarters in England, and there it must have served to promote on the one hand the freedom of empirical scientific inquiry against dogmatic restrictions, and on the other hand the protection of religious needs against the advance of natural science. Previously this purpose was served when religious truth as that which is absolutely irrational was completely separated from empirical science, thus preventing any complications or conflicts with empiricism. Today that is no longer satisfactory, and the absolute irrationality of the *meaning* of all knowledge [Erkenntnis*sinns*]—not simply the "world" conceived as an "object"—must be added in order to create the necessary space for religious interests. Of course, *today* such a motive is not generally valid in this way for James.

The issue is the rational status, following Friedrich Nietzsche's critique of Kant, of *both* moral and religious beliefs *and* empirical science. Both scholars knew Nietzsche's critique and his speculations about *ressentiment*; Weber understood that James had proposed solving the problem experimentally with a working hypothesis about the testing of ideas in practice. "More to the point," Weber continued,

> along with other sources, "pragmatism" typically has a very strong foundation in certain peculiarities of physicalist modes of thought practiced for a long time in England and America, in contrast to France and (until Mach) Germany. These modes of thought are characteristic of Maxwell, for example, as with the use of rationally incompatible, though quite sensually vivid methods of *demonstration* that could never assert the claim to represent the "being" of a physical process. This method of treatment, depicted so nicely by Duhem in contrast to the autochthon continental, and aligned closely with the line of thinking in pragmatism's "economy of thought," leads back in its sources to the beginnings of natural science.

This is an eye-opening comment, among other things, about the range of Weber's and James's intellectual wanderings, both of them citing Ernst Mach, Pierre Duhem, and Wilhelm Ostwald. Weber wrote an entire essay criticizing Ostwald's epistemological "naturalism." For James the epistemological terrain also included a stinging critique of Rickert's neo-Kantian "realist" notion of truth, a position that Weber could not accept either. Such notations are richly suggestive and deserve elaboration; but for now we must set them aside, as we have arrived at the limits of Weber's adventure of the mind in the company of William James.

In his later essays Weber continued to think his way through the problems posed by his encounter with William James and *The Varieties of Religious Experience.* The most important location for the continuing dialogue was actually not so much the second part of *The Protestant Ethic* but the sequel to it: the first synthetic essay he placed at the beginning of his essays on Confucianism, Taoism, and the other world religions, "The Economic Ethic of the World Religions: Comparative Investigations in the Sociology of Religion." Hans Gerth and C. Wright Mills translated the essay, written in 1913, as "The Social Psychology of the World Religions," an exercise in editorial license that at least had the advantage of conveying the true subject, which Weber stated with unusual clarity: "Emphasis will be placed not on the ethical theory of theological compendia that only serve as a means to knowledge (and can be important in some circumstances), but on the *practical impulses for action* [*praktischen Antriebe zum Handeln*] that are grounded in the psychological and pragmatic contexts of religion.

In this thematic announcement from the second paragraph the issue is, once again, the 'drives' motivating action that are understood explicitly in a pragmatic mode."

Pursuing Weber's line of thought in this remarkable and rewarding essay would lead us far afield. But it is essential to point out, nevertheless, that one of his most oft-quoted causal metaphors emerges in the midst of the discussion, where the subject is the Jamesian trinity of the anxious quest for authentic "experience," the thirst for "salvation," and the tasks of the "intellectuals." The formulation is actually an elaboration of one aspect of his comments on James in *The Protestant Ethic*:

Salvation [*Erlösung*] attained a specific significance only where it expressed a systematic and rationalized "image of the world" [*Weltbild*] and represented a stand in face of the world. For the meaning as well as the intended and actual psychological quality of salvation has depended upon such a world image and such a stand. Not ideas [*Ideen*], but material and ideal interests directly govern human conduct. Yet very frequently the "world images" that have been created by "ideas" have, like switches, determined the tracks along which action has been pushed by the dynamic of interest. "From what" and "for what" one wished to be saved and, let us not forget, "could be" saved, depended upon one's image of the world.

Ideas and world images are the province of the saints, the literate virtuosi of the life of the mind and spirit, or the intellectuals. A person's image or picture of the world is not a simple belief system, an attitude or ideology, a perspective or a Weltanschauung, but a mental mapping of the totality of the seen and the unseen, the known and the imagined, the perceptions of cognition and the intuitions of emotion. In Weber's metaphor the world picture is a product of ideas, especially those deeply embedded in a religion. But there is a complication, for the so-called ideal interests are also ideas, fixtures of the mind that provide one of the decisive motivating forces for action. As complicated as the metaphor may seem, it qualifies as a concentrated distillation of Weber's effort to come to terms with the challenge of James's thoroughgoing empiricism and radical insistence on the reality of experience for the spiritual life.

What of Weber's own stance? Does his insistence on *empirical* analysis mirror James's, or should we perhaps not concede too much to the empiricist arguments of pragmatism? Do they leave a space for some kind of "rationality?" The touchstone for an answer is still the Kantian categories. For the science of religion both authors give up the knowledge claims of the transcendental ego, transcendental idealism and the lawlike, legislative compulsion of synthetic a priori truth for human choice. They travel part way with Troeltsch in his assessment of James's reply to Kant. Rationality for James emerges from experience and in cooperation with it: "Instinct leads, intelligence does but follow," is his pithy formula in *Varieties*. James really means "intuition" or "impulsive belief," as distinct from "articulate reason." The role that David Hume assigned to the human passions James gives to our intuitions. But rationality still has a place: it consists in "human ways of thinking that grow up piecemeal among the details of experience because on the whole they work best," as James once reminded Münsterberg. It was precisely *this* "epistemological" claim that Weber found consistent with inner-worldly asceticism's interest in *practical* rationality. For Weber, however, our ideas about "rationality" were notoriously multivalent and multifaceted, affected by complex historical, social and cultural determinants. He wanted to point out, however, that James's "human ways of thinking," once articulated, *could* have an effect (and in the world religions typically *did* have an effect) on the way the world was "experienced." So James's formula has to be completed. Once formed, intelligence could instruct and shape our intuitions. Our experience and intuitions thus became "rationalized," which is emphatically not to claim that the result in thought was therefore "rational" according to an abstract universal standard.

In Weber's hands the Kantian categories have also been superseded, replaced instead by analytic types and directions of social and economic action in particular historical circumstances.

Rationality, in other words, attaches to the science and not to the world. It is a conclusion that William James and Max Weber surely would have applauded.

NINE

AMERICAN MODERNITY

The journey from Boston to New York City by train followed the route through Providence, Rhode Island and New Haven, Connecticut. Writing to Hugo Münsterberg from Philadelphia, Max Weber had expressed the intention of stopping at both Brown University and Yale University, still in search of library holdings related to Puritanism and the Protestant sects. Armed with a recommendation from Münsterberg, he managed only the brief excursion to Brown, with amusing and revealing results. Weber made a point of noting that he was in "the oldest homeland on earth of freedom of conscience (Roger Williams) and the separation of state and church" (November 6; MWP). In search of documentation on this topic, he located the campus librarian who informed him that the university, though founded by Baptists and a few Congregationalists, had decided to erase any connections to its religious and "sectarian" heritage. It had retained no holdings on the history of the Baptists and avoided collecting even modern literature on the founding denominations. This exercise in forgetting the past and becoming nonsectarian and "modern" impressed Weber sufficiently to footnote it in *The Protestant Ethic and the Spirit of Capitalism*, mentioning that if one wanted to know about the American Baptists, then the best library was not at Brown, but at Colgate University, an institution also founded by Baptists.

While in New England the Webers had taken two days to visit another member of their Fallenstein relatives, Max's half cousin Laura, her German immigrant husband Otto von Klock, and their eight children, residing in Wyoming, a community near suburban Medford, north of Boston. It was part of the effort to keep up with the fate of the family's colonial children, as Guenther Roth has shown. Klock had set up a successful typewriter and translation business under Laura's name (L. Fallenstein and Company), and had received commissions from the Astors and other established and wealthy families to conduct genealogical research. For the status conscious, recovering a personal past could sanction pedigree and anchor social prestige, a sign of "Europeanization," Weber maintained. The brief stay turned out to be enjoyable and instructive. Max thought the native-born Klock children had become fully assimilated to American life, despite their father's scorn for "Yankees" and his romanticized longing for a Germany that had disappeared. Secularization had set in, too, as the second generation drifted away from Protestantism, a trend Weber thought was typical in immigrant families.

Arriving for their second stay in New York City a few days before the presidential election, the Webers this time located farther uptown, past Theodore Roosevelt's birthplace to the Holland House at Fifth Avenue and Thirtieth Street. The hotel was four blocks north of D. H. Burnham's recently completed Flatiron Building. The next week in a cost-saving move they relocated to a boarding house at 167 Madison Avenue, closer to the Thirty-third Street Station on the subway that had opened just two weeks earlier. Operated by a Frau von Hilsen, the Madison Avenue residence housed two American couples and several young German businessmen employed in the city. The German immigrants' accounts of life in New York gave Weber another lesson in the attractions of American clubs that found its way into his revised "Protestant Sects" essay and the seminal essay on class and status: outside the work setting, the absolute equality among "gentlemen," regardless of differences in economic class or social status. Alexis de Tocqueville had been impressed by the same phenomenon, though he had not generalized the observation into an analysis of the essential difference between "class" defined economically and "status" defined in terms of social prestige and honor.

Among the American cities, Boston had seemed to the travelers "older, more refined, and more harmonious" than others. The Webers had been especially impressed by Copley Square, bounded by Henry Richardson's Trinity Church on the east side and Charles McKim's Boston Public Library to the west. The church's bold Romanesque adaptation juxtaposed to the library's Italian Renaissance classicism and warm interior seemed especially ingenious and aesthetically pleasing. Marianne wondered what her brother-in-law, the architect Karl Weber, would have thought about it. Now in Manhattan they returned to the sights, sounds, and rhythms of the metropolis that at first had seemed so startling, new and alien. But Marianne's responses had caught up with Max's initial enthusiasms, and she reported feeling "completely at home" amid the strikingly diverse human populations and the architectural variety. Her observations, like her husband's, sometimes turned rhapsodic:

> The view from the Brooklyn Bridge is marvelously fantastic with the evening glow on the illuminated skyscrapers! The mass of enormous structures at the tip of Manhattan, aglow with a million lights, rise up into the glimmering dark red and lilac sky like a strangely shaped mountain. It is as if the spirit that lives in these buildings, striving for financial gains, has embodied itself in glowing streams of gold penetrating the walls like X-rays. A vision like a fairy tale! One could believe that one is looking at the castle of the Holy Grail or some kind of magic palace (November 19; MWP).

Fantastic, magical, strange, mythic, unreal: whether as fairy tale, legend, or science fiction, the language was Marianne's effort to capture the poetry of the modern.

The spirit of the new century had been in evidence during the fall presidential campaign, personified by Theodore Roosevelt. The election fell on November 8, 1904, offering Weber a welcome opportunity for observation. Coincidentally, James Bryce was also in the city as an observer, having just completed his Godkin lectures at Harvard University, "The Study of Popular Government." In Manhattan Judge Alton B. Parker won easily, improving on William Jennings Bryan's margin of victory in 1900. But Theodore Roosevelt captured Brooklyn and carried his and Parker's home state by about 175,000 votes, and the nation with thirty-two states and more than 56 percent of the vote, leading to a comfortable electoral college margin of 336 to 140. Voter turnout in the five boroughs was astounding by today's standards, at 93.7 percent. There was one local surprise: running for another term as a Democrat in the state senate, George Washington Plunkitt of the Tammany Hall machine, famous for his view that "honest graft" is a democratic birthright, was defeated by 344 votes, his first loss in a career spanning more that four decades. Roosevelt's electoral "coattails" may have made the difference. Surveying the presidential results, the *New York Evening Post* editorialized that Roosevelt's commanding victory was a "personal triumph," a tribute to his "personality" that had "captivated the imagination of the American people. His immense instinct for publicity, and his perfect command of the 'grand high pressure of bustle and excitement' which is so powerful a political instrument in a democracy like ours, with his outstanding and taking qualities, have won the general heart and made him the victorious leader he is." In a few lines the *Post* managed to announce the arrival in America of the leader with "charisma," Max Weber's contribution to our political discourse, whose personal qualities overshadow everything else. It is no wonder that when Weber searched for instances of charismatic politicians combating bureaucratized party machines he chose Roosevelt as one of his examples.

During the two weeks in the city the Webers had not only opportunities for observing politics but for taking in cultural and social life. They had the opportunity to feast on a rich cultural fare, starting with the American premier of Gustav Mahler's Fourth Symphony, conducted by Walter Damrosch (negatively reviewed, as in Europe); Richard Wagner's *Parsifal*; a musical version of *The Wizard of Oz*; the play *Alt Heidelberg*, transformed later by Sigmund Romberg into his musical hit *The Student Prince*; Henrik Ibsen's *Hedda Gabler*; the melodrama *Sunday* featuring Ethel Barrymore, who was described in the press as the personification of "ultra-modern refinement"; classics like William Shakespeare's *Hamlet* or *Much Ado about Nothing*; and on and on. The Webers followed the musical and theatrical scene closely, having attended performances of Ibsen in Berlin and Wagner in Paris, for example. But from this menu of choices they selected only the local Yiddish theater. In New York they had other far more important matters on their minds: the settlement houses; the immigrants on the Lower East Side; the social work of Florence Kelley, Lillian Wald, and David Blaustein; Columbia University colleagues, lectures, and the library; the churches and sects; labor relations and the trade unions; and former acquaintances and family contacts. It was dizzying itinerary. Taken in tow by Edwin and Caroline Seligman, and by the brothers Paul and Alfred Lichtenstein and their wives Clara and Hannah, the daughters of Friedrich Kapp, the result was an event-packed schedule and encounters with "as many people as during a year in Heidelberg."

Strange Contradictions

The second day in the city was a Sunday, providing an opportunity to continue the practice of observing religious services. New York offered fertile ground, so the couple divided forces: Marianne selected a Presbyterian service at the old Marble Collegiate Church next to their hotel, while Max traveled uptown to the new First Church of Christ Scientist on Central Park West at Ninety-sixth Street. With a sanctuary dating from 1854, Marble Collegiate had been chartered in 1628 as a Dutch Reformed church and could thus proclaim itself "America's oldest Protestant Church with a continuous ministry." It became famous later in the century through the five decades of preaching and leadership by Norman Vincent Peale, and among its best known parishioners was then lawyer Richard Nixon. The "power of positive thinking" promoted by Peale was a perfect expression of the "mind cure" at its optimistic best as analyzed by William James—a much later chapter in the adventures of worldly asceticism. The service presented Marianne with a contrast to the Haverford Friends Meeting; it was a model of a refined and distinguished denomination, offering parishioners "soft cushions and fans in the pews," in Weber's phrasing.

The leading turn of the century example of "mind cure" for James and Weber was, of course, Christian Science. The Upper West Side church that Max attended, completed in 1903 at a cost of over a million dollars, was designed by John M. Carrère and Thomas Hastings with the aim of capturing the spirit of the new outlook on life, emergent from a sacred past. Trained at the École des Beaux-Arts in Paris, the architects modified the beaux arts style to create a monumental synthesis of the Roman basilica and the New England meeting hall. The massive, unadorned exterior of primary forms seemed modernist, possessing "a degree of force and power that is astonishing" in the words of the *Architectural Record*. For Hastings, the architectural theorist, the modern idiom required finding a compelling language of expression for the uniqueness of the present age while showing sympathy for historical styles of building. "In solving the problems of modern life," he wrote, "the essential is not so much to be national, or American, as to be modern and of our *own* period." The new requirements for the built environment were supposed to match the new universal message for the inner life.

During his travels Weber had puzzled over the evidence of a trend toward secularization in American society. On the one hand, there were signs of movement away from church life and religiosity among the youth, second- and third-generation immigrants, and—in the East—the older generation as well. But on the other hand, summing up impressions at the end of his stay, he found American life "full of secularized offspring of the old Puritan religiosity." Distinguishing the "secular" from the "sacred" could be elusive. In making social contacts and forming friendships, for example, the Lichtensteins reported that the first question often was, "Which church do you belong to?"—at least in "more devout" Brooklyn where they lived, as distinct from a more secular New York City. Religious affiliation still carried weight in social relationships, as the strength of the sects even in the remote Indian Territory had demonstrated. And in contrast to Europe, there were the phenomena of religious revivals and the new religious movements, such as Mormonism and Christian Science. The opposing impressions produced "strange contradictions," Weber concluded, as he described the Sunday event:

> Today I attended a "service" of the "Christian Scientists" (faith healers) here. They have two grandiose churches here, outfitted in the finest manner for religious services. For sermons and the services generally the "Christian Science Quarterly" provides programs, texts of the psalms, passages from the Bible and from the symbolic book "Science and Life." Their "hymnal" is compiled from different national choral works, with melodies from Handel, Haydn, Weber, Mendelssohn, German folk songs and English melodies. The "church" proper, an impressive vaulted space with rostrums and a mighty organ, was stuffed full of people: everyone from "good society" including the middle class. On a raised platform in front of the organ sit 10–12 men and women in tuxedo or white silk, and in front of them two pulpits, from which a man in a tuxedo and a woman in white—about 40, with a garland in her hair and a deep alto voice—conduct the service. First a chorus from the "Messiah" (a wonderful piece), then liturgy: Psalm 38, alternating between the woman preacher and the congregation; then 10 minutes of deep silence for prayer (for the spiritual and physical well-being of one's neighbors), ending with an audible collective "Amen;" then a congregation hymn sung by everyone, leaving quite an impression; then a "sermon," that is, the woman *and* man preacher alternate in readings: *he* from about 30 places in the Old and New Testament, and *she* from the book "Science and Life," drawn apparently from their conception of preaching. Contents: again and again emphasis on "immortality," metaphysically in Plato's sense—or even better, Moses Mendelssohn's "Phaedon"—in short, ceremonial, and slowly spoken maxims; then the sole reality of the "spirit" and the emptiness [*Nichtigkeit*] and transitoriness of matter; God's limitless omnipotence over humanity and the depravity of all who seek

to resist that omnipotence, thereby proving they are not protected by "spirit" and thus blessed with "immortality;" warning about "false friends" (apparently physicians)—45 minutes long, presented without much pathos until it became boring. Then an organ fugue and offertory (i.e., a collection plate covered with dollar bills passed around by men in dark suits); a soprano solo (sung with a lot of tremolo in the English style, unknown to me, probably a modern composition); a congregational hymn and conclusion; and departure to another room for Sunday school by the attractively dressed children, which is a pièce de resistance here, as it is everywhere. There were certainly 800 and perhaps 1000 people in attendance, and their behavior fell unambiguously under the concept "devoutness." The movement hasn't reached its peak yet, and it spreads into all the large cities in the Union (November 6; MWP).

As he had done years earlier in Strasbourg, Weber paid attention not only to the outward forms of devotion but to the selection of appropriate texts and the substance of the spiritual message about the soul's immortality, noticing its similarity to the philosophical attempt to reconcile reason and faith in the German-Jewish Enlightenment.

In *The Varieties of Religious Experience* William James had explored the psychological dynamics of Christian Science's spirituality; he thought the sect represented "the most radical branch of mind-cure in its dealings with evil," an assessment congenial to Weber's views about religious responses to the theodicy of suffering. Indeed, knowledge of the church could well have come from James, who was himself in the city during the week to assist in opening a mental health clinic. James also understood perfectly well the practical effects on conduct of the "mind-cure movement" and the reasons for its popular acceptance. As he wrote in *Varieties*,

> The deliberate adoption of a healthy-minded attitude has proved possible to many who never supposed they had it in them; regeneration of character has gone on an extensive scale; and cheerfulness has been restored to countless homes. The indirect influence of this has been great. The mind-cure principles are beginning so to pervade the air that one catches their spirit at second-hand. One hears of the "Gospel of Relaxation," of the "Don't Worry Movement," of people who repeat to themselves, "Youth, health, vigor!" when dressing in the morning as their motto for the day. . . . The plain fact remains that the spread of the movement has been due to practical fruits, and the extremely practical turn of the American people has never been better shown than by the fact that this, their only decidedly original contribution to the systematic philosophy of life, should be so intimately knit up with concrete therapeutics.

In the last analysis it was not so much refinement of the doctrine of immortality but the *therapeutic* benefits for life conduct that mattered most to the receptive public. Even in James's and Weber's time commercial interests sensed a chance for profit, generating a self-help literature of "insincere stuff, mechanically produced," as James observed, that might induce in avid readers at least an aura of spiritual authenticity.

The following Sunday the Webers continued this line of investigation by attending a service of the Ethical Culture Society, meeting in Carnegie Hall. The Society's founder, Felix Adler, then a professor of social and political ethics at Columbia, delivered a lecture titled "Mental Healing as a Religion," an exercise in coming to terms with Christian Science and similar faith cure and "positive" spiritual tendencies. Marianne found the talk "rather dull," but the corrected manuscript has survived in Adler's papers, so we can judge for ourselves. The German-born Adler knew both Edwin R. A. Seligman and William James—Seligman through their upbringing in German-Jewish circles and the Temple Emanu-El, where Adler's father was rabbi and Seligman's an important trustee; and James because of their shared philosophical interests. James even sought to recruit Adler at Harvard, though without success. Adler's life had been and continued to be a heroic, sustained religious and spiritual quest. His views had migrated from orthodox rabbinical training, through Reform Judaism, to a position somewhere within the orbit of Immanuel Kant's ethical rationalism, and finally to a view of life and world animated by a kind of Emersonian faith and informed by a pragmatic ideal of human perfectibility. Reflecting on Adler's spiritual migration and core beliefs, one of his assistants called Ethical Culture a "creedless religion" that embraced a spare maxim for human conduct: "So act in all your relationships, in the family, in business, in politics, in the professions, as to elicit the best in others, and in so doing you will enhance your own worth." Translating this morality into Benjamin Franklin's idiom, it would have specified a concise code of conduct: helping others is the best policy, because you thereby help not only others but also yourself.

In his Sunday address Adler's starting point was surprisingly a discussion of Lafcadio Hearn's new book, *Japan: An Interpretation* (1904), though with the intention of claiming that Japanese successes in the present age had a "moral" foundation and discipline "furnished principally by their religion." The example served to state a pragmatic criterion of truth: if a religion "manifests good results in the behavior of its followers," then there must be, Adler held, "a certain measure of truth in it." This served as a standard of judgment for mental healing and faith cure, from the old practices at Lourdes, which Weber had beheld with spellbinding fascination, to ancient pilgrimages of the devout, to contemporary attitudes about the treatment of cancer and diphtheria, to the new abstract principles of Christian Science. Of course, Adler objected to Christian Science's metaphysics *and science* concerning the nature of matter and evil. But his chief complaint was its quiescence or inwardness: ascetic, to be sure, but too otherworldly, or, in Max Weber's terms, insufficiently oriented toward employing religious asceticism to master and transform both nature and the world of human affairs. If Adler's interpretation and critical assessment raised questions, then there was an occasion for follow-up, as the Webers dined with Adler and his wife at the Seligmans' Upper West Side home the following evening.

Weber had his own views about the social implications of religious faith and organization. In his work he attempted to search beneath sectarian forms, such as those observed at the Christian Science service, not just for their psychological implications but for their *social* reality—that is, for the rational patterns of sociation and group legitimation of the individual self. The sophisticated liturgical, metaphysical, and musical details of the New York service might seem a world removed from circuit-riding Methodist preaching, the staging of a mountainside Baptist baptism, the expressiveness of an urban African American Baptist church, or the austere silence of a Quaker meeting. In the range of religious experience, no doubt for Weber the contrast between Christian Science extravagance and the spare Haverford Friends Meeting could not have been more starkly drawn. However, these different settings and modes of spirituality were united in the search for "salvation" and the claims upon the self in the sober matter-of-factness of sociation, in the social testing and demonstration of one's moral qualifications before one's peers. The voluntary sects—Methodist, Baptist, Quaker, or Christian Scientist—promoted outcomes having implications for the individual's self-identity and standing in the social order. They also had indirect "political" implications because they were the crucible, Weber thought, in which the idea and practice of democratic associational life took shape.

Becoming American

During these final weeks in New York the Webers moved primarily in German-Jewish and progressive reform circles. Edwin R. A. Seligman, the prominent professor of political economy at Columbia, squired Max around the campus, where he met with colleagues, attended lectures, and used the library. The professional discussions would surely have included John Bates Clark, the economic theorist, who had lectured on the same panel as Jacob Hollander at the Congress of Arts and Science in St. Louis. Caroline Seligman hosted a women's lunch for Marianne, and on the Webers' last day in New York a reception in her honor at the University Club, guiding her on a program of site visits, meetings, and lectures. The Seligmans were closely affiliated with the city's main institutions of social reform and social welfare, from the Ethical Culture Society to the Educational Alliance, and they knew the participants and leadership well. Edwin Seligman's advocacy of municipal reform obviously placed him in direct opposition to Tammany Hall and New York's tradition of machine politics. Discussions in these circles, supported by Friedrich

Kapp's and James Bryce's critical commentaries, would have provided a useful supplement to Weber's thinking about political parties, corruption, and the urban political machines. Passages like those in *Economy and Society* about administrative and civil service reform in the municipalities, or public subsidies for parochial schools, a policy promoted by Boss Tweed's Tammany Hall to ensure loyalty among Catholic voters, should be considered a case in point. Progressive reformers like Seligman advocated administrative reform, and they generally viewed such subsidies as a kind of abridging of the constitutional separation of church and state for electoral gain, thus yet another instance of corruption.

Marianne Weber had an especially strong interest in the settlements and women's contributions to social welfare, evident already in her Buffalo, New York, excursion with Grete Haupt and Johannes Conrad, and the day with Jane Addams and the Women's Trade Union League at Hull House in Chicago. In New York she and Max added three new settlements to their itinerary: University Settlement, Henry Street Settlement, and the Educational Alliance. The oldest was the University Settlement, founded in response to the influx of immigrants by Carl Schurz, Stanton Coit of the Ethical Culture Society, and others in 1886, two years after Toynbee Hall in London and three years before Hull House. It was in the settlements that they met Florence Kelley; Lillian Wald, the cofounder of the Henry Street Settlement; and David Blaustein of the Educational Alliance. Their visits and discussions in these institutions were also the vehicle by which their thoughts about sociation and group activity—the social and political functions of the clubs, orders, and sects in American life—came to a conclusion.

In *Max Weber: A Biography* Marianne made a point of commenting on the self-government of the young boys' and girls' clubs in the settlement houses, the relative freedom from authority of the youth, and the use of the clubs as the most essential "means of Americanization." She also underscored the overriding importance of the model of the voluntaristic sect for civic education and all kinds of citizen-initiated social and political action, quoting one of Max's most unqualified assertions:

> The tremendous increase in the clubs and orders here substitutes for the declining organization of the churches—that is, the sects. Nearly every farmer and a large number of businessmen of medium and lower rank wear their "badge" in the buttonhole, as the French wear little red ribbons, not *primarily* because of vanity, but because it immediately legitimates the wearer as a gentleman, accepted by ballot by a specific group of people who have investigated his character and circumstances. One automatically thinks of our investigation of reserve officers. This is exactly the same service which was rendered a member of the old sects (Baptists, Quakers, Methodists, etc.) by his "letter of recommendation" that his congregation gave him for his "brothers" elsewhere. (November 19; MWP)

Figure 11. Jewish immigrant girls attending a Henry Street Settlement knitting class, similar to scenes the Webers encountered in the Lower East Side settlements of New York City. Courtesy Library of Congress.

While stating the claim in clear language, Marianne's selected passages are unfortunately cobbled together and lifted from different letters and contexts, making this passage appear to come from the Webers' Sunday afternoon in Mt. Airy, North Carolina, earlier in their trip. But it is actually one of Max Weber's summations about New York—and, in particular, the lessons of the settlements on the Lower East Side and their educational programs for Jewish immigrants—that had for him made "the most powerful impression."

The general idea about the sources of social engagement and cohesion that today would be called "social capital" is, of course, not Weber's alone. Tocqueville and Bryce had made similar observations about the penchant for group activity and collective local initiative in American social and political life. Moreover, the settlement movement itself in New York was quite explicit about introducing new arrivals to American life through the self-conscious adaptation of American cultural, social, and political forms: clubs, groups, committees, meetings, voting, majority rule, the right to express one's own opinion, public debate, representation of interests, a structure of elected offices, procedural fairness, impartial parliamentary rules of the game. To become an American was to adopt such public "values" and modes of public conduct, to learn and to internalize these forms and the norms associated with them. The new citizenship meant a turning away from traditionalism and the older sources of authority and identity, such as those rooted in custom, nationality, ethnicity, religion or language, and becoming "equal" and "modern."

In Weber's account the theme of the "cool objectivity of sociation" and social capital is developed in a distinctive way for two reasons: the introduction
of the concept of the "sect," and the treatment of the great triad of modern
social theory: class, race, and gender. The latter set of issues reached its apogee
with the question of the immigrant and immigration. The journey had in a
way started with an awareness of immigration and the exploitation of immigrants aboard the *Bremen*. In the New World the social horizon had been
broadened especially by the days in Chicago; in Muskogee, Indian Territory; at
the Tuskegee Institute in Alabama; in Knoxville, Tennessee; and in Mt. Airy,
North Carolina. New York became the final social laboratory. It completed
the circle: the poor Eastern European steerage passengers crossing the Atlantic
had now returned in the Lower East Side settlements and tenements. What
had become of them?

The most comprehensive summations of the New York settlement experience were actually Marianne's, only partially cited in the biography, though
without admitting her authorship. Max had summed up their impressions
and given them "theoretical" grounding, but the details were hers. Such a
division of labor was not uncommon for the couple, and it reflected their
gendered roles.

As could be expected, Marianne was most impressed by the treatment of
youth and young working women. Commenting on the large number of boys'
and girls' clubs, she noted that they

> already encourage children to organize themselves for common purposes. Creating
> good social relations may well be the main thing, but each of these small clubs also
> engages in social work—for example, collecting money for a hospital or Christmas
> gifts for poor children, handing out helpful pamphlet, or something similar. The
> executive committee of such clubs is always composed of the children. They have
> a Mr. Chairman, a treasurer and recording secretary, and they regularly vote on
> acceptance of members. In short, they use parliamentary forms and in this way en-
> sure that the basic principles of self-government and cooperation are, so to speak,
> imbibed with mother's milk. I think this side of children's life here, so completely
> alien to us, must exert an invaluable influence on their education and upbringing.
> (November 11; MWP)

The comparisons with Germany were never far from her mind. In Boston, Simmons College had reminded her of the Lette Houses, the project in German
cities of Wilhelm Lette to expand vocational opportunities for young women,
especially those who were unmarried. The New York settlements offered an
even better model of combined vocational and social support networks, as an
evening at a young working women's club illustrated:

> The young women from different businesses find social contact, decent entertain-
> ment, also continuing education courses and evening discussions. In Germany the

branch organization of the different professions would make it impossible. The multiplicity of status differences doesn't exist here. The stenographer, salesperson, milliner, and factory worker feel themselves after work to be equal in terms of style and dress. During the evening there was a general discussion on a theme chosen by the chairperson (a "lady" and not a worker), very philosophical and seemingly abstract: "On Ability." But it was quite remarkable how the chair wove the threads together and led the young people into all kinds of questions that would concern them inwardly, from religion to morality. It was even more remarkable that she knew how to get the girls to speak and to engage in a lively exchange of opinions. This woman belongs to those wealthy individuals who with genuine democratic and socially responsible feelings devote all their time and energy to the working class. (November 19; MWP)

The event seemed to Marianne not only a lesson in the leveling of class and status differences through social interaction, group affiliation and educational opportunities but also a lesson in adroitly connecting private concerns with the public persona and the public realm.

Gender differences obviously continued to play a role in the settlements, not only through the organizational structure but in terms of the *content* bearing on the social construction of the self. Having observed a working girls' club in action, she sat in on a boys' club, too. "That was a remarkable event," she wrote,

absolutely absent from our life [in Germany] and probably quite impossible in view of our basic principles of education. The small 12-year-old boys conducted themselves entirely using parliamentary forms: there was a vote on a new member following the report of a "commission" about his character, then a literary part. One boy read a poem he had apparently written himself, and then the most priceless event: a discussion on the political question of whether it would be better to have senators elected by the "people" or, as it is now, by representatives. Two boys each had to argue the case pro and contra, and one of them spoke with gestures and every other skill, "criticizing" the weaknesses of the present system like an experienced adult. The young politicians (entirely Jewish working-class children) showed no signs of being shy around us adults. (November 19; MWP)

The boys' club was a microcosm of the "objective" forms of sociation: the test of personal legitimation, an inquiry into character, disclosure of the self before one's peers, public debate of a contested constitutional issue (the Seventeenth Amendment was ratified nine years later), the confident tone and gestures of modern self-reliance. In these matters class, nationality, religion, and ethnicity—and in this case, age—made no difference. Could there be any more definitive example of schooling for democracy and the institutionalization of political education? Max Weber considered it an instance of *absolute* self-government because all other external authorities were excluded from the group's internal deliberations.

The only element missing, an important one encountered in the girls' and working women's clubs, was the connection that might have been established between the private world of inwardness, the spirit or the "inner life," and the external world of social relations and public affairs. That connection, sometimes carefully forged and other times ignored or absent, has always haunted the American liberal constitutional project with its overlay of Enlightenment rationality.

The conversations with Florence Kelley and Lillian Wald reinforced the visitors' views about the social and political significance of the settlements while reminding them of critical areas in need of social reform, as encountered previously in Chicago. Serving at the time as secretary of the National Consumers League, Kelley impressed them with her engaging presence, "passionate socialism," and sharp social criticism. Attending her speech at the School of Philanthropy, recently opened with a full year program in social work—the nation's first—the Webers heard her critique of the lack of federal labor legislation protecting men, women, and especially children from exploitation. Deploring the consequences of "state particularism" and the confusing and discriminatory patchwork of state labor laws, she also relied on her prior experience at Hull House and her work as the chief inspector of factories in Illinois to excoriate the corrupt practices and collusion of some of the unions, big business, and the state legislatures. Of course, Marianne would have identified, too, with her feminist views about the importance of extending rights to the disadvantaged and about the prospects for lasting social reform. "An ethical gain has been made," Kelley wrote about public policy, "whenever the new intelligence of women has become available to the body politic." Supporting evidence came from the settlement movement itself.

After moving to New York, Kelley had become a member of Lillian Wald's inner circle at the Henry Street Settlement. Wald had established public health nursing as her special mission after graduating from the New York Hospital Training School and studying at the Women's Medical College of New York Infirmary for Women and Children. Funded privately by people like Betty Loeb and her son-in-law Jacob Schiff, Wald's nonsectarian efforts were remarkably successful, both for training nurses and in providing health care to the local population, especially the indigent poor and the working class residents of the tenements. By 1903, after ten years in operation, her Nursing Service boasted eighteen district centers, serving about 4,500 patients per year, to which were added more than 35,000 home visits. The service eventually was extended to cover the entire urban area. The arrangements reminded Marianne, who dined with the women one evening, of a "Diakonisse" like those in Europe managed by the Protestant religious orders, although with profound differences: following Wald's prescriptions, the medical vocation became more attractive to educated women, for it allowed room for individual initiative and personal development and freedom. The Henry Street locations also turned into centers for the wide array of social activities, club meetings, and educational projects characteristic of the settlement movement as a whole. They were a center of community life, a site for sociability, a counterweight to the historical condition Max Weber called "the most fateful force in our modern life: capitalism."

Cultural Pluralism

Capitalism and its beguiling spirit were never far from Weber's consciousness. He had just written about the topic, transported to the scene of its highest development by Benjamin's Franklin's words. In New York there were more than enough daily visual and aural reminders. But Max and Marianne Weber wanted to know about the social and cultural responses, the contours and substance of the life world of the metropolis. The churches and settlement houses told only part of the story. In a city of millions there would always be more byways and niches to explore.

Aside from the Seligmans' invitations and guidance, some of the Webers' afternoons and evenings were taken up with family-related friendships. Helene Weber had suggested they look up Friedrich Kapp's daughters Clara and Hannah, and so they did: Clara was married to Paul Lichtenstein, and Hannah to his younger brother Alfred. The Lichtensteins were successful bankers in Manhattan, residing just across the Brooklyn Bridge in Brooklyn Heights. Max seems to have enjoyed their entertaining company over two dinners, discussing religious attitudes and business affairs, while Marianne chaffed to return to her place among the women social activists. The couple also sought out Otto Weber Jr. and his bride Mabel James, and their family friend, Hermann Rösing. Another one of the cousins, Otto worked in the Wall Street financial firm of G. Amsinck and Company. Of all these connections, however, the most striking was perhaps the afternoon with the Villards—Helen Frances Garrison Villard, the activist liberal reformer and daughter of William Lloyd Garrison, and her daughter-in-law Julia Sandford, recently married to the outspoken son, Oswald Garrison Villard, editor of the *New York Evening Post* and its weekly supplement, *The Nation*. Max had known the Villards in Berlin, where Henry Villard (then Heinrich Hilgard), who had died in 1900, had moved in circles around Weber's father and Friedrich Kapp, and the young Oswald had attended the same Charlottenburg Gymnasium as Max and his brother Alfred. The family's unquenchable zeal and life of determined political engagement was captured best by Oswald's later homage to his mother, writing, "Certain of the triumph of every cause to which she gave her devotion, she was incapable of compromise, without being either a bigot or narrowly puritanical. . . . To modify any position she took for reasons of expediency—that was unthinkable; to shift her ground in order to gain a personal advantage, or to avoid unpleasantness, was as impossible for her as for her father, the strongest lines of whose countenance reappeared, with the years, in hers." Like father, like daughter, and like the daughter, so also the son: the rendezvous was surely a reminder of political struggles in the past, in America and in Germany, some successful and some a failure, and the fading light of the nineteenth century reformers. Helen Villard mentioned that she would still put in an appearance that week at the fashionable fall horse show in Madison Square Garden, a "high society" encomium for the Gilded Age. Max could only imagine with bemused intuition the Vanderbilts and other celebrities on display in their boxes, while the plebian interlopers ogled them and the show.

Among the forays into the city's varied cultural life three more investigations of an entirely different order were particularly instructive. One was a lecture at the League for Political Education by Dr. Yamei Kin, the well-known physician and public speaker, addressing the timely topic, "A Chinese Woman's View of the War in the East." Raised by Protestant missionaries after her parents died in an epidemic, Kin had come to the United States and earned an MD from the Women's Medical College of New York, the first Chinese woman to do so. She knew Lillian Wald and the Henry Street Settlement, sharing Wald's concern for public health, and used the settlement as a model for her hospital work and nurses' training in Tianjin, China. Though there was a war in Asia, "The time is coming," she predicted in her talk, "when there will be different struggles, mind against mind, commerce against commerce, not physical force against physical force." Marianne was charmed by her example and her frankness:

> Remarkably, her sympathies were on the side of the Russians, who would pose no danger for oriental culture, as they can be fully assimilated to it, thus in time would simply become Chinese. What she said was interesting enough, but the attraction was also the charming manner in which she spoke and her petite and graceful appearance in her colorful Chinese costume, which we could use quite nicely as the basis for our reform dresses. I had to agree with her as she scolded the Western European peoples for presuming to force everyone in the world into their capitalist-industrial culture, "so that every nation becomes exactly alike the other," just as one commodity is identical to another. This petite, smart person was at the very least a welcome example. One would not want to see her forced into our forms. (November 15; MWP)

The *New York Times* confirmed Kin's message: "Would you have us all alike?" was her question; "you have done many things," she continued, "made many machines that turn out many things—all just alike. Would you do the same with us? So far you have given us only your vices. But we would like your virtues."

At the top of the list of "virtues" were the basic political goods—the rights of citizenship, the rule of law, equal access to a public realm of communication and action—precisely the values and aims of the settlement movement in creating a new civic life for immigrants. The difficulty, however, was that such a regimen might sit uncomfortably alongside inherited cultural forms and identities, challenging or negating them. Kin was interesting because she recognized the problem, bridging the divide in her own person and anticipating an issue for the twenty-first century.

The Webers spent a quite different evening with a secretary of the local typographical union and his wife, a dinner followed by a tour of a newspaper printing plant. Though neither Max nor Marianne mentioned their host's name, it was probably Jerome F. Healy and his wife, Margaret Ufer Healy. At the time Healy was secretary-treasurer of the New York City Typographical Union No. 6, a biennial elected position in which he had served for eight years. The meeting could have been arranged by Seligman or by Hollander, or especially by labor economics scholar George E. Barnett, who was studying the printing industry and had become an expert on the Typographical Union, the oldest national trade union in the country. The conversation and on-site inspection would have satisfied Weber's curiosity about the modern press and newspapers, expressed a few years later in his Deutsche Gesellschaft für Soziologie proposal for a comparative study of newspapers, news reporting, and journalism. Marianne marveled once again at the relative absence of status distinctions, the working-class typesetter having become a "complete gentleman" and his wife a "well-read lady" of the middle class, the couple owning their own self-built home and traveling every few years to Europe. The style of life upended her notions of hardscrabble working-class existence.

For Max Weber the results came later as he reflected on the topic of political governance, administrative expertise, the progressives' demand for civil service reform, and the problem of corruption in modern democracies. When in a wartime speech on socialism he alluded to having spoken to American workers about the topic, it is surely Healy whom he had in mind. His observations were at least colorful, if somewhat dated, noting, "The genuine American Yankee worker enjoys a high level of wages and education. The pay of an American worker is higher than that of many an untenured professor at American universities. These workers have all the forms of bourgeois society, appearing in their top hats with their wives, who have perhaps somewhat less polish and elegance but otherwise behave just like any other ladies, while the immigrants from Europe flood into the lower strata." Weber's firsthand statistical survey supported the conclusion about status and class differences and the embourgeoisement of the working class: unionized, skilled blue-collar workers did command higher wages than academics, notwithstanding the latter's perceived higher status, and of course they occupied a place in society far removed from the new immigrants. "Whenever I sat in company with such workers," Weber reflected,

> and said to them: "How can you let yourselves be governed by these people who are put in office without your consent and who naturally make as much money out of their office as possible . . . how can you let yourselves be governed by this corrupt association that is notorious for robbing you of hundreds of millions?", I would occasionally receive the characteristic reply which I hope I may repeat, word for word and without adornment: "That doesn't matter, there's enough money there to be stolen and still enough left over for others to earn something— for us too. We spit on these "professionals," these officials. We despise them. But if the offices are filled by a trained, qualified class, such as you have in your country, it will be the officials who spit on us." That was the decisive point for these people. They feared the emergence of the type of officialdom which already actually exists in Europe, an exclusive status group of university-educated officials with professional training.

Plunkitt's recent defeat would have added the reminder that even the best-oiled party machines can grind to a halt in the voting booth. But there was a real issue about democratic accountability and expertise buried in Healy's earthy assessment, one that Weber was to mull over in his critique of bureaucracy and its relationship to a democratic political order. Among Seligman's contemporary progressives, it was especially John Dewey who struggled mightily to reconcile the demand for public accountability with the need and requirements for expert knowledge.

The Webers' tour through the varied urban scene concluded on a high note: an evening with Dr. David Blaustein of the Educational Alliance and a tour of the Yiddish theater in the Bowery District, an institution starting to feel the effects of social change and new forms of entertainment. Like the University and Henry Street Settlements, the Educational Alliance was established as a comprehensive institution for assisting immigrants on their passage into American life. Its focus and clientele was exclusively the Eastern European Jewish population on the Lower East Side, numbering a quarter million, Marianne heard. That estimate was probably low; the U.S. Census Bureau itself recorded 359,000 "Hebrew" immigrants into the city from 1900 to 1904. Blaustein had joined the Educational Alliance as superintendent in 1898, and had quickly set about making it the center of social life for immigrant Jews. Born in Russian Poland and arriving in Boston at age twenty, Blaustein's life story was an inspiring saga of successful "Americanization": graduating with honors from Harvard; serving a Providence, Rhode Island, temple as rabbi; holding a position at Brown as assistant professor of Semitic languages; and then entering the top ranks of community activists and social reformers. His challenge at the Educational Alliance was to bridge the divisions in the fractious community, especially those between the orthodox and the reformed tendencies, and between the older generation and youth. His tireless efforts achieved only a mixed result.

For the evening Blaustein and the Webers were joined by Jacob Michailovitch Gordin, the prolific Ukraine-born playwright, for a performance of *Di emese kraft* (The True Power), with acting that Max found "so magnificent in manner that one completely understood the plot," which he then described:

> A physician who married a "woman of the common folk," the cultural conflicts, an awakening experience, she becomes unfaithful, but a reconciliation at the death bed of his daughter from a first marriage, for whom she's caring. The play, which is not flawless, exhibited a few character types (especially a "socialist" and a rabbinical "scholar") who were splendidly portrayed by the Jewish actors, the best to be found in America, in the most absolute self-caricature. We were of course led behind the scenes to the actors, among them a charming 12 year-old girl, and the gathering with them in the café afterward was quite interesting. (November 19; MWP)

This discussion turned to Yiddish, the community, and Gordin's astounding productivity: novels, short stories, seventy-three plays, eleven children, and an ambitious goal of writing ten plays for each child. Weber hoped he had persuaded Blaustein, the man he called "our special friend" and "the purest of idealists," to write an article for the *Archiv für Sozialwissenschaft und Sozialpolitik*, a hope that unfortunately never materialized.

Blaustein left a strong impression. He had made an effort to achieve the Freemason rank of "master of the chair," but had to withdraw because of the requirement to defend Christianity. The attempt was justified, he told Weber, because of the moral legitimacy it would have conferred, which could in turn have been useful for contacts when traveling or in dealings with business clients. The story provided another "glimpse into the way in which clubs and orders function" in America, Weber thought, alluding to the episode later in a footnote added to his revised essay "The Protestant Sects." It reaffirmed a pattern he observed repeatedly in other contexts.

Having far greater significance, however, was Blaustein's rabbinical training and the line of thought that began to open up in Weber's mind concerning the relationship between Puritanism or the Protestant sects and Judaism. The Educational Alliance's program of "Americanization" presupposed a certain level of compatibility or adaptability between the moral universe of the arriving immigrants and the new host culture. Having negotiated the path of adaptation himself, Blaustein was keenly aware of the pitfalls and the practical issues. He mentioned to Weber that at the Educational Alliance "the first aim of the 'acculturation' process [*Kulturmenschenwerdung*], which it tries to achieve by means of all kinds of artistic and social instruction, [is] 'emancipation from the second commandment'"—that is, the Mosaic Law, Thou shalt not make any graven image! Shedding the commandment seemed a presupposition for adapting to the new "American" identity. Surprisingly, however, the account of Blaustein's remarks was recorded not in Weber's correspondence but in the final chapter of *The Protestant Ethic and the Spirit of Capitalism*. The allusion to the evening with Blaustein and Gordin is in a lengthy note in which the practical issue of educational policy at the Educational Alliance becomes transposed as a theoretical question about the "characterological consequences," using Weber's language, of different religious ethics. Usually Weber restated the question not as one of "characterology" but as an inquiry into the kind of ethos or habitus—the dispositions and ways of conducing one's life—encouraged by a particular spiritual and moral order. His specific concern was the *vocational culture* of American life and the sources of its moral legitimacy.

The question about the consequences for the habitus was woven like a bright thread through Weber's inquiry into the relationship between religious ethics and economic action, and it was enmeshed in the tapestry of his entire sociology of religion. In the final days in New York he had another opportunity to consider the struggle between the reverence for religious tradition and the powerful allure of the "specific and peculiar rationalism" of the modern, though now in relation to the "acculturation" of the immigrant. Turn-of-the-century institutions developed an especially potent approach to forming the new identity of the immigrant citizen, consciously adopting the associational model from American experience. But even so, the practices were worked out on contested terrain in public policy. Today they serve as a reminder of one influential position in a debate about the treatment of the immigrant and cultural differences that continues to provoke debate.

The last two weeks in New York were a quite remarkable tour through the social institutions of the metropolis: Presbyterian and Christian Science churches, the Ethical Culture Society, the University Settlement, the Henry Street Settlement, the Educational Alliance, the School of Philanthropy, the League for Political Education, and the Yiddish theater. Weber had wanted to see the American cities, but he had done much more than that, amassing impressions that would create a vast panorama of a complex and varied sociocultural and political order. Summing up in the last days of their visit, Marianne found the months in the United States "surely by far our most interesting trip" because of the quantity and variety of people they had met and conversed with. Max again pronounced his enthusiasm for the Americans as "a wonderful people," notwithstanding the social problems and political challenges they had encountered—particularly those of race and immigration.

The Webers boarded the liner *Hamburg* on November 18 and sailed for Cherbourg, France, the following day. Max Weber's expectations about returning to the United States were lost in the pressures of work and then were overtaken by a world war. Had he waited a day longer in 1904, he could have heard Woodrow Wilson, then Princeton University's president, lecturing at the Cooper Union on "Americanism." Speaking without notes, Wilson sketched the panorama of American history in a few lines:

> The processes of the development of our country in the present are not the processes of the past. Our development heretofore has been marked by century periods. Our first century was devoted to getting a foothold on the continent; the second was used up in getting rid of the French; and the third was occupied in the making of the Nation; and now we are in the fourth century of our development. We feel that we do not have to prove that we are the greatest country in the world, but, like the lawyer in the story, we admit it. Heretofore we have been in the process of making; we have just come out of our youth, and we are imbued with all the audacity of youth, and sometimes, I fear, with some of its indiscretions. We have had three centuries of beginnings, and what we need now is not the original strength, but the finished education.

"Audacity" and "indiscretion" are a revealing choice of words, signaling both delight in new energies and concern about unanticipated errors of political judgment. But with the energy and impetuousness of youth in mind, what was to be the model for the Wilsonian national project? The future U.S. president found a ready-made answer in the "typical American" as the mythical citizen who could master the frontier, subdue nature, and create social capital—represented, naturally enough, in the person of Benjamin Franklin. For this new model citizen, "I would name Benjamin Franklin rather than Alexander Hamilton," Wilson explained, "for Hamilton, much as I admire him, was a transplanted European in his way of thinking. He was not such a man as could have formed a vigilance committee, but Franklin was the man for the frontier. *If there wasn't any way to live, he would have invented one.*"

Invoking Weber's exemplar for the "spirit of capitalism," Wilson set forth the corollary idea of Americanism as self-reliant worldly action. It was a view of the world and America that emphasized possibility, innovation, command, initiative, self-control, a decisive break with the past. The view merged seamlessly with a "this-worldly" asceticism. For Wilson, after all, mastering the unexpected might require looking to ourselves alone and inventing an entirely new way of life. His extemporaneous message was perfectly pitched. It would be difficult to imagine a more conclusive statement of the American vision of modernity.

TEN

INTERPRETATION OF THE EXPERIENCE

As the *Hamburg* headed for open sea, Max Weber wrote with amusement that New York, the "wonderfully attractive city," now "lies behind us in the mists of a beautiful winter night, and everything is over—'après nous le deluge,' and perhaps 'dans nous' also—for yesterday night we were still in the Jewish quarter until 1:30 a.m." He also did a quick calculation of the costs of the transatlantic passages and the time in America, a total of three months and twelve days from the Heidelberg departure to the return: about 7,000 Marks, minus the Congress of Arts and Science's honorarium of $500, or 2,100 Marks. The travelers had logged around 5,000 miles, mostly on the railroads—180 hours in all.

What of the results? Always attentive to Max's moods and well-being, Marianne delighted in the happiness they had experienced: "I often have the feeling as though I'm bringing a convalescent home, who has again become conscious of the intellectual capital that he has slowly, slowly pulled together." Max did not dispute the assessment, agreeing that a year earlier such a journey would have been impossible, and commenting at one point that "*stimulation* and *engagement* of the mind without excessive intellectual *exertion*" can offer important benefits. At the very end of the correspondence he added a more personal and frank reflection:

> Of course, it cannot be said that for me the "scientific" results of the trip can be compared with the expenses. I have won over a considerable number of interesting contributors for our periodical. I am much better prepared than previously to understand the statistics and government reports in the United States. I shall myself write some critiques of the literature on Negroes and the like, perhaps some other small things. But for my cultural-historical work I haven't seen much more than where the things are that I would need to see, especially the libraries that I would have to use, which are widely scattered across the country in small sects and colleges. Under these circumstances, of course, the trip can be justified in our present situation only from the general point of view of the expansion of the scientific horizon (*and* improvement of my health). In this respect the fruits of the trip can only show themselves after some time has passed. (After November 19; MWP)

To be sure, the results were far from certain and would only become apparent over the coming months and years, even to the very end of Weber's life sixteen years later. There were some disappointments: only W.E.B. Du Bois would follow through with an article for the *Archiv für Sozialwissenschaft und Sozialpolitik*. The literature critiques Weber envisaged would not be written, with his thoughts about race, class, and status absorbed instead into other work, especially the sections in *Economy and Society*. But the opening out of the scientific and scholarly horizon was important. What would it mean for Weber's work?

The Discourse about America

The return to winter in Heidelberg was difficult. Marianne arrived with a cold, Max with complaints about sleeplessness. The demands of work and public life began to accumulate, the usual struggles ensued, and Marianne's anxieties returned. "It would be ironic," she wrote, that if for Max "the quiet measured life here were less tolerable than the roar of life in America" (December 21; DWS). The warm enthusiasms and drama of the journey had been replaced by the cold reality of the everyday. But Max began to manage some events with colleagues, attending a political lecture by the socialist leader Eduard Bernstein, with whom he had corresponded about the Quakers, and appearing at Edgar Jaffé's inaugural lecture "The Methodological Tasks of Political Economy," an effort to expand upon Weber's own essay on the problem of objectivity. Marianne had collected the couple's correspondence from America, all but one misplaced page, and a secretary was typing the transcript for use in lectures and essays. In January the Eranos Circle also resumed, starting with a session at Ernst Troeltsch's home, which ended with long disputations spilling into the street and the night air, putting Max in bed for two days with a cold. The discussion was likely an early round in their disagreements over the typological treatment of church and sect, asceticism and mysticism. Despite the setback, Weber recovered in time for the first main event after the return home: an evening at the Nationalsozialer Verein in Heidelberg on January 20.

The association had scheduled an "America evening" open to the public with announced talks by Marianne Weber, Ernst Troeltsch, and two others: the businessman Otto Nuzinger, and Professor Otto Cohnheim. Marianne had been asked to address the "woman question" in America, a talk she prepared first for her own women's group, the Verein Frauenbildung-Frauenstudium, and then repeated afterward at events in Karlsruhe and Mannheim. The theologian Adolf Deissman, the coorganizer of the Eranos Circle, presided on the occasion. Troeltsch sketched travel impressions, especially of New York and Chicago, while the other speakers addressed the topics of business and labor based on their American experiences. Max Weber was not on the printed program, but with Marianne's encouragement he decided at the last minute to address the packed hotel auditorium. He spoke extemporaneously for an hour until nearly midnight. It was his first public appearance in years.

Starting in the nineteenth century the popular discourse about America in German-speaking Europe had alternated between two poles: on the one side the inspiring romanticism and adventurous spirit of Karl May's popular depictions of the American frontier, surfacing in the multiethnic, multicultural utopia of redemption in Peter Rosegger's *The Last Jacob*, and on the other side the cultural criticism as expressed in Ferdinand Kürnberger's notorious dyspeptic novella *Der Amerika-Müde*, about getting tired or weary of America and everything "American." Weber was aware of both views, as we have seen. He had summoned Rosegger's images while touring the Biltmore estate, reflecting on the despoilment and reclamation of nature. And he had appropriated Kürnberger in the first part of *The Protestant Ethic and the Spirit of Capitalism* in order to stand him on his head, while in doing so pointing to a third possibility, as obvious as it may seem in retrospect: unprejudiced comparison and analysis of the institutions and practices of social and political life under the conditions of a modern capitalism that North America shared with Europe. The "America evening" presentations reflected the effort in this new direction, with speakers addressing the nature of the American cities, industry and business enterprise, labor unions and labor relations, the orientation toward work, the standard of living, the American family, the prospects for a socialist movement, and the position of women in American democracy. The last topic was Marianne Weber's choice, her perspective awaited by the audience "with great anticipation" and given the lion's share of press coverage.

The presentations were a good beginning, though thematically for Max Weber they did not extend as far or probe as deeply as they could have. The Heidelberg press summarized his concluding contribution to the event:

> Greeted with enthusiasm, Prof. Weber spoke for almost an hour about political life in America. During his talk he informed the audience about the essential features and significance of American democracy, policy concerning the Negroes, electoral relationships, the Americans' antipathy toward authority, the different sects, the Congress and the relationship between political representatives and the people, etc., for which he received enthusiastic applause. (*Heidelberger Zeitung*)
>
> In the discussion period Professor Max Weber spoke about *political* life in America, the development of the parties, the *problem of the Negroes*, the system of government, the "Americanization" of the immigrants through democracy, the activity of associations, labor relations, and much more. His inspired and well-informed performance was given the most rapt attention. His criticism of social conditions in *our* country produced great applause. (*Heidelberger Tageblatt*)

Although there is no more complete record of these remarks, it is not difficult to imagine how the record of the journey would have figured in them, from the Indian Territory frontier to the Deep South and the cities of the Midwest and Northeast. All the major themes appear to have been present, with the possible exception of education and the universities. Framed in broadly political terms, Weber's was a perspective that could be used both to improve understanding of the United States and to appeal at home for what *Die Hilfe* characterized as "a politics more oriented to freedom and popular rule," goals congruent with the broader shared political orientation of Progressivism.

In her published account of what women could learn from America, Marianne Weber did expand the field of vision to discuss leading feminists she had met, like Jane Addams and Florence Kelley. She included commentary on social norms, cultural attitudes, and differences among classes and status groups. Relying on her conversations and observations, she extolled the advantages of coeducation in the high schools, the promise of education and the colleges, the social work of the settlements, the prospect of careers and family for working women, the role of the clubs and voluntary associations, and the steps toward women's right to vote in the western states. It was, as reported in the press, a "hymn of praise" that perceived women's higher standing in America compared with Germany, primarily in terms of a *political* difference and its social and personal consequences: the "democratic ideals which the American Constitution embodies: belief in freedom, self-determination of the personality, and equal rights for everyone," quoting Marianne's phrasing. Racial prejudice and the treatment of minorities, as she had seen, belied the lofty promise of the ideals. Nevertheless, her firsthand observations and interpretation served still as a reminder of a central fact and an image of America that had been ignored too often in popular discourse: the United States as the world's oldest self-governing democracy.

During these weeks Max Weber had returned to his unfinished study, *The Protestant Ethic and the "Spirit" of Capitalism*, for the next installment was facing a deadline: it had been scheduled already as a talk for the Eranos Circle. For a meeting of a small group of scholars at the Webers' home in the Hauptstrasse on February 5, Marianne supplied the bodily nourishment of "Burgundy and sliced ham," as she noted, while Max provided the mental repast: the Eranos Circle members heard him talk on "Die protestantische Askese und das moderne Erwerbsleben." The title was an interesting choice: literally it translates as "Protestant Asceticism and Modern Working Life or Employment"—that is, an inquiry into the relationship between asceticism, particularly the "worldly" type characteristic of the Protestant sects, and rational acquisitive economic action in the modern capitalist market economy. The words give the inquiry a practical edge: What does asceticism have to do, if anything, with *earning a living* in the modern world of the money economy, stock and commodity markets, and capitalist production and consumption? Had Weber stayed with the problem and language of "earning a living" his questioning might have been better understood when he put pen to paper for the second part of *The Protestant Ethic*. He had puzzled over the topic in America, noting the "Puritan survivals" and wondering about labor, entrepreneurial initiative, and the culture of capitalism. The announced title is actually closest to the last chapter of the completed text: chapter 5, "Asceticism and Capitalism," revised in 1919 to read "Asceticism and the Capitalist Spirit." The chapter contains the most memorable and most often quoted material in the entire study, including the much-debated imagery of the "iron cage" introduced in Talcott Parsons's translation, the chilling reference to "specialists without spirit," or the allusion to Friedrich Nietzsche's "last men" who invented happiness drawn from *Thus Spake Zarathustra*. We can assume that the earliest formulation of these ideas emerged as Weber brought together the Eranos Circle presentation.

After the presentation Weber proceeded with dispatch. His method of work was not to write in his illegible script and then arrange for a typed transcription, but rather to dictate his thoughts. On March 2 Marianne reported his verbal dictation had begun of "Protestant asceticism" to a Fräulein Hagmann, confirmed a week later when Max wrote to his brother Alfred. The final two chapters began to assume a shape and a direction, and four short weeks later, on April 3, Marianne reported the text completed, scarcely two months after the Eranos Circle meeting. The date coincided appropriately with the opening of the Heidelberg cable car ascending to the heights above the town, the return of chirping birds, and the arrival of spring. Max had dictated chapters 4 and 5, 110 pages in the *Archiv* printing, to add to the 54 pages published before his departure for America. He could now resume his quiet walks along the parapets above the bustling university town.

A Way Out of the Iron Cage?

When he completed *The Protestant Ethic and the "Spirit" of Capitalism* Max Weber suggested that he had made a contribution to cultural history and written as a cultural historian. What kind of imprint, if any, had the American experience made on Weber's thinking in this cultural-historical essay? Had the scientific horizon opened onto new vistas?

In our present age of digital media, there is naturally a quick and easy answer to these questions, readily available by entering search words like *Amerika, Vereinigten Staaten, Franklin,* or *Individualismus* on one of the CD-ROMs of Weber's main collected works, conveniently supplied by the electronic wizardry of Karsten Worm and Thomas Müller. What this engaging exercise will demonstrate is numerous references to the United States, America, and matters American—many more than any other nation (Germany aside, of course) except England or Great Britain. If we turn specifically to the text of part 2 of *The Protestant Ethic and the Spirit of Capitalism*, the original published in the *Archiv*, the results are readily apparent: specific references, often added in footnotes, to (in approximate sequence) Methodism in America;

the secularization of American life; the colleges; Brown University; literature on the American colonies; antiauthoritarian tendencies in America; William James's *Varieties of Religious Experience*; pragmatism; the concept of the "gentleman;" James Bryce on the American college; Benjamin Franklin's autobiography; Anglo-American self-control; toleration in Rhode Island (with reference to Roger Williams), Maryland (Lord Baltimore) and Pennsylvania (William Penn); American sects; Northwestern University; the emotional character of Methodism in America; American Negroes; the Colgate University Library on the Baptists; the lack of respect in America; the Quaker meeting at Haverford College; Franklin twice again, announcing that "honesty is the best policy" and "time is money"; Thorstein Veblen's *Theory of Business Enterprise*; Washington Irving; the self-made man; the "Europeanization" of America; the Educational Alliance and the "Americanization" of immigrants; the trade unions; music and Trinity Church in Boston; the idea of freedom; inheritance in America; capital formation and trade in New England; Pennsylvania and the Revolutionary War; the dry-goods man in Ohio; and finally, capitalism as "sport" in the United States! The sample is intriguing, and no doubt it could not have been compiled before Weber's American trip. Of course, it is amplified in his very next essay "'Churches' and 'Sects' in North America," published a year later in 1906, which starts from a problematic set explicitly in the United States. But we have already considered the content and sources of this commentary, which tends toward tracing the genealogical descent of aspects of American institutions and culture. As suggestive as it may be, a digitized tour tells us very little, as our question is not about engaging examples and key phrases but about the evolving substantive *problematic* of a controversial thesis that continued to take shape in Weber's thinking, even to the end of his life.

America found a place in the thesis of *The Protestant Ethic* for two obvious reasons: amid its polyglot and multilayered culture, the United States offered instances of the ascetic ethos Weber was looking for, the "survivals" of a habitus emphasizing the methodical rationalization of the conduct of life. The religious sects, whatever their denomination, fascinated Weber for precisely this reason: there he came in contact with the human character having some resemblance to the "ideal type" sketched in the pages of *The Protestant Ethic*. The portrait should not be overdrawn. Too often the ascetic strain is modeled on an *American Gothic* motif, the gray on gray of pinched features, furrowed brow, tragic demeanor, and dogged marching to the cadence of hard work and a life of quiet and intense rectitude. But Weber, we should remember, was taken by the enthusiasm, raw energy, taste for adventure, social engagement, creative powers, and sense of humor of his American subjects, a desire to master the self and the world that he even seemed to emulate from time to time. That, too, belonged to the sketch developed in his imagination.

The other reason was equally compelling: because of historical conditions Weber knew all too well, America offered the most fertile ground for the flourishing of the modern market economy, the rational capitalist enterprise and a capitalist culture of seemingly unlimited scope. Capitalism and its "spirit" had existed elsewhere, of course, but in the New World it seemed comparatively unfettered and able to express itself in a concentrated and even exuberant form. Weber had carefully dissected the defining features of the modern capitalist economy, distinguishing enterprises in antiquity and the European Middle Ages from the new modes of rational capital accounting and investment in modern industrial economies with "free" or "self-regulating" commodity, labor, and capital markets. In America he was obviously struck by the dynamism and prospects, for good or ill, of the rapid growth, the expenditure of labor, the massive demographic shifts, the sources of social conflict, and the unsettling transformation of nature into material wealth. The elemental quality of the transformation could not be overlooked in the ports, on the railroads, in the cities, in the immigrant towns, through the Cotton Belt, or on the frontier. Nor could it be missed in the practical, matter-of-fact outlook on life and accomplishments of the most American of social types, the "self-made man." Weber found him—as well as the "self-made woman"—at every turn, as union leader, politician, financier, businessperson, preacher, journalist, administrator, community activist, and social worker. One of these types might even one day climb to the pinnacle of political power as president.

For Weber in America the visible juxtaposition of these two competing forces—the ethical and the material powers—would have been all too obvious, symbolized from the first day in Manhattan by the spire of St. Paul's Chapel set against the towering facade of the Park Row skyscraper. The travelers commented on the symbolic contrast themselves, after all. So we have arrived at the core issue: What does Weber make of this most essential tension between the demands of a certain *kind* of moral life and the competing demands of the "capitalist spirit?" We know how he resolves the contradiction through the "elective affinities" of Parsons's prized detective story, the master narrative of the sacred text. But what about the *American* narrative itself? Has Weber found in his American observations any hint of a reconciliation? Is there a way out of the dilemmas of capitalist modernity? Does the distinctive pattern of associative life in America—*Vergesellschaftung*, once again—offer a possible escape route from the "iron cage" of increasing bureaucratization and the petrifaction of institutions? Can these distinctive social forms counteract the worst excesses of capitalist culture? Properly stated, this is a question not just for Weber but for American historiography as well.

Weber seemed to wrestle with this question through a series of ruminations on the "Europeanization" of American life, an idea surely present in his mind in 1904, and its obverse, the "Americanization" of European institutions, a locution appearing when he turned his attention to the problem of science, the universities, and the quality of associational activity in his own country. In using the phrase the "Europeanization of America" he actually referred to several different phenomena: first, bureaucratization and the unintended consequences for *state development* of progressive civil service reform—the growth of a professional, trained, salaried administrative staff. "In large states everywhere modern democracy is becoming a bureaucratized democracy," was his pithy formulation in the speech "Socialism" in 1918. The trend was institutional and structural, aided in the American case by the distribution of land and settlement of the frontier that he described in St. Louis, Missouri, and viewed in the Indian Territory. The second reference was social and had to do with the intrusion of status-seeking norms of social honor, the "aristocratic" pretensions of the plutocracy that were lumped, even by Americans themselves, under the heading "feudalization." Laura Fallenstein's husband, Otto von Klock, had established a business upon this foundation. The trend was important because it seemed diametrically opposed to the unpretentious practices of the voluntary associations. Third, Europeanization was sometimes a placeholder for the long-term process of secularization that Weber thought was accompanying the massive influx of immigrants from the hinterlands of the Old World. But his judgments about both secularization and immigration vacillated, and his prognostications were often wide of the mark. The final usage was institutional and appeared occasionally when Weber reflected on the emergence of the modern research university devoted to the enterprise of science, such as Jacob H. Hollander's Johns Hopkins or Edwin R. A. Seligman's Columbia, alongside the pedagogical model of the American college with its impressive spiritual genealogy. This final sense of "Europeanization" already reveals the lack of clarity in the concept, however, for—agreeing with Veblen—Weber also realized that the modern research universities also embodied an exactly opposite developmental tendency.

These references were provocative but casual, and hardly the stuff of science. In Weber's thinking, the "Americanization" theme and hypothesis remained even more ambiguous and underdeveloped, perhaps the weakest part of his analysis. There was a good reason, for in Weber's usage the term referred most narrowly either to changes in the political party system and electioneering of the kind Bryce had cataloged in *The American Commonwealth*—that is, the emergence of the mass party as an electoral "machine," a message Weber kept delivering to Robert Michels and repeated in his political essays. In the university setting, especially in the big privately endowed university, it referred to adopting an entrepreneurial—or as Weber said, "capitalist"—model for attracting externally funded research.

Yet, at a deeper level, "Americanization" for Weber alluded to something radically different and much more serious: the development of the dense web of group affiliation, civic culture, and social capital modeled on the voluntary association nurtured at its origins in the crucible of the sect. The idea emerged in his wartime essays, especially "The Suffrage and Democracy in Germany" (1917), a line of reasoning understandably excerpted by Hans Gerth and C. Wright Mills for their Weber reader. In these late essays Weber proposed a number of institutional reforms for the "new Germany," keeping in mind especially American, British, and French examples. But at the level of social relations and *political culture*, the attractions of the American model returned to his imagination. It was actually one of the few positive alternatives Weber pointed to for Germany in the soul searching during the first months of the Weimar Republic, a matter of nothing less in his words than "massive" political education. Fearing misunderstanding, when she published the comment, Marianne Weber added the explanation, "Youth clubs: children are selected into the clubs by their own members, if they conduct themselves properly"! Max's recommendation had nothing whatsoever to do with the cultural leveling, materialism, and consumerism associated in popular stereotypes with "Americanism." Indeed, it came from a radically different alternative, the demanding school of inner-worldly asceticism. But the thought was far too exotic and fell on deaf ears. It was hopelessly ahead of its time.

Today we may have a more satisfactory perspective. In the Adorno Lectures Claus Offe has taken up the challenge of interpreting the results of Weber's American journey. According to his summation, Weber

> brought from America a social-theoretical theme for his life's work: namely, the question of whether US society represented a viable social and political formation that might even be reproduced in Europe; whether this might make it at least possible to avoid the bureaucratization, rationalization, reification, depersonalization, secularization and meaningless occupational and professional specialization (*Berufs- und Fachmenschentum*) encouraged by capitalism; and whether individual freedom could thus be preserved not only . . . for minorities at the *top* of state, party and administrative apparatuses but collectively at the *base* of the citizen body and its associations.

His answer to this question, in brief, is that the alleged "null hypothesis" did not pan out in Weber's work, and that today, in any case, speculations about "convergence" or "divergence" between America and Europe have been overtaken by events. In this view, notwithstanding certain "American anomalies" conditioned by historical differences, there is only one more-or-less consistent and unified model of capitalist development and modernization under the heading of Weber's prized category: "occidental rationalism." There are not alternative paths to the modern world, or multiple modernities. There are no well-lit and well-traveled escape routes from the consequences of capitalist modernity.

This is an important conclusion, and if properly understood, it is the most compelling conclusion we can reach. But it still moves too quickly and too far, for we can penetrate deeper into the biography of the work by acknowledging that Weber took a major, fully developed theme with him to America—a hypothesized relationship, an "elective affinity," between an ethos based in religious conviction, a type of worldly orientation exemplified in Benjamin Franklin's sayings, and "capitalist" economic activity—and then returned with both persuasive evidence supporting the postulated relationship, and new questions about the implications of a novel *type* of social formation: the "cool objectivity of sociation" in the voluntary association. It is only in America, and nowhere else, that Weber confronts this social phenomenon. What then forms in his mind is the typological accentuation of the *possibility* of its realization. At the center of this "ideal type" is the moral personality of the *Berufsmensch*, the person committed to a calling or identified through vocation. Socially, this type of person is made possible only by a particular form of civil society, in which voluntaristic associational activity involves the self-governing selection and moral testing of group members. A robust, authentic civil society in this kind of democracy thus requires a specific social construction of the modern self, a particular kind of "characterology." It is striking to realize that Weber thought the "Americanization" of immigrant youth that he witnessed in clubs and small groups took precisely this form, or that his characterization of the American "college" was tailored to such social requirements. In his view these small local microcosms merely replicated and in turn reinforced a pattern firmly established in the larger social order.

It would be dramatic and satisfying to suppose that this ideal typical pattern of sociation and type of civil society, constructed on the template of the sect, could offer a way out of the grinding rationalization and disenchantment of life produced by the forces unleashed by capitalism. Weber wisely refrained from ever giving this social formation a name. Since *bürgerliche Gesellschaft* with its "bourgeois" connotations is out of the question, Sung Ho Kim has proposed calling it "sectlike society," a phrase that is sociologically accurate but linguistically inelegant and opaque. Whatever the term, in the actual historical world of group affiliation the route of escape, the great alternative, is hardly ever found, and its discovery only becomes a possibility, paradoxically, within the parameters of the self-governing and self-sustaining association. Beyond those boundaries, the usual conceptual antinomies—the choices among diametrically opposed action orientations that Parsons, standing on Weber's shoulders, called the "pattern variables"—will always apply. The history of communal movements in America to the present day, both religiously inspired and secular, is replete with efforts to suppress such choices and remain true to the "warrantable calling," using the Puritans' long-forgotten term. We know how the impulse arises. The incubator for these movements has already been faithfully described, with a nod to Weber's "Protestant ethic," in Perry Miller's classic *The New England Mind*. As for the prospects of planting such a seed on foreign soil, we have only to remember Weber's skeptical warnings about the prospects for liberal democracy in Russia.

America in Weber's Work

Aside from the possibility of distinctive American forms of association, there is the further question about the expanded scientific horizon of Weber's work, for repeatedly after 1905 his thinking comes back to American examples, models, and comparisons, especially in the public setting. The topics and contexts are remarkably varied: the debates in the Verein für Sozialpolitik over trusts, cartels, the state, bureaucracy, and productivity; the discussions in the Deutsche Gesellschaft für Soziologie of the press, the modern media, the sociology of voluntary associations, race, religiosity, the sects, the conceptual and sociological complexity of legal entities like "the United States," and the problem of conceptualizing the "nation" and national identity; the replies to Felix Rachfahl about the sects, acquisitiveness and the "capitalist spirit," which he calls a *habitus* for the first time; the speeches and articles on higher education triggered by disputes over "academic freedom," the politics of university administration under Friedrich Althoff in the Prussian Ministry of Education, and the discussions at the German Association for Higher Education (Deutscher Hochschullehrertag); the unsuccessful discussions with Georg Jellinek over a proposed Institute for Comparative Politics and Jurisprudence at the University of Heidelberg, funded by Andrew Carnegie; and finally, of course, repeatedly in the political essays of 1917 to 1919, the references to American political and social conditions finding their way even into Weber's comments as a member of Hugo Preuss's committee for drafting the Weimar constitution.

The thread woven through all these commentaries is the appropriation of American institutions and social practices as a logical anchor point, a point of departure, or a baseline for comparison in a pattern of observation or a process of reasoning. The construction of contrasts, oppositions, alternatives, or antinomies was in any case the hallmark of Weber's restless typological cast of mind. Sometimes the intention is polemical, as in the attack on Gustav Schmoller's defense of cartels in Germany and dismissal of American antitrust legislation. On other occasions the message is didactic—for example, in the report to the Deutsche Gesellschaft für Soziologie proposing a large-scale study of associations (*Vereinswesen*), Weber's language suggests nothing less than a comparative inquiry into civil society and the sources of social capital. As he moves from generalization to examples—bowling clubs, choral societies, political parties, voluntaristic sects, artistic cults—it becomes clear that the *quality* of associational activity is essential to the character and strength of civil society and that the American practices of "selection" and demonstrating "proof" of character serve as a yardstick for measurement: "How does this compare with the way things are here in Germany? Can we find analogous examples here, and, if so, what is their nature and extent? Where, and with what consequences? Where not, and why not?" And, adding to the farrago, "How does a certain associational membership influence the inner workings of the individual members or the personality as such?" Weber's excitability is palpable in this outpouring: In what direction does a particular form of sociation move the individual—toward passive and quiescent subjection, or toward active and engaged citizenship? This is not just a question about the formation of social capital but a question about the construction of the kind of person appropriate to a democratic social order.

Nowhere is such insistent questioning more obvious than in the two well-known speeches, "Science as a Vocation" and "Politics as a Vocation." Considering the context and the audience for these talks to students in Munich on November 7, 1917, and January 28, 1919—a struggling but still undefeated nation at war, and a city torn apart by political upheaval after the armistice—it must seem extraordinary that they are framed in part by thoughts about America. In Weber's vision the "internal," inward conditions and requirements for an absolute commitment to the pursuit of knowledge or an unqualified choice for the political vocation are not bounded by time and space. Such matters belong to a conversation for the ages. They could be called *transcendent*. But the "external" institutional and material circumstances for the practice of science or politics as vocations are determined by historical and social conditions. So, he asks, what do we find today? Regarding "external" conditions, we find in the community of science the rapid shift of universities away from the old model of cultivated learning or *Bildung* based on principles of collegiality to a bureaucraticized and capitalized enterprise oriented toward competition, production, and the separation of the scientist/worker from the means of production; and we find in the political realm the replacement of politics as an avocation for notables by the professional politician, the party as a machine, and the ascendency of the "plebiscitarian principle" for leadership selection, as Weber calls it. Let us strip away the illusions and drop all pretense, he counsels; in these developments American institutions point the way. Sometimes he is blunt: "In very important respects German university life is being Americanized, as is German life in general." Yet at other times he only extends an invitation: "Permit me to take you once more to America, because there one can often observe such matters in their most massive and original shape." The word Weber chooses is *Ursprünglichkeit*—the true source, the most original, native and *natural* form.

Yet with this summons we have been led across a boundary, for the last sentence is not about mere "externals" but about the *inward calling*, the problem of the *meaning* of science in the totality of life. We might ask, What arsenal of concepts would William James have brought to solve *that* problem? Weber's words that follow supply the answer: the message is a bracing dash of cold water, a sudden plunge into the stream of pragmatism, a lesson in practicality and the "cash value" of ideas and the pursuit of knowledge. The problems of meaning are resolved not transcendentally but with a matter-of-fact appeal to "self-clarification" and the sense of "responsibility"—in science, responsibility for knowledge and its uses, and in politics, responsibility for the exercise of power and its consequences for history.

There are, of course, other words left untouched by this resolution: principally the chapters, sections, and fragments collected posthumously as *Economy and Society*. But they are appropriately a part of the work in America.

PART 2

THE WORK IN AMERICA

It gripped my intense interest immediately and I read it straight through . . .
as if it were a detective story.

—Talcott Parsons, on reading *The Protestant Ethic and the Spirit of Capitalism*
in Heidelberg in 1925

ELEVEN

THE DISCOVERY OF THE AUTHOR

Author and Audience

Max Weber's present reputation is dependent importantly on his reception in the English-speaking world. Yet the American reception—the translation, publication, reading, and diffusion of his work, and its effect on the disciplines, on scholarship, and intellectual life generally in the United States—was a lengthy and unusually complex affair, one that continues to this day. His writings were essentially unknown during his lifetime. Then, in the 1920s, the beginnings of an interest in Weber's work led to the gradual translation and incorporation of his thought into the social science disciplines, college and university curricula, and even public discourse. Leaving aside professional publications, today it is no longer uncommon to have Weber appear in popular literature, such as John le Carré's *Absolute Friends*, or to find his ideas mentioned on editorial pages, in the blogosphere, or in places like the *New York Review of Books*, the *New Yorker*, the *Atlantic Monthly*, *Harper's*, or the *Chronicle of Higher Education*, much as Karl Marx or Sigmund Freud might have been in previous decades. Only Alexis de Tocqueville seems to have survived in this public sphere of discourse as well. Perhaps it goes without saying that Weber would have been astounded by such a development. He did not seek this kind of reputation himself, nor would he or anyone else have thought it possible in 1920. A true "combination of circumstances"—to speak with Weber, both intended results and entirely fortuitous events, or readings of his work that some time ago Guenther Roth aptly called "creative misinterpretations"—have contributed to bringing about this success.

Of course, fascination with Weber's writings or the popularization of some of his ideas, such as charisma and "charismatic authority," bureaucracy and bureaucratic rule, or the ubiquitous "work ethic," does not necessarily translate into widespread positive "influence" or "paradigmatic" status in disciplines like sociology and political science, characterized today by seemingly intractable disagreements, fragmentation, and compartmentalization of specialties. Even to speak of a "successful" reception is problematic and points to the complexities inherent in assessing what contemporary disciplines credit to a predecessor like Weber. Not surprisingly, there is a full range of opinion about what or how much the social science disciplines—and sociology, in particular—actually do owe to Weber's work. Some have argued for the vitality of a distinctive "Weberian" perspective, paradigm, or research program while others have seen little substance behind such claims and categories. Such disagreements point to confusion on two fronts: First, there is lack of agreement about the application and use of words like *reception, influence, dissemination* or *diffusion*. Commentaries are vague regarding the kind of evidence that would support claims attached to such vocabularies. Second, in the American disciplines the nature of Weber's contribution itself is still contested or poorly formulated. This circumstance surely reflects in part the complicated history of the translation and incorporation of his work into the social science canon, and disputes over the division of labor within the emerging social science disciplines themselves.

As an initial step toward clarity, one can suggest that there were minimally three necessary conditions for the successful reception and propagation of Weber's work: the development of professional networks for cultivating and sustaining interest in his writings; the translation and publication of the most important parts of the work; and the "institutionalization" of his thought, research problems, and conceptual language in curricula, undergraduate courses, and advanced graduate research seminars in American colleges and universities. In addition, to these three conditions one must add two further considerations that have a special character in the American context: the disciplinary needs of the newly emergent social sciences—especially sociology—in the modern research university and in a professional context in which Weber's work seemed to supply answers and guidance; and a certain resonance or convergence of Weber's basic assumptions and questions with American conditions and with issues having prominence in American social and intellectual life, including an extraordinarily potent cultural narrative of achievement and atonement.

The last consideration cannot be underestimated; one of the most remarkable features of the work was that it unintentionally tapped the most fundamental of American narratives: the possibility of emancipation in pursuit of a better life—remaking the self, gaining a second chance, atoning for past failure, striving for a lasting reconciliation with God and world. Weber described the pattern in exacting detail especially in the pages of *The Protestant Ethic and the Spirit of Capitalism*. Astute readers could not miss the moments of recognition. The characters were all too familiar. It was a story about ourselves. For that reason the cultural narrative was the deepest source of attachment to Weber's words and of fascination for his work.

Networks of Scholars

To assist in understanding the reception and dissemination of Weber's work into the important decade of the 1960s, it is useful to bear in mind developments at the center of American university life and intellectual culture in the social sciences, as well as developments that were more peripheral to the established disciplines and institutions. Both were equally important in their own way. It is also essential to identify and distinguish among the important "clusters" of scholars who came to constitute the larger network of academics, teachers, and intellectuals who contributed to diffusion of knowledge about Weber. The effectiveness of these clusters came about through their location in the topography of American intellectual life, their institutional prestige, their leadership in educational policy, and their role in educating and supporting successive generations of teachers and scholars. The clusters also played a part in the formation of a larger educated public. Such schematic generalizations probably oversimplify a complex set of relationships, to be sure, but they are nevertheless helpful for orienting our discussion.

With regard to the early work on Weber, five core institutions were important: the University of Chicago, Harvard University, the University of Wisconsin, Columbia University, and the New School for Social Research—three well-established private universities, one distinguished land-grant public university, and a small new urban institution. Each of the different "clusters" of scholars in which intensive discussion occurred had a base in one or more of these universities.

The first grouping of any significance, forming in the second half of the 1920s, were the scholars at Chicago and Harvard: Frank Knight in economics and Louis Wirth in sociology at Chicago, joined by Edward Shils as a graduate student, and Talcott Parsons at Harvard starting in 1927. To this quartet one should add Melchoir Palyi and Alexander von Schelting, both of whom were at the University of Chicago by 1933, Palyi as a lecturer in economics and Schelting as a Rockefeller fellow. In addition, one should include Edward Hartshorne, an undergraduate with Parsons and a graduate student at Chicago who served as a kind of go-between, bringing Schelting into Parsons's orbit once again. Parsons had met Schelting earlier while studying in Heidelberg, and the renewed intellectual exchanges proved unusually fruitful because Parsons was writing *The Structure of Social Action*, first published in 1937.

Within this circle, Parsons had written his Heidelberg dissertation on Weber, Sombart, and the problem of capitalism, so was well-versed in the debates in German scholarship. Wirth played a role primarily as an activist in professional circles and as a teacher, mentoring both Shils and later Reinhard Bendix. Knight's interest in matters Weberian reached its apogee in the mid-1930s, but then declined as he turned more attention to disputes in economic theory, and after a parting of the ways with Parsons in 1940, his presence became less significant. Schelting was affiliated briefly with Howard Becker at the University of Wisconsin, and then settled into the Columbia University faculty. Among these scholars, it was particularly Parsons and Shils who continued to carry the Weber torch to the end of their lives.

The second notable cluster, essential for the work of translation, formed around Hans Gerth, who arrived at the University of Wisconsin in 1940. Assisted by his association earlier with Karl Mannheim in Heidelberg and Frankfurt, then in exile in London, Gerth was befriended by both Parsons and Shils, arriving in the United States first in December 1937 for the American Sociological Society annual meeting in Atlantic City, New Jersey, for what has been called "refugee conversations." Gerth brought with him a wealth of knowledge about social thought that included involvement with the Mannheim circle, a year studying with Harold Laski at the London School of Economics, and engagement with Theodor Adorno, Max Horkheimer, and others at the Institut für Sozialforschung in Frankfurt. After some temporary lectureships, arranged in part with Shils's assistance, Gerth attracted the attention of Howard Becker and arrived in Madison, Wisconsin, with the unfortunate and ambiguous legal status of "enemy alien." His brilliant idiosyncrasies and learning quickly attracted the attention of two ambitious sociology graduate students, C. Wright Mills and Don Martindale. As Martindale recalls the encounter,

> During the lecture the majority of students had experienced a mixture of bewilderment and frustration. They sat with notebooks open and pens poised, realizing the something momentous was happening but unable to find a beginning or a stopping place—some had been unable to take a single note. During the lecture a powerfully built young man sitting near me, however, had no trouble. He watched the lecturer with bright, hard, appraising eyes and, though never missing a word or gesture, was taking quick careful notes. On the way out of class we found ourselves side by side. I observed, "That was the most extraordinary performance I have ever seen." "Gerth," [Mills] replied, "is the only man worth listening to in this department."

This episode prefigured the pattern and the roles played by each member of this dynamic threesome that evolved into two unusual and productive partnerships. Subsequently, after a brief stint at the University of Maryland, Mills moved on to Columbia with Robert Merton and Theodore Abel as colleagues, while Martindale had a lengthy career at the University of Minnesota.

The third, more loosely knit group one should mention is the émigré scholars of the 1930s—particularly those in New York affiliated with the New School for Social Research, such as Emil Lederer, Albert Salomon, or Hannah Arendt, where Weber's work was widely cited and discussed. There is inevitably some overlap with these émigré scholars and the previously identified clusters, most obviously in the case of Hans Gerth. It was generally the case that as late arrivals these intellectuals were also more marginal to the social science disciplines, not having had American roots or strong institutional and professional connections in the United States. They were also quite widely dispersed, especially through the state university systems—for example, Paul Honigsheim at Michigan State, Arthur Salz at Ohio State, Eric Voegelin at Louisiana State and the University of Alabama, and Karl Loewenstein at the University of Massachusetts. However, some were recruited later to prestigious locations, such as Franz Neumann to Columbia University or Leo Lowenthal to the University of California–Berkeley. Notwithstanding their dispersion and relative marginality, these scholars still served the purpose of spreading knowledge of Weber's work more widely than would have been the case otherwise, particularly among the regional public universities.

As one might anticipate, patterns of cooperation and competition relating to Weber and his work began to take shape within this network and its three main clusters of ambitious scholars. There was some sharing of knowledge and texts, but also interpretative disagreement and competition over access to texts, with mastery of the German language as a mechanism of control and a source of disagreement and criticism. There were also "priority" disputes, typical of the sciences, and rivalries over informal "rights" to translations. The situation involving both cooperation and competition was rendered more complex by the fact that knowledge of Weber and translation of his work proceeded at two distinct levels: at the level of the publicly accessible discourse over his thought, fed by published, copyrighted work; and at the level of privately or semipublicly produced texts and knowledge about Weber, accessible to select audiences and giving rise to a kind of hidden or "fugitive" literature.

There is only one notable outlier and exception among these clusters: Lowell Bennion, a man who is scarcely remembered, though he corresponded with Becker and Schelting, and Parsons knew his work. Bennion had studied with Eric Voegelin in Vienna, the context for his first encounter with Weber's work. In 1933 he published the first book on Max Weber in English, *Max Weber's Methodology*, a well-informed discussion of the subject written as a dissertation under Maurice Halbwachs at the Université de Strasbourg, the man who helped introduce Weber in France. Returning to the United States, Bennion sought an academic home in sociology and failing to find one in the years of the Depression, instead took up an administrative position in the Mormon Church, where he sought to reform and liberalize its practices in the spirit, as he saw it, of Weber's rectitude and defense of the individual against authoritarian control. Resigning finally in disappointment, Bennion resurfaced in the 1960s at the University of Utah and for a decade returned to his first love, annually teaching a well-received Weber seminar that exercised a grip on the imagination of a new generation of students. Remarkable in its own terms, Bennion's intellectual journey illustrates the larger point about the scholarly networks: it evokes the pattern of engagement that characterized the entire generation of scholars which emerged in the late 1920s and '30s.

Translation History

These generalizations are illustrated by the record of publication. Over slightly more than three decades leading up to 1960, eleven major texts by Max Weber had been translated into English, all by six scholars at the center of these networks: Knight, Parsons, Shils, Gerth, Mills, and Martindale—one economist

TABLE 1
Max Weber's Work in English Translation: The Main Publications, 1927–58

Year	Title	Translator(s)
1927	*General Economic History*	Frank Knight
1930	*The Protestant Ethic and the Spirit of Capitalism* (GARS 1:1–206)	Talcott Parsons
1946	*From Max Weber: Essays in Sociology*	Hans Gerth and C. Wright Mills
1947	*The Theory of Social and Economic Organization* (EaS, part 1, chaps. 1–4)	A. M. Henderson and Talcott Parsons
1949	*The Methodology of the Social Sciences* (GAW, 146–290, 451–502)	Edward Shils and Henry Finch
1951	*The Religion of China: Confucianism and Taoism* (GARS 1:276–536)	Hans Gerth
1952	*Ancient Judaism* (GARS 3)	Hans Gerth and Don Martindale
1954	*On Law in Economy and Society* (EaS, part 2, chap. 8)	Max Rheinstein and Edward Shils
1958	*The Religion of India* (GARS 2)	Hans Gerth and Don Martindale
1958	*The City* (EaS, part 2, chap. 16)	Don Martindale and Gertrud Neuwirth
1958	*The Rational and Social Foundations of Music*	Don Martindale, Johannes Riedel, and Gertrud Neuwirth

and five sociologists—only occasionally with assistance from other specialists (see table 1).

A few shorter Weber texts were also available, published separately as articles or chapters: "Class, Status and Party" and selections on bureaucracy and charisma from *Economy and Society*, and "The Hindu Social System" from Weber's sociology of religion. These translations meant that after more than three decades, the English-language readership could devour all of Max Weber's *Gesammelte Aufsätze zur Religionssoziologie* (Collected Essays in the Sociology of Religion); some sections of *Wirtschaft und Gesellschaft* (Economy and Society); major portions of *Gesammelte Aufsätze zur Wissenschaftslehre* (Collected Essays in the Philosophy of Science); and a few miscellaneous texts, such as the two essential lectures "Science as a Vocation" and "Politics as a Vocation" and, of course, Knight's version of *Wirtschaftsgeschichte* (General Economic History), though without Weber's conceptual introduction. These texts appeared without a clear understanding of the sequence and context of the work, a fact bemoaned by the translator-authors themselves, and a regrettable source of confusion that persists to this day, especially for the sociology of religion.

TABLE 2

Early Translations of Weber's Work, in Typescript, Mimeograph, or Microform Format

Year	Title	Translator(s)
c. 1934–35	*"Objectivity in Social Science and Social Policy" (GAW, 146–214) *"The Meaning of Ethical Neutrality" (GAW, 451–502) "Critical Studies in the Logic of the Cultural Sciences" (GAW, 215–90) "Roscher and Knies" (GAW, 1–145) "Critique of Stammler" (GAW, 291–357) *"Science as a Vocation" (GAW, 524–55) *"Politics as a Vocation" (GPS, 493–548) "Socialism" (GASS, 492–518) "The Reichspraesident" (GPS, 486–89) *"Parties" (from EaS, part 2, chap. 3) *"Classes, Estates, Parties" (from EaS, part 2, chap. 9)	Edward Shils
c. 1935	"Sociology of the Press and Associations" (DGS 1910, in GASS, 431–49)	Everett Hughes
1937–38	*Economy and Society*, part 1, ch. 1 (Soziologische Grundbegriffe)	Alexander von Schelting and Camilla Kample; Edward Shils and Alexander von Schelting; Talcott Parsons
1938	*Sociology of Law* (EaS, part 2, chap. 8)	(Frank Knight), Edward Shils
1939	*Economy and Society*, part 1, chaps. 1–4	A. M. Henderson, Talcott Parsons
c. 1940	"Politics as a Vocation" (partial)	Gabriel Almond

*Texts introduced in 1939 at the University of Chicago as required reading in the second year (sophomore) required social science survey course.

The major project left unfinished by this first wave of translations was, of course, the complete text of *Economy and Society*, published in three volumes by Guenther Roth and Claus Wittich in 1968, based largely on the previous partial translations, including Parsons's influential version of part 1, *The Theory of Social and Economic Organization* (1947). The editors' lengthy introduction and the inclusion as an appendix of most of the wartime essay "Parliament and Government in a Reconstructed Germany" (1917) linked Weber's work to a larger intellectual and political context. What has occurred since then is a piecemeal filling in of the textual gaps: mainly Weber's dissertation on commercial partnerships in the Middle Ages, his essays on Russia, the debates over the "Protestant Ethic" thesis with Karl Fischer and Felix Rachfahl, his commentaries on the universities, the treatises on the stock and commodities exchanges, the lengthy handbook article on agrarian relations in antiquity, and the remaining essays on methodological issues in the social sciences that had been avoided by Edward Shils and Henry Finch. This outpouring may have lacked coordination and coherence, but it succeeded in extending and deepening the reach of Weber's ideas.

With regard to the early translations, the neat tabulation of activity is somewhat misleading, for the actual history of these translations and their availability is far more complex than it may appear. Following publication of Parsons's rendition of *The Protestant Ethic and the Spirit of Capitalism* in 1930, there were several efforts at translation over the next decade. By his own account, Shils began translating several texts, ending with a total of at least eleven, drawn mainly from the *Wissenschaftslehre* but including two selections from *Economy and Society* and three political writings (see table 2).

Recalling his motivations, Shils noted retrospectively,

> It is difficult for me to explain why I began to translate the essays from the *Wissenschaftslehre*. Perhaps I was just too lazy to do something more serious on my own. The truth is that I adored those writings. I could never understand why people said that Max Weber was an obscure and difficult writer, except for the treatment of *Sinn*—which I found, and still find, unsatisfactory! For the rest, his sentences were sometimes very strenuous to master, but once mastered, one felt one had solved a problem. It was gratifying to see the parts fall into place. . . .
>
> I had no particular reason to translate these writings of Max Weber. I had no arrangements or plans for publishing them; I just did them. (ESP)

Shils was not alone in his enthusiasm. Everett Hughes translated Weber's 1910 Deutsche Gesellschaft für Soziologie commentary on a sociology of the press and associations; Gabriel Almond, the political scientist, tried his hand at "Politics as a Vocation"; and several other people began translating parts of *Economy and Society*: Schelting teamed with Camilla Kample to work on the famous first chapter, then collaborated with Shils on the task, and their work was in turn passed along to Parsons at his request as he labored over the draft text produced by Alexander M. Henderson of the first two chapters. Most surprising of all, while on leave from teaching in 1938, Frank Knight had hired a graduate student to translate the sociology of law (*Rechtssoziologie*) chapter in *Economy and Society*, a rough copy transferred to Shils and later Max Rheinstein, professor in the University of Chicago law faculty, thus becoming the basis for the 1954 publication under the title *On Law in Economy and Society*.

How were these texts used? The record is not entirely clear, nor can we be certain that these were the only works that constituted a kind of subterranean shelter for Weber's writings. To cite two examples, in corresponding with Frank Knight, Marianne Weber noted that "a few years ago the pub-

lisher [Mohr/Siebeck] and I granted permission to an American to translate
the sociological categories section (Part I [of *Economy and Society*]). I wrote an
introduction for it, but the translator apparently couldn't find a publisher, and
the work never appeared" (March 13, 1937; FKP). According to Edith Hanke,
the Mohr/Siebeck Archiv reveals the mystery translator as the well-known
American sociologist George Simpson. Shils recalled that while serving as
Wirth's research assistant he lent copies of some of his own translations to an
unnamed friend, who proceeded to make additional copies and circulate them
among graduate students, alarming the ever-cautious Shils to the extent that
he recalled his translations!

Clearly there was growing interest in these materials when Knight taught
his seminar on the German text of *Economy and Society* in 1936, attended
by Shils and a handful of other Knight devotees, including at least some of
the time Milton Friedman, as Shils remembered. The seminar preparations
prompted Knight to ask Parsons about his further plans concerning Weber:

> [Melchoir] Palyi has just told me that you are definitely engaged in translating
> *Wirtschaft und Gesellschaft*. I had been meaning to write & learn what might be
> back of rumors. I'm putting a seminar through the work (as far as we get!) and
> have been thinking toward making the substance available in English in the best
> way, which I thought would not be by complete & close translation, anyway I'd
> like to know what your plans are and how far they are advanced, *especially* whether
> you now have any considerable part of it in MS and if we could get hold of this
> just to enable us to make faster progress. It would be helpful even if not in finished
> form and I could have copies made and possibly make suggestions on specifically
> economic problems. And in this connection, what about the essays on *Wissen-
> schaftslehre*? I have been "thinking" about doing something about some of those
> also. (April 13, 1936; TPP)

Palyi was mistaken about Parsons's scholarship at this stage; engagement
with *Wirtschaft und Gesellschaft* translations came three years later. Replying
to Parsons's disappointing response, Knight noted, "I had already tentatively
arranged with a couple of students to make rough translations of parts of it,
which I hope to have for use in my class in economic institutions" (May 1,
1936; TPP). Pursuing the pedagogic utility of the translations, Knight had
already taken the opportunity to identify one of his neophyte translators, noting, "there is a youngster here [Edward Shils] in sociology who is working on
a book of selections from Weber for a wider audience. Do you know about
him?" (April 13, 1936; TPP). Through this offhand query Talcott Parsons was
introduced to Edward Shils. Knight's mediation is also the earliest indication
of Shils's intentions well before his priority dispute with Gerth and Mills.

Notwithstanding his instinctive caution, Shils did circulate some translations among colleagues, including Hans Gerth. When the *Economy and Society* chapters became available, Parsons seems to have been generous, sharing

drafts and even a microfilm copy at least with Howard Becker, Robert Merton, and Eric Voegelin (not to mention Shils and Schelting, whose work he had used), all of whom appear to have provided access to students. Of these colleagues, Becker's position at the University of Wisconsin would have been especially useful for encouraging a new and important audience, beyond the established circles at Chicago and Harvard.

Clearly the most crucial development to emerge from these activities was the outcome at Chicago of the discussion of reforming the undergraduate social science curriculum in the college (the first two years of undergraduate education), advanced by the celebrated educator and the university's president, Robert Hutchins. Frank Knight had already engaged with this issue in 1936, remarking to Parsons that "the 'talk' hereabouts runs largely in terms of breaking down and bridging over the departmentalization of social science. It seems obvious to me that if the talkers mean anything of what they say, this matter of doing something about Max Weber to make his material available for students ought to be a leading item in the actual program" (May 1, 1936; TPP). Knight thought the climate was encouraging, with support coming from Robert Redfield, the anthropologist who then served as dean for social sciences. And indeed, three years later six Weber texts, translated by Shils and mimeographed for student use, became part of the general education curriculum for the required social sciences core course for sophomores.

The Chicago reforms were the first true "institutionalization" of Weber's thought in an American university. Given Chicago's prominence in American higher education, it served as a kind of model for subsequent instructional and curricular innovations. At the university itself the incorporation of Weber texts affected students like Reinhard Bendix, who as an undergraduate was reading Weber's original articles in the *Archiv für Sozialwissenschaft und Sozialpolitik*, and it provided a laboratory for instructors recruited to the college, among them Daniel Bell, Milton Singer, Morris Janowitz, and David Riesman.

Yet Max Weber's emergence as a thinker worthy of attention—worth translating, studying in graduate seminars, teaching in the undergraduate curriculum, citing in the public forum—was by no means a certainty in the American university and beyond. How did the emergence and growing prominence of Weber come about?

The Disciplines

To answer this question is like piecing together parts of a puzzle. When Max Weber's work began to attract attention in the mid-1920s, it was appropriately at the University of Chicago, home to one of the oldest sociology departments in the United States and to the world's oldest sociology journal, the

American Journal of Sociology. Before then, early American sociology in the Midwest had paid considerable attention not to Weber but to Georg Simmel. Albion Small, chair of the Chicago department, was responsible for translating and publishing nine of Simmel's essays in the *American Journal of Sociology* between 1896 and 1910. By contrast, the only major article of Weber's to appear in English before 1927 was his presentation to the Congress of Arts and Science in St. Louis, Missouri, in 1904, buried in the conference proceedings. We have learned only recently that two brief articles under Weber's name also appeared, in English, in the *Encyclopedia Americana* for 1907–8—minor essays that passed unnoticed for nearly a century. It is difficult to believe that Small, as an organizer of the St. Louis Congress and host to Weber and the other delegates from Europe who visited Chicago beforehand, would have missed Weber's work appearing at the time and afterward, such as the important essay on "Objectivity" or *The Protestant Ethic and the "Spirit" of Capitalism.* Nevertheless, no translation projects or committed readership emerged in these early decades.

The change in fortune for Weber's work had to do partly with the improved availability of his texts in German, thanks to the labors of Marianne Weber and others such as Oskar Siebeck and Melchoir Palyi. It also had to do in part with increasing interest at Chicago in the methodological foundations of social science and large-scale comparative work, an impatient reaction in some quarters to the parochialism and triviality of narrowly focused, unsystematic, and atheoretical observational reporting. In their retrospective assessments from the 1960s, both Hugh Duncan and Irving Louis Horowitz noted the earlier "rather parochial world of American social science," the dramatic postwar improvements due partly to the availability of inexpensive translations in social theory, and Weber's oppositional role as an alternative to mere localism and provincialism and as a "cosmopolitan" scholar who "sees things in grand world historic terms." This view was apparent earlier among the key figures at Chicago; in his 1926 review of modern German conceptions of sociology, for instance, Wirth maintained that Weber was the "best-known and certainly most quoted sociologist in Germany," citing with approval especially his work in the comparative sociology of religion and his efforts to advance the cause of science and to define the subject matter and methodology of sociological inquiry. Heeding his colleague's comment about Weber's "most quoted" status, the following year Knight published his translation of the *General Economic History,* based on the lecture notes published in 1923 by Hellmann and Palyi, whose preface he also translated.

Wirth, an immigrant himself as a teenager in 1911 and fluent in German, would certainly have followed developments on the Continent with interest, although his scholarly contributions were mainly to American urban studies and social policy. He also played an important role as a teacher, organizer and public figure of note. Knight, on the other hand, was a skilled economic theorist and critic of institutional economics, drawn to Weber because of his own eclectic interest in methodological issues, the social context of economic action, the uses and limits of analytic theoretical approaches for understanding *Homo economicus*, and the distinctiveness and origins of modern capitalism and the market economy. Though religiously "unmusical," as Weber said of himself, through his evangelical Christian upbringing Knight was also fascinated by religion and its socioeconomic effects. Weber must have seemed in some ways a kindred spirit. Knight was also a Germanist, having written his master's thesis at the University of Tennessee on Gerhart Hauptmann. With his excellent command of German, he translated the *General Economic History* on his own, consulting the economic historian A. P. Usher, his former teacher. Encouraged in the project by Allyn Young, his economics dissertation director at Harvard, Knight published the translation with the small firm of Greenberg in New York in its Adelphi economic series. Having this accomplishment to his name, Knight attracted Oskar Siebeck's attention as a possible translator for *The Protestant Ethic and the Spirit of Capitalism*, although he was never asked and was not interested in assuming responsibility for a second translation. When Parsons inquired about Knight's commitments, it was actually through Paul Douglas, Knight's Chicago economics colleague, an inquiry that led to more than a decade of fruitful exchanges between the two scholars.

Wirth's reference to Weber as a sociologist rather than an economist or economic historian was an important choice, for it reflected changes occurring at Chicago in the social science disciplines, and in particular the separation of sociology from economics, followed somewhat later by further differentiation between sociology and anthropology and between political science and history. The nascent interest in Weber's role in sociology, fueled by methodological concerns, was apparent in Theodore Abel's *Systematic Sociology in Germany* (1929). Indeed, the changes in the disciplines were felt generally in major American teaching and research universities by the late 1920s and early '30s. At Harvard, for example, we should remember that Talcott Parsons's first appointment was as a tutor in economics (1927–30) followed by an instructorship in sociology, which emerged as a new department from the Committee on Sociology and Social Ethics (only in 1931), amid a debate over whether it should be considered a social science discipline at all. The shift in disciplinary boundaries, in general more highly articulated in American universities compared with European institutions, permitted or even encouraged assimilating Weber's work to some newly emergent lines of inquiry.

In this period of transition within economics, and with economic history already ceding ground to economic theory, Weber's *General Economic History* might well have had a limited appeal. However, these late lectures did contribute to the contemporary discussion of capitalism and the kind of "rationality" associated with capital accumulation and market exchange. Thus, in his article comparing Sombart and Weber on "modern capitalism," a brief treatment of the same topic as Parsons's dissertation, Knight underscored the significance of the discovery by these two economists of what he labeled "*quantitative rationality* as a phase of the modern social mind," a concept more commonly discussed today by Jürgen Habermas and others as "instrumental" rationality. Briefly reviewing the "Protestant ethic" debate, Knight summed up his assessment of Weber's importance:

> Whatever one may think of his Puritanism theory, there is surely one respect in which Max Weber towers above all the other writers noticed; he is the only one who really deals with the problem of causes, or approaches the material from that angle which alone can yield an answer to such questions, that is, the angle of comparative history in the broad sense. It seems to the writer that the question of the origin of capitalism would gain by being stated in negative form: why did capitalism *not* develop (in the sense in which it did not) in other times and places than modern Western Europe? Especially, why was there no development comparable to that of modern times in the classical and ancient civilizations? Max Weber discusses these questions. His *General Economic History* is a mere sketch, available only in an editorial patchwork from students' lecture notes, but in this fundamental regard it stands in a class by itself.

It was in the spirit enunciated by Knight that Weber was read at the time as an economist and economic historian.

Even as an economist, however, Knight later taught his Weber seminar not on topics in economic history and the nature and origins of capitalism but on *Economy and Society*. By then the perspective had shifted, and it was the "interdisciplinary" Weber bridging the social science disciplines who now attracted attention.

Described by Shils as a close analysis of the text, Knight's 1936 seminar became an intense intellectual engagement and for an enthusiast like Shils a powerful formative experience:

> We read a fair amount of *Wirtschaft und Gesellschaft*, line by line, commenting on it as we went along, raising questions about it, trying to understand the text. It was a serious intellectual experience. In its way, the seminar was almost as intense as the discussions about *Wirtschaft und Gesellschaft* which von Schelting and I had some years later in New York when we scrutinized that first chapter. In a very important respect it was much better because Frank Knight repeatedly made very profound observations about matters which Weber's text called to his mind. Sometimes, too, he would break out in his old-fashioned rustic wonderment with, "That's mighty fine stuff." (Undated, ESP)

It was this particular seminar encounter, reading Weber through Knight's eyes, that provoked Shils's important and revealing later self-reflection. "I was overpowered when the perspectives opened up by Weber's concepts brought together things which hitherto had never seemed to me to have any affinity with each other," he commented. "I could not assimilate it all or bring it into a satisfying order. But reading Max Weber was literally breathtaking. Sometimes, in the midst of reading him I had to stand up and walk around for a minute or two until my exhilaration died down." Precisely this kind of *experience* in reading Weber's work far from its point of origin—in Chicago or elsewhere, in German and then as part of an English-language discourse—is essential to understanding the fascination with Weber, the effect on his readers, and the character of his American reception. The same intense response appears repeatedly, best exemplified in Knight, Shils, and Parsons.

The experience of reading transcended the pedagogical debates over the uses of the work and the disputes over disciplinary boundaries. Immersion in Weber's writings set off the kind of intellectual enthusiasm that led to sustained engagement, encouraging a movement of thought beyond routine inquiry and parochial perspectives and satisfying the thirst for large questions and unanticipated and novel connections. The work seemed to offer something for a wide range of readers—the economist, sociologist, historian, political scientist, anthropologist, classicist, or methodologist. Multivalent and open-textured, it refused to conform to a standard disciplinary nomenclature. But more than that, in Shils's telling the work was overwhelming and disorienting, yet exhilarating and compelling. It promised intellectual emancipation. Like the New World itself, it opened onto new possibilities for the journey of the intellect.

TWELVE

THE CREATION OF THE SACRED TEXT

Of all of Max Weber's texts, one stands alone for its special significance as an expression of his originality and as the basis for his reputation: *The Protestant Ethic and the Spirit of Capitalism* (hereafter in this chapter *PESC*), a truly canonical book that has been called sociology's "most famous" work, published in 1930 with Talcott Parsons as the translator. It was the second of Weber's works to appear in English, following Knight's translation of *General Economic History*, and the two were the only translated texts widely available until the postwar cascade of translations, beginning with the selection of writings translated and edited by Hans Gerth and C. Wright Mills, *From Max Weber: Essays in Sociology*. *PESC* not only appeared early but achieved impressive longevity: for seventy-two years the version attributed to Parsons reigned as the sole authority for the Anglophone world. The situation changed only with the publication of new translations by Peter Baehr and Gordon Wells, based on Weber's original *Archiv für Sozialwissenschaft und Sozialpolitik* essays of 1904–5, and by Stephen Kalberg, using Weber's 1920 revised text, favored by Parsons.

Translation is a risky affair, as devotees of poetry, narrative fiction, and social theory well know. As Vladimir Nabokov once wrote in "On Translating *Eugene Onegin*":

> O, Pushkin, for my stratagem:
> I traveled down your secret stem
> And reached the root, and fed upon it;
> Then, in a language newly learned,
> I grew another stalk and turned
> Your stanza, patterned on a sonnet,
> Into my honest roadside prose—
> All thorn, but cousin to your rose.

As someone has remarked, all translations are in some measure a violation and distortion of the original; if we want to know what an author *really* meant to say then we must read the original work, remove the pain of the thorn for the pleasure of the rose. But the discussion and dissemination of ideas would be a slow and uninspired labor if we were to follow such advice slavishly. Translations, however imperfect, are an indispensable aid to communicating knowledge, even if they may contribute to creative misinterpretation.

Indeed, *mis*interpretations just as much as allegedly faithful readings have always played a role in the reception of an author's work, the development of a reputation, and the advancement of ideas.

Nowhere among Weber's writings has the disputation over translation been more sharply joined than with *PESC*—centered, of course, on the text's alter ego: the young Talcott Parsons. Acknowledgment of Parsons's accomplishment, combined in varying degrees of generosity with reservations and complaints about his translation, have been commonplace for some time. Revisionist readings have been encouraged as well by reactions against the "Parsonizing" of Weber that began with *The Structure of Social Action* (1937), written with the unfortunate guidance of Alexander von Schelting's methodological critique of Weber. These matters have been given greater urgency recently as the work of translation has expanded in new directions and to new circles of scholars having interests rather different from those of Parsons and his generation. In sum, though the issues of translation will always defy consensus there is surely agreement, citing recent representative judgments, that this first translation of the most famous sociological investigation "has been enormously influential in the reception of Weber's work in the English-speaking world," even though today "most scholars accept that Parsons's translation is seriously defective." The presence of a text that is both influential and defective, widely authoritative and deeply flawed, should in itself provoke curiosity and demands for an explanation. How could such a situation come about?

The story of the first translation and publication of *PESC* is a chapter in the sociology of knowledge or, more specifically, the politics and sociology of Weber translations, an unusually complicated episode. The history of the translation provides a lesson in the social construction of a text, and equally important, a precise answer to the questions that are central to any general sociology of translation: Who translated the work, and why? When, and where? As we shall see, the text we know as *PESC* is a product, to be sure, of intellectual decisions Parsons arrived at as translator, but it is also significantly the result of social forces and relationships at work at the time. Indeed, strictly speaking, it is not actually Parsons's intended translation tout court, but his proposed text as influenced by social circumstances and modified by editorial fiat and "correction." The effect of these circumstances and modifications was to create an English-language Weber text that from a contemporary perspective was less satisfactory than Parsons's original. Thus, some (though not all) of the criticism of Parsons has been misdirected. Those aspects of the translation regarded as "unsatisfactory" today had to do, in part, with a context and relationships beyond the control of the designated translator. Ironically, aspects of the subsequent criticism only echo some of Parsons's own concerns and criticisms at the time he struggled with the challenges of producing a reliable and readable manuscript.

An American in Heidelberg

Talcott Parsons's effort to translate Weber's work in the sociology of religion dates from late 1926 and began in earnest early in 1927, as he was writing his dissertation while on a temporary year appointment in economics at Amherst College, his undergraduate alma mater. It ended three years later, following extended negotiations and complications, with the publication of the text in London and New York.

For the young Talcott Parsons in 1920s, whether as a student in London or Heidelberg, or as a young instructor at Amherst College or Harvard University, the problem was, in a word, *capitalism*. It was not a problem unique to his perceptions, needless to say, but one that was widely shared by many others, including Frank Knight and Allyn Young, among leading economists. Parsons's own encounter with Weber on this multifaceted "problem" came about as it did entirely as a matter of chance. Having graduated from Amherst and spent a year at the London School of Economics, attending lectures by R. H. Tawney, Morris Ginsberg, L. T. Hobhouse, and Bronislaw Malinowski, he was fortunate to receive a fellowship in a new post–World War I exchange program with Germany for the 1925–26 academic year and was simply assigned to the University of Heidelberg, having no say in the matter and knowing little about the faculty. As he acknowledged later, "I had never heard Weber's name mentioned during the whole year I was in London, but he still was clearly the dominant figure at Heidelberg and I got extraordinarily interested in him very fast." Though Tawney was working on *Religion and the Rise of Capitalism*, he apparently had avoided any discussion of Weber's work in his lectures. Thus, in Parsons's words, "the decisive turning point for me was going to Germany and falling under the aegis of Weber. If I had gone to either Columbia or Chicago in the late 1920s, I don't think I would have absorbed Weber, at least not for another ten or fifteen years. Among other things, I wouldn't have known German well enough to read Weber in German, and the translations would not have begun coming out for quite a while."

Arriving in Heidelberg in the fall after language preparation in Vienna, not having read Max Weber's work before, Parsons was thrown into courses with Alfred Weber, Karl Jaspers (on Immanuel Kant), and Karl Mannheim, who was teaching a seminar on Weber. During the year he also studied with the two economists, Emil Lederer and Edgar Salin, eventually choosing the latter as his major advisor for a dissertation on the concept of "capitalism," a degree opportunity he had not even imagined during his first months in residence. Advised early on by Arnold Bergstraesser, he immediately got the point that Weber was the person to read.

Parsons began reading Weber when the university semester began, first during long hours in the library. But he quickly purchased the first edition of *Wirtschaft und Gesellschaft* (1922), the *Gesammelte Aufsätze zur Wissen-schaftslehre* (1922), and at least the first volume of the *Gesammelte Aufsätze zur Religionssoziologie* (also the 1922 printing). The marginalia and extensive underlining in these books and his notes from the period suggest that Parsons was a voracious and careful reader, devouring the Weber texts and establishing the direction for his early labors if not his entire career. As he later commented, through such texts a spiritually present Weber "served, in a very real sense, as my teacher." Like Edward Shils, he carried with him a vivid memory of this initial encounter, writing, "I don't think it was mere chance that the first of Weber's works which I read was his study, *The Protestant Ethic and the Spirit of Capitalism*. I don't know how surprising it will be for others, however, that this reading had an immediate and powerful impact on me. It gripped my intense interest immediately and I read it straight through—that is, subject to the limits of library hours, since I did not yet own a copy—*as if it were a detective story*." Whose footprints and which clues was Parsons following? In his personal copy, among the copious marginalia that he wrote, one in particular points to the answer—a simple "Uncle Frank" that he scribbled alongside a sentence Weber quoted from Benjamin Franklin's *Advice to a Young Tradesman*, which Parsons had underlined: "Neben Fleiß und Mäßigkeit trägt nichts so sehr dazu bei, einen jungen Mann in der Welt *vorwärts zu bringen*, als Punktlichkeit und Gerechtigkeit bei allen seinen Geschäften," or, in his later original typescript translation, "After industry and frugality, nothing contributes more to the *raising of a young man in the world* than punctuality and justice in all his dealings." (Parenthetically, he reproduced Weber's italics, inserting a note that they were Weber's emphasis, not Franklin's; but the published text, as occurred throughout, eliminated the italics and the footnote, following the editorial recommendations of Tawney.) Immersed in the text, Parsons was now on the trail of the people he knew, their ethos, their moral personalities, himself among them. The author's message to his detective-reader should have been *de te narratur fabula* (this story is about you), a line Weber actually did use elsewhere. The cultural significance of the "Protestant ethic" and the "spirit of capitalism" for Americans like Parsons, this retelling of the most compelling narrative of the founding of "America" and its moral order, its "habits of the heart" in Alexis de Tocqueville's words, is one of the essential clues to understanding the Weber phenomenon in the United States.

For Parsons what emerged from this extraordinarily productive year, most obviously, was the D. Phil. dissertation under Salin, defended on a return to Heidelberg the following year on July 29, 1927 (though awarded only in April 1929), and the publication soon afterward of its third chapter in two parts, "'Capitalism' in Recent German Literature," in the *Journal of Political Economy*, edited at the University of Chicago. But the foundation for translating Weber and working toward *The Structure of Social Action* (1937) was laid in

Heidelberg as well. The proposal to translate Weber actually surfaced in late 1926 or early 1927, before Parsons had completed his dissertation, with the stimulus coming not from a publisher but from professor Harry Elmer Barnes, the sociologist-historian then at Smith College and later on the New School for Social Research faculty. Parsons's serious interest in the idea was first expressed in an informative handwritten letter he sent to Marianne Weber (whom he knew already from the year in Heidelberg) that contained a courteous and important request for support—one he was to repeat seven months later. He wrote in German in April 1927 (undated):

Sehr verehrte Frau Professor:

Vor mehreren Monaten ist mir vorgeschlagen worden etwas von Max Weber ins Englische zu übersetzen. Der Vorschlag war mir ausserordentlich angenehm und ich habe Verhandlungen mit verschiedenen Leuten darüber aufgenommen.

Eine Reihe von Büchern wird jetzt herausgegeben unter dem Titel "History of Civilization Series" die in England vom Verlag Kegan, Paul & Co. Ltd, London, und in den Vereinigten Staaten vom Verlag Alfred Knopf, New York publiziert wird. Man schlägt vor die "Protestantische Ethik" von Max Weber mit der "Vorbemerkung" und wahrscheinlich auch dem Aufsatz "Die protestantischen Sekten usw", d.h. die ersten 236 Seiten vom Band I der Religionssoziologie darin als ein Band für sich erscheinen zu lassen.

Neulich habe ich mit dem Redakteur der Reihe, Mr. C. K. Ogden und auch mit dem Verlagshaus Knopf gesprochen und beide haben dem Vorschlag genehmigt. Jetzt hängt alles davon ab wie die Sache von deutscher Seite angesehen wird.

Hätten Sie gerne dass diese Arbeit Max Webers im Englischen erscheinen solle? Ich weiss nicht ob ich genügend in der Arbeit Max Webers und in der deutschen Sprache eingewachsen bin um der Aufgabe gewachsen zu sein. Trotzdem werde ich mein Bestes tun da ich glaube dass gerade diese Schrift für uns in Amerika von ausserordentlicher Wichtigkeit ist und viel weiter bekannt zu werden verdient.

Die Angelegenheit der Übersetzungsrechte bleibt, wie ich verstehe, in den Händen der Englischen Firma, Kegan Paul. Sie ist bereit die üblichen Betrag für die Rechte eines wissenschaftlichen Werkes, etwa $100 zu bezahlen. Mehr können Sie nicht leisten da dies ja keine kommerzielle Unternehmung ist. Glauben Sie dass der Verlag Mohr damit einverstanden sein wird? Und wenn Sie die Übersetzung gern sehen würden könnten Sie vielleicht so freundlich sein ein Wort an den Verlag zu schreiben? Ich glaube es würde die Verhandlungen sehr erleichtern.

Mit vorzüglicher Hochachtung

Ihr Ergebener, Talcott Parsons

[Several months ago it was proposed to me to translate something from Max Weber into English. The proposal was extremely attractive to me and I started negotiations with several people. A series of books with the title "History of Civilization Series" will be published now in England by Kegan, Paul & Co. Ltd, London, and in the United States by Alfred Knopf, New York. They are proposing to print as a single volume Max Weber's "Protestant Ethic" with the "Introduction" and probably also the essay "The Protestant Sects etc," i.e. the first 236 pages of volume 1 of the Sociology of Religion. Recently I have spoken with the series editor, Mr C. K. Ogden, and also with Knopf Publishers, and both have approved the proposal. Now everything depends on how the matter will be viewed from the German side. Would you like to see this work of Max Weber appear in English? I do not know whether I am sufficiently well-versed in Max Weber's work and the German language to be equal to the task. Nevertheless I will do my best, as I believe that precisely this text is extraordinarily important for us in America and deserves to be more widely known. The matter of translation rights remains, as I understand, in the hands of the English firm, Kegan Paul. The firm is prepared to pay the amount of about $100 for the rights to a scientific work. More than that is not possible, as this is not a commercial undertaking. Do you think that Mohr Publishers will agree to this? And if you would like to see the translation appear, would you perhaps be good enough to send a supportive note to the publisher? I believe it would make the negotiations a lot easier.] (TPP)

Parsons threw himself into this project with enthusiasm and determination, speaking with Ogden, who was then in the United States, and with Paul B. Thomas at Knopf. He already sensed that difficulties might arise and therefore enlisted Marianne Weber's assistance, perhaps with the knowledge that earlier in 1922 a proposal from Routledge had foundered on the Siebeck/Mohr preference for an English-language edition of all *three* volumes of the *Religionssoziologie*. The other obvious weakness was his status and bona fides: barely out of graduate study in 1927 at the age of twenty-four, an unknown and very junior scholar, not a published word to his name, without a doctoral degree, without permanent university employment. Under the circumstances it is remarkable he was considered at all! And in fact, at first he barely was, and even to the very end other unnamed "expert translators" were invited by the publishers to intervene and evaluate his work.

For her part, when Parsons informed her, Marianne Weber was interested in moving the project forward, inviting him to Sunday afternoon tea when he arrived in Heidelberg that summer to complete and defend the dissertation. Their meeting occurred on June 26, 1927, and it led Parsons to a follow-up conversation with Oskar Siebeck, who reportedly "had a very good impression of him" (August 22, 1927; VAMS). Both Marianne Weber and Oskar Siebeck were committed to finding the best possible translator, with Marianne especially concerned about using someone unschooled in the sociology of religion discussions and fretting over the dismal experience of her friend Marie Luise Gothein, whose book A *History of Garden Art* had been mangled in translation. Siebeck considered himself not only a representative of the firm but also an advocate for Marianne Weber's editorial and financial interests. Parsons quickly became Marianne's candidate and her support was strong and consistent; indeed, she spoke of him with great warmth to the end of her life in 1954. What they shared throughout decades of contact and friendship, interrupted only by the war, was the love for Max Weber and his work. Without this special relationship—without Parsons's stubborn dedication and Marianne Weber's unwavering support, accepted by Siebeck—it is highly improbable the translation would have appeared at all, and certainly not when it did.

Parsons Translates *The Protestant Ethic and the Spirit of Capitalism*

Aside from the obvious matters of the choice of a translator, legal rights, and financial terms, the questions raised for translating the text that came to be known as *The Protestant Ethic and the Spirit of Capitalism* were set very early: Which text or texts would be translated? Who would write the introduction, and what kind of introduction to the work and the author would it be? Who would have overall editorial control? The publication rights had to be negotiated with English and American firms: Kegan Paul and Allen and Unwin in London, Alfred A. Knopf in New York, and eventually, at the very end, Charles Scribner's Sons in New York. The first three publishing houses figured in the discussions with Mohr/Siebeck from the very beginning. Among the editors from these firms, it is important to note that Oskar Siebeck had close ties only with Stanley Unwin, a factor that turned out to be decisive.

As for the text itself, Siebeck had for some time favored translating all three volumes of Weber's *Religionssoziologie* and, interesting enough, Parsons agreed with him on scholarly grounds, commenting later to Frank Knight, "The Protestant Ethic is quite impossible to understand apart from its place in the wider framework" of Weber's *Religionssoziologie*, a view he always held and repeated over the years (June 5, 1936; TPP). From his standpoint, the more of the three volumes one could translate, the better. But repeated attempts to convince Kegan Paul and Knopf ended in failure, marked finally in the summer of 1927 by an apparent agreement on a reduced format of *Gesammelte Aufsätze zur Religionssoziologie* (hereafter, GARS) volumes 1 and 2 in Kegan Paul's series, the publication outlet favored initially by Harry Barnes and proposed to C. K. Ogden, the series editor, now back in London: "We shall be willing to publish in English translation (with the American market) at least the equivalent of the two volumes out of the three volumes of Max Weber's 'Gesammelte Aufsätze zur Religionssoziologie' in the History of Civilization Series on the terms you name," read the press's communication to Siebeck (July 26, 1927; VAMS).

A series of tortured negotiations through the rest of the year led to the collapse of this apparent agreement. The reasons for the failure are difficult to fathom, as the parties were not far apart. The correspondence among Parsons,

Ogden, Thomas, Siebeck, and Marianne Weber suggests there was a clash between "material" commercial and "ideal" academic interests, and an irresolv-
able dispute over the ownership of translation rights. The correspondence also
suggests that the politics of interwar publishing played a role, with a certain
amount of suspicion, obfuscation, and "buck passing" among the English and
American firms. Caution was combined with scarcely concealed hostility concerning the translation of European authors, especially German and French
ones—a legacy of World War I. Explaining the situation to Parsons, Ogden
once remarked that "it is impossible to pay more for a German book than an
English one as we do at present, except on a non-commercial basis ('in order
to have some of these foreigners')" (June 23, 1927; TPP)! Misgivings persisted
about using an American translator. To make matters worse, Ogden eventually concluded that Siebeck was a "hopeless" negotiating partner, provoking
Parsons's defense of the publisher with "I still think that he [Oskar Siebeck]
is right on that [not publishing "The Protestant Ethic" alone in translation]. I
do think that the work as a whole is essentially a unit, and that for the proper
understanding of Weber's work it would be too bad to break it up. Also I think
that it would prove to be popular and that when the one part became known
there would be a considerable demand for the rest. Around here people are
talking about it a good deal and I think it would be widely read" (November
12, 1927; TPP). It is true that Oskar Siebeck made every effort to negotiate
the most favorable terms, partially to protect Marianne Weber's financial interests during this period of economic uncertainty. While in the process he
may have sacrificed some good will, there is no evidence that he was incapable
of reaching a reasonable agreement. In the end he did exactly that, acceding
to terms with Stanley Unwin at Allen and Unwin close to those initially proposed by Ogden at Kegan Paul, with one key exception: the decision concerning *what* to translate.

This failure and the backtracking by Kegan Paul and Knopf could have terminated the entire project. Instead, Parsons persisted, urging that the proposed
translation be scaled back to *GARS* volume 1 (1–275): the Vorbemerkung, or
prefatory remarks, from 1920; the "Protestant Ethic" essays; the essay on the
Protestant sects; and the Einleitung, or introduction, to the subsequent series
of essays on the world religions. But the Einleitung was eventually dropped,
and then the essay on the sects—a process of textual "downsizing" under editorial pressure that left what we now have. Even retaining the Vorbemerkung
required a special defense. With Marianne Weber arguing the case, and Oskar
Siebeck using his relationship with Stanley Unwin to advantage, finally in
September 1928—nearly two years after the idea surfaced—Parsons submitted
a rough draft (or as the publisher called it, a "specimen" or "sample translation") of the first "Protestant Ethic" essay (*GARS* 1:17–62) to Allen and
Unwin in London. He explained that he was aiming for what we could call a

"semantic" translation, urging that the unavoidable problems of textual meaning and the work's larger significance be addressed in a critical introdution:

> In general I have tried to be faithful to the text rather than to present a work of art as far as English style is concerned. It would be impossible to do anything else without almost completely recasting the whole manner of exposition. . . . It also seems to me it would be very undesirable to have the thing published without a critical introduction which set forth its significance for Weber's sociological work as a whole and Weber's place in the social thought of Germany. In Germany itself it has been very gravely misunderstood, and I fear that without such a safeguard the same process would be repeated for English readers. (September 24, 1928; TPP)

Because of R. H. Tawney's reputation and following, assisted by the publication in 1926 of his Holland Memorial Lectures as *Religion and the Rise of Capitalism*, Stanley Unwin had from the beginning viewed him as the best choice for the introduction or foreword, urging Siebeck that Tawney's presence "should help materially in securing an adequate reception for the book both in the press and scholastic circles" (July 22, 1927; VAMS). So the nod went to Tawney, who unfortunately appears not to have kept abreast of developments in German scholarship. His exchange of letters with Unwin and Siebeck in 1930, for example, shows that he was entirely unaware of Marianne Weber's major biography of her husband published in 1926.

Furthermore, Tawney paid little attention to Weber's actual arguments, with his own interests ascendant instead in the uninspired and modest fourteen-page foreword that he did produce at the last minute, delaying publication of the translation while Stanley Unwin waited impatiently for his introductory comments. Indeed, Tawney appears to have been slow to grasp Weber's significance, with his most incisive commentary on Weber coming not in the foreword to Parsons's translation of *PESC* but in the 1937 preface to the second edition of his own book. This outcome confirmed Parsons's fears about the consequences of not publishing a critical introduction. As Lutz Kaelber, a skilled translator, has noted, "Tawney's misrepresentations set a precedent for careless reading of Weber's work among sociologists and scholars in neighboring disciplines alike, especially until other writings by Weber became available in English translations and Tawney's foreword became replaced with one that actually presented Weber's argument in its strengths and weaknesses and addressed the argument's contexts."

Notwithstanding the completion of a first installment, the nourishment and birth of Parsons's complete translation was still far from assured. Stanley Unwin had initially consulted Tawney about a suitable translator, had ruled out Frank Knight, whose translation of the *General Economic History* he had agreed to distribute in Britain, and then wondered about other possible "expert" translators. Despite his favorable impression of Knight's achievement, "It is *not* our intention," Unwin had written Siebeck, "to turn to America for a translator of 'Die Protestantische Ethik'" (July 25, 1927; VAMS). Nevertheless, that is what occurred. But Unwin never reconciled himself to Marianne Weber's choice of Parsons, as becomes evident through the continuous exchange of questioning and complaints, as if to remind her and Oskar Siebeck of the risk of acceding to her wishes and his generosity in doing so. As late as the end of October 1929, Unwin accompanied Tawney's report on the translation to Siebeck with an affirmation of its purpose—namely, "to show you some of the difficulties with which you have presented us by insisting upon an American translator. It bears out our repeated experience, viz. that a knowledge of the technique of translation is necessary as well as a knowledge of the subject and a mastery of the language. We shall no doubt eventually pull through, but we think you will now more readily understand our reluctance to employ translator[s] of whose work we have no previous experience" (October 29, 1929; VAMS). Parsons must have sensed the doubts and tensions, as he took the highly unusual step of having his friend and London School of Economics compatriot, the economist Arthur R. Burns, appear at the Allen and Unwin offices to check on the situation while vacationing in England. Burns provided some measure of reassurance, although he acknowledged to Parsons having been quizzed about his friend's reputation and accomplishments. On his side, to protect editorial discretion, Unwin recruited R. H. Tawney as the final arbiter of any disputes that might arise, actually writing that provision into the contract Parsons signed, and in addition reserving the right to revise the text at the translator's expense.

Parsons's "sample translation" in typescript was in reality a test of his merits. It was read by at least six people: three unidentified in-house readers for Allen and Unwin, plus Stanley Unwin himself, Oskar Siebeck, and, most surprising, Marianne Weber. The publishers' response was at best grudging acceptance of a rough draft badly in need of revision, at worst a challenge to the entire enterprise. A translator with less fortitude and thinner skin might have walked away at this point. Marianne Weber's reply to Siebeck (forwarded to Unwin) revealed her own frustration, which must have been matched by that of Parsons:

> It is very difficult for me to judge Parsons's translation, as I read it with a feel for the German rather than the English language. For me it is thoroughly readable and stylistically acceptable, and in any case it should be considered a basis for revision. In a number of places better formulations might be found, but doubtless only with a translator who is at home in history and political economy. I notice immediately on p. 1 of section 2 a question mark about the concept "historical individual." The German word "historisches Individuum" is a familiar philosophical concept in Germany, given its character by H. Rickert, that in my view cannot

be translated differently. But if Parsons's text is not understandable to readers of English, then in my opinion we must authorize the English firm to have it revised, to be sure by someone schooled in the science who takes on the task of remaining as true to the content as possible. Of course it is the concentrated content of the sentences that produces such difficulties (1) of understanding and (2) of translation. (November 26, 1928; VAMS).

Such questioning of standard conceptual language says a great deal about the level of complaint concerning the quality of Parsons's work. But Unwin had made his point and agreed to proceed, though with the insertion of Tawney for protection.

When the completed translation arrived at the offices of Allen and Unwin in mid-1929, criticism resumed, of course. By now, well into the third year after Barnes's initial contact, Parsons was aiming for a readable and reliable text, avoiding complex formulations and conceptual terminology that might be misunderstood and lead to further delay. Even the previous summer he had become frustrated, writing to Ogden, "it has dragged out so long that I shall be willing to take any publisher who will bring the matter to a decision" (June 10, 1928; TPP). But he also sought accuracy, so was careful to include almost all of Weber's many italicized words and phrases, as well as his legendary and copious use of quotation marks or inverted commas around key words and phrases. Whenever possible, he kept Weber's paragraphs intact, and for good measure he included in the margins the page references to the original GARS, volume 1, text, thus facilitating a kind of dual language comparison by the curious reader.

Tawney read the typescript first, followed by two more professional translators (copy editors were an invention for the future). The American publisher of record, now Charles Scribner's Sons, was thankfully absent from these discussions, as arrangements with that firm had been initiated not by Allen and Unwin but surprisingly by Ralph Barton Perry, Parsons's senior Harvard colleague in philosophy and a series advisor for Scribner's, who was on the lookout for an inexpensive student-friendly "Weber source book" in a new social science series. In any case, for contractual reasons it was Tawney's judgments that were binding. "With regard to Parsons' translation of Weber," he wrote,

I have read more of this. I cannot, as I told you, assume responsibility for the accuracy of the translation, as to compare the English and German sentence by sentence would be a very long job.

I think that, as a piece of English, it will pass, provided that certain alterations are made, viz. (1) The translator has reproduced the German italics throughout. This, I fear, must be altered. German writers use italics for emphasis where they are unnecessary, and, indeed, would appear quite out of place in English. The effect on the English reader of finding them in every other line, on some pages, would not be good. I suggest that the translation should be read by someone who will delete them, wherever, in English eyes, they are unnecessary.

(2) Somewhere the same comment applies to the use of inverted commas, though not to the same extent.

(3) The paragraphing and stopping require attention.

(4) Sometimes, though not very often, Mr. Parsons' English appears to me shaky. Here, again, the changes required are usually quite simple. The alteration of the order of the words would, in some cases, put the matter right.

Much the weakest part of the translation, as a piece of English, is the Introduction, the reason presumably being that the German of it is the more abstract and difficult. I think this needs particular attention. (September 28, 1929; TPP)

With the advantage of hindsight, Tawney's alarm over "Mr. Parsons' English" and the 1920 introduction or prefatory remarks appears somewhat overstated. As a representative example of the issues, consider the original typescript form of 1929 and Parsons's rendition of Weber's first two sentences:

A child of modern European civilization will necessarily and rightly treat problems of universal history in terms of this question: [to] what combination of circumstances may the fact be attributed that in western civilization and only in it, cultural phenomena have appeared, which—nevertheless as we like to think at least—lie in a line of development having *universal* significance and value?

Only in the west does "*science*" exist at a stage of development which we recognize today as "valid."

The editorial correction in the actually published text then read:

A PRODUCT of modern European civilization, studying any problem of universal history, is bound to ask himself to what combination of circumstances the fact should be attributed that in Western civilization, and in Western civilization only, cultural phenomena have appeared which (as we like to think) lie in a line of development having *universal* significance and value.

Only in the West does science exist at a stage of development which we recognize to-day as valid.

What is the result of this intervention? One simple change in syntax introduces a first sentence that is easier to scan, but Parsons's more precise statement of Weber's central question, the all-important *Fragestellung*, is needlessly sacrificed. Equally telling, the carefully crafted typography or form of Weber's text, faithfully reproduced in Parsons's second sentence, has now been seriously compromised.

The changes to the typography of Parsons's draft were indeed considerable and extensive. Most significant, following Tawney's suggestions, nearly all of Parsons's faithfully rendered italics and inverted commas were eliminated. For example, in the Vorbemerkung alone, to use a quantitative measure,

Weber had italicized eighty-three words and used inverted commas fifty times, nearly all reproduced by Parsons. But the published text retained only ten of the former, and it eliminated *all* of Weber's and Parsons's use of inverted commas. Paragraphs and sentences were divided and simplified further. And finally, the marginal pagination references to the German original were dropped on the grounds that by shifting Weber's voluminous footnotes to endnotes (an editorial decision that seems not to have been discussed with Parsons at all!), such a reference system became confusing. Alteration of Parsons's intended textual typography was not a trivial matter, for in the end the text that was actually published, compared with his original submission, had lost something of the emphasis, qualification, nuance, and *meaning* of Weber's text that it otherwise would have had, as present-day scholars have noted.

As for the celebrated conceptual terminology, after all these readings—probably at least nine people altogether orchestrated by the press, plus unspecified others Parsons said he consulted—the basic vocabulary for which Parsons is so famous remained intact: typically "conduct" or simply "life" for *Lebensführung*, "life" or "way (also 'type' and 'manner') of life" for *Lebensstil*, "elimination of magic from the world" for *Entzauberung der Welt*, "historical individual" for *historisches Individuum*, the egregious "correlations" for *Wahlverwandtschaften* ("elective affinities"), and. most important, "iron cage" for *stahlhartes Gehäuse* (literally, "a casing as hard as steel"). The familiar concise and powerful drumbeat cadences, such as those found in the concluding pages, were authentically Parsons's invention as well; for example, "The Puritan wanted to work in a calling; we are *forced* to do so," or "No one knows who will live in this cage in the future, or whether at the end of this tremendous development entirely new prophets will arise, or there will be a great rebirth of old ideas and ideals, or, if neither, mechanized petrification, embellished with a sort of convulsive self-importance. For, of the last stage of this cultural development [*Dann allerdings könnte für die "letzten Menschen" dieser Kulturentwicklung*], it might well be truly said: 'Specialists without spirit, sensualists without heart; this nullity imagines that it has attained a level of civilization never before achieved.' No editor would want to revise that language, steeped in pathos. For once, even the inverted commas survived, though not the italics. But all readers still overlooked with the translator Weber's crucial philosophical-cultural reference to Friedrich Nietzsche's "last men" who "invented happiness," an integral part of his argument, with Parsons's revisionist phrasing (viz. "the last stage of this cultural development") signaling the limits of his imagination and interests. It remains a striking paradox nevertheless that Parsons's English prose often achieved a level of clarity, power, and concision while engaging with Weber's German text that was unmatched in the much-maligned leaden style of his subsequent work. It is as if Weber's language and thought had fired his imagination and provoked a more vivid and supple style. The fortunate beneficiaries in this specific respect were, of course, Weber and his English-language audience.

When considering what we regard today as key Weberian concepts, it is important to point out that in his reading notes from his student days in Heidelberg, written in German, Parsons often enough (but not always!) wrote out phrases like "Systematik der Lebensführung," "Entzauberung der Welt," or "Methodische Lebensführung in USA" when reading PESC or the ensuing essay "The Protestant Sects and the Spirit of Capitalism." It is not as though he missed this terminology altogether or failed to see it as part of the text. Rather, his problem from the very beginning was "capitalism"—the *concept* of capitalism—or, as he wrote in his notes, the problem of the "breeding of capitalist qualities" (*Züchtung kapitalistischer Qualitäten*), and much later in print, "'capitalism' as a socioeconomic system." Parsons's central question was thus framed unsurprisingly through the intellectual discourse and economics of his time, instead of through formulations such as "the discourse of the modern" or the problematics of the cultural sociology and cultural criticism of our own age.

More specifically, Parsons suggested in his dissertation chapter that one rationale for making Weber's text available was to explore an alternative to the "individualistic," "rationalistic," and "unilinear" evolutionary assumptions operative in Anglo-American economic thought, a framing of the issue derived from the work of his dissertation director, Edgar Salin. Salin, however, a grand nephew of Jacob Schiff who as a teenager had sojourned with the wealthy in New York at his uncle's invitation, was known not only as an economist but also as an esthete and follower of Stefan George. The aesthetic sensibility becomes apparent in his overdrawn distinction between two mutually exclusive points of view in economics: one abstract and individualistic, the other concretely historical and "organic" with roots in German romanticism. For Salin both Karl Marx and Max Weber emerged from the latter orientation. Yet neither could be squeezed into such a highly schematic format without considerable distortion, and indeed Parsons completely abandoned it a few years later when writing *The Structure of Social Action*. When translating PESC, moreover, these framing dichotomies could hardly have assisted his choice of language and categorical distinctions.

With respect to the problem of capitalism itself, Weber's treatise had two major advantages for Parsons. First, it critically addressed the "economic interpretation of history" and demonstrated that the problems of modern capitalism must be grasped not only with tools of abstract economic theory, but also with the intellectual resources and methods of comparative history and sociological investigation. Second, it gave a clarifying answer to the "problem" of capitalism itself, which for Parsons (as for Weber) was a matter of understanding *modern* capitalism's "peculiar rationality." That rationality consisted in Parsons's brief retelling of Weber's account in (1) rational organizational and institutional forms, such as bureaucracy, rational law, rational accounting practices, and the rational organization of formally "free" labor; and (2) the distinctive "adaptation of the whole way of life of modern man to a particular set of values" summed up in the phrase "the spirit of capitalism." The result was a socioeconomic system that Parsons described in his dissertation as "objective"—that is, existing independently of our individual will; "mechanistic," or based on contractual relationships; "ascetic" in the sense of affirming supra-personal norms of action, such as "productivity" and "service"; "autonomous" because it followed its own laws of development; and "rational" in the dual sense of adapting means to ends, and demanding "the extreme discipline and self-control of the whole life of every individual."

The more "psychologically" and "culturally" resonant language that Weber sometimes used was subordinated to the purpose of ferreting out modern capitalism's special features and rationale, as Parsons's own notational outline of the "Vorbemerkung" (GARS 1:1–12) reveals, complete with page references to the German text, transcribed exactly as he wrote it (TPP):

Staatsbegriff: 4
Kap. die schicksalsvollste Macht unsres modernen Lebens, 4
Unmittelbar danach
Charakteristik des Kapitalismus 4–5
Anmerkung gegen Brentano 4–5
    Simmel, Sombart
Begriff des Kapitalismus überhaupt 6
Spezifische Eigenart des modernen Kapitalismus 6–7
   Rationale Organisation 7
   Trennung von Haushalt u. Betrieb 8
   Rationale Buchführung 9
   Kap. Arbeitsorganisation 9
   Rat. Sozialismus 9
   Das Zentrale Problem 10
      Entstehung des Bürgertums
      Eigenart der mod. Wissenschaft
Wichtige Quellen des Kapitalismus 11
   Recht
   Rationalismus des okzidentalen Kultur, 11
   Religiöse und magische Mächte 12
Asketischer Protestantismus

The concept of *Lebensführung*, or "life conduct," does indeed appear in these revised pages that Weber published in 1920, though in this instance not in Parsons's notes, where it is implicitly subordinated to the "rationalism of occidental culture." In this respect the modern objections to Parsons's intellectual choices are important and correct: they alert us to a level of meaning

he obscured. All the rich conceptual language Weber constructed in compound nouns based on "life," so essential to the fifth chapter of PESC—life
conduct (*Lebensführung*), lifestyle (*Lebensstil*), life ideal (*Lebensideal*), life outlook (*Lebensanschauung*), life conception (*Lebensauffassung*), life atmosphere
(*Lebensluft*), life mood (*Lebensstimmung*)—was played down in Parsons's more
muted vocabulary. Perhaps it was the Simmelian cast to this terminology, a reminder of the last chapter on the "Style of Life" in Georg Simmel's *Philosophy
of Money*, that suggested to Parsons the advisability of sharpening a theoretical
boundary, in these instances by using a less culturally and psychologically suggestive terminology or by ignoring Weber's inventions altogether.

Notwithstanding such choices as a translator, it is also the case that Parsons's
reading captured accurately the overarching terminology of rationalism, rationality, and rationalization that was central to Weber's account of asceticism
and the capitalist "spirit." This was the theoretical language that has survived
as one of the most distinctive signposts of Weberian thought, having achieved
by now a life of its own. In this respect Parsons's orientation was perspicacious:
it remained true to what Weber would have called the "culturally relevant"
problem complex of the modern world—namely, the "peculiar rationalism" of
Western capitalist culture and the problematic character of modern capitalism
as a "fateful force," a dynamic socioeconomic system in the age of, as we now
say, "globalization."

For Parsons the translation of *PESC* was an episode at the very beginning of
his career, like a military boot camp best forgotten and left behind. His only
later reflection on the three-year project was dramatically understated; after
receiving Marianne Weber's support and introduction to Oskar Siebeck, he
noted, "I went to see Siebeck and worked out the arrangement. He in turn
arranged publication of the English version by Allen and Unwin of London. It
appeared, after a few vicissitudes, in the early summer of 1930."

The result of these "few vicissitudes," however, was a text, strictly speaking,
that was not Parsons's intended version but an intervention that had made
matters worse, a true *Verschlimmbesserung*, an "incorrect correction" or "dis-
improvement" in the fine German oxymoron. But the text had been created,
an enduring accomplishment, though an untimely one, for just as it was published its problem focus—capitalism and its "spirit"—seemed headed for self-
destruction. The New York Stock Exchange crash in October 1929 coincided
with the final proofreading, complaints from the typesetters, and Parsons's last
attempts to correct the corrections, provoking a warning "that your allowance
of 10 per cent for author's corrections will be exceeded" (January 27, 1930;
TPP). While the worldly problem of capitalism had arrived in full force, a
scholarly exploration of the "work ethic" and its cultural-religious sources by
a German author may well have seemed a distraction with excessive panache.
Capitalism's "spirit" had assumed too sinister a form. Allen and Unwin's Lon-

don director subsequently reported total sales of only 1,009 through 1933. "There is now very little demand for the book," he mused, "and it is unlikely that we shall ever sell as many as 2,500 copies"—a Depression-era prognosis wildly off the mark in light of postwar developments. Parsons's work of translation, also representing an unintended interpretation, awaited a new generation of readers in vastly changed circumstances.

Today we *should* reassess Parsons's *PESC*, but not simply because it is riddled with errors. We should do so because it is important as a socially constructed artifact, an exemplar of the vagaries of "authorship." Of course, each generation reads a text with its own problems in mind, and a new generation will read it differently and feel the need understandably to render the original more intelligible, more vivid and more accessible to the zeitgeist. But what does this adverb *more* conceal? Are new readings to be preferred to their predecessors? Would a different text with fidelity to Parsons's original italics, inverted commas, and pagination to *GARS*, volume 1, in the margins have altered the understanding and interpretation of Weber, even to a slight degree? In the *actually existing* translation attributed to Parsons, Weber's text has certainly lost something in subtlety, texture, emphasis, conceptual precision, and meaning. It became accessible to new English-language readers, but as a simpler and more mechanical treatise that it otherwise would have been. The careful reader could not be alerted to the kind of linguistic qualifications, problematic or borrowed notions, and authorial distance that Weber wished to convey in developing his cultural history and "explanation" of the relationship, the "elective affinity" between the "Protestant ethic" and the "spirit" of capitalism. Side-by-side comparison of original and translation was rendered extremely difficult, as anyone knows who has made the effort to find, say, the four places in which Weber used the phrase *Entzauberung der Welt* (disenchantment of the world) that Parsons actually translated in slightly different ways. Perhaps with Parsons's original and more faithful typography we would have come sooner to the kind of questioning that has breathed life into Weber's ideas. Perhaps we would have avoided fruitless debates over positions attributed to Weber that he actually never advocated and sometimes explicitly repudiated. Perhaps, perhaps . . .

Yet, hold on! Since we have Parsons's original typescript, bearing an anonymous archivist's scribbled notation, "This should be preserved as a historical document of considerable value," some enterprising spirit could even now issue the *authentic* Parsons translation of Weber's text, which with truly minor alterations in response to his posthumous critics—a word here, a phrase there—might well become the definitive version of sociology's most famous work. And why would we want to do this? What purpose—intellectual, scientific, social, cultural, historical, or personal—would such an exercise serve? In defense of the labor of translation, long on labor and short on appreciation, perhaps it is sufficient to answer, paraphrasing our authors, that even the detectives among us can never know with certainty when the light of the great cultural problems will shift and move on, and with which as yet unexpressed textual resources and innovative readings, misreadings, and rereadings.

THIRTEEN

THE INVENTION OF THE THEORY

The fate of Max Weber's *Protestant Ethic and the Spirit of Capitalism* is a compelling chapter in the sociology of knowledge. The social forces affecting Talcott Parsons's translation offer a larger lesson about the politics and sociology of the articulation, presentation and dissemination of Weber's thought. The lesson applies to subsequent developments as well—especially the second and third crucial steps forward for Weber's American and Anglophone readership: the timely postwar publication in 1946 of Hans Gerth's translations, assisted by C. Wright Mills, of some of the most important texts from the Weber corpus in *From Max Weber: Essays in Sociology*; and in the following year Talcott Parsons's final major investment in translating Weber, the first part of *Economy and Society* that was published under the ambitious Parsonian imprimatur of *The Theory of Social and Economic Organization*, a title connected only vaguely to Weber's original manuscript.

While Parsons's version of the *The Protestant Ethic* surely deserves a special place in the pantheon of Weber's works, the two texts of 1946 and 1947 extended knowledge of Weber into new and uncharted domains. *From Max Weber* offered a concise tour of central texts on politics, science, the sociology of religion, bureaucracy, charisma, and other topics lifted from *Economy and Society*, while *The Theory of Social and Economic Organization* posed on its paperback cover as "The most extensive general exposition of Max Weber's sociological theory and its applications to the broad empirical problems of historical structure and change." Parsons meant every word of this promotional blurb: Behold, at last, Weber the general theorist! The claim has prospered and acquired a life of its own. When a few years ago the International Sociological Association decided to canvass opinion concerning the most important books of the twentieth century in sociology, the uncontested winner turned out to be not *The Protestant Ethic and the Spirit of Capitalism*, which finished a close fourth, but Weber's *Economy and Society*. It is an astonishing outcome for a treatise cobbled together mostly from manuscripts and notes never prepared for publication as a coherent whole by the author himself.

Gerth and Mills Publish a Weber "Source Book"

From Max Weber: Essays in Sociology arrived with the postwar American universities and the social sciences entering a new phase of unprecedented expansion. Gerth and Mills's choice of a "reader" format for their selections, a text designed for classroom use that opened with an informative and dramatic introduction to Weber's life and work, revealed their superior editorial savvy, supported by marketing expertise at the Oxford University Press. Even Edward Shils, who threatened to delay the project or cause it to wither on the vine, as Guy Oakes and Arthur Vidich have shown, was moved later to pen his grudging admiration. But he did so behind the scenes, so to speak, and not in a text intended for publication during his lifetime, writing, "Although I think that the translations that Gerth and Mills made from Max Weber are not very good, still, they are the works which really put Max Weber 'on the map' in America and England. Prior to the appearance of that miscellany, the writings of Max Weber available in English were rather peripheral, although very fine in their own way. But Gerth and Mills did make some rather important writings widely available, albeit in a very melodramatic interpretation and in a selection biased in that direction." Even when meting out praise in a private memoir, Shils could not avoid the caustic aside, enjoying jabs at Gerth's "incoherence" and "unintelligibility," or in his most delicious swipe at Mills, writing that he "would have been an ordinary, vigorous, semi-literate and productive ruffian if it had not been for the civilizing influence of Gerth's knowledge of Max Weber." This salvo from Shils's arsenal must rank as the most original form of praise Weber has ever received. It is understatement to say that there was little quarter given by these competitors during and after the publication of *From Max Weber*.

Oakes and Vidich have recorded and traced in detail the remarkable record of initial cooperation, followed by competition, concealment, bad faith, and professional jealousy that eventually ruined the relationship between Gerth and Shils. As Oakes and Vidich have concluded, agreeing with Mills's own judgment, the new Weber reader could only have been published at the cost of the collegial friendship between Gerth and Shils. In this regard two considerations were decisive. First there was the episode they rightly call the "Shils affair" which was in its most serious aspects a struggle over "priority" claims in science. In this tangled relationship Gerth had entered onto a terrain first occupied by Shils with his mania for translating difficult Weber texts. The entry was in a sense fortuitous, for by his own account Gerth found himself in Madison, Wisconsin, a registered alien during wartime not allowed beyond the city limits without special permission. In a therapeutic effort to relieve boredom and perhaps coincidentally to improve his English, he turned to translating Weber texts. From his point of view Shils had already taken up the difficult task of translating Karl Mannheim, completing *Ideology and Utopia* (1936) with Louis Wirth, then moving on to *Man and Society in the Age of Reconstruction* (1940). In the publishing world of all the major German language predecessors it was still Weber who remained essentially untouched. From Gerth's perspective what better task than to begin filling this gaping omission. But for

Shils this apparent division of labor hardly squared with his personal sense of mission. Gerth was in the nature of things a dangerous competitor, trespassing on sacred ground. Both by education and working relationships with people like Mannheim, and importantly because of his linguistic competence, he was in a position to supplant Shils altogether.

Second, Gerth's casual account of his entry into the Weber field concealed a disciplined pedagogical intention identical to that of Knight and Shils at the University of Chicago: providing good new texts on important subjects to his students, expanding their reading and enhancing his teaching. He also employed a similar method, enlisting graduate students as copy editors to produce a perfected and idiomatic draft, approved by Gerth after careful comparison with the original, and then mimeographed for class use and distribution. In the University of Wisconsin sociology department Mills became one of these favored students. Thus, what began as a pedagogical exercise was slowly transformed over several semesters into a local publishing venture for Weber texts, in the course of which the editorial relationship and division of labor between Gerth and Mills was defined.

As strange as it may seem, Mills's role in the priority dispute and the management and promotion of Gerth's talent was a major contributing factor to the promotion of knowledge about Weber and his work. Left to his own disorganized brilliance, Gerth would most likely never have compiled a set of Weber texts that would have attracted the attention of a major prestigious press. But with Mills's entrepreneurial bent, career ambitions, feel for audience and publishing markets, and sheer chutzpah and "street smarts" the senior immigrant scholar and the erstwhile University of Texas undergraduate Charlie Mills became a formidable team.

What emerged from this collaboration, then, was exactly the kind of "Weber source book" that Ralph Barton Perry had envisioned when Parsons was translating *The Protestant Ethic and the Spirit of Capitalism*—a text that was, of course, nothing like a compendium of Weber's thought. There was a need in Perry's view for an inexpensive reader useful for meeting the pedagogical needs of American higher education, where the teaching function was essential and where, in the best of circumstances, the introductory lecture and the reading and analysis of texts were connected to larger purposes in a competitive environment: attracting an audience, recruiting promising students, and promoting graduate education and programs of research. It was in this sense and this context that *From Max Weber* was able to "put Max Weber on the map," as Shils noted.

Furthermore, the Gerth and Mills partnership led to an outpouring of publications, including the collaborative work in social psychology, *Character and Social Structure* (1953), but mainly the popular treatises Mills assembled with the assistance of borrowings from Gerth's fertile field of ideas, such as *White Collar: The American Middle Classes* (1951) and *The Power Elite* (1956).

Figure 12. C. Wright Mills in his Columbia University office in 1954, with the Weber translations behind him, photographed for *Life Magazine* as the celebrated author of *White Collar*. Photograph by Fritz Gorro. Reproduced by permission from Getty Images.

Reworking the theory, Mills's masterstroke was to demonstrate the ways in which elements of Weber's thought could be elaborated into a "Weberian" critique of social class, status, power, and organization in modern America. To be fair to Mills regarding his relationship with Gerth, however, he did strongly encourage his comrade in thought to take the next giant step forward regarding Weber's work. "Why don't *you* do the definitive intellectual biography of Weber?" he challenged Gerth. "Why in God's name don't you get onto it? You're the obvious man to do it. It would be the way, the royal way, to consolidate all your work in translation. If you did decide to do it, please know that as far as the English is concerned, I should be glad to edit the manuscript with no mention of my name in any way. I mean that. Do think upon it. As far as the publisher is concerned, just now that would be no problem" (December 22, 1959). Gerth did follow up with the Oxford University Press, but he also allowed teaching and the trivia of everyday life to clutter his days, and then with Mills's sudden death the project lost its impresario. We are, it seems, still awaiting the great definitive work.

Parsons's "Theory of Social and Economic Organization"

The collaboration begun at the University of Wisconsin, centered around Hans Gerth, did produce the completion of the project Oskar Siebeck and Talcott Parsons had in mind in the 1920s, though not at all in their preferred form: the complete translation of Weber's three-volume *Gesammelte Aufsätze zur Religionssoziologie*. At least these *Collected Essays in the Sociology of Religion* became available in the English language, though they were scattered out of sequence through five different books, including Gerth and Mills's own reader. What remained unavailable still was the formidable body of work many considered Weber's magnum opus: the collection of material known as *Economy and Society*. The summons to rectify that omission landed once again on the desk of Talcott Parsons.

The project of publishing the totality of *Wirtschaft und Gesellschaft*, much less translating it, is a tangled affair. Most of the German text, drawn from unfinished manuscripts left on Weber's desk, was published posthumously by Marianne Weber with the assistance of Melchoir Palyi. The editorial complications have only been exacerbated with the passage of time because of several factors: the disappearance of large blocks of Weber's handwritten original; the problem of the work's location in the *Grundriss der Sozialökonomik*, the multivolume basic outline of social economics that Weber himself had supervised over the last decade of his life as the general editor for Oskar Siebeck; the relationship of Weber's contributions to that encyclopedic enterprise; and finally, the fact that Marianne Weber's edited text, modified by Johannes Winckelmann, has come under critical scrutiny and been challenged for accuracy, even as to the very title of the work. The current reconstruction by the editors of the *Max Weber Gesamtausgabe* promises to bring a resolution of these difficulties, at least for the German text.

Encountering Weber in the 1920s and working on the problems of his thought in the 1930s, Parsons was oblivious to such editorial issues. He first bought and read the text of *Wirtschaft und Gesellschaft* while a student in Heidelberg, the 1922 edition published in the third section of the *Grundriss der Sozialökonomik*, the text edited by Marianne Weber and Palyi with the intention of presenting a systematic and coherent treatise. The book preserved in his papers, with the notation "Talcott Parsons Heidelberg 1925" in his own hand, contains considerable underlying (in four colors of pencil!) and numerous marginalia in both German and English. Presumably the German phrases were written earlier, though we cannot be certain. In any case, the text was well worked over—many times over.

If Parsons read *The Protestant Ethic and the Spirit of Capitalism* rapidly like a detective story, then he must have worked his way gradually through *Economy and Society* as a monumental epic like Homer's *Odyssey* or Leo Tolstoy's *War and Peace*, if not, as Wolfgang Mommsen has suggested, "like a Chinese book." This was an eye-opening exercise entirely unlike the encounter with *The Protestant Ethic*. But Parsons continued the same practice begun previously of jotting succinct marginalia: for example, *sehr wichtig* and *Anknüpfung an Sombart*—"very important" and "in reference to Sombart"—are penned alongside the heavily underlined characterization by Weber of Henry Villard's "blind pool" maneuver against the stock of the Northern Pacific Railroad as an example of "robber capitalism":

> The structure and spirit of this robber capitalism [*Beutekapitalismus*] differs radically from the rational management of an ordinary capitalist large-scale enterprise and is most similar to some age-old phenomena: the huge rapacious enterprises in the financial and colonial sphere, and "occasional trade" with its mixture of piracy and slave hunting. The double nature of what may be called the "capitalist spirit," and the specific character of modern routinized capitalism with its professional bureaucracy [*der spezifischen Eigenart des modernen, 'berufsmäßig' büreaukratisierten Alltagskapitalismus*], can be understood only if these two structural elements, which are ultimately different but everywhere intertwined, are conceptually distinguished.

The example drawn from the Weber family chronicles and America's Gilded Age posed a question about the "rationality" of mature capitalism, raised also by Sombart. It caught the young Parsons's attention, for in passages like these he found not only the familiar but also a formulation of the concept of modern capitalism—the "specific peculiarity of modern 'vocational' bureaucratized everyday or ordinary capitalism," when read literally. The concrete became abstract, for Parsons also saw in Weber's text a theoretical analysis of the larger, more general problem of "rationality" as such—especially the rationality of *all* social action.

As we have seen, various efforts at translation of *Wirtschaft und Gesellschaft* involving Knight, Shils, Alexander von Schelting, and others gained headway in the 1930s. Declining earlier entreaties, Parsons finally took up the task in 1939, and only then, as he acknowledged, through an inquiry from Friedrich von Hayek, with Fritz Machlup, the University of Buffalo economist, serving as intermediary. Having left Vienna for the London School of Economics, Hayek had encouraged a young economist, Alexander Henderson, to translate the first two chapters of the text. Concerned about the quality of the translation, he then approached Parsons for advice. Parsons found the work deeply flawed and expressed his initial misgivings to the editor, James Hodge in London:

> [T]his work [*Wirtschaft und Gesellschaft*], particularly the first chapter, presents one of the very few most difficult problems of translation which I can imagine. Some of the main reasons are the following: It is a highly technical work, and Weber is presenting the barest outline of a conceptual framework without all the detailed explanation and application which would serve to make it much more readily intelligible. Then, particularly in its methodological parts, it builds upon a development of thought, and discussions around its problems, which have had no direct counterpart in the English-speaking world. Hence many terms and references would be intelligible to the initiated German reader which have no near equivalents in English at all. Weber built upon this tradition and gave many of these terms a further specification of meaning which accentuates the problem. Then finally Weber's own style is, apart from these considerations, peculiarly difficult. (January 26, 1939; TPP)

In view of these reservations Parsons went on to question "the advisability of even attempting a direct translation." He thought the effort might be worthwhile, however, but only with careful editing, close attention to subject matter and conceptual language, and a comprehensive introduction—a brief for his own intervention.

Parsons's response could be considered self-serving, but he obviously had a point about Weber's language. Conceptual building blocks like *Zweckrationalität* (instrumental, purposive, or means-to-ends rationality), *Vergemeinschaftung* (the process of forming communal relationships), *Vergesellschaftung* (the process of forming social relationships; sociation, or association), or even the common adjective *sinnvoll* (meaningful) presented special difficulties that had to be addressed. In Parsons's view Henderson's apparent penchant for using "end-rational" for *zweckrational* or "significant" for *sinnvoll* only added new levels of obscurity. Nevertheless, though his defensiveness cannot be surprising, Henderson was surely correct in seizing on the essential issue: as he wrote to Hodge, "Weber makes his reader think in terms of concepts which are new to the English reader and if the concepts are to be used a new terminology must come too, and it does not greatly matter whether new technical meanings are given to ordinary words or whether new words are coined, but there is no escape from the alternative" (undated, but prior to March 14, 1939; TPP). In other words, the task at hand, both men agreed, was the invention of a new conceptual language, an edifice of interconnected nouns, verbs, and adjectives that would capture the structure and content of Weber's thinking.

In the correspondence that followed Parsons acceded to Hodge's request to revise Henderson's draft of chapters one and two of *Economy and Society* while also persuading the editor to include chapters three and four and thus complete part 1 of the text, arguing correctly that it was a conceptual whole that should not be split apart. Part 1 was in fact the "Conceptual Exposition" or the "soziologische Kategorienlehre" that Weber had written last, in 1919 and 1920, and prepared for publication himself. A decade had passed since Parsons's struggles with Stanley Unwin and R. H. Tawney, and with the success of *The Structure of Social Action* (1937) to his credit, he was in a position to impose his will on the project. The roles were now reversed, with Parsons assuming Tawney's mantle as arbiter and judge. Called to military service, Henderson faded from view, never submitting the translation of chapters 3 and 4 that Parsons had requested. Left to the field himself, Parsons completed a draft translation in about four months, adding in a note to Robert Merton that he was also finishing his "theoretical essay" or introduction to the whole (September 28, 1939; TPP).

World War II delayed publication for eight years. In the meantime Parsons had the text microfilmed, sending copies to Merton at Columbia University and Howard Becker at the University of Wisconsin for their department libraries. In preparing the text he consulted with Professor Edwin Gay, the economic historian and his Harvard University colleague, about the terminology in the lengthy second chapter on the sociological categories of economic action that has too often been overlooked, though revived recently through the efforts of Richard Swedberg. In addition, he used the earlier translation by Shils and Schelting.

Parsons's larger purposes were twofold: first, the abstraction from Weber's empirical interests of a theoretical point of view. Commenting on his practice as a translator to Louis Wirth, Parsons put the matter succinctly:

> Weber's theoretical analysis is most definitely bound up with the empirical interest in capitalism. It seems to me that this comes out in most striking fashion in the classification of the types of action in which the two rational types are very clearly the center and the two non-rational types essentially residual in character. The same applies to the whole typological system of *Wirtschaft und Gesellschaft*. My careful working through of the early part of that book in connection with the translation strongly confirms this impression. At every crucial point, Weber is concerned with the problem of what constitutes rationality of action and of the conditions on which it is dependent. In the famous classification of the types of *Herrschaft* it seems to me quite clear that rational, legal Herrschaft is the conceptual starting point and that the other two types are formulated primarily as antitheses of this in different respects. (October 6, 1939; TPP)

If the translation laid bare the logic of Weber's thinking and underscored his contributions as a theorist, then it also accomplished a second purpose: introducing the audience to an altogether different Weber. The aim became explicit in Parsons's introduction to the work, for there, as he explained to Eric Voegelin,

I have dealt with some methodological problems of Weber's work, but have given by far the largest amount of space to what might be called his institutional sociology in the economic and political spheres, with special reference to his interpretation of the modern western social order and its sources of instability. It seemed to me particularly important to lay stress on this aspect of his work since Weber is, as you know, known here either as the naïve idealist of the *Protestant Ethic* or the methodologist of the ideal type. This institutional aspect of his work has hardly penetrated the English-speaking world. (August 1, 1941; TPP)

Parsons's own work had unintentionally assisted in promoting the earlier partial impressions of Weber's thought. The new translation offered an opportunity for correction, setting forth a comprehensive theoretical vocabulary designed for institutional and structural analysis.

Parsons succeeded with the publication of *The Theory of Social and Economic Organization*, a title he suggested to Hodge, in presenting the scientific Weber with an appropriate conceptual terminology. He replaced the more colloquial and literal language often favored by Shils and Schelting with more abstract and generalized locutions: for example, "application to subjective processes" for *innerlich* (inward, inner) or "the objective point of view" for *äusserlich* (outer, external). He proposed the elaborate conceptual terminology for identifying the types of social action, the bases of legitimacy, the categories of social and economic action, and the system of social stratification. Almost all of it has remained in the complete text of *Economy and Society* that is read today, with the exception of the ill-advised and awkward choice of "imperative control" or "coordination" for *Herrschaft*, penciled late into Parsons's typescript, rather than the by-now-standard terminology of "domination" or "authority." In the rarified atmosphere of modern social theory *Zweckrationalität* has earned a life of its own, most often as "instrumental rationality" in the authoritative translations of Jürgen Habermas's work. And an elusive concept like *Vergesellschaftung*, which Parsons rendered variously as "associative relationship" or "organized activity," simply has no settled solution and never will. Parsons's initial skepticism was well founded; pried loose from their linguistic matrix, some concepts lose too much of their original connotation.

Fortuitously, the four chapters Parsons translated were as close as we can come to Weber's last words in social theory. The expansive world-historical perspective of the sociology of religion remained intact, copiously illustrated with historical examples, but now in *The Theory of Social and Economic Organization* there was a different ambition. These chapters offered something remarkably novel: a monumental edifice of ideal types of social action ranging from wholly formal and legal rationality to purely affective action and routine habituation, as Parsons remarked. Weber's intellectual penchant for identifying diametrically opposed positions and extreme alternatives in order comparatively to set forth different institutional possibilities was on full display. Any evolutionary or developmental scheme that might have surfaced was dissolved in the proliferation of an apparently endless supply of pure types that could be used for empirical investigation and assessment of actual social structure and social organization. Moreover, the situation of social action was clarified: the individual was now confronted with possible choices for action and its consequences. The translation accomplished its goal: Weber's work had acquired a new level of significance for general theory.

Weber among the Émigrés

The roles played by Hans Gerth and Talcott Parsons and the extended arc of Weber's gathering reputation and knowledge of his work brings us back to the third significant and somewhat dispersed grouping of scholars with a stake in the universities, the development of the social sciences, and the course of intellectual life in America: the interwar émigré generation of scholars and university professors, the "Weimar intellectuals" and exiles from Nazi Germany. They, too, had a part to play in the struggle over the mastery of Weber, the man many considered "the most important thinker in their lifetimes" who had "set the terms of debate" in the social sciences, citing the judgment of historians of the New School for Social Research. However, unlike the first two clusters of scholars discussed previously, the émigré community was hardly a cohesive grouping or network. The term *cluster*, implying minimal cohesion, could hardly apply. Because of its variety, dispersion, and internal tensions, this group must be approached as a complicated, multilayered, and contested patchwork of disparate and sometimes overlapping social and professional networks.

Viewed expansively, the emigration from Germany relative to the social sciences in the second, third, and fourth decades of the twentieth century actually spanned several academic generations, from Louis Wirth, who emigrated as a teenager in 1911, to one of his most important students at the University of Chicago, Reinhard Bendix, who arrived as a twenty-two year old undergraduate in 1938. But the more specific political term *émigré* concealed a variety of routes to American shores: a more-or-less voluntary decision to emigrate permanently under the pressure of events, forced (and perhaps temporary) exile, flight as a refugee, persecution as a Jew, or expulsion for political and ideological reasons by Nazi authorities after 1933. Whatever the individual motives and reasons, sometimes significant for social differentiation and status within the émigré community, it was most specifically those arriving in the 1930s from German-speaking Europe with careers already underway, thus suddenly disrupted and possibly ruined, who gave some sense of identity and "shared fate" to this multifaceted configuration. What they shared above all was the experience of displacement that Theodor Adorno referred to as the "damaged life."

A sense of the nature of this disruption and the ambiguous feelings it provoked is revealed in an unusual way by one of the many postwar exchanges between Karl Jaspers, a Weber devotee, and Hannah Arendt. On April 19, 1950, two days before what would have been Max Weber's eighty-sixth birthday, Jaspers had a dream at his home in exile in Basel. As he reported it in a letter to Arendt, "I had a remarkable dream last night. We were together at Max Weber's. You, Hannah, arrived late, were warmly welcomed. The stairway led through a ravine. The apartment was Weber's old one. He had just returned from a world trip, had brought back political documents and artworks, particularly from the Far East. He gave us some of them, you the best ones because you understood more of politics than I." About to complete *The Origins of Totalitarianism*, Arendt replied, "Prompted by your dream I've read a lot of Max Weber. I felt so idiotically flattered by it that I was ashamed of myself. Weber's intellectual sobriety [*Nüchternheit*] is impossible to match, at least for me." She added the self-reflection, "With me there's always something dogmatic left hanging around somewhere," and then the parenthetical "(That's what you get when Jews start writing history)."

In ways he could not have appreciated from his Swiss sanctuary, Jaspers's intuition in the dream sequence proposed an unusual answer to the question, Why Weber in America? It evoked the archaic image of the mythic scholar-*theoros*, thrown into the alien world like the émigrés themselves, collecting and documenting, returning home as guide, mentor, observer of the unknown. The place assigned Weber lay deep within the intellectual milieu of the émigré community and what we might call the social psychology of the refugee scholar, the immigrant, and the exile in America. Weber and his work could thus function in two ways: both as a bridge to the new, to the world of capitalist modernity, and a road to an acceptable cosmopolitan "liberal" historical past, to the intellectual world Jaspers and many others had experienced in the Weber residence on the Ziegelhäuser Landstrasse in Heidelberg, the home built by Weber's grandfather Fallenstein, the meeting place for Georg Gottfried Gervinus and the 1848 Frankfurt liberals, who had become by 1933 the outsiders, exiles, and outcasts of modern German history.

So it was Weber the cosmopolitan and self-described "outsider" who could give legitimacy and weight to the intellectual orientations and problems thought to be significant for the community in exile: the relations between politics and culture, the moral foundations of the social and economic order, the problem of "rationality" and the irrationality of action, the place for historical thinking or the "historical sensibility," the "value" problem, the meaning of science as a vocation, the fate of the intellectual and the Jewish scholar. It was this Weber who could cushion the negative shock of what was often perceived as America's "intellectual and cultural provincialism," quoting Leo Lowenthal, and establish for the émigré scholar and intellectual the historical task of assisting in the development of American intellectual and cultural life. At the same time, the presence of a *different* Weber in America, already an established interest of scholars like Frank Knight, Talcott Parsons, and Edward Shils, created not just opportunities but difficulties for the European newcomers. The previous American reading and incorporation of Weber's work had abstracted it from the contextualized and political Weber, the view of Weber as an "intellectual desperado," that was so important to the émigré perspective. What would become of the work amid the contending strains of émigré thought and action?

As in Jaspers's dream, Arendt had indeed arrived late—too late to answer this question. She never met Max Weber, only attending a few of the Heidelberg *jours* Marianne Weber continued to host into the 1920s and '30s. But there were, of course, those from a more senior generation in this strikingly diverse community of émigré scholars who, like Jaspers, knew Weber personally, such as Emil Lederer at the New School, or Paul Honigsheim at Michigan State University, and Karl Löwenstein at the University of Massachusetts. There can be no doubt that their work and teaching was affected by the long shadow of Weber's scholarship and personality, as they often acknowledged. Honigsheim is a perfect case in point, as his sociology of music is quite explicitly an extension of ideas generated in conversations with Weber. The Weber legacy obviously affected his life as a scholar and teacher in every question he pursued and in his very demeanor with students in seminars and in the classroom. Others, such as Alfred Schutz, Albert Salomon, or Arnold Brecht at the New School, had read Weber's work and then used it for their own purposes—Schutz in phenomenology and Brecht in political theory. They also published work expounding, interpreting, or appropriating some of Weber's ideas, always taking for granted the politicoeconomic dimension of his work. Salomon had already published on Weber in Germany, characterizing him somewhat misleadingly as the "bourgeois Marx," a phrase that resonated in certain quarters for decades. Among his New School peers the characterization was important because it provided a kind of intellectual connection to Weber for those such as Franz Neumann, Otto Kirchheimer, and even Lederer, whose critical neo-Marxist outlook had traveled with them across the Atlantic, typically becoming modified during the exile years. In the United States Salomon's authoritative introductory essays on Weber, published in the first two volumes of *Social Research*, reveal his earlier command of the philosophical and sociological underpinnings of Weber's work but now expand the scope to the entire range of issues confronting the social sciences, as if to say, If one wants to participate in the theoretical discourse of the modern social sciences, Weber's work is the place to begin.

In the empirical studies of the New School faculty it is characteristic that when Weber is actually cited it tends to be the Weber of political economy or political sociology who is credited with an insight. This is no less true of Franz Neumann in his masterwork *Behemoth*, although his affiliation with the Institute of Social Research often put him at odds with New School intellectuals. Even émigré scholars as far apart in basic orientation as Paul Lazarsfeld and Theodor Adorno allow similar parts of Weber's work as an inspiration. Among the faculty's larger monograph-length research projects, Frieda Wunderlich's late publication on the German agrarian economy shows its debt to Weber's earliest studies on the nineteenth-century agrarian economy of Germany east of the Elbe. But as an "institutional" economist working with ideal types and a typology of rational action instead of formal models of marginal utility or mathematical models of choice, Weber had little effect on the emerging field of economic theory and the work of the professional economists, figures like Ludwig von Mises, Albert Hirschman, or Oskar Morgenstern.

Beyond the walls of the New School there were still other scholars, such as Melchoir Palyi at Southern Illinois University, Arthur Salz at Ohio State University, Erich Voegelin at the University of Alabama, or Leo Strauss at the University of Chicago who were well-versed in Weber's thought. For Voegelin and Strauss the response to Weber's work ranged from ambivalence to hostility. Voegelin, a Laura Spelman Rockefeller Fellow in the United States from 1924 to 1927, part of the time at the University of Wisconsin, had published an earlier positive discussion of Weber before his emigration. In *The New Science of Politics* (1952), however, he went on the offensive against social science, anticipating Strauss's well-known attack on Weber in *Natural Right and History* (1953). Strauss's views should be read in the context of the University of Chicago social science curriculum favored by Knight and Shils. His critique became generalized in a standpoint juxtaposing "social science" or simply "the social" with "political philosophy," a reification of positions also found in Voegelin's work, and in a highly individual and novel version modified by "existentialist" concerns in Hannah Arendt as well. Arendt thought Voegelin's book was "on the wrong track, but important nonetheless. The first fundamental discussion of the real problem since Max Weber", and she summarized her opinion of Strauss: "He is a convinced orthodox atheist. Very odd. A truly gifted intellect. I don't like him"—a sentiment reciprocated by Strauss and his followers in this frequently contentious environment.

Conflict and hostility is sometimes the stuff of social life, now and then with interesting consequences. In the émigré community there was also what could be called a Weber "nonreception" in the 1930s, worth taking into account because of subsequent developments in postwar American intellectual life. In New York the configuration was evident early in the sometimes uncomfortable institutional (and personal) relationships among the three intellectual centers: Columbia University, the New School for Social Research, and the Institute of Social Research transported to Manhattan from Frankfurt. Edward Shils captured the essence of this situation in his inimitable politically charged style, commenting from a distance of four decades on the year he spent in the city, affiliated with Columbia. At the New School, he noted, "was a rather nice lot of refined liberal and social-democratic Germans, very unfanatical, cultivated and very pleasant to get on with" who knew Weber's work well. On the other hand, uptown in Morningside Heights he found the "Frankfurt gang," as he called them,

> a very mean lot: terribly edel, radical, cliquish, self-promoting. They were spreading as well as they could their pernicious *Kritische Philosophie*, i.e., fancied-up Marxism. I used to go to their seminars at 429 West 117th Street. I never heard Max Weber mentioned there in the year 1937–38, and I cannot recall any of them writing about Weber. . . . Horkheimer had no interest in Weber, nor did Marcuse, nor Adorno, nor Pollock. Even Wittfogel, who was then one of them, and thus very close to communism, did not pay attention to Weber in his *Wirtschaft und Gesellschaft Chinas* (1927). At least, I don't think so.

One can imagine Shils's hyperawareness of the names "Weber" and "Weberian," as this was the year in which, having just emerged from Knight's Weber seminar at Chicago, he was committing a good deal of attention to a similar seminar with Schelting at Columbia, the context for their initial efforts to translate the first chapter of *Wirtschaft und Gesellschaft*.

Neither by temperament nor inclination could Shils have bridged the divide separating these three institutions and groups of scholars. Toward the end of the decade Franz Neumann and Otto Kirchheimer performed that function to some extent, as did Paul Lazarsfeld from an autonomous position in his Bureau for Applied Social Research. Even though he thought of himself as a "European positivist," Lazarsfeld by the late 1930s was actually closely involved in the "empirical" work of the institute, then moving himself and his restructured bureau to Columbia. He also knew Weber's concept of action and his empirical work, giving it credit for some of his own interests.

The reality of the relationship vis-à-vis Weber's writings and reputation was of course much more complicated than Shils's acerbic portrayal suggests. Furthermore, the situation within the émigré groups changed somewhat over the years. Memories faded of Weber as the "bourgeois Marx" in the European context and they were replaced even in the same minds by a Weber retooled for the social sciences in the New World. Furthermore, some "elective affinities" concerning historical and comparative perspectives emerged in the American environment of the kind that Bendix recalled in his own experience. Building on such affinities, Franz Neumann even thematized the vocation of the émigré scholar—namely, bringing to bear hard-earned historical perspective and theoretical grounding on the dangers lurking in the American outlook, as reflected in the social sciences: too much optimism about an ability to change the world, too much faith in the self-justifying value of collecting raw empirical data, and too much eagerness in pursuit of the kind of financial support that compromises intellectual integrity and independence. What the American experience offered, in return, was a bracing pragmatic lesson in reconciling or tempering theory with experience, a perfect point of entry for the fascination with Weber. As for Weber's work itself, Franz Neumann's judgment was prescient: "It is characteristic of German social science that it virtually destroyed Weber by almost exclusive concentration upon the discussion of his methodology. Neither his demand for empirical studies nor his insistence upon the responsibility of the scholar to society were heeded. *It is here, in the United States, that Weber really came to life.*" For Neumann it was as if, in the land of Benjamin Franklin and William James, Weber's thirst for empirical and intellectual sobriety, his *Sachlichkeit*, had found a home.

It should not be surprising that the wide range of scholarship and opinion among the émigrés and their dispersion across the vast landscape of American intellectual life produced an exceptionally complex intellectual, social, and institutional history. Notwithstanding their sometimes marginal status or the less prestigious standing of institutions such as the New School, it is nevertheless important to stress that over time the scholars in exile added a new dimension to the understanding of Weber's work and to interest in it. Their concerns and their uses of Weber spilled over to a variety of institutionalized settings, as developments in the immediate postwar years illustrate.

One such setting was the organized discussions at Columbia University. The faculty Seminar on the State offered an important instance of the new postwar uses of Weber's thought across different social science disciplines. Franz Neumann had joined the Columbia faculty in political science, and joined by Karl Wittfogel from the émigrés, along with Robert Merton and others, he participated in this important interdisciplinary seminar, a gathering later attended by C. Wright Mills, Daniel Bell, S. M. Lipset, David Truman, Richard Hofstadter, and Peter Gay. The émigrés had merged into the mainstream of American academia. As evidence of the way some of Weber's ideas permeated the environment, it should be noted that by 1946 in the minutes of the Seminar's biweekly discussions, it is commonplace to find Weber's work on rational-legal authority and bureaucratic forms of organization serving as a shared point of departure and framework for analysis. Knowledge of Weber's ideas from *Wirtschaft und Gesellschaft*, just starting to appear in translation, became a common point of reference for participants. Contrasting positions on the bureaucratic rationalization of the state, past and present, East and West, democratic and authoritarian, were even articulated through commentary on Weber. The problems in these discussions had to do not with the interpretation of Weber's work as such but with particular issues such as the workings of bureaucracy in the Soviet Union, for which Weber's writings simply offered useful guidance and a compelling theoretical perspective.

The discourse of the Columbia Seminar on the State can be regarded as typical: the use of Weber's work as a mode of argumentation, as a text for articulating, clarifying, and distinguishing one's own interpretive and theoretical position. It was increasingly this use of Weber, addressing contested topics not his own, that as much as anything helped create social "carriers" for his ideas and intellectual environments in which those ideas could be restated, criticized, reinterpreted, and thus renewed.

Weberian Sociology and Social Theory

The substantial body of translations principally considered here—namely, Parsons's *The Protestant Ethic and the Spirit of Capitalism*, Gerth and Mills's *From Max Weber: Essays in Sociology*, and Parsons's *The Theory of Social and Economic Organization*—became the basis for the postwar permeation of Weber's work into the social sciences, and especially into the subfield specializations of sociology. To these we can add the three essays from Weber's philosophy of science, the *Wissenschaftslehre*, published finally by Edward Shils with Henry Finch as *The Methodology of the Social Sciences* (1949), a supplemental text that was poorly edited. Some of its neologisms, such as the woolly "ethical neutrality" for the more precise *Wertfreiheit*, have bedeviled discussions ever since and obscured the intention behind Weber's insistence that moral indifference has nothing whatsoever to do with the ideals of rational criticism and "intersubjectivity" in science. Only a few perspicacious thinkers at the periphery, such as Maurice Merleau-Ponty, have understood the existential and intellectual demands this kind of "freedom" imposes.

In the universities by the end of the 1950s, Weber's texts had become standard fare in the sociology of religion, political sociology, studies of bureaucracy and organization, investigations of inequality and social stratification, the comparative historical analysis of social institutions, and the discussions of modernization. This diffusion of the work in sociology was only part of the story, however, for in terms of the major social science disciplines Weber's ideas were also introduced in the same period into political science, cultural anthropology, and some areas of history, philosophy, and the humanities. They became part of the contentious disputes over "positivism," the so-called *Positivismusstreit*, and the philosophical, methodological, and political debate over "value judgments" and "objectivity" in science that was gathering energy by the early 1960s. At the same time it was this somewhat improbable translation, reading, and propagation of Weber's work in America rather than in Europe—as noted recently by Uta Gerhardt—that then made possible Weber's equally improbable and surprising return to his place of origin. Having kept the flame burning in North America, scholars like Parsons and Bendix, even Horkheimer and Adorno, along with many others, would live to see it transported back to Germany, though not under conditions any of them might have chosen.

Nearly half a century has passed since the three conferences held on both sides of the Atlantic in 1964 to commemorate the centennial of Max Weber's birth: those of the Midwest Sociological Society in Kansas City, the International Sociological Association in Montreal, and the Deutsche Gesellschaft für Soziologie in Heidelberg. Reviewing these proceedings today, especially those in Heidelberg, is like entering the superheated, misty cultural and ideological battlefields of the 1960s, with Weber and his work serving as a stand-in for conflicting positions, agendas, and accusations, some of them from a past that was refusing to pass. These conferences represented a kind of caesura in the recovery and reconstruction of Weber's thought. They brought into sharp focus a number of issues in the social sciences, the academic disciplines, and the universities that had concerned Weber and received attention in some of his most important texts, such as "Science as a Vocation" and "Politics as a Vocation": the duties of the teacher and scholar; the critical assessment of political and economic power; the social and cultural effects of capitalism; the uses of scientific inquiry and human reason in an age dominated by big science, vast bureaucracies, and impersonal market forces; the prospects for social justice or socialism; and our responsibility for history. In the most visible venues, however, these issues played out as a hostile face-off between competing intellectual orientations, with orthodox "Weberians" on the one side, such as Parsons and Bendix, and proponents of a "critical theory," such as Adorno and Marcuse, on the other. Protagonists like Raymond Aron seemed caught between contending parties in the *querelles allemandes*.

In the decades since then the underlying issues connected to Weber's thought have never entirely vanished, and those defined by the problem of "rationality" and the "most fateful force in our modern life, capitalism," have returned with a vengeance in the first decade of the twenty-first century. But from the perspective of the present, as the abbreviated twentieth century from 1914 to 1991 has come to a close, such fundamental and enduring themes have been joined by an eclectic mix of preoccupations conditioned by numerous intellectual, cultural, and political factors, including the decline of Parsons and Shils's general theory of action, the demise of structural functionalism in the social sciences, the collapse of Marxism, the "cultural" turn in the social sciences and humanities, the end of the Cold War and its accompanying realignments, and the social tensions and confusions of the most recent fin de siècle. In the rush into our current century only a few monuments and points of reference from the mid-twentieth century have been left standing; Weber's thought is one of them.

Figure 13. Talcott Parsons later in life in his Harvard University study, the battles
in the 1960s over Weber's legacy and the seriousness of the times etched on
his countenance. Harvard University Archives, call # UAV 605.295.7, Box 3.
Reproduced by permission.

Taking stock of what remains has assumed different forms. Weber's work as
a whole has at last come under scrutiny, with the laborious compilation and
editing in Germany of the authoritative collected works as a critical edition,
the *Max Weber Gesamtausgabe*, accompanied by a gold mine of unpublished
correspondence and cultural landmarks from the still poorly understood Wilhelmine era. With this effort the opportunities for historical and biographical
contextualization have expanded enormously. Itself a product of Cold War
competition, the *Max Weber Gesamtausgabe* has outlived the reasons for its
birth to open vistas onto deeper and richer prospects for comprehending the
biography of the work.

In the academic disciplines the emphasis has often been on assimilating the work, extending it in different directions, and applying it to a startling range of contemporary problems, such as those encountered in the application of law, the administration of justice, the formation of institutions in the European Union, the operations of the modern corporation, the nature of "rationality" in modern market capitalism, the character of modernizing regimes in the developing world, or the problems of the modern habitus and living in a "disenchanted" world. Among these newer interpretations, the stylish apotheosis of the Weberian thesis of disenchantment—the phenomenal world has become rationalized, calculable, denuded of magical and mysterious forces—and its mirror image, the promise of "reenchantment," is a telling case in point. The specification of the "disenchanted" condition and the ensuing discussion plays out as an affirmation, argument, elaboration, explication, extension, amplification, critique, or denial of the viewpoint Weber enunciated.

Judging from numerous collections of articles that have appeared over the past decade, there has also been considerable attention directed toward specifying the basic features not just of Weber's work but of the "Weberian" outlook or position in social theory. In America, sociological theory may still figure as the "ground zero" for such disputations, but elsewhere the conversations have migrated beyond porous disciplinary boundaries to a generalized interest in "social theory" wherever it appears. The rediscovered author has now come of age and spawned a movement of thought, an adjective before the noun, a perspective or theoretical approach, or in the words of one prominent group of scholars, a "research program" or "paradigm."

What can Weberian "theory" or a Weberian "research program," "paradigm" or "perspective" possibly signify? It would be an exaggeration to maintain that general agreement has been achieved on answering such a question, or that consensus exists even on the very project of abstracting a "Weberian theory" from Weber's incomplete, exploratory, and unsystematic writings. One of the attractions and strengths of the work has always been its unrivaled scope, variety, and indeterminacy. But the contours of an emergent perspective, if not the precise contents, have become discernable amid the recent outpouring of books, articles, collections, and commentaries. To delineate these contours is to synthesize and condense dramatically the underlying structure of Weber's thinking—which is by its nature, we should not forget, always problem-oriented rather than oriented toward articulating a general "theory" or specifying a methodological position.

With this caveat in mind, for those in search of "theory" it seems self-evident that Weber's central questions were always directed toward investigating developmental dynamics and understanding their consequences for the conduct of life in different sociohistorical contexts. In his work such questioning is indeed obsessive and singular. Viewed through the lens of an expository synthesis, such as that proposed by M. Rainer Lepsius, Weberian investigations thus can be thought of as displaying an interest in "dynamic processes"— that is, developmental dynamics driven by conflicting social forces that are open-ended in terms of type, duration, pace, direction, and consequences. Following Weber's lead, developmental dynamics can be conceptualized in terms of a three-part relationship among structure, action, and meaning, to use the terminology of the moment in the social sciences. Stated somewhat more elaborately, Weberian analysis is thought to be concerned with three central problems and their relationship: the problem of the external *structure* or material form in which action occurs; the problem of the *rationality* of action and association, or the forming of social relationships; and the problem of *cultural* "meanings" and "significance," including the meaning of action for both subjects and observers. This tripartite orientation seems to emerge even in the opening sections of *Wirtschaft und Gesellschaft*.

From the perspective of theory and the elusive "research program" or "paradigm," to state the matter in this way is important, for it suggests that Weber's work bridges the analytic approaches in the social sciences that are often proposed as alternatives: the structural, the institutional, the rational action or action-oriented, and the cultural modes of inquiry. Furthermore, it now becomes possible to point out that in the Weberian view the relationship among the three problem complexes is worked out at different levels of analysis: at the *individual* level of the actor and action orientations, at the *social* level of associations, institutions, and organizations; and at the *cultural* level of legitimation processes and disputes over "values" and the "normative" order. The entire sociology of legitimate authority or domination is filled with such variations. No single problem complex or level of analysis can claim logical priority either, for to do so would be to prejudge the relationships any investigation aims to reveal. This insistence on a configurational, "multicausal" and "multilevel" analysis, using the language of contemporary social science, amounts to a recommendation always to search for the unique particulars and the differences in any configuration of events, the "combination" or "concatenation of circumstances" Weber referenced that accounts for large-scale sociohistorical transformation.

Summarized in this way and abstracted from its concrete problematics, the Weberian project thus has been shown to be capable of suggesting modes of analysis and paths of investigation applicable to the most varied problems and problem complexes. In this view the extension of the conceptual language— from asceticism to *Zweckrationalität*, so to speak—is constrained only by the investigator's imagination. From such a perspective, completing the process Parsons set in motion, Weber's work has thus become an authoritative voice not only in the settled domains of sociology and other established social sciences, but also in the rarified atmosphere of "social theory" with all its exotic possibilities and alternatives, from the reflections of George Herbert Mead to the inquiries of Pierre Bourdieu. The identity of the "Weberian" theory, research program, or perspective has finally come of age.

Weber beyond Weberian Sociology

Setting forth such a general and abstract claim can be intellectually satisfying. It encourages us to recognize that Max Weber did achieve an intellectual synthesis, as Parsons maintained, though not a synthesis of concepts and categories confined solely to the general theory of action. It was rather a complex synthesis formed from combining structural and institutional analysis, notions of rationality, propositions about social action, awareness of cultural particularities, and a deep appreciation for historical inquiry and evidence, or as Weber wrote in the final sentence of *The Protestant Ethic and the Spirit of Capitalism*, a single-minded pursuit of that elusive construction, "historical truth." Such a synthesis was justified not by its stand-alone generality as theory but by its heuristic promise in grasping and clarifying significant puzzles, problems, and questions about the phenomena of the social and historical world. The synthesis was brought to life by its nuanced qualities, varied applications, and problem-centered specificity, not by its drive toward systematicity.

Notwithstanding their elegance, the efforts to recast Weber's work as canonical for the social sciences and central to its current agendas must always remain radically incomplete, for it fails to capture the new edges of excitement and agitation that will always grip those kinds of inquiry notable not for their well-defended paradigms but for their "eternal youthfulness," to borrow Weber's suggestive phrase.

The recent struggle for the mastery of Weber has charted a double course. One direction has seen an expansion of the horizon for Weber's ideas beyond the boundaries of sociology to the commanding vistas of the Western philosophical and political tradition, of which modern sociology is but one constituent element. From these heights of thought the partners in conversation for Weber are not so much Parsons and Mills but figures like Thucydides, Plato, Aristotle, Niccolò Machiavelli, Immanuel Kant, G.W.F. Hegel, Alexis de Tocqueville, Karl Marx, John Stuart Mill, and Friedrich Nietzsche, as well as the entire tradition of civic republicanism, liberalism, and liberal democratic thought. In this view Weber arrives very late, coming at the end of more than two millennia of reflection on matters of civic and philosophical import. The lessons of the Western tradition concerning ethics and politics receive a trenchant summation in his most consequential, penetrating, and socially engaged writing. The work circles back to the starting points in antiquity, retrieving the questions about what we should do and how we should live, though posed now in a radically different rationalized and disenchanted modern world that demands novel, complex, honest, and often unsettling answers.

The spirit animating this perspective has encouraged a subtle reorientation, a shift in focus toward Weber's preoccupation with the human condition, with "statecraft and soulcraft." If we ask what were Weber's deepest concerns, then the answer from this standpoint is, in a phrase, the formation of the personality and character of the individual within the different orders of life. The Weberian concepts of *Lebensführung* and *Lebensordnung*, of "conduct of life" and the "orders of life," are elevated to the status of master concepts. The concentrated synthesis of ideas from the sociology of religion, the highly charged "Zwischenbetrachtung," or "Intermediate Reflection," which Gerth and Mills retitled "Religious Rejections of the World and Their Direction," becomes the master text, drawing together the scattered strands of Weber's thought. It offers an unusual adventure of the mind: a guided tour, complete with historical illustrations and comparisons, through the practices of the self in Western civilization.

Weber's relationship to predecessors in the Western tradition plays out thematically in his emphasis on the importance of moral and political judgment, the ethic of responsibility, the interaction between charisma and political education, the institutions for cultivating citizenship, and the creation of an active civil society through the power of association—precisely the themes of his American journey. The emphasis could be seen as a singular "preoccupation with ethical characterology and public citizenship in a modern mass democracy," as an effort to retrieve the classical political tradition and breathe new life into the practice of what Machiavelli used to call civic *virtù*. This particular Weberian project is indeed deeply enmeshed in the political and philosophical traditions of Western thought, a reminder in the biography of the work of Weber's admiration for the thinkers of Greek antiquity and his attraction to Rome and attachments to the civilization of the Renaissance in Italy.

The other direction in the encounter with Weber recapitulates in a very different world and under quite different circumstances the kind of enthusiasms experienced by readers like the young Talcott Parsons and Edward Shils, for today Weber's thought has traveled beyond American sociology to other perspectives, social contexts, and modes of thought, pressing against the boundaries of the recognized disciplines. The Americanized Weber of the founding clusters of scholars in the social sciences has given way to an international dialogue of impressive scope, ranging far beyond American shores to Eastern Europe, Russia, Spain, Latin America, the Middle East, China, Korea, Taiwan, and Japan. This surprising journey of a body of thought has occurred not merely because Weber wrote in an original idiom, or because his subjects actually *were* the various cultures, religions, and economies of the world, East and West, but because the grammar, concepts and *problematic* of the thought continue to capture the drama of the times and to inspire a response. The light of the great cultural problems may have moved on, but Weber's thought has moved with them.

Of the great cultural problems, one continues to remain central and to connect us to the past: the rationalization processes in the life orders of the world, to use Weber's formulation—or, in more informal terms, the problem of "modernization" and the inescapable conflict between traditionalism and the forces of the modern world, the very heart of Weber's problematic in numerous texts, including especially *The Protestant Ethic and the Spirit of Capitalism.* Thus, when Weber's ideas appear amid debates in a country like contemporary Iran, it is not surprising to find the question of "legitimate domination" raised with reference to "patrimonialism," a traditional type of rule salient there and missing or obscured elsewhere. Or when the issue is the creation of "social capital" and the relationship between civil society and the state, whether in Lithuania or Korea, Weber's commentaries about associational life can offer a clarifying perspective and a way of confronting the conflicts caused by the grinding forces of the modern world of rationalization, especially in societies experiencing jarring dislocations and social transformations.

Nowhere has the dynamic effect of reading Weber been more evident than in Japan, where an independent reception of the work has been in progress dating from the era of Knight and Parsons. (In China, by contrast, the encounter with Weber's work is recent, relying almost entirely not on the original texts, but on the English-language translations transcribed into Chinese.) The Japanese fascination with Weber has a compelling explanation, for in the words of one authority, the deep and lasting impact of Weber's writings

> since the 1920s should be ascribed to the fact that a large segment of social and cultural science has interpreted the modern history of Japanese society as a special case of partial modernization or, in Weberian terms, of partial rationalization. In Weber's work scholars encountered in ideal-typical form the autonomous development of personality in civil society. They took this model out of its cultural context and applied it as a method and value to the analysis of Japanese society . . . and the Asian world . . . For Japanese "modernists" (*kindaishugisha*) Weber's work and person showed a path out of the magic garden of religious and political salvation doctrines and let them see with new eyes the world from which they came and which they entered.

This different reading of Weber has little to do with a program of research, instead revealing a much more urgent search for an orientation to the world, for knowledge of how to act and what to do. In this respect it shares an aspect of the effort to place Weber's thought within the Western political and philosophical tradition.

Max Weber in Japan offers a kind of template. The experience of Japan's opening to the West—that is, to the forces of "rationalization" or "modernization"—continues to be repeated everywhere. There is no escape, and there are no exceptions. It is always a journey from the magical, romanticized past to the rationalized, disenchanted present and future, from the poetic to the prosaic. As in the Indian Territory of 1904, so in other times, places, and cultures: with lightening speed everything standing in the way of capitalist culture is swept aside. Then as now, the question always becomes, How will individuals respond, and how will a society and a culture adapt to the new forces unleashed by the modern project?

Weber's work will continue to resonate in those times and places where the encounter with rationalization persists and the stresses of the transformation of tradition are keenly felt, for the work is attuned not only to the dynamics of rationalization but also to the range and types of possible responses, the allure of all manner of escape routes from the aporias of modernity: mastery of the world; flight from the world; reconciliation with opposed forces; quiescent surrender to fate; revival of old beliefs; return to venerated traditions; escape into aestheticism, intellectualism, eroticism, or some other solipsistic way of leading one's life; transcendence through the power of the extraordinary, through charisma; the call of "revolution." The possibilities are always renewable; there can be no final accounting of the all-too-human search for alternatives.

Max Weber in America—the journey and the dissemination of the work—contributed to launching multiple projects that are still underway and far from complete. It is thus worth remembering that the attention given to Weber's writings and to matters Weberian will continue to depend, as it always has, upon the richness, brilliance, complexity, and open-ended quality of the thought. The context and audience for reading the work may change, but the confusions of the present will always remain, addressed in a bewildering variety of ways. In such circumstances one of the most fruitful and compelling choices continues to be, as it has been in the past, the fresh encounter with the work itself. Only in that way can the thought remain alive, connected to the great cultural problems of the times, and capable of renewal.

APPENDIX 1

Max and Marianne Weber's Itinerary
for the American Journey in 1904

August 17	Departure from Heidelberg
August 20	Departure from Bremen, Germany, aboard the *Bremen*
August 29	Arrival in New York Harbor; the *Bremen* is sighted "south of Fire Island at 7:30 p.m."
August 30	Passengers disembark
August 30–September 4	New York City; Astor House at Broadway and Vesey Street; visit to the Stock Exchange, Brooklyn Bridge, Green-Wood Cemetery in Brooklyn, Fifth Avenue mansions; discussions with Professor William Hervey, Columbia University
September 4	Train to Niagara Falls with Ernst Troeltsch
September 5–9	Niagara Falls: Hotel Kaltenbach; joined by Paul Hensel
September 6	Visit North Tonawanda, New York; the German Reform Church; meet Hans and Grete Conrad Haupt
September 7	Meet Professor Edmund James, president of Northwestern University, his wife Anna Margarethe Lange, and their sons
September 8	Marianne visits Buffalo, New York, settlements with Professor Johannes Conrad and Grete Conrad Haupt
September 9	Train to Chicago
September 9–17	Chicago, Auditorium Building Hotel, Michigan Avenue
September 11	Hull House visit, meet Jane Addams; Marianne attends WTUL Meeting
September 14	Northwestern University, Evanston, Illinois; attend Methodist Chapel, probably with Professor James Taft Hatfield
September 15	Congress of Arts and Science invitees visit the University of Chicago and the Field Museum; reception at Reynold's Club, possibly meeting Albion Small
September 16	Max visits the stockyards; evening banquet for Congress participants, Auditorium Building
September 17	Train to St. Louis, Missouri; Max to stay until September 26, Marianne until October 1; stay with August Gehner and family, 4498 Lindell Boulevard
September 18	Troeltsch visits the Gehners
September 19	Congress of Arts and Science begins

September 20	Max and Marianne's eleventh anniversary
September 21	Max's lecture, "The Relations of the Rural Community to Other Branches of Social Science" (official translated title)
September 22	Marianne attends the Woman's Club dinner ("Science Section of the Wednesday Club"); Max probably attends Jacob Hollander's lecture, "The Scope and Method of Political Economy"
September 25 or earlier	Breakfast with W.E.B. Du Bois
September 26	Max travels to Oklahoma Territory by night train
September 27	Max arrives in Guthrie, Oklahoma at the Hotel Royal, 11:40 a.m., and stays one hour, according to the *Daily Oklahoman*; he then travels to Muskogee, Indian Territory
September 27–October 1	Max in Muskogee at McFarland's Hotel and Café
September 28	Max has lunch with Robert Latham Owen and his mother, Narcissa Chisholm Owen; meetings with Col. Clarence B. Douglass, editor of the *Muskogee Phoenix*; J. Blair Shoenfelt, Indian agent; J. George Wright, Indian inspector; and Tams Bixby, chair of the Dawes Commission
September 29–30	Max takes trip to Fort Gibson Clubhouse
September 29	In St. Louis, Marianne visits a coeducational high school with Pauline Gehner Mesker
September 30	Max observes a land auction
October 1	Max observes the Creek payment; stops in South McAlester, Indian Territory; Max and Marianne travel separately to Memphis, Tennessee, by night trains
October 2	Max and Marianne rendezvous in Memphis at the Peabody Hotel, and continue to New Orleans
October 3–5	New Orleans
October 5	Train to Tuskegee, Alabama
October 5–7	Tuskegee; meetings with Margaret Washington, Jane Clark, and the staff of the Tuskegee Instutute; Marianne attends the Tuskegee Women's Club; encounter with Dr. S. Becker von Grabil
October 8	Train through Atlanta, and Chattanooga, Tennessee, to Knoxville, Tennessee
October 9–12	Knoxville with William F. (Bill) Miller and family; discussions with John P. Murphy, Miller's law partner
October 12–13	Asheville, North Carolina, at the Manor, Albemarle Park; visit to the Vanderbilt estate Biltmore
October 14	Stop in Greensboro, North Carolina; lunch at Hotel Huffine after leaving Asheville at 5 a.m.; continue by train to Mount Airy, North Carolina

October 14–16	Mount Airy with Jim and Jeff Miller and relatives
October 16	Attend Methodist church service, Mt. Airy, with Miller relatives in the morning; Baptist sevice in the afternoon
October 17	Train to Richmond, Virginia
October 18	Tour of Richmond in the morning; train from Richmond to Washington, D.C.
October 18–24	Washington, D.C., at the Raleigh Hotel; visits to Mount Vernon, Arlington National Cemetery; Max meets Samuel Gompers
October 23	Attend African American church service at Nineteenth Street Baptist Church
October 24	Train to Philadelphia
October 24–28	Philadelphia at the Aldine Hotel, 1910 Chestnut Street
October 25	Max visits the Johns Hopkins University in Baltimore, attends Jacob Hollander's lecture and seminar; meets George E. Barnett
October 26	Marianne visits Bryn Mawr College and meets Martha Carey Thomas; Max visits Haverford College and its library, and meets Professor Don Carlos Barrett
October 27	Attend the Quaker service at Haverford Friends Meeting, hearing Allen Clapp Thomas speak on the saints
October 28	Train to Boston
October 28–November 4	Boston, at Young's Hotel
October 29	Attend a football game: University of Pennsylvania defeats Harvard University, 11–0
October 30	At Hugo Münsterberg's home, 7 Ware Street, Cambridge, Massachusetts; meeting with William James;
October 31–November 1	To Melrose, northern Boston suburb; visit with Laura Fallenstein and Otto von Klock
November 2–3	Max uses the Harvard University Library; probably meets John Brooks, William Ripley; Marianne visits Wellesley College (twice) with Ethel Dench Puffer, and attends a lecture by Ethel Dench Puffer; also visits Simmons College; Max and Marianne pay another visit to the Münsterberg home
November 4	Train to New York City via Providence, Rhode Island (Max visits Brown University Library there) and New Haven, Connecticut
November 5–19	New York City, at the Holland House, Fifth Ave. and Thirtieth Street (November 4–7), and at 167 Madison Ave. (November 7–19)
November 6	Max attends a service at the First Church of Christ Scientist, Central Park West at Ninety-sixth Street; Marianne

	attends a Presbyterian Service at the Marble Collegiate Church, Fifth Avenue at Twenty-ninth Street
November 8	Theodore Roosevelt elected president
November 10	Dinner with a trade union secretary and his wife, probably Jerome F. and Margaret Ufer Healy
November 11	Dinner at Paul Lichtenstein's, 182 Amity Street, Brooklyn
November 12	Visit to University Settlement, meet Lillian Wald; attend a lecture by Dr. Yamei Kin, "A Chinese Woman's View of the War in the East"
November 13	Attend Ethical Culture Society meeting, Carnegie Hall; Felix Adler speaks on "Mental Healing as a Religion"
November 14	Dinner at Edwin and Caroline Seligman's home with colleagues and friends, including Felix Adler
November 7–18	Meet Florence Kelley, hear her speak at the School of Philanthropy meet Otto Weber and his wife, and Hermann Rösing; meet Helen Frances Garrison Villard; Marianne attends a "working girls' club" meeting and dines with Lillian Wald at one of the settlements; also attends a boys' club meeting at the settlement; Max at Columbia University, working in the library and attending lectures
November 17	Dinner at Alfred Lichtenstein's, 201 Columbia Heights, Brooklyn
November 18	Reception in honor of Marianne at the Columbia University Club; attend a performance of Jacob Gordin's play *Di emese kraft* at the Yiddish Theater with Gordin and David Blaustein, the latter the leader of the Educational Alliance
November 19	Departure from New York aboard the *Hamburg*
November 27	Arrival in Cherbourg, France; train via Paris to Heidelberg

APPENDIX 2

Max Weber, Selected Correspondence with American Colleagues, 1904–5

Note: Correspondence is listed alphabetically by correspondent.

W. E. B. DU BOIS

Max Weber to W.E.B. Du Bois, 8 November 1904
New York City
handwritten (incomplete)
Du Bois Papers, reel 3; Du Bois Library, University of Massachusetts–Amherst
[letterhead:] Holland House, 5th Avenue and Thirtieth Street

167 Madison Avenue
(until 18th Nov[ember], afterwards: Heidelberg, Germany)

Dear Sir—

I learned from you at St. Louis that you hoped to be back at Atlanta after the 20th of October. Unfortunately my wife could not stand the climate of the South and so I failed to see your University and to make your acquaintance,—the few minutes at St. Louis not counting in this respect. I hope to be allowed to do so another time.

To-day I beg you to take into consideration a request I have to make as editor (together with Prof. Sombart) of the "Archiv für Sozialwissenschaft und Sozialpolitik". Until now, I failed in finding in the American (and, of course, in any other) litterature [sic] an investigation about the relations between the (so-called) "race-problem" and the (so-called) "class-problem" in your country, although it is impossible to have any conversation with white people of the South without feeling the connection. We have to meet to-day in Germany not only the dilettantic litterature [sic] à la H[ouston] St[ewart] Chamberlain & Com., but a "scientific" race-theory, built up on purely anthropological fundaments, too,—and so we have to accentuate especially those connections and the influence of social-economic conditions upon the relations of races to each-other. I saw that you spoke, some weeks ago, about this very question, and I should be very glad, if you would find yourself in a position to give us, for our periodical, an essay about that object. So I bid you to write me, whether you should be willing to do so, and at what time?

Max Weber to W.E.B. Du Bois
17 November 1904
New York City
handwritten
Du Bois Papers, reel 3; Du Bois Library, University of Massachusetts–Amherst

Dear Sir—
I received your kind letter dated Nov. 8th and am indeed very glad, that you are dis-
posed to give us the essay I asked you for. I shall with pleasure read the studies about the
race problem you kindly promised to send me, and hope to be allowed to ask you also
for a report and schedule of the lectures of the Atlanta University, showing if possible
the text books used in the social-science-lectures, *if* I could get them.

I am quite sure to come back to your country as soon as possible and especially to the
South, because I am absolutely convinced that the "colour-line" problem will be the
paramount problem of the time to come, here and everywhere in the world.
    My German address is, simply: Prof. M[ax] W[eber], Heidelberg. I am going there
this Saturday, and am
    Yours very respectfully
    Max Weber

Max Weber to W.E.B. Du Bois
30 March 1905
Heidelberg
handwritten
Du Bois Papers, reel 3, Du Bois Library, University of Massachusetts–Amherst

Dear Sir,
I was glad to receive your kind letter. When, at the 15th, your article was not yet at
hand, I supposed you might perhaps be prevented of writing the same now, and so we
had to dispose about the space of the next number of the "Archiv." So, your article
will be published at the head of the number to be edited *November 1st* of this year,—it
would be hardly possible at any earlier time. —

Your splendid work: "The souls of black folk" ought *to be translated in German*. I do not
know, whether anybody has already undertaken to make a translation. *If not*, I am au-
thorized to beg you for your authorisation to Mrs. Elizabeth *Jaffé* = von Richthofen here,
a scholar and friend of mine, late factory inspector at Karlsruhe, now wife of my fellow-
teacher and fellow-editor Dr. Jaffé. I should like to write a short introduction about Negro-
question and -litterature [sic], and should be much obliged to you for some information
about your life: viz. only: age, birthplace, descent, positions held by you,—of course, only
if you give your authorization. I think Mrs. Jaffé would be a very able translator, which
will be of some importance, your vocabulary and style being very peculiar: it reminds me
sometimes of Gladstone's [idioms], although the spirit is a different one. —

I should like to give in one of the next numbers of the "Archiv" a short review of the recent publications about the "race problem" in America. Besides your own work and the "Character-Building" of Mr. Booker Washington, I got only the book of Mr. Page ("The Negro, the Southerner Problem"—very superficial me thinks), the "Occasional papers" of your Academy and the article of Mr. Wilcox in the Yale Review. If there is anything else to be reviewed, I should be much obliged to you for any information. (Of course I saw the article of Viereck in the official publication). —

Please excuse my bad English—I seldom here had the opportunity to speak it, and realize a language in speaking and writing it is very different.

Yours very respectfully

Professor Max Weber

Max Weber to W.E.B. Du Bois

17 April 1905

Heidelberg

handwritten

Du Bois Papers, reel 3; Du Bois Library, University of Massachusetts–Amherst

Dear Sir —

your manuscript came to my hands to-day. We shall provide for the translation as soon as possible, and it will be printed in the number of November 1st of this year. I hope you have received my letter on behalf of Frau Dr. Jaffé.

I thank you very much for your very useful article and am

Yours very respectfully

Prof. Max Weber

W.E.B. Du Bois to Max Weber

18 April [1905]

handwritten copy (incomplete)

Du Bois Papers, reel 3; Du Bois Library, University of Massachusetts–Amherst

My Dear Professor Weber:

It is very kind for you to offer Madame Jaffa [sic]-von Richthofen's services in the translation of my book & if the necessary business arrangements can be made I shall be delighted to accept her services. I have written my publishers, Messrs. A. C. McClurg & Co., in whose name my book is copyrighted & told them of your offer. They reply that they are negotiating for a French translation with their Paris representative, M. Terquem & that thru him they will take up your proposition & see if they can interest some German publishers.

Meantime may I ask if you know of any German publisher who would probably be willing to undertake the publishing of a German translation. If you do kindly let me know. I will write you on this matter again as soon as I hear further.

I trust my manuscript is by this time in your hand. It is a rather hurried piece of work & if it is not just what you want do not hesitate to cut it down or reject it.

As to literature on the Negro problem the recent publications include:

Sinclair: Aftermath of Slavery (Sewell Maynard & Co.)

Johnson: Light Ahead for the Negro (Grafton Press)

Collins: Domestic Slave Trade (Broadway Pub. Co.)

Max Weber to W.E.B. Du Bois
1 May 1905
Heidelberg
handwritten
Du Bois Papers, reel 3; Du Bois Library, University of Massachusetts–Amherst

My dear colleague!

I thank you very much for your kind letter. *We have engaged* a publisher—Dr. P[aul] Siebeck (Firma: J. C. B. Mohr), Tübingen, the publisher of the "Archiv für Sozialpolitik" —, *of course* with reservation of your previous consent to the making of the translation. I beg you to inform your publisher and hope there will be no difficulties.

The library of our University will certainly be very glad to have your University publications. I thank you very much for your useful informations.

Will you not have your "Sabbath-year" one of the next years? I hope you will come to Germany then, once more, and visit us. As to me, [perhaps] I shall come to the United States, I think, 1907 or 8.

Yours very respectfully
Prof. Max Weber

JACOB H. HOLLANDER

Max Weber to Jacob Hollander
27 October 1904
Philadelphia, Aldine Hotel
handwritten
Hollander Papers, series I, box 11; Eisenhower Library, the Johns Hopkins University

Dear Professor Hollander—

Allow me to express, again, how much I enjoyed my visit in your seminary, the acquaintance I made of your students and of your assistant fellow-teacher. I was deeply impressed by the intensity of the work done in your department and, before all, learned with pleasure, that—at least in your university—the ambition to get the largest *number* of students, so dangerous even now to almost all our German universities—is not allowed to lower the high standard of scientific investigation. In Germany we suffer much more than you are able to imagine from that illness resulting out of our system of paying the teacher by taxes paid by the students for each lecture.—When I come again after some years—as I hope to do—[I] think my English will be improved so that I will be more able to express myself. —

I talked with you about the questions of the Indian Territory and asked you, during our conversation, if you would be inclined to give us for the "Archiv für Sozialwissenschaft u. Sozialpolitik" an essay about the development of these questions during the time since the treaties giving existence to that territory. Do you think to be able to fulfill my request and—perhaps—to inform me about the time, at which you will probably be able to do so?

I should be even more happy, if I could get from you for our periodical an essay about the present development of economic investigation in America. I agreed so much with your statement—at St. Louis—that the rapid progress of the scientific work done in your country is almost unknown in Germany, even by many specialists in economic science. I am quite sure that critics of *single* works of American writers would not change the situation, if not our problem, *before* reading such critics as we hope to give in the future in our periodical, but get some broader information about the evolution of American economic investigation as *a whole*, the different methods used, the "schools" and their relations to European "schools" etc.—I don't know where to apply if not to you and should indeed by very happy if you could give us an essay of this character. I beg you to take this request in consideration and hope to get from you a promise. I am informed that you have recently published some articles about objects like this. —

Do you think I should be able to get some recent reports of the Johns Hopkins University and, if possible, the rules for taking the Ph.D. degree, by simply applying to the Secretary of the President? or are the[y] sold by the bookseller? I should be much obliged for any information about that and am sorry having forgotten to ask you in Baltimore.

Yours very respectfully

Max Weber

(Young's Hotel, Boston or: Holland House, New York)

P.S. For your information about the formalities of our periodical: we pay for essays 80 Mark (= ca. 19$) for each 16 pages, maximum 240 Mks. for the single essay.

Max Weber to Jacob Hollander
3 November 1904
Young's Hotel, Boston
handwritten
Hollander Papers, series I, box 11; Eisenhower Library, the Johns Hopkins University

Dear Professor Hollander

I received with thanks your letter of Nov. 2d and am glad to see, that you are willing to contribute to our periodical. We should be interested to get specially a sketch of the *present* tendencies of development in American economic investigation and should be very glad if you would develop your essay in that direction—the *earlier* history of American economic thoughts being today rather *better* known in Germany than their *present* conditions. I beg you to write me to Heidelberg, or—if you are able to inform me already now—to New York, Holland House, at *what time* you think we shall have to expect your essay and how large it (approximately) will be (longer or shorter than your essay in the Yale Review). I am at N. York until 18th November.

I will *try* to make arrangements for an exchange of our publications so as you kindly suggest. The difficulty is that our library and our seminary *both are* subscribers to the Johns Hopkins Studies and, of course, the Breslau library to[o] and the number to our disposition for exchanges are very limited now—we exchange, I think, with at least 8–10 American *periodicals*,—and so my fellow-editors Sombart a[nd] Jaffé might perhaps not yield to your proposal. I write you about that from Germany. Sombart is—I was surprised to be informed so here—gone back to Germany October 28th.

Yours very respectfully,
Max Weber

EDWIN R. A. SELIGMAN

Max Weber to Edwin R. A. Seligman
19 November 1904
New York
handwritten
Seligman Papers, Columbia University Rare Book and Manuscript Library

Sehr geehrter Herr Kollege!
Wir können New York nicht verlassen, ohne Ihrer Frau Gemahlin und Ihnen nochmals unsren verbindlichsten Dank auszusprechen für die ganz außerordentliche Liebenswürdigkeit, mit der Sie uns aufgenommen und uns hier die Wege geebnet haben. Eine ganze Reihe von genuß- und lehrreichsten Abenden verdanken meine Frau und ich ausschließlich Ihrer freundlichen Fürsorge und Vermittlung.

Ich werde voraussichtlich im Lauf der nächsten Jahre die V. Staaten noch einmal besuchen, und hoffe dann nicht in dem Maße wie jetzt in der Eile und überdies durch meine ungenügende Beherrschung der englischen Sprache und außerdem durch meine auch hier gelegentlich noch recht fatal fühlbare Krankheit gehemmt zu sein.

Ich bitte Sie nochmals, die selbst für "Dutchmen" außergewöhnliche Formlosigkeit, mit der wir uns hier betragen haben, zu verzeihen,—es war tatsächlich nicht anders möglich gegenüber dem überwältigenden Maße von persönlichen Beziehungen, die sich hier alsbald entwickelten. Ich hoffe, Ihre Frau Gemahlin und Sie geben uns recht bald die Ehre eines Besuches in Heidelberg—vielleicht während Ihres "Sabbathjahres"? Ich erlaube mir, Ihnen demnächst einige Essays zu schicken, die Sie vielleicht im Anschluß an unsere Unterhaltungen interessieren.

Mit ausgezeichneter Hochachtung und collegialem Gruß
sowie angelegentlichster Empfehlung an Ihre Frau Gemahlin
Ihr ergebenster
Max Weber und Frau

[We could not leave New York without again expressing our deepest thanks to you and your wife for the extraordinary kindness you showed in receiving us and paving the way for us. Thanks to your friendly concern and assistance my wife and I enjoyed a whole series of the most enjoyable and informative evenings.

I will probably visit the United States again in the course of the coming years, and hope then not to be rushed to such an extent, and not to be constrained by my inadequate command of English, or the unfortunate illness that I feel occasionally.

Please excuse again our uncommon informality, even for us too as "Dutchmen." Anything else was quite impossible in view of the overwhelming number of personal relationships that developed so quickly here. I hope you and your wife will soon give us the honor of a visit in Heidelberg, perhaps during your sabbatical? I shall send you several essays that may interest you in light of our conversations.]

Max Weber to Edwin R. A. Seligman
18 December 1905
Heidelberg, Hauptstrasse 73
handwritten
Seligman Papers, Columbia University Rare Book and Manuscript Library

Sehr geehrter Herr College!
Sie haben mir durch Übersendung Ihres Werkes ("Principles of Economics") eine große Freude und Überraschung bereitet und ich beneide Sie sehr um die bedeutende Arbeitskraft, welche in dieser Leistung sich ausspricht. Ich habe erst einen Teil Ihrer Darlegungen lesen können, da ich tief in logischen Arbeiten stecke, und darf mir daher kein Urteil erlauben. Mich freut es, daß Sie ebenso wie dies überhaupt in den V. St. geschieht, das Übermaß von Historismus, welches durch den starken Einfluß Schmoller's auf uns lastet, entschlossen bei Seite lassen und das gute alte Prinzip: "qui bene distinguit, bene docet," nach wie vor gelten lassen. Bei uns ist zur Zeit fast jeder Muth zu theoretischer Arbeit und die Unbefangenheit in der Prägung klarer Begriffe dahin, und Sombart's Arbeiten—so *sehr* hoch ich sie stelle—haben darin keine Wandlung gebracht.

Ich kann leider Ihre Sendung vorerst kaum mit einem noch so bescheidenen Gegengabe erwiedern, da meine Studien sich auf sehr entlegenen Gebieten bewegen.

Eine besondere Freude wäre es mir, und sicherlich auch Sombart, wenn Sie gelegentlich Veranlaßung nähmen, sich einmal in unserem "Archiv" zu äußern,—jetzt wo Sie diese große Arbeit abgeschloßen haben, ist ja Ihre Arbeitskraft wieder freier als bisher.

Ihr Werk wird selbstverständlich in unserer Zeitschrift eingehend besprochen werden, nur bedarf es etwas Zeit, da unser Raum zur Zeit übermäßig besetzt ist und es auch nicht leicht ist, einen geeigneten deutschen Rezensenten zu finden. Doch werden wir alle Mühe aufwenden.

Mit den besten Neujahrs-Gratulationen und Empfehlungen, auch meine Frau, an Ihre Frau Gemahlin und Sie.

bleibe ich
Ihr hochachtungsvoll ergebenster
Max Weber

[I am very pleased and delighted to have received your book ("Principles of Economics"), and I am envious of the substantial labor and effort evident in this accomplishment. I have been able to read only a part of your exposition, as I am deeply immersed in logical work, and thus have to withhold an evaluation. I am pleased that you decisively set aside the excesses of historicism—as occurs generally in the United States, and that weighs on us because of the strong influence of Schmoller—and accept as valid the good old principle: "qui bene distinguit, bene docet" (he who distinguishes well, teaches or learns well). At the moment in Germany the courage to engage in theoretical work and the impartiality required to develop clear concepts is at a standstill. In that respect Sombart's work, as *much* as I admire it, has not brought about a change.

Unfortunately I can't respond to your book with even a modest work of my own, as my studies lie in rather remote fields.

It would be a real pleasure for me and surely Sombart as well, if you could find the occasion to contribute to our "Archiv." You may have a freer work schedule than previously, now that you have completed the great work.

Your book will obviously be comprehensively reviewed in our journal, though it may take a while, as our space is overloaded at the moment, and it also isn't easy to find a suitable German reviewer. But we will make every effort.]

BOOKER T. WASHINGTON

Max Weber to Booker T. Washington
25 September 1904
St. Louis
handwritten
Washington Papers, containers 96–97, reel 88; Library of Congress

Dear Sir,

Being here a speaker at the Congress of Arts and Science, I should be very glad to visit—if I am allowed to do so—your world-known Normal and Industrial School at Tuskegee. I am going now to Oklahoma and the Indian Territory and shall come, I think, the 1st October to New Orleans, so that I could be October 3d at Tuskegee. I should be very obliged to you, if you kindly would write me to *New Orleans, St. Charles Hotel*, if I may have the honour to visit you and see your Institute. I made here the acquaintance of Mr. Dubois [sic], from Atlanta, and am *exceedingly* interested in your great and humanitary work.

Yours very respectfully
Max Weber
Professor of social science
at the University of
Heidelberg, Germany

Booker T. Washington to Max Weber
30 September 1904
typescript copy
Washington Papers, containers 96–97, reel 88; Library of Congress

Mr. Max Weber,
St. Charles Hotel, New Orleans, Louisiana

My dear Sir:

I write to assure you that we shall be very glad to have you include Tuskegee in your itinery [sic] and shall expect you to be here September 3rd [sic]. It will give us great pleasure to have you accept the hospitality of the school while here and for you to remain just as long as you possibly can. We shall afford you every opportunity to look into the work we are doing at Tuskegee. If you will be good enough to advise me as to just when you will reach Tuskegee, I shall see that you are met at the Station.

I think I ought to say that it is very probable that I myself shall not be here at the time of your visit, but the Acting Principal and all of the officers of the Institute will take pleasure in seeing that you are given opportunity to thoroughly investigate our work and in making your stay pleasant and profitable.

Very truly yours

Max Weber to Booker T. Washington
6 November 1904
167 Madison Avenue, New York
handwritten
Washington Papers, Containers 96–7, reel 88; Library of Congress

Dear Sir,

I was, some weeks ago, at Tuskegee, and my wife and myself were so deeply impressed by all we saw and learned there, that we hoped to be in a position to come again before leaving the country. I should especially have been very glad to meet you, yourself, after having read your works and seen your work. But my wife could not stand the climate of the South and so we went back and have now, the 19th, to cross the ocean to Germany.

Before going, allow me to express our respectful and hearty thank[s] to Mrs. Washington and to the officers and teachers of your Institute, especially 1) Mr. Warren Logan, 2) Mr. Taylor, 3) the professor of Agriculture and 4) Miss Clark. I hope to come again after some 2 or 3 years latest and then to have the opportunity to express [to] you the high admiration and consideration, which I, as I think everybody who saw Tuskegee, feel for you and your important work. It was—I am sorry to say that—*only* at Tuskegee I found *enthusiasm* in the South at all.

I hope to get some reports of your Institute here by the booksellers; if not, I hope not to trouble too much your secretary in applying to him.

With high respect

Yours very truly

Professor Max Weber

Booker T. Washington to Max Weber

[10] November 1904

typescript copy

Washington Papers, Containers 96–7, reel 88; Library of Congress

Prof. Max Weber

167 Madison Ave., New York, N.Y.

My dear Sir:

I am very glad indeed to have your letter of a few days ago and to learn that you so thoroughly enjoyed the short time that you spent at Tuskegee. I am very sorry that I myself was not here to have the pleasure of meeting you, but I have been very glad to hear so much of you from those here who did meet you. Our only regret is that you were not able to spend a longer time at Tuskegee and to look more thoroughly into the work that we are trying to do. I am very glad however to know that you hope to visit Tuskegee again, and assure you we shall be very glad to receive you at any time you can come.

I am sending a copy of my last Annual Report, and other printed matter, which contains information with reference to our work.

Very truly yours,

Enc.

ARCHIVES AND COLLECTIONS CONSULTED

Bayerische Staatsbibliothek, Munich
   Deponat Weber-Schäfer (Max and Marianne Weber Papers)
Boston Public Library, Special Collections
   Hugo Münsterberg Papers
Bryn Mawr College Archives
   Martha Carey Thomas Papers
Bundesarchiv Koblenz
   Lujo Brentano Papers
   Georg Jellinek Papers
Cincinatti Historical Society, Cincinatti, Ohio
   Hans and Margarethe Conrad Haupt Papers
Columbia University Rare Book and Manuscript Library
   Felix Adler Papers
   Edwin R. A. Seligman Papers
Deutsche Staatsbibliothek Handschriftenabteilung, Berlin
   Adolf von Harnack Papers
Geheimes Staatsarchiv Preussischer Kulturbesitz, Berlin
   Werner Sombart Papers
   Max Weber Papers
George Allen and Unwin Archive, University of Reading Library
Harvard University Archives and Houghton Library
   Charles W. Eliot Papers
   William James Papers
   Talcott Parsons Papers
   William Z. Ripley Papers
   Helen Frances Garrison and Oswald Garrison Villard Papers
Haverford College Library, Special Collections
   Rufus Matthew Jones Papers
   Isaac Sharpless Papers
The Johns Hopkins University, Milton S. Eisenhower Library Archives
   Jacob C. Hollander Papers
Knox County, Tennessee Public Library, McClung Historical Collection
Library of Congress, Special Collections and Archives
   Simon Newcomb Papers
   Robert Latham Owen Papers
   Booker T. Washington Papers
Michigan State University Library, Special Collections
   Paul Honigsheim Papers
Missouri Historical Society, St. Louis

Northwestern University Library, Special Collections
  Edmund J. James Papers
  James Taft Hatfield Papers
Oklahoma Historical Society, Oklahoma City
  Robert Latham Owen Papers
Radcliffe College, Schlesinger Library
  John Graham Brooks Papers
  Morgan-Howes Family Papers (Ethel Dench Puffer Howes)
St. Louis Art Museum Archives
  Louisiana Purchase Exposition
University of Chicago Regenstein Library, Special Collections
  William R. Harper Presidential Papers
  Frank Knight Papers
  Edward Shils Papers
  Albion Small Papers
University of Massachusetts W.E.B. Du Bois Library, Special Collections
  W.E.B. Du Bois Papers
University of Tennessee Library, Special Collections
Verlag Archiv Mohr/Siebeck, Tübingen, Germany
Washington D.C. Historical Society

BIBLIOGRAPHIC NOTES

ABBREVIATIONS

I have used the following abbreviations for frequently cited editions of Max Weber's work, in both the original German and English translation:

Baehr & Wells — *The Protestant Ethic and the "Spirit" of Capitalism and Other Writings*, ed. and trans. Peter Baehr and Gordon Wells. New York: Penguin, 2002.

EaS — *Economy and Society: An Outline of Interpretive Sociology*, ed. Guenther Roth and Claus Wittich. New York: Bedminster Press, 1968. Berkeley and Los Angeles: University of California Press, 1978.

GARS — *Gesammelte Aufsätze zur Religionssoziologie*. 3 vols. Tübingen, Germany: Mohr (Siebeck), 1920.

GASS — *Gesammelte Aufsätze zur Soziologie und Sozialpolitik*, ed. Marianne Weber. Tübingen, Germany: Mohr (Siebeck), 1924.

GAW — *Gesammelte Aufsätze zur Wissenschaftslehre*. 3rd ed., ed. Johannes Winckelmann. Tübingen, Germany: Mohr (Siebeck), 1968.

GPS — *Gesammelte Politische Schriften*. 2nd enlarged ed., ed. Johannes Winckelmann. Tübingen, Germany: Mohr (Siebeck), 1958.

Gerth & Mills — *From Max Weber: Essays in Sociology*, ed. and trans. Hans Gerth and C. Wright Mills. New York: Oxford University Press, 1946.

Lassman & Speirs — *Political Writings*, ed. Peter Lassman and Ronald Speirs. Cambridge: Cambridge University Press, 1994.

MWG — *Max Weber Gesamtausgabe*, ed. Horst Baier, M. Rainer Lepsius, Wolfgang J. Mommsen, Wolfgang Schluchter, and Johannes Winckelmann. Tübingen, Germany: Mohr (Siebeck), 1984—

PESC — *The Protestant Ethic and the Spirit of Capitalism*, trans. Talcott Parsons. New York: Charles Scribner's Sons, 1958 (1930).

Shils & Finch — *The Methodology of the Social Sciences*, trans. Edward A. Shils and Henry A. Finch. Glencoe, IL: Free Press, 1949.

WuG — *Wirtschaft und Gesellschaft: Grundriss der verstehenden Soziologie*, ed. Johannes Winckelmann. Köln, Germany: Kiepenheuer and Witsch, 1964.

I have also used the following abbreviations for archives cited more than once in the text:

BAK — Bundesarchiv Koblenz
DWS — Deponat Weber-Schäfer, Bayerische Staatsbibliothek

ESP   Edward Shils Papers, University of Chicago Regenstein Library,
                Special Collections
FKP   Frank H. Knight Papers, University of Chicago Regenstein
                Library, Special Collections
MWP   Max Weber Papers, Geheimes Staatsarchiv Preussischer Kul-
                turbesitz
TPP   Talcott Parsons Papers, Harvard University Archives
VAMS   Verlag Archiv Mohr/Siebeck

Note: in the quotations in text, all emphasis is in the original documents unless noted
otherwise.

INTRODUCTION

Marianne Weber, *Max Weber: Ein Lebensbild* (Tübingen, Germany: Mohr [Siebeck],
1926) has persisted as the standard source for Weber's biography. It was translated
by Harry Zohn as *Max Weber: A Biography* (New York: John Wiley and Sons, 1975),
and reissued in 1988 (New Brunswick, NJ: Transaction) with a new introduction by
Guenther Roth, "Marianne Weber and Her Circle." Joachim Radkau's controversial
reassessment emphasizing the psychological dramas of Weber's life is *Max Weber: Die
Leidenschaft des Denkens* (Munich: Carl Hanser, 2005), translated in abridged form by
Patrick Camiller as *Max Weber: A Biography* (Cambridge: Polity Press, 2009).

The classic historical investigation of Alexis de Tocqueville's journey to America
in relation to his thought is George Wilson Pierson, *Tocqueville in America* (Baltimore: Johns Hopkins University Press, 1996 [1938]). Alexander Schmidt, *Reisen in
die Moderne: Der Amerika-Diskurs des deutschen Bürgertums vor dem Ersten Weltkreig
im europäischen Vergleich* (Berlin: Akademie Verlag, 1997) discusses German views of
America before 1914. For a broader view, see James W. Ceaser, *Reconstructing America:
The Symbol of America in Modern Thought* (New Haven, CT: Yale University Press,
1997), esp. chaps. 7–8 for German perceptions.

Page(s)
1 Weber's recently recovered *Americana* articles, "Germany—Agriculture and Forestry," and "Germany—Industries," are reprinted in the *Kölner Zeitschrift für Soziologie und Sozialpsychologie* 57 (2005): 139–56, and in *Max Weber Studies* 6, no. 2
(2006): 207–30, preceded by Guenther Roth's critical introduction; see also MWG
I/8, Ergänzungsheft (2005).
6 Weber's reference to capitalism as "the most fateful force in our modern life" is in the
1920 introduction to *Collected Essays in the Sociology of Religion*, in PESC, 17; GARS
1:4.
6 For Weber's St. Louis speech see my discussion in chapter 4 of the present volume;
the speech is reprinted in Gerth & Mills as "Capitalism and Rural Society in Germany"; quotations herein on 369, 385.
6 "Permit me to take you once more to America . . ." is in Max Weber, "Science as a
Vocation," in Gerth & Mills, 149. The comments about America are in PESC, 182;
GARS 1:204.

CHAPTER 1

Thoughts about America

For Progressivism in the United States and Europe, see the classic study by James T. Kloppenberg, *Uncertain Victory: Social Democracy and Progressivism in European and American Thought, 1870–1920* (New York: Oxford University Press, 1986); see also James T. Kloppenberg, *The Virtues of Liberalism* (New York: Oxford University Press, 1998), esp. chap. 6. In addition, see Melvin Stokes, "American Progressives and the European Left," *Journal of American Studies* 17 (1983): 5–28; Dorothy Ross, *The Origins of American Social Science* (Cambridge: Cambridge University Press, 1991); Daniel T. Rodgers, *Atlantic Crossings: Social Politics in a Progressive Age* (Cambridge: Belknap Press, 1998); and Axel R. Schäfer, *American Progressives and German Social Reform, 1875–1920: Social Ethics, Moral Control, and the Regulatory State in a Transatlantic Context* (Stuttgart: Steiner Verlag, 2000). In the vast literature on American progressivism useful studies are Eldon J. Eisenach, *The Lost Promise of Progressivism* (Lawrence: University Press of Kansas, 1994); Steven J. Diner, *A Very Different Age: Americans of the Progressive Era* (New York: Hill and Wang, 1998); Michael E. McGerr, *A Fierce Discontent: The Rise and Fall of the Progressive Movement in America* (New York: Free Press, 2003); Shelton Stromquist, *Reinventing "The People": The Progressive Movement, the Class Problem, and the Origins of Modern Liberalism* (Urbana: University of Illinois Press, 2006); and, most recently, Maureen A. Flanagan, *America Reformed: Progressives and Progressivisms, 1890s–1920s* (New York: Oxford University Press, 2007).

There is a voluminous literature, much too vast to cite, on the "Protestant ethic," Weber's "thesis," and the problems of its historical and empirical foundations. For details see Alan Sica, ed., *Max Weber: A Comprehensive Bibliography* (New Brunswick, NJ: Transaction, 2004). Useful for my purposes are Peter Ghosh, "Max Weber's Idea of 'Puritanism': A Case Study in the Empirical Construction of the Protestant Ethic," *History of European Ideas* 29 (2003): 183–221; and Peter Ghosh, "Max Weber in the Netherlands 1903–7: A Neglected Episode in the History of *The Protestant Ethic*," *Bijdragen en Medeelingen betreffende de Geschiednis der Nederlanden* 119 (2004): 358–77; both are now in Peter Ghosh, *A Historian Reads Max Weber: Essays on the Protestant Ethic* (Wiesbaden, Germany: Harrassowitz, 2008), chaps. 1 and 2. See also Guenther Roth, "Zur Entstehungs- und Wirkungsgeschichte von Max Webers 'Protestantische Ethik,'" *Vadecum zu einem Klassiker der Geschichte Ökonomischer Rationalität* (Düsseldorf: Verlag Wirtschaft und Finanzen, 1992), 43–68; and Peter Hersche, "Max Weber, Italien und der Katholizismus," *Quellen und Forschungen aus italienischen Archiven und Bibliotheken* 76 (1996): 362–82. Hartmut Lehmann, *Max Weber's 'Protestantische Ethik'* (Göttingen, Germany: Vandenhoeck and Ruprecht, 1996) provides an authoritative and insightful discussion; see also Wilhelm Hennis's insightful *Max Weber: Essays in Reconstruction*, trans. Keith Tribe (London: Allen and Unwin, 1988), and a second edition under the title *Max Weber's Central Question* (Newbury, England: Threshold Press, 2000.) Among edited collections see Hartmut Lehmann and Guenther Roth, eds., *Weber's Protestant Ethic: Origins, Evidence, Contexts* (Cambridge: Cambridge University Press, 1993); Hans G. Kippenberg and Martin Riesebrodt, eds., *Max Webers "Religionssystematik"* (Tübingen, Germany: Mohr Siebeck, 2001); Hartmut Lehmann and J. M. Quédraogo, eds., *Max Webers Religionssoziologie in interkultureller Perspektive* (Göttingen, Germany:

Vandenhoeck and Ruprecht, 2003); and, most recently, William Swatos and Lutz Kaelber, eds., *The Protestant Ethic Turns 100: Essays on the Centenary of the Weber Thesis*
(Boulder, CO: Paradigm, 2005), esp. the essays by Hartmut Lehmann, William Swatos,
and Peter Kivisto.

The most thorough discussion of Weber's knowledge of Alexis de Tocqueville's *Democracy in America* is Martin Hecht, *Modernität und Bürgerlichkeit. Max Webers Freiheits-
lehre im Vergleich mit den politischen Ideen von Alexis de Tocqueville und Jean-Jacques Rous-
seau* (Berlin: Duncker and Humblot, 1998), esp. 12–13, 153–66, 199–235. On Weber
and America more generally, see Georg Kamphausen, *Die Erfindung Amerikas in der
Kulturkritik der Generation von 1890* (Weilerswist, Germany: Velbrück, 2002), esp.
chap. 5; see also Claus Offe, *Reflections on America: Tocqueville, Weber and Adorno in the
United States*, trans. Patrick Camiller (Cambridge: Polity Press, 2005), esp. chap. 3.

Page(s)

11 Gunnar Myrdal's remarks about Weber are in the unabbreviated edition of his classic, *An American Dilemma: The Negro Problem and Modern Democracy* (New York:
Harper and Brothers, 1944), 952, 1429 n. 43.

12 The colorful account of Max Weber Sr.'s Northern Pacific Railroad trip is in Paul
Lindau, *Aus der Neuen Welt: Briefe aus dem Osten und Westen der Vereinigten Staaten*
(Berlin: Rütten and Loening, 1990 [1884]).

12 For the "cosmopolitan bourgeoisie" see Guenther Roth, *Max Webers deutsch-
englische Familiengeschichte 1800–1950* (Tübingen, Germany: Mohr Siebeck, 2001),
esp. chap. 1. James Bryce, *The American Commonwealth* (London: Macmillan,
1988). 2 vols.; Bryce's popular work went through numerous editions, and it is likely
Weber used one of the earlier complete editions, such as the third revised edition
of 1893. Weber's copy of Franklin's *Autobiography* in translation as *Sein Leben, von
ihm selbst beschrieben*, with Kapp's introduction and December 1875, dedication to
young Max is in the Winckelmann Library of the Max-Weber-Gesamtausgabe in
Munich.

12–13 Max Weber, *Jugendbriefe*, ed. Marianne Weber (Tübingen, Germany: Mohr [Sie-
beck], 1936), 29, 140–42, 255, 314.

13 "My questioning deals with the origins of the *ethical* 'style of life'. . ." is found
in Max Weber, "Second Reply to Karl Fischer" (1908), reprinted in Johannes
Winckelmann, ed., *Die Protestantische Ethik II. Kritiken und Antikritiken* (Munich:
Siebenstern, 1968), 55; Baehr & Wells, 241; and *The Protestant Ethic Debate: Max
Weber's Replies to His Critics, 1907–1910*, ed. David J. Chalcraft and Austin Harrington (Liverpool: Liverpool University Press, 2001), 50; I have modified the
translations.

13–14 James T. Kloppenberg, *Uncertain Victory: Social Democracy and Progressivism in
European and American Thought, 1870–1920* (New York: Oxford University Press,
1986), 321.

15 Hugo Münsterberg, *Die Amerikaner* (Berlin: Mittler und Sohn, 1904). 2 vols., and
the abbreviated English edition in one volume, *The Americans*, trans. Edwin B. Holt
(New York: McClure, Phillips, 1905). The German edition was reviewed by Albion
Small in *American Journal of Sociology* 10, no. 2 (1904): 245–52.

17 The first edition of Karl Baedeker's famous North American travel guide appeared in
1893 in both German and English, intended for Chicago's World Fair. The second

English edition was published in 1899, and the third edition prior to the St. Louis Exposition in 1904 in English and German.

18 Unfortunately, knowledge of the Eranos Circle is limited; see M. Rainer Lepsius, "Der Eranos-Kreis Heidelberger Gelehrter 1904–1908," in *Jahrbuch der Heidelberger Akademie der Wissenschaft für das Jahr 1983* (Heidelberg: Carl Winter, 1984), 46–48; and Klaus Kempter, *Die Jellineks 1820–1955. Eine familienbiographische Studie zum deutschjüdischen Bildungsbürgertum* (Düsseldorf: Droste, 1998), 277–79.

20 The quotation from *The Protestant Ethic and the "Spirit" of Capitalism* is from the original 1904–5 text, in Baehr & Wells, 36; compare *PESC*, 91–92, and *GARS* 1:83. Upon its first publication in two parts in 1904–5, Weber's work originally appeared with "Spirit" (*Geist*) in quotation marks: *The Protestant Ethic and the "Spirit" of Capitalism*; these were subsequently dropped from the title in Weber's 1920 version, and in Talcott Parsons's translation (*PESC*). In the present volume, when I refer to or quote the original edition in German, I retain the quotation marks around "Spirit."

22 Edwin Seligman's extensive lecture notes in five notebooks are in his Papers, Box 86 (quotes from notebook 2, Heidelberg winter semester, 1880–81). His correspondence with Weber began in 1897.

24 Martin Luther's statement comes from *The Sermons of Martin Luther* (Grand Rapids, MI: Baker, 1983), 1:270, §34.

CHAPTER 2

The Land of Immigrants

The *Yearbook of Immigration Statistics* issued annually by the U.S. Department of Homeland Security provides accurate comparative historical data on immigration. Detailed immigration data by nationality for the decade from 1900 to 1909 were reported in the *New York Times*, October 16, 1910, and May 19, 1912. The passenger manifests for ships arriving in New York can be found at http://www.ellisisland.org.

Weber's extensive writings on the stock and commodity exchanges have been collected as *Bösenwesen. Schriften und Reden 1893–1898*, in MWG I/5, ed. Knut Borchardt with Cornelia Meyer-Stoll (Tübingen, Germany: Mohr [Siebeck], 1999, 2000). A partial translation by Steven Lestition is available as "Stock and Commodity Exchanges" and "Commerce on the Stock and Commodity Exchanges," *Theory and Society* 29 (2000): 305–71. The proceedings of the Reich commission on the stock exchange are *Verhandlungen des provisorischen Börsenausschusses im Reichsamt des Innern* (Berlin: Reichsdruckerei, 1896), esp. 31, 33, 34, 66–67, 128–29, 165–67 for Weber's remarks about German and other exchanges, such as those in New York, Chicago, and London.

Hans Rollmann's account of the American journey is "'Meet Me in St. Louis': Troeltsch and Weber in America," in *Weber's Protestant Ethic: Origins, Evidence, Contexts*, ed. Hartmut Lehmann and Guenther Roth (Washington, DC: German Historical Institute and Cambridge University Press, 1992), 357–83. Hans Haupt's two monographs are *Die Eigenart der amerikanischen Predigt* (Giessen, Germany: Töpelmann, 1907), and *Staat und Kirche in den Vereinigten Staaten von Nordamerika* (Giessen, Germany: Töpelmann, 1909). For the literary record of the Haupt family, see Hans Haupt, *Out of My Life* (1941), and Margarethe Conrad Haupt, *Life Stories and Memories* (1930), both in the

Cincinnati Historical Society; see also Walter H. Haupt, *A Myopic View of the Twentieth Century, or an Autobiography*, formerly in the possession of Hildegard Haupt Babbs. For Pauck's comments on Hans Haupt, see Wilhelm Pauck, *Harnack and Troeltsch: Two Historical Theologians* (New York: Oxford University Press, 1968), 72. A respected German theologian, Pauck was well informed about the German Evangelical and Reform congregations; as an aside, he ordained my father as a Congregational minister in 1940.

Weber's articles on religion in America are "'Kirchen' und 'Sekten," *Frankfurter Zeitung*, April 13 and 15, 1906; revised as "'Kirchen' und 'Sekten' in Nordamerika, eine kirchen- und sozialpolitische Skizze," *Christliche Welt* 20 (1906); further revised in 1920 as "Die protestantischen Sekten und der Geist des Kapitalismus," *GARS* 1:207–36. The 1906 version is translated as "'Churches' and 'Sects' in North America: An Ecclesiastical and Sociopolitical Sketch," in Baehr & Wells, 203–20; and the 1920 revision appears as "The Protestant Sects and the Spirit of Capitalism," in Gerth & Mills, 302–22.

A brief account of city planning and Olmsted's work in Buffalo is available in Francis R. Kowsky, ed., *The Best Planned City: The Olmsted Legacy in Buffalo* (Buffalo, NY: Burchfield Art Center, 1992). Considerable information is now available on the Internet. Verlyn Klinkenborg's *The Last Fine Time* (New York: Alfred A. Knopf, 1991; reissued University of Chicago Press, 2004) treats only the decades in Buffalo following World War I, but still captures the consequences of industrialization and economic dislocation starting in the 1890s.

Page(s)
25 Max Schlichting's painting, *Strandvergnügen*, has been on display recently in the National Gallery in Berlin; see the exhibit catalog, *Berliner Impressionismus. Werke der Berliner Secession aus der Nationalgalerie*, ed. Angelika Wesenberg (Bonn: GH Verlag, 2006), 99.
33 Quotation from Gerth & Mills, 302–3; *GARS* 1:208.
33 The definitions of "church" and "sect" are in Gerth & Mills, 314; *GARS* 1:221.
35 Many of Weber's writings on universities are collected in *Max Weber on Universities*, trans. and ed. Edward Shils (Chicago: University of Chicago Press, 1974), quotation herein on 37, from a 1911 newspaper article.
36 Weber's 1918 speech to Austrian officers is "Der Sozialismus," in *GASS*, 492–518, quotation herein on 497; translated as "Socialism" in Lassman & Speirs, 278–9; translation modified.

CHAPTER 3

Capitalism

For the Webers' letters quoted in this chapter I have used Harry Zohn's translation, but corrected and modified it according to the original German texts.

Page(s)
39 For Bryce's comment, see James Bryce, *The American Commonwealth* (Indianapolis, IN: Liberty Fund, 1995), 2:1456. Sandburg's lines are the first stanza from

"Chicago" (1916), which can be found online at http://carl-sandburg.com/chicago.htm.

40 Weber's comment about the modern metropolis is in remarks to the Deutsche Gesellschaft für Soziologie in 1910; in GASS, 453.

43 Lincoln Steffens, "Chicago: Half Free and Fighting On," McClure's 21, no. 6 (1903): 563–77; quotations herein on 563, 564; see also The Autobiography of Lincoln Steffens (Berkeley, CA: Heyday Books, 2005 [1931]), 428, on Chicago.

43 Information about the Hull House maps and papers, including the kind of demographic charts and maps the Webers saw, are available on a Northwestern University website at http://homicide.northwestern.edu/pubs/hullhouse/Maps/.

44 Marianne Weber's commemoration for Jane Addams is "Jane Addams. Zu ihrem 70. Geburtstag," Frankfurter Zeitung, September 9, 1930, evening edition, 1–2. The detailed protocols and minutes of the Heidelberg chapter of the Verein Frauenbildung-Frauenstudium, 1897 to 1905, are in Marianne Weber's Papers, DWS Ana 446, Box 22; the association sponsored a Heidelberg visit and lecture by Charlotte Perkins Gilman in March 1905.

45 Karl Baedeker's description of the Chicago stockyards is in The United States, 2nd rev. ed. (Leipzig: Karl Baedeker/New York: Charles Scribner's Sons), 1904, 357. In addition to Philip S. Foner's classic, History of the Labor Movement in the United States, vol. 3, The Policies and Practices of the American Federation of Labor, 1900–1909 (New York: International Publishers, 1964), the 1904 stockyards strike is discussed in David Brody, The Butcher Workmen: A Study of Unionization (Cambridge, MA: Harvard University Press, 1964); James R. Barrett, Work and Community in the Jungle: Chicago's Packinghouse Workers, 1894–1922 (Urbana: University of Illinois Press, 1990), esp. chap. 5 on the rationalization of work; and Rick Halpern, Down on the Killing Floor: Black and White Workers in Chicago's Packinghouses, 1904–54 (Urbana: University of Illinois Press, 1997), esp. chap. 1.

47 Max Weber's 1908 Verein-sponsored study of industrial labor, Zur Psychophysik der industriellen Arbeit, is reprinted with a methodological introduction in GASS, 1–255, and in MWG I/11 (1995).

48 The University Record of the University of Chicago 9, no. 6 (1904): 229–30, mentions the events associated with the Congress of Arts and Science. The comments about the Hatfields, father and son, are in "Memorial Meeting to James Taft Hatfield" (December 14, 1945) and "James Miller Hatfield"; J. T. Hatfield Papers, Northwestern University Archives.

50 The Northwestern University rules for student conduct are printed in the Bulletin of Northwestern University. General Catalogue, 1904–05 (Evanston, IL: Northwestern University, 1904); see 174 for "religious worship." The Chicago Daily Tribune story is "Says Character Is Capital, David R. Forgan, Vice President of the First National Bank, Talks at Athenaeum," Chicago Daily Tribune, September 10, 1904. Theodore Roosevelt's speech at Northwestern on April 2, 1903, is discussed in Estelle Frances Ward, The Story of Northwestern University (New York: Dodd, Mead, 1924), 242–43. The story of the visiting scholars from Germany was "German Savants Come," Evanston Index, September 17, 1904. See also Judy Hilkey, Character Is Capital:

Success Manuals and Manhood in Gilded Age America (Chapel Hill: University of North Carolina Press, 1997), for the cultural history of the topic.

51–52 Weber's writings on the American and German universities are conveniently collected in translation in Max Weber, *Max Weber on Universities*, trans. and ed. Edward Shils (Chicago: University of Chicago Press, 1974); see 23–24 for the quoted remarks from 1911.

CHAPTER 4

Science and World Culture

The seven volumes of proceedings, *Congress of Arts and Science: Universal Exposition, St. Louis, 1904*, ed. Howard J. Rogers (Boston: Houghton, Mifflin, 1905–6) are conveniently available online at http://books.google.com/books. Weber's speech was delivered in German and translated for publication as "The Relations of the Rural Community to Other Branches of Social Science" by Charles Seidenadel, also the translator of Sombart's talk. Published in volume 7 of the proceedings, the Seidenadel translation was reprinted with revisions and a misleading title ("Capitalism and Rural Society in Germany") in Gerth & Mills, 363–85. Peter Ghosh's improved corrected text that I cite is "Max Weber on 'The Rural Community': A Critical Edition of the English Text," *History of European Ideas* 31 (2005): 327–66; see also Ghosh's companion article "Not the *Protestant Ethic*? Max Weber at St. Louis," *History of European Ideas* 31 (2005): 367–407, revised as "Capitalism and *Herrschaft*: Max Weber at St. Louis," chapter 4 in Peter Ghosh, *A Historian Reads Max Weber: Essays on the Protestant Ethic* (Wiesbaden, Germany: Harrassowitz, 2008). As Ghosh points out, the most accurate title would be "Rural Society in Its Relation to the Other Branches of Society." A critical version of the text is also published in MWG I/8 (1998): 212–43.

Hans Rollmann's account of the 1904 Congress of Arts and Science is "'Meet Me in St. Louis': Troeltsch and Weber in America," in *Weber's Protestant Ethic: Origins, Evidence, Contexts*, ed. Hartmut Lehmann and Guenther Roth (Washington, DC: German Historical Institute and Cambridge University Press, 1992), 357–66. Robert W. Rydell, *All the World's a Fair: Visions of Empire at American International Expositions, 1876–1916* (Chicago: University of Chicago Press, 1984), places the Louisiana Purchase Exposition in political and historical context. For a recent critical study, see James Gilbert, *Whose Fair? Experience, Memory, and the History of the Great St. Louis Exposition* (Chicago: University of Chicago Press, 2009).

Page(s)

55 Hugo Münsterberg published defenses of his plan for the Congress in the *Atlantic Monthly* 91 (1903): 671–84, quotations herein on 673, 676, 684; *Science* 18 (1903): 559–63; and the *Journal of Philosophy, Psychology and Scientific Methods* 1 (1904): 1–8. For a summary of Münsterberg's views see Matthew Hale, *Human Science and Social Order: Hugo Münsterberg and the Origins of Applied Psychology* (Philadelphia: Temple University Press, 1980), esp. chap. 6.

56 Albion Small's most astute reply to Münsterberg is an unpublished and undated (probably February 1903) memorandum to the organizing board for the Congress of Arts and Science; in the Simon Newcomb Papers, No. 39; quotation herein on 5.

56 Small's letter to Harper, January 24, 1903, is in the University Presidents' Papers, University of Chicago. John Dewey's critique and reply to Münsterberg is in *Science* 18 (1903): 275–78, 665. William James's June 28, 1906, letter to Münsterberg is part of a larger critical discussion of neo-Kantian philosophy and pragmatism in the William James Papers. Du Bois also wrote a scathing critique of the confusions about "sociology" at the Congress, but left it unpublished: "Sociology Hesitant," in the Du Bois Papers, reel 82.

58 Max Weber, "Die 'Objektivität' sozialwissenschaftlicher und sozialpolitischer Erkenntnis" (1904), in *GAW*, 146–214; Shils & Finch, 49–112; see also the superior recent translation by Keith Tribe, "The 'Objectivity' of Knowledge in Social Science and Social Policy," in *The Essential Weber: A Reader*, ed. Sam Whimster (London: Routledge, 2004), 359–404; quotation herein on 383.

58 Weber's texts are "Roscher und Knies und die logischen Probleme der historischen Nationalökonomie" (1903–1906), *GAW*, 1–145; see 70–92 for the critique of Münsterberg; quotation herein on 72; translated by Guy Oakes as *Roscher and Knies: The Logical Problems of Historical Economics* (New York: Free Press, 1975).

59 James Kloppenberg, *The Virtues of Liberalism* (New York: Oxford University Press, 1998), 84.

59 Weber, "The Objectivity of Knowledge in Social Science and Social Policy," in *The Essential Weber: A Reader*, ed. Sam Whimster (London: Routledge, 2004), 371, 403; *GAW*, 166, 213–14.

60 For a recent comment on the discussion of modernization and "multiple modernities" (a concept attributed to S. N. Eisenstadt) in relation to the United States, see Wolfgang Knöbl, "Of Contingencies and Breaks: The U.S. American South as an Anomaly in the Debate on Multiple Modernities," *Archives européennes de sociologie* 47, no. 1 (2006): 125–57.

61–66 Max Weber, "Max Weber on 'The Rural Community': A Critical Edition of the English Text," trans. Peter Ghosh, *History of European Ideas* 31 (2005): 327–66; quotations herein on 329–31, 333, 335–36, 344–46. Tocqueville's discussion of "individualism" is in Alexis de Tocqueville, *Democracy in America*, vol. 2, sec. 2, chaps. 2–4, 8; his chapter "How an Aristocracy May Be Created by Manufactures," is in Alexis de Tocqueville, *Democracy in America*, vol. 2, sec. 2, chap. 20. Werner Sombart's *Why Is There No Socialism in the United States?* first appeared in 1905 as an article in the *Archiv für Sozialwissenschaft und Sozialpolitik*, then the following year as a book, *Warum gibt es in den Vereinigten Staaten keinen Sozialismus?* (Tübingen, Germany: Mohr [Siebeck], 1906). A convenient survey of the "exceptionalism" debate is Seymour Martin Lipset and Gary Marks, eds., *It Didn't Happen Here: Why Socialism Failed in the United States* (New York: W. W. Norton, 2000). See Thorstein Veblen, *The Theory of the Leisure Class: An Economic Study of Institutions* (New York: Macmillan, 1902 [1899]); and William J. Ghent, *Our Benevolent Feudalism* (New York: Macmillan, 1902).

67 The conflict over German art at the 1904 International Exposition is discussed in Peter Paret, *The Berlin Secession: Modernism and Its Enemies in Imperial Germany* (Cambridge: Belknap Press, 1980), chap. 4; quotation herein on 149.

68 Photographs of the rooms in the Varied Industries Building are in the *Descriptive Catalogue of the German Arts and Crafts at the Universal Exposition, St. Louis 1904* (Berlin: Imperial German Commission, 1904). In the official documents there are two instructive reports on architecture, arts, and crafts: Friedrich von Thiersch, "Architektur und Kunstgewerbe," 2:179–98, and Hermann Muthesius, "Das Kunstgewerbe, insbesondere die Wohnungskunst," 2:263–96, in *Amtlicher Bericht über die Weltausstellung in St. Louis 1904 erstattet vom Reichskommissar* (Berlin: Carl Heymanns Verlag, 1906).

69 Guenther Roth, "Marianne Weber als liberale Nationalistin," in Juergen Hess, Hartmut Lehmann, and Volker Sellin, eds., *Heidelberg 1945* (Stuttgart: Steiner, 1996), 310–26. On Frank Lloyd Wright, Joseph Maria Olbrich, and the St. Louis Exposition, see Anthony Alfonsin, *Frank Lloyd Wright: The Lost Years, 1910–1912: A Study of Influence* (Chicago: University of Chicago Press, 1993), 12–40.

70 The description of Gehner is in *The City of St. Louis and Its Resources* (St. Louis, MO: Continental, 1893). For the history of the Mesker Brothers Iron Works, see the publication of the Illinois Historic Preservation Agency, *Historic Illinois* 28 (April 2006), conveniently online at www.illinoishistory.gov/gotmesker/Historic_Illinois_Meskder.pdf; a 1903 wedding party photograph of the Gehner family appears on p. 5. As an ironic postscript, in 1960 the Gehners' stylish red granite German baroque mansion was razed to make room for the headquarters of the Optimist Club International.

71 The definitive study of public school reform and the role of Calvin Woodward in St. Louis is Selwyn K. Troen, *The Public and the Schools: Shaping the St. Louis System, 1838–1920* (Columbia: University of Missouri Press, 1975); the quotation from Harris is on 162. William J. Reese, *Power and the Promise of School Reform: Grassroots Movements During the Progressive Era* (Boston: Routledge and Kegan Paul, 1986), discusses the controversies over schooling in the Progressive Era.

CHAPTER 5

Remnants of Romanticism

For evidence of Weber's prior knowledge of the American West see his *Jugendbriefe*, 75, and *Die römische Agrargeschichte*, MWG I/2, ed. Jürgen Deininger (1986): 145. Max Sering's study is *Die Landwirthschaftliche Konkurrenz Nordamerikas in Gegenwart und Zukunft* (Leipzig: Duncker and Humblot, 1887); see 107 for his remark about colonization. The journalist Paul Lindau published an account of the railroad trip arranged by Henry Villard that included Max Weber Sr.; see Lindau, *Aus der neuen Welt* (Berlin: Rütten and Loening, 1990), chap. 6. Guenther Roth discusses the purposes of the trip in *Max Webers deutsch-englische Familiengeschichte 1800–1950* (Tübingen, Germany: Mohr Siebeck, 2001), 478–85. In 1855 Kapp had published an account of the German settlements in Texas, reprinted in Friedrich Kapp, *Aus und über Amerika. Thatsachen und Erlebnisse* (Berlin: Springer, 1876), 243–90. For the Indian Territory's history, see Jeffrey Burton, *Indian Territory and the United States, 1866–1906* (Norman: University of Oklahoma Press, 1995).

Page(s)

73 The quoted letters from 1904 are from the Simon Newcomb Papers (September 20), the Georg Jellinek Papers (September 24), the Booker T. Washington Papers (September 25), and the William Harper Papers, University of Chicago Regenstein Library, Special Collections (October 7).

73–74 The report on the White House reception is "Delegates at White House," *Washington Post*, September 28, 1904.

75 Weber's letter of October 27, 1904 (see appendix 2) is in the Jacob Hollander Papers.

76 Hollander's letter of July 18, 1904, is in the Edwin Seligman Papers. Hollander reported on the Indian Territory in "A Report on School Taxation in Indian Territory," 58th United States Congress, 3rd Session, House of Representatives, Document 34 (1904); quotation herein on 2. The St. Louis presentations Weber likely attended were John Bates Clark, "Economic Theory in a New Character and Relation," 47–56; Jacob H. Hollander, "The Scope and Method of Political Economy," 57–67; William Z. Ripley, "Problems of Transportation," 95–112; and Edwin R. A. Seligman, "Pending Problems in Public Finance," 190–200; in *Congress of Arts and Science Universal Exposition, St. Louis*, vol. 7, ed. Howard J. Rogers (Boston: Houghton, Mifflin, 1906).

77–78 The Guthrie incident was reported in "Wouldn't Stay: German Professor's Visit at Guthrie was Suddenly Terminated," *Daily Oklahoman*, September 29, 1904; the Berlin press account comes from Marianne Weber's Papers (DWS), a clipping inserted by Helene Weber into her letter of October 2, addressed to Max and Marianne in Boston; my thanks to Sam Whimster for alerting me about this copy. Weber's arrival in Muskogee is mentioned in "A Distinguished Visitor," *Muskogee Phoenix*, September 28, 1904.

79–81 Clarence B. Douglas, *Oklahoma in the Making from the Twin Territories* (El Reno, OK: El Reno American, 1951), 28.

81 For Robert Owen, see the anonymous article "Senator Owen and the Halo of Romance," *Current Opinion* 56 (1914): 350; and Wyatt W. Belcher, "Political Leadership of Robert L. Owen," *Chronicles of Oklahoma* 31 (1953): 361–71.

82 For the statements about Bixby, Wright, and the Dawes-Bixby Commission, see Kent Carter, "Tams Bixby," *Chronicles of Oklahoma* 78 (2000): 412; Kent Carter, "A Faithful Public Servant," *Chronicles of Oklahoma* 81 (2003), 55, 64; and Kent Carter, *The Dawes Commission and the Allotment of the Five Civilized Tribes* (Orem, UT: Ancestry. com, 1999), esp. chaps. 8 and 11; quotation herein on 175.

85–86 Owen's Congressional testimony is "Remarks before the Committee on the Territories of the House of Representatives," in *Statehood for Indian Territory and Oklahoma* (Washington, DC: Government Printing Office, 1904), quotes herein on 5–6, 8.

87–88 See Narcissa Chisholm Owen, *Memoirs* (Oklahoma City: Oklahoma Historical Society, 1907), esp. 102–4; Janet Shaffer, "The Indian Princess at Point of Honor," *Lynch's Ferry: A Journal of Local History* 7 (1994): 15–23; and Joni L. Kinsey, "Cultivating the Grasslands: Women Painters in the Great Plains," in *Independent Spirits: Women Painters of the American West, 1890–1945*, ed. Patricia Trenton (Berkeley and Los Angeles: University of California Press, 1995), 264–65, 268.

92 See Jean Hector St. John de Crèvecoeur, *Letters from an American Farmer* (New York: Signet, 1963), 36–37.

93 Zohn's comment is in Marianne Weber, *Max Weber: A Biography*, trans. Harry Zohn (New Brunswick, NJ: Transaction, 1988), 291 n. 22. D. H. Lawrence, *Studies in Classic American Literature* (New York: Penguin, 1977), 55, 69.

94 See John F. McDermott, "Introductory Essay," in Washington Irving, *A Tour on the Prairies* (Norman: University of Oklahoma Press, 1956), xxii. Weber's comments about Irving are in *PESC*, 261 n. 10, 275 n. 73; Baehr & Wells, 177–78, 194; *GARS* 1:167 n. 2, 188 n. 2.

95 Weber's statement about "ethical style of life" and capitalism is in Max Weber, "Second Reply to Fischer," in *The Protestant Ethic Debate: Max Weber Replies to His Critics, 1907–10*, ed. David J. Chalcraft and Austin Harrington (Liverpool, England: Liverpool University Press, 2001), 50.

95–96 Weber commented about the similarity between Roman and North American colonization in Max Weber, *The Agrarian Sociology of Ancient Civilizations*, trans. R. I. Frank (London: New Left Books, 1976), 269–70, 307, 309. The quotations are from "'Churches' and 'Sects' in North America," in Baehr & Wells, 204–6; cf. "The Protestant Sects and the Spirit of Capitalism," in Gerth & Mills, 310; *GARS* 1:215; *EaS*, 926, 932–33, 971, 984–85, 991; *PESC*, 255–56 n. 178; *GARS* 1:154–55 n. 3. For an analysis of Weber's ideas about the sects and their significance see Sung Ho Kim, *Max Weber's Politics of Civil Society* (Cambridge: Cambridge University Press, 2004), esp. chap. 3.

97 Weber's letter to Jaffé, January 10, 1914, is in *MWG* II/8 (2003): 465–66; see also Edgar Jaffé, "Das englisch-amerikanische und das französische Bankwesen," in *Bankwesen. Grundriss der Sozialökonomik* vol. 2 (Tübingen, Germany: Mohr [Siebeck], 1915), esp. 209–14.

97 Weber's concluding remarks are in Max Weber, "Max Weber on 'The Rural Community': A Critical Edition of the English Text," trans. Peter Ghosh, *History of European Ideas* 31 (2005): 345–46; Gerth & Mills, 385; *PESC*, 181; Baehr & Wells, 121; *GARS* I, 203. I have revised the translations. Weber writes "fossilen *Brennstoffs*," the generic word for "fuel" or "petrol," as Baehr and Wells indicate, but Parsons translated it as "coal," an unfortunate, though minor, slip.

CHAPTER 6

The Color Line

The literature on race relations in America familiar to Weber was Friedrich Kapp, *Geschichte der Sklaverei in den Vereinigten Staaten von Amerika* (New York: Hauser, 1861); James Bryce, *The American Commonwealth*, vol. 2 (Indianapolis, IN: Liberty Fund, 1995), chaps. 93–94, though a much more extensive discussion was added later in chap. 95; Hugo Münsterberg, *Die Amerikaner*, vol 1 (Berlin: Mittler und Sohn, 1904), esp. 261–88. Münsterberg's book was reviewed by Albion W. Small in the *American Journal of Sociology* 10 (1904), 250, which quoted the author's comment that "the negro question is the one really black cloud on the horizon of the public life of the American nation" (Munsterberg, 1:282) as an example of an exaggerated and unbalanced opinion. Karl Bücher, *Arbeit und Rhythmus*, 3rd. ed. (Leipzig: Teubner, 1902), 217–33, has a section with scores and texts of African American field songs.

The discussion of race in Weber's work begins with the essay of a German émigré, Ernst Moritz Manasse, "Max Weber on Race," *Social Research* 14, no. 2 (1947): 191–221, and continues in two partial translations (by Jerome Gittleman) of Weber's 1910 remarks at the Deutsche Gesellschaft für Soziologie, with commentaries published by Benjamin Nelson: "Max Weber on Race and Society," *Social Research* 38, no. 1 (1971): 30–41; and "Max Weber, Dr. Alfred Ploetz, and W.E.B. Du Bois," *Sociological Analysis* 34, no. 4 (1973): 308–12. Karl-Ludwig Ay, "Max Weber und der Begriff der Rasse," *Aschkenas. Zeitschrift für Geschichte und Kultur der Juden* 1 (1993): 189–218, is the most thorough assessment. Among the important early studies of race in America, see Hortense Powdermaker, *After Freedom: A Cultural Study in the Deep South* (Madison: University of Wisconsin Press, 1993 [1939]), which adopts a sociological approach; John Dollard, *Caste and Class in a Southern Town* (Garden City, NY: Doubleday, 1988 [1937]), uses a psychological framework and advances the "frustration aggression" hypothesis. A recent critical reassessment is Jane Adams and D. Gorton, "Southern Trauma: Revisiting Caste and Class in the Mississippi Delta," *American Anthropologist* 106, no. 2 (2004): 334–45. The peculiarities of economic development in the South have been addressed repeatedly by historians. For a recent contribution, see Wolfgang Knöbl, "Of Contingencies and Breaks: The U.S. American South as an Anomaly in the Debate on Multiple Modernities," *Archives européennes de sociologie* 47 (2006): 125–57.

For Booker T. Washington, see Louis R. Harlan's unsurpassed two-volume biography *Booker T. Washington: The Making of a Black Leader, 1856–1901* (New York: Oxford University Press, 1972); and *Booker T. Washington: The Wizard of Tuskegee, 1901–1915* (New York: Oxford University Press, 1983). Margaret (Mrs. Booker T.) Washington's brief account of her work is "The Tuskegee Woman's Club," *Southern Workman* 49, no. 8 (1920): 365–69. Weber read *Up from Slavery* (New York: Doubleday, 1901), which he cites in the "Protestant ethic" debate of 1910, and surely the collection of Washington's Sunday evening talks at Tuskegee, *Character Building* (New York: Doubleday, 1902.)

W.E.B. Du Bois's classic *The Souls of Black Folk* (Chicago: A. C. McClurg, 1903), brings together several of his previous publications. His monograph *The Philadelphia Negro: A Social Study* (Philadelphia: University of Pennsylvania Press, 1899) was reissued by the University of Pennsylvania Press in 1995, and the Atlanta University Publications are now available online at http://fax.libs.uga.edu/E185x5xA881p/aupmenu. html. The American Negro Academy Occasional Papers have been reissued (New York: Arno Press, 1969), and they include Du Bois's "The Conservation of Races" (1897). His article "The Relation of the Negroes to the Whites in the South" is in the *Annals of the American Academy of Political and Social Science* 18 (1901), 121–40. Du Bois's article in the *Archiv für Sozialwissenschaft und Sozialpolitik* 22 (1906): 31–79, has been translated recently by Joseph Fracchia; see "Die Negerfrage in den Vereinigten Staaten (The Negro Question in the United States) (1906)," *CR: The New Centennial Review* 6 (2006): 241–90. The definitive biography of W.E.B. Du Bois is David Levering Lewis's two volume study: *W.E.B. Du Bois: Biography of a Race, 1868–1919* (New York: Henry Holt, 1993), and *W.E.B. Du Bois: The Fight for Equality and the American Century, 1919–1963* (New York: Henry Holt, 2000). For the relationship between Du Bois and Max Weber, see the detailed exposition in Nahum D. Chandler,

"The Possible Form of an Interlocution: W.E.B. Du Bois and Max Weber in Correspondence, 1904–1905," CR: The New Centennial Review 6 (2006); 193–239, and 7 (2007): 213–72, together with extensive discussion of recent perspectives on Du Bois in that same volume of the same journal. Axel R. Schäfer, "W. E. B. Du Bois, German Social Thought, and the Racial Divide in American Progressivism, 1892–1909," Journal of American History 88 (2001): 925–49, is alert to the ambiguities within progressivism in the United States.

Page(s)

100 "The problem of the twentieth century is the problem of the color line..." opens Du Bois's essay, "The Freedmen's Bureau," Atlantic Monthly 87 (1901): 354; revised as chapter 2 in The Souls of Black Folk ((Chicago: A. C. McClurg, 1903).

100 See appendix 2 for Weber's correspondence with W. E. B. Du Bois and Booker T. Washington.

102 I would like to thank Guenther Roth for bringing to my attention Else Jaffe's letter to Du Bois, November 10, 1905, expressing her interest in the translation project and doubts about bringing it to fruition.

104 Dorothy Ross, The Origins of American Social Science (Cambridge: Cambridge University Press, 1991), discusses the importance of the German universities for the nascent social sciences in America; quotation herein on 439.

104 Weber's statement about the South's problems as "essentially ethnic and not economical" is in his St. Louis speech. See Max Weber, "Max Weber on 'The Rural Community': A Critical Edition of the English Text," trans. Peter Ghosh, History of European Ideas 31 (2005): 329.

105 "Caste in America" is reprinted as "Caste: That is the Root of the Trouble," in Writings by W.E.B. Du Bois in Periodicals Edited by Others, ed. Herbert Aptheker (Millwood, NY: Kraus-Thompson, 1982), 1:231–34.

106 Carl Schurz's article is "Can the South Solve the Negro Problem?" McClure's 22 (1904): 259–75. Weber knew about Schurz through his father, who had traveled with him across the United States, and from Friedrich Kapp, his political ally. There is no evidence, however, that he met Schurz in New York City.

107 Myrdal's classic is an important early exception to the absence of a sociology of race; see Gunnar Myrdal, An American Dilemma: The Negro Problem and Modern Democracy, with the assistance of Richard Sterner and Arnold Rose (New York: Harper and Brothers, 1944); quote herein on 952–53.

107 W.E.B. Du Bois, "The Relation of the Negroes to the Whites in the South," Annals of the American Academy of Political and Social Science 18 (1901): 121–40.

108 Weber's letter to Karl Bücher, February 1, 1909, is in MWG II/6 (1994): 46–50; and his comment on the talent for music in Negro churches comes from the 1905 text of The Protestant Ethic and the Spirit of Capitalism; see Baehr & Wells, 192; PESC, 272.

109 Marianne Weber, Max Weber: A Biography, trans. Harry Zohn (New Brunswick, NJ: Transaction, 1988), 295.

111 Booker T. Washington, Character Building: Being Addresses Delivered on Sunday Evenings to the Students of Tuskegee Institute (New York: Doubleday, Page, 1902), 91, 290.

112 Weber's reference to Washington's Up from Slavery is in his second reply to Rachfahl (1910), translated in The Protestant Ethic Debate: Max Weber's Replies to His

Critics, 1907–1910, ed. David J. Chalcraft and Austin Harrington (Liverpool, England: Liverpool University Press, 2001), 129 n. 19. Andrew Zimmerman, "Decolonizing Weber," *Postcolonial Studies* 9 (2006): 53–79, is a hostile attack that sheds more heat than light on the issue of race. His article on Washington and the Tuskegee Institute, "A German Alabama in Africa: The Tuskegee Expedition to German Togo and the Transnational Origins of African Cotton Growers," *American Historical Review* 110 (2005): 1362–98 (forthcoming as a monograph, *Inventing the Color Line: The Tuskegee Expedition to German Togo and the Globalization of the New South*), is more useful for pointing to the ambiguities in the Tuskegee program.

112 W.E.B. Du Bois, "Die Negerfrage in den Vereinigten Staaten (The Negro Question in the United States) (1906)," trans. Joseph Fracchia, *CR: The New Centennial Review* 6, no. 3 (2006): 285.

112 See Max Weber, "Diskussionsbeiträge in der Debatte über Alfred Plötz: Die Begriffe Rasse und Gesellschaft und einige damit zusammenhängende Probleme," *GASS*, 456–62 (abridged text) and the original in *Verhandlungen des Ersten Deutschen Soziologentages vom 19–22 Oktober 1910 in Frankfurt a. M.* (Tübingen, Germany: Mohr [Siebeck], 1911), 151–65. The partial translation by Jerome Gittleman is cited above.

113 Weber's remarks at the 1912 meeting of the Deutsche Gesellschaft für Soziologie are reprinted in *GASS*, 489; this text has not been translated.

113 Ernst Moritz Manasse, "Max Weber on Race," *Social Research* 14, no. 2 (1947): 191.

114 Weber's 1898 outline of course lectures has been reissued as *Grundriss zu den Vorlesungen über Allgemeine ("theoretische") Nationalökonomie* (Tübingen, Germany: Mohr [Siebeck], 1990); see esp. §6, 9–10; and the lectures from 1894 to 1898 are in *MWG* III/1 (2009).

114–15 Max Weber's most pertinent texts are *EaS*, part 1, chap. 4, "Status Groups and Classes," esp. 302–7; part 1, chap. 5, "Ethnic Groups," 385–98; and part 2, chap. 9, "Political Communities," section 6, "The Distribution of Power within the Political Community: Class, Status, Party," 926–40; quotations herein are on 42, 389, 394–95; the passages on "ethnic communities" are in *MWG* I/22.1 (2001): 169–90; see esp. 178–79 on status honor and "poor white trash"; see also *MWG* I/22.5 (1999): 254.

CHAPTER 7

Different Ways of Life

Max Weber's American relatives are discussed in Guenther Roth, *Max Webers deutsch englische Familiengeschichte, 1800–1950* (Tübingen, Germany: Mohr Siebeck, 2001), esp. 94–95, 354–70, 531–32. For the Mt. Airy relatives, see the 2006 video edited by Larry G. Keeter and Steven Hall, *Max Weber Visits America*, at video.google .com/videoplay?docid=3847257290288473322; see also Larry G. Keeter, "Max Weber's Visit to North Carolina," *Journal of the History of Sociology* 3, no. 2 (1981): 108–14; Larry G. Keeter, "Max Weber: A Spy!" *ASA Footnotes* 8, no. 6 (1980): 7; and William H. Swatos, "Sects and Success: *Missverstehen* in Mt. Airy," *Sociological Analysis* 43, no. 4 (1982), 375–79.

The important classic studies for Southern politics and history of the period are V. O. Key, *Southern Politics in State and Nation* (New York: Alfred A.Knopf, 1949), esp. chap. 4 on Tennessee; and C. Vann Woodward, *Origins of the New South, 1877–1913* (Baton Rouge: Louisiana State University Press, 1951), esp. chap. 14. Among the many works on progressivism, there are useful discussions in Arthur S. Link and Richard L. McCormick, *Progressivism* (Arlington Heights, IL: Harlan Davidson, 1983), and Richard L. McCormick, *The Party Period and Public Policy: American Politics from the Age of Jackson to the Progressive Era* (New York: Oxford University Press, 1986), 269–88. The politics of the New South and Colyar's role are discussed in Thomas Woodrow Davis, "Arthur S. Colyar and the New South, 1865–1905" (PhD diss., University of Missouri–Columbia, 1962). Among the books Murphy gave to Weber was Arthur St. Clair Colyar, *Life and Times of Andrew Jackson: Soldier—Statesman—President*, 2 vols. (Nashville, TN: Marshall and Bruce, 1904), now in the library of the Max-Weber-Edition in Munich, as its director, Edith Hanke, has informed me.

There is no satisfactory social history of Knoxville. For my purposes the most useful sources are Verton M. Queener, "The East Tennessee Republican Party, 1900–1914," *East Tennessee Historical Society's Publications* 20 (1950): 94–127. Morgan J. Kousser, *The Shaping of Southern Politics: Suffrage Restriction and the Establishment of the One-Party South, 1880–1910* (New Haven, CT: Yale University Press, 1974), 104–23; Lucile Deaderick, ed., *Heart of the Valley: A History of Knoxville, Tennessee* (Knoxville: East Tennessee Historical Society, 1976); William R. Majors, *Change and Continuity: Tennessee Politics since the Civil War* (Macon, GA: Mercer University Press, 1986), esp. chap. 2; Dewey W. Grantham, "Tennessee and Twentieth-Century American Politics," in *Tennessee History: The Land, the People, and the Culture*, ed. Carroll Van West (Knoxville: University of Tennessee Press, 1998), 343–72; Paul H. Bergeron, *Antebellum Politics in Tennessee* (Lexington: University Press of Kentucky, 1982); and Paul H. Bergeron, Stephen V. Ash, and Jeanette Keith , *Tennesseans and Their History* (Knoxville: University of Tennessee Press, 1999), chap. 9.

Page(s)

124 William R. Majors, *Change and Continuity: Tennessee Politics since the Civil War* (Macon, GA: Mercer University Press, 1986), 32, describes political contests as "bitter and confusing."

125 Murphy's campaign statement was reported in "Deputy Sheriff Yarnell Interrupted the Meeting," *Knoxville Sentinel*, October 10, 1904. Max Weber, "Politics as a Vocation," in Gerth & Mills, 103; MWG I/17 (1992): 204.

126 I allude to the classic formulation by Louis Hartz, *The Liberal Tradition in America: An Interpretation of American Political Thought since the Revolution* (New York: Harcourt, Brace and World, 1955), esp. chap. 1.

127 This is a reference to Thorstein Veblen, *The Theory of the Leisure Class* (New York: Macmillan, 1902 [1899]). The Biltmore estate is discussed in Witold Rybczynski, *A Clearing in the Distance: Frederick Law Olmsted and America in the Nineteenth Century* (New York: Charles Scribner's Sons, 1999), 379–84.

128–29 Peter Rosegger, *Jakob, der Letzte. Eine Waldbauerngeschichte aus unseren Tagen*, 13th ed. (Leipzig: L. Staackmann, 1904), quotation herein on 372. For the cultural significance of the *Heimat* literature, see Peter Blickle, *Heimat: A Critical Theory of the German Idea of Homeland* (Rochester, NY: Camden House, 2002).

130 Weber's references to the Mt. Airy episode are in Max Weber, "'Kirchen' und 'Sekten,'" *Frankfurter Zeitung*, April 13 and 15, 1906; Max Weber, "'Kirchen' und 'Sekten' in Nordamerika. Eine kirchen- und sozialpolitische Skizze," *Die Christliche Welt*, June 14 and 21, 1906; translated by Colin Loader as "'Churches' and 'Sects' in North America: An Ecclesiastical Socio-Political Sketch," *Sociological Theory* 3, no. 1 (1985): 7–13. The final revision is Max Weber, "The Protestant Sects and the Spirit of Capitalism" from *GARS I*, trans. Hans Gerth in Gerth & Mills, 302–22.

130 Weber's comment about music in American churches is in *PESC*, 272 n. 64; and Baehr & Wells, 191–92 n. 278. Useful ethnographic studies, including interviews with a few of Weber's relatives, are James L. Peacock and Ruel W. Tyson Jr., *Pilgrims of Paradox: Calvinism and Experience among the Primitive Baptists of the Blue Ridge* (Washington, DC: Smithsonian Institution Press, 1989); and Beverly Bush Patterson, *The Sound of the Dove: Singing in Appalachian Primitive Baptist Churches* (Urbana: University of Illinois Press, 1995).

131–32 Max Weber, "'Kirchen' und 'Sekten,'" *Frankfurter Zeitung*, April 13, 1906; my translation. In the correspondence Weber cites Jeff Miller referring to one of the men who is being baptized as "Bem," but in the subjunctive mood, thus leaving the time and circumstance unclear: "Jeff, who thought the entire business was 'nonsense,' said that he would have asked one of them, 'Didn't you feel pretty cold, Bem?' Answer: 'I thought of a pretty hot place (hell, of course) Sir, and so I didn't care for the cool water'" (October 19, MWP; the quoted comments in English).

133 Max Weber, "The Protestant Sects and the Spirit of Capitalism," from *GARS I*, in Gerth & Mills, 305, 308; *GARS I*, 211, 213–14. For pertinent issues in the sociology of religion, see William H. Swatos, "Baptists and Quakers in the USA," in *Max Webers Religionssoziologie in interkultureller Perspektive*, ed. Hartmut Lehmann and Jean Martin Quédraogo (Göttingen, Germany: Vandenhoeck and Ruprecht, 2003), 257–70, and the reply by Hermann Wellenreuther, "On the Curious Relationship between Words and Realities: Some Remarks on 'Baptists and Quakers in the USA,'" in the same volume, 271–77.

134 Max Weber, "'Kirchen' und 'Sekten,'" *Frankfurter Zeitung*, April 15, 1906; "'Churches' and 'Sects' in North America: An Ecclesiastical Socio-Political Sketch," trans. Colin Loader, *Sociological Theory* 3, no. 1 (1985); 10–11; translation modified here. An excellent recent discussion of Weber's theory of the sects and its modern implications is Sung Ho Kim, *Max Weber's Politics of Civil Society* (Cambridge: University of Cambridge Press, 2004).

CHAPTER 8

The Protestant Ethic

Page(s)

138 Sombart's extensive reviews are in Werner Sombart, "Quellen und Literatur zum Studium der Arbeiterfrage und des Sozialismus in den Vereinigten Staaten von Amerika (1902–1904)," *Archiv für Sozialwissenschaft und Sozialpolitik* 20 (1905): 633–703; and Werner Sombart, "Studien zur Entwicklungsgeschichte des nor-

damerikanischen Proletariats," *Archiv für Sozialwissenschaft und Sozialpolitik* 21 (1905): 210–36, 308–46, 556–611, which opens with the declaration, "The United States of America has become fashionable. It has become 'interesting.'"

138 Weber's commentaries on labor relations are in replies to presentations at the Verein für Sozialpolitik, reprinted in GASS, 394–430; see esp. 402–6, from September 1905.

140 In addition to the Congress of Arts and Science presentation, Hollander had recently published "Political Economy and the Labor Question," *North American Review* 176 (1903): 563–70; and "Economic Investigation in the United States," *Yale Review*, May 1903, 25–31; quotes herein on 26, 29. His reassessment of economics in America a decade later is "Economic Theorizing and Scientific Progress," *American Economic Review* 6, no.1, supplement (1916): 124–39. The academic program in economics is described in Jacob H. Hollander and George E. Barnett, eds., "The Economic Seminary, 1904–1905," *Johns Hopkins University Circular*, new ser., no. 6 (1905), 1–43. George Barnett's early work, *The Printers: A Study in American Trade Unionism* (Cambridge, MA: American Economic Association, 1909), was a pioneering study of the typographic union. The text they were using is John A. Hobson, *The Evolution of Modern Capitalism: A Study of Machine Production*, 2nd ed. (London: Walter Scott, 1901 [1894]).

141 Martha Carey Thomas's St. Louis speech, "The College," is in the proceedings *Congress of Arts and Science, Universal Exposition, St. Louis, 1904*, vol. 8, ed. Howard J. Rogers (Boston: Houghton, Mifflin, 1907), 133–50; reprinted in *Educational Review*, January 1905, 1–23; quotation herein on 17. The study that launched her national reputation is Martha Carey Thomas, *Education of Women* (Washington, DC: U.S. Department of Education, 1900), a monograph series edited by Nicholas Murray Butler. The book was reprinted in 1904 for the St. Louis Exposition, and it must have served as an essential source for Marianne Weber. For the debate over gender difference and education, see Martha Carey Thomas, "Should the Higher Education of Women Differ from that of Men?" *Educational Review*, January 1901, 1–10. Marianne Weber's presentation in Berlin on the participation of women in science is "Die Beteiligung der Frau an der Wissenschaft," in *Der Internationale Frauen-Kongress in Berlin 1904*, ed. Marie Stritt (Berlin: Verlag C. Habel, 1904), 105–15; this is followed by Martha Carey Thomas, "The University Education of Women in the United States of America, with Special Reference to Coeducation," in the same volume, 124–30. The definitive biography is Helen Lefkowitz Horowitz, *The Power and the Passion of M. Carey Thomas* (New York: Alfred A. Knopf, 1994).

143 Weber's reference to Rufus M. Jones is in a note added to the final revision of *The Protestant Ethic and the Spirit of Capitalism*, PESC, 253 note 169; GARS 1:151 note 4.

144–45 Weber mentions Allen Clapp Thomas's Haverford talk twice, though never with attribution; see PESC, 258 note 193; Baehr & Wells, 104, 175–76 n. 220; quotations herein are on 101, 104, 105. In the 1919–20 revision Weber adds "at Haverford College," GARS 1:162 note 4. The second reference is in "The Protestant Sects and the Spirit of Capitalism," in Gerth & Mills, 317–18.

147 Weber's brief remarks about the sociology of sports is in *PESC*, 166–67; Baehr & Wells, 113. For the coverage of the Harvard-Penn football game and statements about the Penn victory, see the *Philadelphia Inquirer*, October 26, 30, 31, and November 1, 1904, esp. the articles "Joy at Old Penn" (October 30), "Students Scored by Magistrate" (October 31), and "University Students Put in a Day and Night of Violent Celebration, Winding Up with the Night Shirt Dance and a Snake Dance Down Town" (November 1); the *Baltimore Sun*, October 30, 1904; and the *Globe* (Boston), October 30, 1904.

148 Hugo Münsterberg's major treatise, *Die Grundzüge der Psychologie* Leipzig: J. A. Barth, 1900), was better received in Germany than in the United States, partly because it was oriented to methodological issues raised in the *Methodenstreit*. For Münsterberg's place in psychology see Matthew Hale, *Human Science and Social Order: Hugo Münsterberg and the Origins of Applied Psychology* (Philadelphia: Temple University Press, 1980).

149 Ethel Puffer, "Studies in Symmetry," *Psychological Review* 4, no. 1 (1903), 467–539, reports on her work in experimental psychology at Harvard's Psychological Laboratory. Her treatise, *The Psychology of Beauty* (Boston: Houghton, Mifflin, 1905), quotation herein on 39, was a study in aesthetics as well as psychology. Her later essays of interest—as Ethyl Puffer Howes—include "The Great Refusal," *Atlantic Monthly* 108 (1911): 625–33; "Accepting the Universe," *Atlantic Monthly* 129 (1922): 444–53; "Continuity for Women," *Atlantic Monthly* 130 (1922): 731–39; and "The Meaning of Progress in the Woman Movement," *Annals of the American Academy of Political and Social Science* 143 (1929): 14–20. The Institute for the Coordination of Women's Interests is covered in "An Institute to Coordinate Women's Interests Launched," *Christian Science Monitor*, October 22, 1925. For discussions of Ethel Puffer Howes as a "material feminist" or "pragmatist feminist" see Betty Friedan, *The Second Stage* (New York: Summit Books, 1981), esp. 292–97; Dolores Hayden, *The Grand Domestic Revolution: A History of Feminist Designs for American Homes, Neighborhoods, and Cities* (Cambridge, MA: MIT Press, 1981), esp. 267–77; Elizabeth Scarborough and Laurel Furumoto, *Untold Lives: The First Generation of American Women Psychologists* (New York: Columbia University Press, 1987), chap. 3; Elizabeth Scarborough, "Continuity for Women: Ethel Puffer's Struggle," in *Portraits of Pioneers in Psychology*, ed. Gregory A. Kimble, Michael Wertheimer, and Charlotte White (Washington, DC: American Psychological Association, 1991), 105–19; and Charlene Haddock Seigfried, *Pragmatism and Feminism: Reweaving the Social Fabric* (Chicago: University of Chicago Press, 1996), esp. 46, 63–65. An imaginary dialogue concerning the meaning of "beauty" and set in William James's library with James, Puffer, Santayana, Münsterberg, and others as dramatis personae was broadcast on the radio by the U.S. Office of Education in the series *Gallant American Women* on January 2, 1940.

149 For Ernst Troeltsch's St. Louis presentation, see "Main Problems of the Philosophy of Religion: Psychology and Theory of Knowledge in the Science of Religion," *Congress of Arts and Science, Universal Exposition, St. Louis 1904*, ed. Howard J. Rogers, vol. 1 (Boston: Houghton, Mifflin, 1905), 275–88; see also his review of the book in *Deutsche Literaturzeitung* 25, December 10, 1904, 3021–27. Troeltsch's appreciation of James is "Empiricism and Platonism in the Philosophy of Religion:

To the Memory of William James," *Harvard Theological Review* 5 (1912): 401–22; reprinted in translation in Ernst Troeltsch, *Gesammelte Schriften. Zur religiösen Lage, Religionsphilosophie und Ethik*, vol. 2 (Aalen, Germany: Scientia Verlag, 1962), 364–85.

152 Weber's explicit references to William James are in GARS 1:112–3 n. 4, and 213 n. 1; the latter reference is translated in Gerth & Mills, 308 (the editors incorporate the footnote in the text); *PESC*, 232–33; trans. Peter Baehr and Gordon Wells, in Baehr & Wells, 144–45. Weber's comment in this note on the psychological implications of Nietzsche's idea of "eternal recurrence" was added in the 1920 edition. The other reference to James is in Weber's review of Adolf Weber, *Die Aufgaben der Volkswirtschaftslehre als Wissenschaft*, in *Archiv für Sozialwissenschaft und Sozialpolitik* 29, no. 2 (1909), 615–20. For important studies, see Wilhelm Hennis, *Max Weber's Science of Man: New Studies for a Biography of the Work*, trans. Keith Tribe (Newbury, England: Threshold Press, 2000), esp. 46–65; and Hartmut Lehmann, "Max Webers 'Protestantische Ethik' als Selbstzeugnis," in *Max Webers 'Protestantische Ethik'* (Göttingen, Germany: Vandenhoeck and Ruprecht, 1996), 109–27. For a skeptical point of view, see Peter Ghosh, "Max Weber and William James: 'Pragmatism,' Psychology, Religion," in *A Historian Reads Max Weber: Essays on the Protestant Ethic* (Wiesbaden, Germany: Harrassowitz, 2008), chap. 8.

152 William James, *The Varieties of Religious Experience* (New York: Vintage, 1990 [1902]), quotations herein in lecture 1, 13. William James to Charles Eliot, August 13, 1902, in the Charles W. Eliot Papers, Box 125A.

152 Baumgarten's observations about James are in Eduard Baumgarten, *Max Weber: Werk und Person* (Tübingen, Germany: Mohr [Siebeck], 1964), 313.

153 William James, *The Varieties of Religious Experience* (New York: Vintage, 1990 [1902]), lectures 4–5, "The Religion of Healthy-Mindedness," p. 105; lecture 6, "The Sick Soul," 128–29; lecture 8, "The Divided Self, and the Process of Its Unification," 155.

153 Weber's oft-quoted remark, "Denn ich bin zwar religiös absolut 'unmusikalisch' . . . Aber ich bin, nach genauer Prüfung, weder antireligiös, *noch irreligiös* [For I am really absolutely 'unmusical' religiously . . . But I am on close examination neither antireligous *nor irreligious*"] is in Max Weber to Ferdinand Tönnies, February 19, 1909, MWG II/6 (1994): 65. *PESC*, 104, 105, 108; GARS 1:93, 95, 98; Baehr & Wells, 73, 74; I have restored the original emphases from Weber's 1905 text.

153 Baehr & Wells, 69, 86; *PESC*, 97–98, 126; GARS 1:86, 125. Referring to the "psychological drives," Weber added the clarifying phrase "originating in religious belief and the practice of religion [Praxis des religiösen Lebens]" in the 1920 edition. Weber notes that "the idea of *being put to the test* [Bewährungsgedanke]" as the "psychological starting point for methodical morality" is fundamental to his inquiry; I am citing the original 1905 text, in Baehr and Wells's translation.

154 Baehr & Wells, 87; *PESC*, 128; GARS 1:128.

154 Max Weber to Adolf von Harnack, January 12, 1905, in the Adolf von Harnack Papers.

155–56 Baehr & Wells, 144 n. 113, their translation; *PESC*, 232 n. 66; GARS 1:111–2 n. 4.

157 See Weber's review in the *Archiv für Sozialwissenschaft und Sozialpolitik* 29, no. 2 (1909), 615–20.

158–59 Max Weber, "Die Wirtschaftethik der Weltreligionen," is in GARS 1:237–75; translated by Hans Gerth as "The Social Psychology of the World Religions," in Gerth & Mills, 267–301; and recently translated by Sam Whimster as "Introduction to the Economic Ethics of the World Religions," in *The Essential Weber: A Reader* (London: Routledge, 2004), 55–80; quotations herein on 56, 69; I have retranslated these passages using Weber's original.

159 William James, *The Varieties of Religious Experience*, lecture 3, 74; William James to Hugo Münsterberg, March 16, 1905, in the William James Papers. Martha Nussbaum, *Upheavals of Thought: The Intelligence of Emotions* (Cambridge: Cambridge University Press, 2001), is a recent discussion of the problem of the rationality of emotion and experience. On pragmatism generally, see Lewis Menand's excellent *The Metaphysical Club: A Story of Ideas in America* (New York: Farrar, Straus and Giroux, 2001).

CHAPTER 9

American Modernity

Aspects of the Webers' second stay in New York are discussed in Guenther Roth, "Transatlantic Connections: A Cosmopolitan Context for Max and Marianne Weber's New York Visit 1904," *Max Weber Studies* 5, no. 1 (2005): 81–112. Tracing the family connections, he reports that Paul and Clara (Kapp) Lichtenstein lived at 182 Amity Street, Brooklyn, in the neighborhood now renamed Cobble Hill (a few doors away from the birthplace of Winston Churchill's mother, Jennie Jerome), while Alfred and Hannah (Kapp) Lichtenstein lived in Brooklyn Heights at 201 Columbia Heights. The Webers dined at their homes on November 11 and 17, 1904, respectively. See also Guenther Roth, *Max Webers deutsch-englische Familiengeschichte 1800–1950* (Tübingen, Germany: Mohr Siebeck, 2001), 354–70, 486–89, for the family history.

Page(s)

161–62 Weber's oblique references to Otto von Klock and to the conversations in the Madison Avenue boarding house are in the final version of "The Protestant Sects and the Spirit of Capitalism," GARS 1: 215, 216 nn. 1, 2; Gerth & Mills, 310–11, and "Class, Status, Party," *EaS*, 932; MWG I/22.1 (2001): 260; Gerth & Mills, 187.

163 Weber characterizes Theodore Roosevelt as a charismatic politician in Max Weber, "Charisma and Its Transformation," *EaS*, 1130–32; *WuG*, 849–50; the references are to Roosevelt's 1912 campaign, which Weber apparently followed with interest. For a recent discussion of Weber's ideas about charisma and their applicability see Peter Baehr, *Caesarism, Charisma and Fate: Historical Sources and Modern Resonances in the Work of Max Weber* (New Brunswick, NJ: Transaction, 2008).

164 Weber's reference to the Marble Collegiate Church is in GARS 1:215 n. 1; Gerth & Mills, 310.

164 See Jean-Pierre Isbouts, *Carrère and Hastings: Architects to an Era* (PhD thesis, Rijksuniversiteit Leiden, 1980), esp. 144–48; and Mark Alan Hewitt, Kate Lemos, Wil-

liam Morrison, and Charles Davock Warren, *Carrère and Hastings, Architects* (New York: Acanthus Press, 2006). Carrère and Hastings also designed the New York Public Library and the U.S. Senate and House of Representatives office buildings in Washington, D.C. Hastings's theory of architecture is summarized in Thomas Hastings, "Modern Architecture," in Ralph Adams Cram, Thomas Hastings, and Claude Bragdon, *Six Lectures on Architecture: The Scammon Lectures for 1915* (Chicago: University of Chicago Press, 2003 [1917]), 98–122; quotation herein on 98.

166 James's statements about "mind cure" are in William James, *The Varieties of Religious Experience* (New York: Vintage, 1990) 92–93, 103, lectures 4 and 5 on the religion of healthy-mindedness.

167 For an overview of the Ethical Culture Society, see the book by Adler's assistant, David S. Muzzey, *Ethics as a Religion* (New York: Frederick Ungar, 1951), quote herein on 3–4; also Horace L. Friess, *Felix Adler and Ethical Culture: Memories and Studies*, ed. Fannia Weingarner (New York: Columbia University Press, 1981). Adler's twenty-page sermon "Mental Healing as a Religion" is in the Felix Adler Papers, Box 61.

169 Weber's comments about municipal reform and support for Catholic schools are in *EaS*, 961, 1195–96. The issues are also discussed in James Bryce's chapters on the party system generally in Bryce, *The American Commonwealth* (Indianapolis, IN: Liberty Fund, 1995), 2:683–906, as well as "The Tammany Ring in New York City,"1023–46, and "The Churches and the Clergy," 1370–85, in the same volume.

173 Florence Kelley, *Some Ethical Gains through Legislation* (New York: Macmillan, 1905), quotation herein on 172, presents a concise statement of her socialist and progressive feminism. The most recent biography is Kathryn Kish Sklar, *Florence Kelley and the Nation's Work: The Rise of Women's Political Culture, 1830–1900* (New Haven, CT: Yale University Press, 1995), the first of two volumes on Kelley. The transatlantic dialogue among women reformers is covered in Kathryn Kish Sklar, Anja Schuler, and Susan Strasser, eds., *Social Justice Feminists in the United States and Germany: A Dialogue in Documents, 1885–1933* (Ithaca, NY: Cornell University Press, 1998), although Marianne Weber's role should be amplified. For more on Lillian Wald, see Doris G. Daniels, *Always a Sister: The Feminism of Lillian D. Wald* (New York: Feminist Press, 1989); Lillian Wald's reader *Lillian D. Wald: Progressive Activist*, ed. Clare Coss (New York: Feminist Press, 1989); and Beatrice Siegel, *Lillian Wald of Henry Street* (New York: Macmillan, 1983).

174–75 The Villard family history is found in Henry Villard, *Memoires of Henry Villard: Journalist and Financier, 1835–1900*, 2 vols. (Boston: Houghton, Mifflin, 1904); Fanny Garrison Villard, *William Lloyd Garrison on Non-Resistance, Together with a Personal Sketch, and a Tribute by Leo Tolstoi* (New York: Nation Press, 1924); and Oswald Garrison Villard, *Fighting Years: Memoirs of a Liberal Editor* (New York: Harcourt, Brace, 1939), quotation herein on 21. See also Michael Wreszin, *Oswald Garrison Villard: Pacifist at War* (Bloomington: Indiana University Press, 1965), and for the deeper sources of the family's civic zeal and nonconformist support of women's causes, African Americans, and the peace movement, Henry Mayer, *All on Fire: William Lloyd Garrison and the Abolition of Slavery* (New York: St. Martin's Press, 2008 [1998]).

175–76 Yamei Kin's speech at the Committee on Political Education (in the little theater of the Berkeley Lyceum) was reported in "China a Real Power, Dr. Kin's Prediction," *New York Times*, November 13, 1904; see also James Kay MacGregor, "Yamei Kin and Her Mission to the Chinese People," *Craftsman* 9 (1905): 242–49.

176–77 Weber's remarks about American workers' attitudes toward corruption are in Max Weber, "Socialism" (1918), in *GASS*, 496; and Lassman & Speirs, 277; I have revised the translation.

177–79 On Blaustein's work, see David Blaustein, *Memoires of David Blaustein, Educator and Communal Worker*, ed. Miriam Blaustein (New York: McBride, Nast, 1913). Daniel Soyer, *Jewish Immigrant Associations and American Identity in New York, 1880–1939* (Cambridge, MA: Harvard University Press, 1997), is an excellent historical account. Jonathan M. Hess, *Germans, Jews and the Claims of Modernity* (New Haven, CT: Yale University Press, 2002), discusses the discourse of Jewish emancipation and the promise, limits, and contradictions of Enlightenment universalism. Weber's references to Blaustein are in *GARS* 1:181–82 n. 2, 212 n. 3; *PESC*, 166, 270–71; Baehr & Wells, 112, 189; "The Protestant Sects," Gerth & Mills, 307; *EaS*, 623; *MWG* I/22.2 (2001): 432. Weber's phrase "specific and peculiar 'rationalism' of occidental culture," which I have adapted, is in *PESC*, 26; *GARS* 1:11.

180 Woodrow Wilson's Cooper Union speech is covered in "Wilson Says Elasticity Saves the Constitution," *New York Times*, November 20, 1904; emphasis added.

CHAPTER 10

Interpretation of the Experience

Page(s)

181 Weber's last letter from the journey is undated, but written on November 19 or later (MWP).

182 On Troeltsch's threefold distinction among church, sect, and mysticism, see Arie L. Molendijk, *Zwischen Theologie und Soziologie. Ernst Troeltschs Typen der christlichen Gemeinschaftsbildung: Kirche, Sekte, Mystik* (Gütersloh, Germany: Gütersloher Verlagshaus, 1996); see also the journal *Troeltsch-Studien* 9 (1996).

183 The *Heidelberger Zeitung* and *Heidelberger Tageblatt* reports of the "America evening" on January 20, 1905, are reprinted in *MWG* I/8 (1998): 381–85, quotations herein on 384–85. Marianne Weber's presentations were published as "Was Amerika den Frauen bietet," *Centralblatt des Bundes deutscher Frauenvereine* 6 (1905): 170–72, 177–79, 186–88; quotation herein on 170. Jeffrey L. Sammons, *Ideology, Mimesis, Fantasy: Charles Sealsfield, Friedrich Gerstäcker, Karl May, and Other German Novelists of America* (Chapel Hill: University of North Carolina Press, 1998), is a useful discussion of the literary images of America.

185 The CD-ROM selections from Weber's work (a partial selection only) are *Max Weber. Das Werk*, ed. Thomas Müller (Berlin: Heptagon, 2000), and *Max Weber im Kontext*, ed. Karsten Worm (Berlin: InfoSoftWare, 2001).

188 Weber's line about bureaucracy and democracy appears in Max Weber, "Socialism," in Lassman & Speirs, 279; GASS, 497.

189 See Max Weber, "Wahlrecht und Demokratie in Deutschland" (1917), in GPS, 233–79; Gerth & Mills, 386–95; MWG I/15 (1984). Weber's statement about the importance of American clubs is in a letter to Friedrich Crusius, November 24, 1918, in Max Weber, Gesammelte Politische Schriften, ed. Marianne Weber (Munich: Drei Masken Verlag, 1921), 483.

189 Offe's interpretation is in Claus Offe, "Max Weber: American Escape Routes from the Iron Cage?" in Reflections on America: Tocqueville, Weber and Adorno in the United States, trans. Patrick Camiller (Cambridge: Polity Press, 2005), quotation herein on 49, which relies in part on Georg Kamphausen, Die Erfindung Amerikas in der Kulturkritik der Generation von 1890 (Weilerswist, Germany: Velbrück Wissenschaft, 2002).

190 Sung Ho Kim, Max Weber's Politics of Civil Society (Cambridge: Cambridge University Press, 2004), esp. 6, 91–3, 173–80.

190 Perry Miller, The New England Mind: From Colony to Province (Cambridge, MA: Harvard University Press, 1953), discusses the "Protestant ethic" in chapter 3, applying the idea to John Cotton's The Way of Life (London: n.p., 1641).

191–92 Many of Weber's important writings about universities and educational policy were collected and translated by Edward Shils in Max Weber on Universities: The Power of the State and the Dignity of the Academic Calling in Imperial Germany (Chicago: University of Chicago Press, 1973); the tantalizing and little-known pre–World War I proposal for a Carnegie-sponsored institute at Heidelberg is discussed in Weber's correspondence with Jellinek: MWG II/6 (1994), esp. the letters of July 15, 25, August 19, and September 12, 1909. Marianne Weber published most of her husband's contributions to the Verein and Deutsche Gesellschaft für Soziologie debates in GASS, 394–491; they are also now in MWG I/8 (1998). Weber's proposal to study voluntary associations, "Voluntary Associational Life (Vereinswesen)," presented at the 1910 Deutsche Gesellschaft für Soziologie, is translated by Sung Ho Kim with a translator's introduction in Max Weber Studies 2, no. 2 (2002): 186–209; quotations herein on 202.

192 The definitive editions of "Science as a Vocation" and "Politics as a Vocation" are now in MWG I/17 (1992), edited by Wolfgang J. Mommsen and Wolfgang Schluchter. Hans Gerth and C. Wright Mills published their translation in Gerth & Mills, 77–156; quotes herein on 131, 149. The most recent translation is Max Weber, The Vocation Lectures, trans. Rodney Livingstone, ed. David Owen and Tracy B. Strong (Indianapolis, IN: Hackett, 2004), with an introduction by the editors.

CHAPTER 11

The Discovery of the Author

Page(s)

197 For typical examples of Weber's popular reach, see John Le Carré, Absolute Friends (Boston: Little, Brown, 2003), 352, 390; Patrick R. Keefe, "Iraq: America's Private Armies," New York Review of Books (August 12, 2004); Earl Shorris, "Ignoble Liars:

Leo Strauss, George Bush, and the Philosophy of Mass Deception," *Harper's* 308 (2004): 65–71; Charles Kurzman, "Reading Weber in Tehran," *Chronicle Review*, November 1, 2009, available online at http://webcache.googleusercontent.com/ search?q=cache:E8IY5ofu0qQJ:chronicle.com/article/Social-Science-on-Trial-in/ 48949/+Charles+Kurzman,+"Reading+Weber+in+Tehran&cd=1&hl=en&ct= clnk&gl=us&client=safari; see also Matthew Yglesias's December 19, 2009, blog entry at http://yglesias.thinkprogress.org.

197 Roth's comments about "creative misinterpretations" are in Guenther Roth and Reinhard Bendix, *Scholarship and Partisanship: Essays on Max Weber* (Berkeley and Los Angeles: University of California Press, 1971), 35; and Guenther Roth, "Max Weber: Family History, Economic Policy, Exchange Reform," *International Journal of Politics, Culture and Society* 15, no. 3 (2002): 509.

197 An apt example of "Weberian theory" in American sociology is Randall Collins, *Weberian Sociological Theory* (Cambridge: Cambridge University Press 1986); for a contrasting skeptical assessment of Weber's import or "influence" see David Zaret, "Max Weber und die Entwicklung der theoretischen Soziologie in den USA," in *Max Webers Wissenschaftslehre: Interpretation und Kritik*, ed. Gerhard Wagner and Heinz Zippian (Frankfurt: Suhrkamp, 1994), 332–66. *Das Weber Paradigma: Studien zur Weiterentwicklung von Max Webers Forschungsprogramm*, ed. Gert Albert et al. (Tübingen, Germany: Mohr Siebeck, 2003), argues for a "Weberian paradigm" or "research program" in the social sciences today, a view taken up from a very different perspective in Mark I. Lichbach, "Thinking and Working in the Midst of Things," in *Comparative Politics: Rationality, Culture, and Structure*, ed. Mark I. Lichbach and Alan S. Zuckerman, 2nd ed. (Cambridge: Cambridge University Press, 2009), 18–71.

199 Parsons's dissertation is Talcott Parsons, "'Capitalism' in Recent German Literature: Sombart and Weber," originally published in two parts in the *Journal of Political Economy* 1928–29, and reprinted in *Talcott Parsons: The Early Essays* (Chicago: University of Chicago Press, 1991), 3–37. The best source for the early Talcott Parsons is Charles Camic, "Introduction: Talcott Parsons before *The Structure of Social Action*," in *Talcott Parsons: The Early Essays* (Chicago: University of Chicago Press, 1991), xxx–xliv. See also Uta Gerhardt, *Talcott Parsons: An Intellectual Biography* (Cambridge: Cambridge University Press 2002), which emphasizes his public and political involvements. Hartshorne's life ended tragically in August 1946 when he was assassinated on the Autobahn by Nazi partisans. Serving as a denazification officer for Bavaria, Hartshorne had visited Marianne Weber on May 16, 1945, a conversation recorded in her *Lebenserinnerungen* (Bremen: Storm Verlag, 1948), 483–91; she "responded warmly to the name of Talcott Parsons," Hartshorne recorded in his diary. Uta Gerhardt generously provided access to the diary.

200 David Kettler and Volker Meja, *Karl Mannheim and the Crisis of Liberalism* (New Brunswick, NJ: Transaction, 1995), 220–26, discusses the "refugee conversations."

200 Don Martindale, *The Monologue: Hans Gerth (1908–1978), A Memoir* (Ghaziabad, India: Intercontinental Press, 1982), is a work of refreshing candor that Guenther Roth brought to my attention; quotation herein on 2.

201 Lowell Bennion, *Max Weber's Methodology* (Paris: Les Presses Modernes, 1933); see also Laurie N. DiPadova, "Max Weber and Lowell Bennion: Towards an Un-

derstanding of Hierarchy and Authority," *Dialogue: A Journal of Mormon Thought* 30 (1997): 1–24.

202 Weber's selected shorter texts are "Class, Status and Party," trans. Hans H. Gerth and C. Wright Mills, *Politics* 1 (1944): 272–78; "The Hindu Social System," trans. and ed. Hans H. Gerth and Don Martindale, in *Bulletin No. 1, Historical Series*, vol. 1 (Minneapolis: University of Minnesota Sociology Club, n.d.); and "The Essentials of Bureaucratic Organization: An Ideal-Type Construction," 18–27, "The Presuppositions and Causes of Bureaucracy," 60–68, and "The Routinization of Charisma," 92–100, in Robert K. Merton, Alisa P. Gray, Barbara Hockey, and Hanan C. Selvin, eds., *Reader in Bureaucracy* (Glencoe, IL: Free Press, 1952).

204 Shils's unpublished autobiographical reflections are found in "Some Notes on Max Weber in America" (1975–76); quotes herein on 28, 30, in ESP.

204 Parsons corresponded about translation issues with Dumas Malone, director of the Harvard University Press (February 25, 1939), Knight (May 17, 1939), Shils (May 17, 1939), Schelting (July 12, 1939), and Professor F. Gay (August 17, 1939)—all in TPP. See also Knight to Malone, May 20, 1939, in TPP.

204–5 Marianne Weber's March 13, 1937, letter is in FKP, Box 62; her "introduction" has apparently not survived. Correspondence a decade earlier on translation issues includes Oskar Siebeck to Marianne Weber, July 21, 1927 (VAMS), and an exchange between Parsons and Douglas, November 13 and December 7, 1927, TPP.

207 See Hugh D. Duncan, "The Uses and Misuses of Max Weber's Types of Legitimation in American Sociology," 316–43 (quote herein on 316), and Irving L. Horowitz, "Max Weber and the Spirit of American Sociology," 344–54 (quotes herein on 346, 350), in "Weber Symposium," special issue, *Sociological Quarterly* 5 (1964); and Louis Wirth, "Modern German Conceptions of Sociology," *American Journal of Sociology* 32 (1926): 461–67; quotation herein on 464. See also Guenther Roth, "Heidelberger kosmopolitische Soziologie," in *Das Weber-Paradigma: Studien zur Weiterentwicklung von Max Webers Forschungsprogramm*, ed. Gert Albert, Agathe Bienfait, Steffen Sigmund, and Claus Wendt (Tübingen, Germany: Mohr Siebeck, 2003), 23–31.

208 See Theodore F. Abel, *Systematic Sociology in Germany: A Critical Analysis of Some Attempts to Establish Sociology as an Independent Science* (New York: Columbia University Press, 1929).

209 Knight's assessment is Frank Knight, "Historical and Theoretical Issues in the Problem of Modern Capitalism," *Journal of Economic and Business History* 1 (1928): 119–36; quotations herein on 130, 134. For examples of Weber read as an economist, see Georg Brodnitz, "Recent Work in German Economic History, 1900–1927," *Economic History Review* 1 (1928): 322–45; or the comments not only on the *General Economic History* but also on Weber's habilitation of 1891, *Die Römische Agrargeschichte*, by a Johns Hopkins University classicist writing on the economic history of ancient Rome, Frank Tenney, "Recent Work on the Economic History of Ancient Rome," *Journal of Economic and Business History* 1 (1928): esp. 110. For the economics audience, see also Carl Diehl, "The Life and Work of Max Weber," *Quarterly Journal of Economics* 38 (1923): 87–107.

209 See Edward Shils, "Some Notes on Max Weber in America," 41–42, ESP.
210 See Edward Shils, "Some Academics, Mainly in Chicago," *American Scholar* 50 (1981): 179–96; quotation herein on 184.

CHAPTER 12

The Creation of the Sacred Text

This chapter relies on correspondence primarily from two sources: the Talcott Parsons Papers (HUGFP 42.8.2 and 42.45.2), cited as TPP; and the Verlags Archiv Mohr/Siebeck (Nrs. 432, 439, 447, 455), cited as VAMS. I have also used the George Allen and Unwin Archive (1930 correspondence) at the University of Reading. I appreciate the efforts of Mike Bott, University of Reading, and especially Edith Hanke of the MWG and the Bayerische Akademie der Wissenschaften, for assisting with access to the archives in Reading and in Tübingen, Germany.

Two recent translations into English are *The Protestant Ethic and the "Spirit" of Capitalism and Other Writings*, ed. and trans. Peter Baehr and Gordon C. Wells (New York: Penguin, 2002); and *The Protestant Ethic and the Spirit of Capitalism*, ed. and trans. Stephen Kalberg (Los Angeles: Roxbury, 2002), now in an expanded fourth edition. Peter Ghosh is also planning a third new translation. The discussion of translation and textual interpretation can be followed in numerous studies, among them Peter Ghosh, "Some Problems with Talcott Parsons's Version of "The Protestant Ethic," *Archive européennes de sociologie* 35 (1994): 104–23; Peter Ghosh, "Translation as a Conceptual Act," 59–63, as well as David J. Chalcraft, Austin Harrington, and Mary Shields, "The Protestant Ethic Debate: Fischer's First Critique and Max Weber's *First Reply* (1907)," 15–32 (quotation herein on 20); Gordon C. Wells, "Issues of Language and Translation in Max Weber's Protestant Ethic Writings," 33–40; and Stephen Kalberg, "The *Spirit of Capitalism* Revisited: On the New Translation of Weber's *Protestant Ethic* (1920)," 41–58, all in *Max Weber Studies* 2, no. 1 (2001). See also Peter Baehr, *Founders, Classics, Canons: Modern Disputes over the Origins and Appraisal of Sociology's Heritage* (New Brunswick, NJ: Transaction, 2002), 185–204; Lutz Kaelber, "Max Weber's Protestant Ethic in the 21st Century," *International Journal of Politics, Culture and Society* 16, no. 1 (2002): 133–46 (quotation herein on 133); Lutz Kaelber and Stephen Kalberg, "An Exchange," *International Journal of Politics, Culture and Society* 17, no. 2 (2003): 329–32; Lutz Kaelber, "Introduction: Max Weber's Dissertation in the Context of His Early Career and Life," in Max Weber, *The History of Commercial Partnerships in the Middle Ages*, trans. Lutz Kaelber (Lanham, MD: Rowman and Littlefield, 2003), 38–40; Sam Whimster, "Translator's Note on Weber's 'Introduction to the Economic Ethics of the World Religions,'" *Max Weber Studies* 3, no. 1 (2002): 74–98; Richard Swedberg, *The Max Weber Dictionary: Key Words and Central Concepts* (Stanford, CA: Stanford University Press, 2005); the translation of PESC into French by Jean-Pierre Grossein as *L'Éthique protestante et l'esprit du capitalisme* (Paris: Gallimard, 2003); Jean-Pierre Grossein, "Max Weber 'à la française'? De la nécessité d'une critique des traductions," in "Lire Max Weber," ed. François Chazel and Jean-Pierre Grossein, special issue, *Revue française de sociologie* 46, no. 4 (2005): 883–901; Keith Tribe, "Talcott Parsons as Translator of Max Weber's Basic Sociological Categories," *History of European Ideas* 33 (2007): 212–33;

David Chalcraft, "Why Hermeneutics, the Text(s) and the Biography of the Work Matter in Max Weber Studies," in David Chalcraft, Fanon Howell, M. L. Menendez, and Hector Vera, eds., *Max Weber Matters: Interweaving Past and Present* (Farnham, England: Ashgate, 2008), 17–40; and the Norton critical edition of Max Weber, *The Protestant Ethic and the Spirit of Capitalism*, trans. Talcott Parsons, ed. Richard Swedberg (New York: W. W. Norton, 2009).

Page(s)

212 The comment is Lutz Kaelber's in "Max Weber's Protestant Ethic in the 21st Century," *International Journal of Politics, Culture and Society* 16, no. 1 (2002): 133.

213 Talcott Parsons's three reflections on his encounter with Weber's work are in "A Short Account of my Intellectual Development," *Alpha Kappa Deltan* 29, no. 1 (1959), 3–12; "Dialogues with Parsons (1973–4)" ed. Martin Martel, in *Essays on the Sociology of Talcott Parsons*, ed. G. C. Hallen, *Indian Journal of Social Research* 17 (1976): 1–34, quotations herein on 4–5; and "The Circumstances of My Encounter with Max Weber," in *Sociological Traditions from Generation to Generation*, ed. Robert K. Merton and Matilda White Riley (Norwood, NJ: Ablex, 1980); quotations herein on 38, 39, emphasis added. For the biography of the work, see also Guy Rocher, "Talcott Parsons: A Critical Loyalty to Max Weber," in *Max Weber's "Objectivity"Reconsidered*, ed. Laurence McFalls (Toronto: University of Toronto Press, 2007), 165–83.

214 For Weber's Franklin quotation, see *PESC*, 49; *GARS* 1:32. The phase *de te narratur fabula* is used in Max Weber, "The Social Causes of the Decay of Ancient Civilization," trans. Christian Mackauer, *Journal of General Education* 5 (1950): 76; *GASW*, 291.

219 The correspondence between Tawney and Stanley Unwin is in the George Allen and Unwin Archive.

219 See R. H. Tawney, *Religion and the Rise of Capitalism* (New York: Mentor, 1963), 3–9, for his preface to the 1937 edition. Kaelber's assessment is Lutz Kaelber, "Max Weber's Protestant Ethic in the 21st Century," *International Journal of Politics, Culture and Society* 16, no. 1 (2002): 137.

220 Marianne Weber's original reads, "Es ist für mich sehr schwierig, die Parsons'sche Uebersetzung zu beurteilen, da ich sie mit deutschem, nicht englischem Sprachgefühl lese. Für mich ist sie so durchaus lesbar u. auch stilistisch erträglich, u. ich glaube als Grundlage einer Überarbeitung dürfte sie jedenfalls in Betracht kommen. Für eine Anzahl von Stellen werden sich sicher bessere Formulierungen finden lassen, aber zweifellos nur durch einen Uebersetzer, der in der Geschichte und in der Nationalökonomie zu Hause ist. Ich bemerke gleich auf S. 1 von Abschnitt 2 in Fragezeichen bei dem Begriff, 'historical individual'. Das deutsche Wort 'Historisches Individuum' ist ein in Deutschland bekannter von H. Rickert geprägter philosophischer Begriff, der m.E. night anders übersetzt werden kann. Wenn aber der Parsons'sche Text für englische Leser unverständlich ist, so müssen wir dem englischen Verlag m.E. die Befugnis geben, ihn überarbeiten zu lassen, allerdings durch eine wissenschaftlich geschulte Persönlichkeit, die sich die Aufgabe stellt, den Inhalt möglichst getreu wiederzugeben. Es ist natürlich der konzentrierte Gehalt der Sätze, der solche Schwierigkeiten 1) des Verstehens 2) des Uebersetzens macht."

222 *PESC*, 13; *GARS* 1:1. Weber's introduction/prefatory remarks originally read, "Universalgeschichtliche Probleme wird der Sohn der modernen europäischen Kulturwelt unvermeidlicher- und berechtigterweise unter der Fragestellung behandeln: welche Verkettung von Umständen hat dazu geführt, daß gerade auf dem Boden des Okzidents, und nur hier, Kulturerscheinungen auftraten, welche doch—wie wenigstens wir uns gern vorstellen—in einer Entwicklungsrichtung von *universeller* Bedeutung und Gültigkeit lagen? Nur im Okzident gibt es 'Wissenschaft' in dem Entwicklungsstadium, welches wir heute als 'gültig' anerkennen."

223 Parsons's phrasings about being forced to work in a calling and the "specialists without spirit" are in *PESC*, 181, 182; *GARS* 1:203, 204.

224 Salin's views are expressed in Edgar Salin, *Geschichte der Volkswirtschaftslehre*, 4th ed. (Tübingen, Germany: Mohr [Siebeck], 1951 [1923]; reissued Berlin: Springer-Verlag, 2007), esp. 62–102 [1923]).

225 See Talcott Parsons, "'Capitalism' in Recent German Literature: Sombart and Weber," in *Talcott Parsons: The Early Essays*, ed. Charles Camic (Chicago: University of Chicago Press, 1991), esp. 3–4, 22–32; originally published in 1928–29 in the *Journal of Political Economy*.

226 Talcott Parsons, "The Circumstances of My Encounter with Max Weber," in *Sociological Traditions from Generation to Generation*, ed. Robert K. Merton and Matilda White Riley (Norwood, NJ: Ablex, 1980), 40.

227 See Guenther Roth, "Max Weber at Home and in Japan: On the Troubled Genesis and Successful Reception of His Work," *International Journal of Politics, Culture and Society* 12, no. 13 (1999): 521, for comments on the sales of *The Protestant Ethic and the Spirit of Capitalism* in a letter of July 30, 1934, from the governing director of Allen and Unwin to J.C.B. Mohr.

227 The four "disenchantment of the world" passages that Weber added in 1919–20 are *PESC*, 105, 117, 147, 149; *GARS* 1:94, 114, 156, 158.

CHAPTER 13

The Invention of the Theory

Under the heading "Weberian theory," see the quite varied offerings from Randall Collins, *Weberian Sociological Theory* (Cambridge: Cambridge University Press, 1986); Harvey Goldman, *Max Weber and Thomas Mann: Calling and the Shaping of the Self* (Berkeley and Los Angeles: University of California Press, 1988); Wolfgang Schluchter, *Rationalism, Religion, and Domination: A Weberian Perspective*, trans. Neil Solomon (Berkeley and Los Angeles: University of California Press, 1989), and *Paradoxes of Modernity: Culture and Conduct in the Theory of Max Weber*, trans. Neil Solomon (Stanford, CA: Stanford University Press, 1996); Lawrence A. Scaff, *Fleeing the Iron Cage: Culture, Politics, and Modernity in the Thought of Max Weber* (Berkeley and Los Angeles: University of California Press, 1989); Steven Kalberg, *Max Weber's Comparative-Historical Sociology* (Chicago: University of Chicago Press, 1994); Peter Breiner, *Max Weber and Democratic Politics* (Ithaca, NY: Cornell University Press, 1996); Richard Swedberg, *Max Weber and the Idea of Economic Sociology* (Princeton, NJ: Princeton University Press, 1998); Wilhelm Hennis, *Max Weber's Central Question*, 2nd ed., trans. Keith Tribe (Guildford, England: Threshold, 2000), and *Max Weber's*

Science of Man: New Studies for a Biography of the Work, trans. Keith Tribe (Guildford, England: Threshold, 2000); Zenonas Norkus, *Max Weber and Rational Choice* (Marburg, Germany: Metropolis, 2001); Alan Sica, *Max Weber and the New Century* (New Brunswick, NJ: Transaction, 2004); Sung Ho Kim, *Max Weber's Politics of Civil Society* (Cambridge: Cambridge University Press, 2004); and Peter Baehr, *Caesarism, Charisma and Fate: Historical Sources and Modern Resonances in the Work of Max Weber* (New Brunswick, NJ: Transaction, 2008).

Recent collections are Stephen Turner, ed., *The Cambridge Companion to Weber* (Cambridge: Cambridge University Press, 2000); Gert Albert, Agathe Beinfair, Steffen Sigmund, and Claus Wendt, eds., *Das-Weber-Paradigma: Studien zur Weiterentwicklung von Max Webers Forschungsprogramm* (Tübingen, Germany: Mohr Siebeck, 2003); William H. Swatos and Lutz Kaelber, eds., *The Protestant Ethic Turns 100: Essays on the Centenary of the Weber Thesis* (Boulder, CO: Paradigm, 2005); Charles Camic, Philip S. Gorski, and David M. Trubek, eds., *Max Weber's Economy and Society: A Critical Companion* (Stanford, CA: Stanford University Press, 2005); Javier Rodriguez Martinez, ed., *En el centenario de La ética protestante y el espíritu del capitalismo* (Madrid: CIS, 2005); Wolfgang Schluchter and Friedrich Wilhelm Graf, *Asketischer Protestantismus und der 'Geist' des modernen Kapitalismus* (Tübingen, Germany: Mohr Siebeck, 2005); Michel Coutu and Guy Rocher, eds., *La légitimité de l'État et du droit. Autour de Max Weber* (Québec: Presses de l'Université Laval, 2005); Karl-Ludwig Ay and Knut Borchardt, eds., *Das Faszinosum Max Weber: Die Geschichte seiner Geltung* (Konstanz, Germany: UVK Verlagsgesellschaft, 2006); Laurence McFalls, ed., *Max Weber's "Objectivity" Reconsidered* (Toronto: University of Toronto Press, 2007); and David Chalcraft, Fanon Howell, M. L. Menendez, and Hector Vera, eds., *Max Weber Matters: Interweaving Past and Present* (Farnham, England: Ashgate, 2008).

For helpful comments on Weber's effect on subfields of sociology, see Guenther Roth and Reinhard Bendix, "Max Webers Einfluss auf die amerikanische Soziologie," *Kölner Zeitschrift für Soziologie und Sozialpsychologie* 11 (1959): 38–53; Guenther Roth, "Vergangenheit und Zukunft der historischen Soziologie," in *Max Weber heute: Erträge und Probleme der Forschung*, ed. Johannes Weiss (Frankfurt: Suhrkamp 1989), 417–23; and Uta Gerhardt, "Die Rolle der Remigranten auf dem Heidelberger Soziologentag 1964 und die Interpretation des Werkes Max Webers," in *Zwischen den Stühlen? Remigranten und Remigration in der deutschen Medienöffentlichkeit der Nachkriegszeit*, ed. Claus-Dieter Krohn and Axel Schildt (Hamburg: Christians Verlag, 2002), 216–43.

The literature concerning the émigrés and exiles from Nazi Germany is far too extensive to cite in full. Useful for my purposes are Hans Gerth, *Politics, Character, and Culture: Perspectives from Hans Gerth*, ed. Joseph Bensman, Arthur J. Vidich and Nobuko Gerth (Westport, CT: Greenwood Press 1982). Paul Honigsheim's career in sociology is extensively documented in the Paul Honigsheim Papers, Michigan State University Special Collections, particularly the material on modern philosophy, religion, music, ethnology, and social stratification—the main fields of his teaching and research. His own commentary is in Paul Honigsheim, *On Max Weber*, trans. Joan Rytina (New York: Free Press, 1968); and Paul Honigsheim, *The Unknown Max Weber*, ed. Alan Sica (New Brunswick, NJ: Transaction, 2000). See also Karl Löwenstein, *Max Weber's Political Ideas in the Perspective of Our Time*, trans. Richard and Clara Winston (Amherst: University of Massachusetts Press, 1966); and Emil Lederer, "Freedom and

Science," *Social Research* 1 (1934): 219–30. The "Contested Legacies" special issue of the *European Journal of Political Theory* 3, no. 2 (2004), contains useful analysis, esp. the articles by Peter Breiner, "Translating Max Weber: Exile Attempts to Forge a New Political Science," 133–49; and John Gunnell, "Reading Weber: Leo Strauss and Eric Voegelin," 150–66.

For work at the New School, see Albert Salomon, "Max Weber's Methodology," *Social Research* 1 (1934): 147–68; Albert Salomon, "Max Weber's Sociology," *Social Research* 2 (1935): 60–73; and Albert Salomon, "Max Weber's Political Ideas." *Social Research* 2 (1935): 368–84; see also Albert Saloman, "Max Weber," *Die Gesellschaft* 3 (1926): 131–53. For Salomon' slife, see Ulf Matthiesen, "'Im Schatten einer endlosen Zeit': Ettapen der intellektuellen Biographie Albert Salomons," in *Exil, Wissenschaft, Identität: Die Emigration deutscher Wissenschaftler, 1933–1945*, ed. Ilja Surbar (Frankfurt: Suhrkamp, 1988), 299–350. See also Arnold Brecht, *Political Theory: The Foundations of Twentieth-Century Political Thought* (Princeton, NJ: Princeton University Press, 1959); Frieda Wunderlich, *Farm Labor in Germany 1810–1945* (Princeton, NJ: Princeton University Press, 1961).

For Voegelin and Strauss, see Eric Voegelin, "Über Max Weber," *Deutsche Vierteljahrsschrift für Literaturwissenschaft und Geistesgeschichte* 3 (1925): 177–93; Eric Voegelin, *The New Science of Politics* (Chicago: University of Chicago Press 1952); Eric Voegelin, *Autobiographical Reflections*, ed. Ellis Sandoz (Baton Rouge: Louisiana State University Press, 1989); Leo Strauss, *Natural Right and History* (Chicago: University of Chicago Press 1953), chap. 2; Hannah Arendt, *The Human Condition* (Chicago: University of Chicago Press 1958), and her views in Hannah Arendt and Karl Jaspers, *Correspondence 1926–1969*, ed. L. Kohler and H. Saner, trans. Robert and Rita Kimber (New York: Harcourt Brace, 1992), 148–50, 203, 244, 548–51. For Lazarsfeld, see Paul F. Lazarsfeld, "An Episode in the History of Social Research: A Memoir," in *The Intellectual Migration: Europe and America, 1930–1960*, ed. Donald Fleming and Bernard Bailyn(Cambridge, MA: Belknap Press, 1969), 270–337; and Paul F. Lazarsfeld and Anthony R. Oberschall, "Max Weber and Empirical Social Research," *American Sociological Review* 30 (1965): 185–99. See also Reinhard Bendix, *Unsettled Affinities*, ed. John Bendix (New Brunswick, NJ: Transaction 1993), esp. 12–14; Franz L. Neumann, "The Social Sciences," in *The Cultural Migration: The European Scholar in America*, ed. Franz L. Neumann, Henri Peyre, Erwin Panofsky, Wolfgang Köhler, and Paul Tillich (Philadelphia: University of Pennsylvania Press 1953), 4–26.

Page(s)

229 The International Sociological Association reports the complete results of its reputational survey, "Books of the Century" at http://www.isa-sociology.org/books.

230 Edward Shils, "Some Notes on Max Weber in America," 32–33, 36–38; ESP, Box 46.

230 For the discussion of the Gerth, Mills, and Shils troika see Guy Oakes and Arthur J. Vidich, *Collaboration, Reputation, and Ethics in American Academic Life: Hans H. Gerth and C. Wright Mills* (Urbana: University of Illinois Press 1999), esp. 21–37; and Guy Oakes and Arthur J. Vidich, "Gerth, Mills, and Shils: The Origins of *From Max Weber*," *International Journal of Politics, Culture and Society* 12, no. 3

(1999): 399–433. See also Donald A. Nielsen, "Hans H. Gerth, C. Wright Mills, and the Legacy of Max Weber," *International Journal of Politics, Culture and Society*, 13, no. 4 (2000): 649–61.

231 Perry wrote three notes to Parsons about the Weber "source book": December 7, 1928; and January 25 and June 10, 1929; TPP.

232–33 Mills's letter to Gerth, December 22, 1959, is in C. *Wright Mills, Letters and Autobiographical Writings*, ed. Kathryn Mills and Pamela Mills (Berkeley and Los Angeles: University of California Press 2002), 282.

233 There is a lengthy discussion of the composition and editorial interventions in *Economy and Society*, all of it pointing to the difficulties in compiling a text that lives up to Weber's intentions and conveys accurately his concepts, expositions, and arguments. A readable summation of these issues is Wolfgang J. Mommsen, "Max Weber's 'Grand Sociology': The Origins and Composition of *Wirtschaft und Gesellschaft. Soziologie*," *History and Theory* 39 (2000): 364–83; see also MWG I/24, ed. Wolfgang Schluchter (2009). The most complete discussion of Parsons's translation of *Wirtschaft und Gesellschaft* is Keith Tribe, "Talcott Parsons as Translator of Max Weber's Basic Sociological Categories," *History of European Ideas* 33 (2007): 212–33.

234 Weber's text is in *EaS*, 1118; *WuG*, 838.

236 See Richard Swedberg, *Max Weber and the Idea of Economic Sociology* (Princeton, NJ: Princeton University Press, 1998), and Max Weber, *Essays in Economic Sociology*, ed. Richard Swedberg (Princeton, NJ: Princeton University Press, 1999).

237 The Shils and Schelting translation of the opening pages of *EaS*, 3–22, *WuG*, 3–15, is in FKP, Box 53; they used the overarching title "The Methodological Foundations of Sociology," a heading Parsons retained.

237 On the uses of "instrumental rationality," see Jürgen Habermas, *The Theory of Communicative Action, Volume One: Reason and the Rationalization of Society*, trans. Thomas McCarthy (Boston: Beacon Press, 1984), chap. 2, 143–271.

238 The characterization of Weber as the "most important German thinker" is in Peter M. Rutkoff and William B. Scott, *New School: A History of the New School for Social Research* (New York: Free Press, 1986), 201; see also Lewis Coser, *Refugee Scholars in America: Their Impact and Experience* (New Haven, CT: Yale University Press, 1984); Claus-Dieter Krohn, *Intellectuals in Exile: Refugee Scholars and the New School for Social Research*, trans. Rita and Robert Kimber (Amherst: University of Massachusetts Press, 1993); Rolf Wiggershaus, *The Frankfurt School: Its History, Theories, and Political Significance*, trans. Michael Robertson (Cambridge: MIT Press, 1994); and Martin Jay, *The Dialectical Imagination: A History of the Frankfurt School and the Institute of Social Research, 1923–1950*, 2nd ed. (Berkeley and Los Angeles: University of California Press, 1996).

239 Hannah Arendt and Karl Jaspers, *Correspondence 1926–1969*, ed. L. Kohler and H. Saner, trans. Robert and Rita Kimber (New York: Harcourt Brace, 1992), 148–50. The compelling anecdote has been noticed by others and used for different purposes; see, for example, Peter Baehr, "The Grammar of Prudence: Arendt, Jaspers, and the Appraisal of Max Weber," in *Hannah Arendt in Jerusalem*, ed. Steven E. Aschheim (Berkeley and Los Angeles: University of California Press, 2001), 306–24.

240 Leo Lowenthal, *An Unmastered Past: The Autobiographical Reflections of Leo Lowenthal*, ed. Martin Jay (Berkeley and Los Angeles: University of California Press, 1987), 148. The appellation "Intellectual desperado" is ascribed to Siegfried Krakauer: see Rolf Wiggershaus, *The Frankfurt School: Its History, Theories, and Political Significance*, trans. Michael Robertson (Cambridge: MIT Press, 1994), 69.

241 Hannah Arendt and Karl Jaspers, *Correspondence 1926–1969*, ed. L. Kohler and H. Saner, trans. Robert and Rita Kimber (New York: Harcourt Brace, 1992), 203, 244.

242 Edward Shils, "Some Notes on Max Weber in America," 37–38; ESP, Box 46.

243 Neumann, "The Social Sciences," in *The Cultural Migration: The European Scholar in America*, ed. Franz L. Neumann, Henri Peyre, Erwin Panofsky, Wolfgang Köhler, and Paul Tillich (Philadelphia: University of Pennsylvania Press 1953), quotation herein on 22; emphasis added.

243 For the Columbia University Seminar on the State, see the Minutes for 1946–47 (Columbia University Seminars Office Archive), esp. October 18, and November 1 and 29, 1946, and January 17, 1947; I want to thank David Kettler for bringing this record to my attention. See also the commentary in Ira Katznelson, *Desolation and Enlightenment: Political Knowledge after Total War, Totalitarianism, and the Holocaust* (New York: Columbia University Press, 2003), 121–34.

244 Merleau-Ponty's judgments about Weber are in Maurice Merleau-Ponty, "The Crisis of the Understanding" (1955), in *The Primacy of Perception and Other Essays*, ed. James M. Edie (Evanston, IL: Northwestern University Press, 1964), 193–210.

245 The records of presentations at the conferences in 1964 are "Max Weber: A Symposium," special issue, *Sociological Quarterly* 5, no. 4 (1964), and *Max Weber and Sociology Today*, ed. Otto Stammer, trans. Kathleen Morris (New York: Harper and Row, 1971); see also Guenther Roth, "Heidelberg und Montreal: Zur Geschichte des Weberzentenariums 1964," in *Das Faszinosum Max Weber. Die Geschichte seiner Geltung*, ed. Karl-Ludwig Ay and Knut Borchardt (Konstanz, Germany: UVK, 2006), 377–91, and Guenther Roth, "Reminiscences of the Weber Centenary 1964, Its Prehistory and Aftermath: Lessons in Academic Politics," in *Max Weber Matters*, ed. David Chalcraft, Fanon Howell, M. L. Menendez, and Hector Vera, eds. (Farnham, England: Ashgate, 2008), 41–52. See Uta Gerhardt, "Die Rolle der Remigranten auf dem Heidelberger Soziologentag 1964 und die Interpretation des Werkes Max Webers," in *Zwischen den Stühlen? Remigranten und Remigration in der deutschen Medienöffentlichkeit der Nachkriegszeit*, ed. Claus-Dieter Krohn and Axel Schildt (Hamburg: Christians Verlag, 2002), 216–43; and Uta Gerhardt, "Worlds Come Apart: Systems Theory versus Critical Theory. Drama in the History of Sociology in the Twentieth Century," *American Sociologist* 33 (2002): 5–39.

247 On "disenchantment" see the very different approaches in Anne Harrington, *Reenchanted Science: Holism in German Culture from Wilhelm II to Hitler* (Princeton, NJ: Princeton University Press, 1996); Richard Jenkins, "Disenchantment, Enchantment and Re-Enchantment: Max Weber at the Millenium," *Max Weber Studies* 1 (2000), 11–32; Jane Bennett, *The Enchantment of Modern Life: Attachments, Crossings, and Ethics* (Princeton, NJ: Princeton University Press, 2001); Wolfgang Schluchter, *Die Entzauberung der Welt* (Tübingen, Germany: Mohr

Siebeck, 2009); George Ritzer, *Enchanting a Disenchanted World: Continuity and Change in the Cathedrals of Consumption*, 3rd ed. (Thousand Oaks, CA: Pine Forge Press, 2010).

248 M. Rainer Lepsius, "Eigenart und Potenzial des Weber-Paradigmas," in *Das-Weber-Paradigma: Studien zur Weiterentwicklung von Max Webers Forschungsprogramm*, ed. Gert Albert, Agathe Beinfair, Steffen Sigmund, and Claus Wendt (Tübingen, Germany: Mohr Siebeck, 2003), 32–41.

248 A recent example of a "Weberian" perspective put to good use, including explicit "ideal types," is Chris Wickham's magisterial *Framing the Early Middle Ages: Europe and the Mediterranean, 400–800* (Oxford: Oxford University Press, 2005). For an earlier generation of scholars employing Weber's arguments, see Moses I. Finley, *The Ancient Economy* (Berkeley and Los Angeles: University of California Press, 1973).

249 See Max Weber, "The 'Objectivity' of Knowledge in Social Science and Social Policy," in *The Essential Weber: A Reader*, ed. Sam Whimster, trans. Keith Tribe (London: Routledge, 2004), 398: "But there are sciences destined to eternal youthfulness, and that includes all *historical* disciplines, all those disciplines to which the eternally advancing flow of culture poses new problems"; Shils & Finch, 204; GAW, 206.

250 "Statecraft and soulcraft" is used in Sung Ho Kim, *Max Weber's Politics of Civil Society* (Cambridge: Cambridge University Press, 2004), chap. 6; quotation herein on 180.

251 Wolfgang Schwentker, *Max Weber in Japan: Eine Untersuchung zur Wirkungsgeschichte 1905–1995* (Tübingen, Germany: Mohr Siebeck, 1998), 14–15; quoted in Guenther Roth, "Max Weber at Home and in Japan: On the Troubled Genesis and Successful Reception of His Work," *International Journal of Politics, Culture and Society* 12, no. 13 (1999): 518; see also the essays in *Max Weber und das moderne Japan*, ed. Wolfgang Schwentker and Wolfgang J. Mommsen (Göttingen, Germany: Vandenhoeck und Ruprecht, 1999).

APPENDIX 2

Max Weber, Selected Correspondence with American Colleagues, 1904–5

Page(s)

257 Weber's first letter to Du Bois consists of two pages and is incomplete; it is written on Holland House stationary. Weber wrote the address of the boarding house, 167 Madison Avenue in New York, where he would be staying after November 7.

258 Weber's third letter to Du Bois was reproduced, with minor errors, in *The Correspondence of W.E.B. Du Bois*, ed. Herbert Aptheker (Amherst: University of Massachusetts Press, 1973), 1:106–7.

259 The works mentioned in Weber's third letter to Du Bois are Booker T. Washington, *Character Building* (New York: Doubleday, 1902); Thomas Nelson Page, *The Negro: The Southerner's Problem* (New York: Charles Scribner's Sons, 1904); *American Negro Academy Occasional Papers*, nos. 1–11 (1896–1905); and Walter F. Wilcox, "The Census Statistics of the Negro," *Yale Review*, May 1904, 274–86. "Viereck" must be Louis Viereck, the German immigrant and member of the

Deutsche Gesellschaft der Stadt New York, though I have not been able to identify the publication.

259 The two-page transcription of the original of Du Bois's letter is incomplete. Du Bois's letters have not been found in Max or Marianne Weber's papers.

260 In Weber's last letter to Du Bois, the word "perhaps" is crossed out in the original.

INDEX